学亦有益

海关英语学习随笔拾集

Learning is Important

A Selection of Essays on the Study of Customs English

孙毅彪◎著

2018年3月10日，北京人民大会堂，参加中国人民政治协商会议第十三届全国委员会第一次会议。

March 10, 2018, the Great Hall of the People in Beijing, at the First Meeting of the Thirteenth National Committee of the Chinese People's Political Consultative Conference.

自 序

Author's Note

"Learning is important." It is from a chapter in *Shuoyuan* (literally A Place of Sayings), a collection of stories mainly reflecting Confucian philosophy and ideas, authored by Liu Xiang during the Western Han Dynasty. The story was about a conversation between Confucius and Zi Lu, one of his disciples. Zi Lu asked Confucius, "Is learning important?" Confucius pursued the question and guided Zi Lu through profound ideas using brief terms to come to the conclusion that "you have to learn to become a Noble Person (Jun Zi)." Zi Lu was convinced and understood it was wrong to think otherwise. The story is an example of plain Materialism, and the idea that acquired knowledge is more important still guides our behaviors today. "We are not born with knowledge. We acquire knowledge in life." It means that besides inherited intelligence, we still

"学亦有益"，选自于中国古代西汉刘向编的《说苑·建本》。记载的是孔子与其学生子路最初相见时的一段对话。子路问："学亦有益乎？"面对子路的疑惑，孔子循循善诱，简明而深入地纠正了子路的观点，最后得出了"君子不可以不学"的结论。子路无可辩驳，惭愧自醒。这个故事包含着朴素的唯物主义思想，至今仍有深刻的借鉴意义，即强调后天学习的重要作用。"人非生而自知者，学而自知者也。"也就是说，人不能光凭天赋，还

need constant learning and practice to improve ourselves.

要勤奋学习，多加实践，才能不断提高自我。

Looking back on my experience from work, I've always believed that "learning is important" no matter where I am or what my work is. In addition to political theories, I have always been learning about customs operation and its related knowledge, as well as the English language.

回顾我的工作经历，不管岗位调动和职位变迁，我始终铭记"学亦有益"的深刻道理。除了加强政治理论学习外，还不断学习海关专业及相关理论知识，其中包括英语学习。

The load was heavy when I invested all my time and effort into working and learning English. But it was a bittersweet experience, because learning and working are inseparable, and the knowledge that I have learned can be conducive to solving problems at work. Particularly when I was with foreign customs colleagues, companies or friends, speaking English made the communication easy and smooth, and brought us closer. When I started working in Shanghai in 2004, I began to take pieces of English notes about important events or interesting people during my work or foreign exchange activities. After that, I would gather more information in my spare time to compare, think, explore and comment, and come up with my own feelings or opinions about the subject.

边工作边自学英语，自然忙碌不堪，但苦中有乐。因为这种学习是与实际工作紧密结合的，是能解决实际问题的。尤其在与外国海关同事、外企和朋友们交往的过程中，能直接使用英语交流，双方都会感到十分的自在、亲近、明了和容易沟通。自2004年我到上海海关工作后，我开始试着用英语作笔记，也就是把平时在外事活动中或在工作学习生活中自己觉得有意义或感兴趣的事和人以随笔的方式用英语把它们记录下来，逐渐形成了若干文字片段。事后等一有空，再查阅相关资料，对比、思考、拓展、评述，形成一些心得体会和感想。

Towards the end of 2009, I was relocated to Beijing and took office as Member

2009年底，我调到北京工作，任国家海关总署党组成

of Board and Vice Minister of the General Administration of China Customs (GACC). One of my responsibilities is customs international cooperation. It brings more interactions with foreign counterparts, and English came to be an essential tool in my line of work. Over the years of frequent visits to foreign countries, meetings, exchanges and my own study on issues of interest, I've kept taking notes of events in English, and put pieces of them together into complete articles when I am free. These articles are not confined to specific topics and my goal is to learn. I paid a lot of efforts into collecting and expanding basic information, accumulated a fair number of English materials about customs and other subjects, and have gradually improved my reading and writing skills.

员、副署长。由于分管的工作中涉及海关国际合作，使用外语的机会就更多了，英语就成了我对外交往必不可少的重要语言工具。几年来，在大量的外事出访、会晤、交流以及平时对一些感兴趣的问题研究过程中，我始终保持用英语记事的习惯。只要一有空，就把它们整理成完整的文章。不限题材、只求积累，注重基础、逐渐拓展。结果积累了大量的海关专业等英文基础材料，同时也渐渐地提升了自己英语的读写能力。

I am very grateful to my organization for the two English training programs. The first one was a short training course in August 2009 at the Wharton School of the University of Pennsylvania and University of California, Los Angeles (UCLA); the other was a three and a half months' advanced English class (IETP-7) in 2012. The trainiag gave me a lot of guidance in learning English and opportunities to practice, which made me more interested in learning the language.

在这里，我要特别感谢组织上曾给予我两次英语学习的机会。一次是2009年8月赴美国宾夕法尼亚大学沃顿商学院和加州大学洛杉矶分校进行短期培训；另一次是2012年参加了为期三个半月的省部级领导干部英语强化班（IETP-7）学习。这两次培训给了我很多学习指引和实践锻炼，也更激发了我对英语学习的兴趣，收获颇丰，终生难忘。

Over the past decade or so, I have written more than a hundred articles. Every time when I read them, it brings me back to working with my colleagues day and night for the country's reform and opening-up, economic and social development, and for a new era of China Customs operations and its international cooperation, leaving me immersed in the memory.

随着积累，十多年里我写下的英文文章已有100多篇。每当我重阅自己记录下的行行文字，就不禁会回想起与同事们朝夕相处、共同为国家的改革开放和经济社会发展、开创海关事业和海关国际合作新局面而不懈努力的工作经历及人和事。触景生情、回想联翩、回味无穷。

When my colleagues came to know about these articles, they asked me to publish them, to give an overview of the China Customs' innovative work and achievements in supporting reform and opening-up under the correct leadership of the CPC Central Committee and the State Council; let more people know the past and achievements of China Customs international cooperation; and provide more standard English expressions concerning customs operations; as well as to share my experience with those who are keen on learning English.

我的同事们知道了此事后，纷纷要求我把这些文章奉献出来，既为回顾总结这些年来在党中央国务院的正确领导下，海关围绕服务国家改革开放发展大局所采取的一系列改革创新举措及取得的成就；又能真实反映中国海关在国际舞台上加强海关国际合作所走过的路程及取得的成果；也为进一步丰富和规范海关专业英语提供借鉴；同时，与爱好英语学习的人士分享我的学习体会。

This book is a compilation of 60 articles among those I wrote over the past years, including essays of study, commentaries on work, reflections on life, personal opinions on various issues, and references for customs technical terms. These articles are mainly

本书收入了我曾撰写的60篇文章。内容主要有学习随笔、工作心得、生活感悟、观点评述及海关专业词汇释义等。以坚定正确的政治方向、海关改革创新、海关国际合作

about upholding the correct political direction, customs reform and innovation, customs international cooperation, while some also cover politics, economy and foreign trade. Meanwhile, in order to build a larger glossary, I've also written a few articles related to technology, environmental protection, culture and sports. For the readers to better understand these articles, I've translated them into Chinese, and all articles will be shown in both languages.

My English teachers Mr. David Robyak (American), Mr. Norman Pritchard (British) and Ms. Wang Xiaomei (Head of the Teaching Group of IETP-7, Associate Professor of Beijing Foreign Studies University) are kind enough to have given me guidance during my course of writing. And my colleagues, friends and family have supported and helped me during the editing, compiling and checking of this book. My sincerest gratitude goes to them all.

Surely learning English is a process of long-term accumulation and constant practice. I am still a fresh learner and my knowledge in some specific areas is limited, so some of the content might be inaccurate or incomplete, and I sincerely welcome any suggestions and comments.

Summer, 2018

内容为主，政治、经济、外贸等也占一定篇幅。与此同时，为拓展英语词汇，也涉及少量有关科技、环保、文化、体育等方面的内容。为便于大家阅读和理解，我把英文都译成了中文，以英中对照的形式与大家见面。

在上述文章写作过程中，我的英文老师David Robyak先生（美籍）、Norman Pritchard先生（英籍）和王小梅女士（IETP-7教学组组长，北京外国语大学副教授）等给予了我悉心的指导。在本书编辑、整理、校对过程中，我的同事、朋友以及家人也给予了大力的支持和帮助，在此一并表示衷心的感谢！

当然，英语学习是一个长期积累和不断运用的过程。鉴于我对英语学习还是初步的，且对一些专业问题研究还不是很深，难免有挂一漏万、不妥当抑或不准确之处，敬请广大读者批评指正。

2018年夏

contents

contents

contents

光辉的思想　实践的指引

——学习《习近平谈治国理政》

2017年12月29日

Glorious Thought and Practical Guide

——Studying *Xi Jinping: The Governance of China*

December 29, 2017

Thought is the precursor of action and guidance for practice. The 19th CPC National Congress decided the Xi Jinping Thought on Socialism with Chinese Characteristics for a New Era to be the guiding philosophy that must be upheld for a long time to come, and to be included in the CPC Constitution, which is of far-reaching realistic and historical significance.

思想是行动的先导，是实践的指南。党的十九大将习近平新时代中国特色社会主义思想确立为我们党必须长期坚持的指导思想并写入党章，这具有十分重大的现实意义和深远的历史意义。

The Xi Jinping Thought on Socialism with Chinese Characteristics for a News Era is the Party's guiding principle and guidance for actions, makes clear the major contents in 8 aspects and lists 14-point fundamental principles of upholding and developing

习近平新时代中国特色社会主义思想是我们党的理论纲领和行动指南。这一思想的"八个明确"和新时代坚持和发展中国特色社会主义基本方略的"十四个坚持"，极大地

socialism with Chinese characteristics in the new era. It is a significant addition to the latest achievement in adapting Marxism to the Chinese context, an important component of the theoretical system of socialism with Chinese characteristics, and the scientific truth proven by practice. It provides guidance for us to fully implement the Party's basic theory, guideline and policy.

丰富了马克思主义中国化的最新理论成果，成为中国特色社会主义理论体系的重要组成部分，为全党全面贯彻党的基本理论、基本路线、基本方略提供了指导。

In September 2014 and November 2017, the first and second volume of *Xi Jinping: The Governance of China* were published by China International Publishing Group both at home and abroad. The two volumes contain a compilation of 178 of General Secretary Xi Jinping's talks, interviews, speeches, instructions and correspondence from November 2012 to September 2017, along with notes and related photographs.

2014年9月和2017年11月，中国外文出版社分别向海内外发行了《习近平谈治国理政》第一卷和第二卷，收录了习近平总书记在2012年11月至2017年9月期间的重要著作，共有讲话、谈话、演讲、批示、贺信等178篇，并附有注释和图片。

I have studied the important two volumes earnestly and thoroughly, and I am deeply impressed by the books' lofty conception, extensive content, important propositions and far-reaching significance. It depicts the grand cause of the CPC Central Committee with Comrade Xi Jinping at its core unifying and leading the whole Party and the people of all ethnic groups in China in upholding and developing socialism with Chinese characteristics. It reflects the evolution of Xi

我认真地研读了这两卷重要的著作，深深地体会到《习近平谈治国理政》立意高远、内涵丰富、博大精深、意义深远。它生动地记录了以习近平同志为核心的党中央团结带领全党全国各族人民在新时代坚持和发展中国特色社会主义的伟大实践，集中反映了习近平新时代中国特色社会主义思想的发展脉络和主要内容，充分

Jinping Thought on Socialism with Chinese Characteristics for a New Era, embodies the Chinese wisdom and Chinese solutions of the Party to the great rejuvenation of the Chinese nation, building a community of shared future for mankind and promoting world peace and development, and opens a clear window for the world to get to know China.

体现了我们党为中华民族伟大复兴和推动构建人类命运共同体、促进人类和平与发展事业贡献的中国智慧和中国方案，也为世界了解和认识中国打开了一扇明亮的窗口。

The 178 works cover theories related to socialism with Chinese characteristics, the building of a moderately prosperous society in all respects and the Chinese Dream; practical requirements such as new development concepts, the new normal of economic development, deeper reform, the wellbeing of the people and the building of beautiful China; major topics including the rule of law, socialist democracy, cultural confidence, and the all-out effort to enforce strict Party discipline; as well as topics that respond to the call of our times, including China's diplomacy as a major country, peaceful development, a community of shared future, military development, and national reunification.

这178篇著作既有坚持和发展中国特色社会主义、决胜全面建成小康社会、实现中华民族伟大复兴的中国梦的理论指引，又有坚定不移贯彻新发展理念、适应把握引领经济发展新常态、将改革进行到底、保障和改善民生、建设美丽中国的实践要求；既有建设社会主义法治国家、发展社会主义民主政治、坚定文化自信、推动全面从严治党向纵深发展的重要内容，又有推进中国特色大国外交、坚持和平发展、推动构建人类命运共同体及强军兴军、推进祖国统一的时代强音。

Studying the above had me thinking further and renewed my understanding of some issues.

通过学习，我对一些问题的理解有了更深的思考和更新的体会。

1. Adhere to the right path and uphold the guidance of thoughts.

In volume one of *Xi Jinping: The Governance of China*, "Uphold and Develop Socialism with Chinese Characteristics" thoroughly elaborates on the significance of adhering to the path of socialism with Chinese characteristics and upholding the truth of Marxism. In this article, General Secretary Xi Jinping pointed out that "which path should we follow? This is the paramount question for the future of the Party and the success of its cause. Socialism with Chinese characteristics is the integration of the theory of scientific socialism and social development theories of Chinese history. Socialism has taken root in China. It reflects the views of the people and meets the development need of the country and the times. It is a sure route to success in building a moderately prosperous society in all respects, in the acceleration of socialist modernization, and in the great renewal of the Chinese nation".

In my opinion, this is a clear announcement to the world: The Communist Party of China must uphold and develop socialism with Chinese characteristics and follow the path of socialism with Chinese characteristics. Since the advent of modern times, from the Taiping Tianguo Uprising to the Westernization

（一）坚定正确道路，坚持思想指引。

《习近平谈治国理政》第一卷中《毫不动摇坚持和发展中国特色社会主义》一文，深刻阐明了坚持走中国特色社会主义道路、坚守马克思主义真理的重要意义。习近平总书记指出："道路问题是关系党的事业兴衰成败第一位的问题，道路就是党的生命。中国特色社会主义，是科学社会主义理论逻辑和中国社会发展历史逻辑的辩证统一，是根植于中国大地、反映中国人民意愿、适应中国和时代发展进步要求的科学社会主义，是全面建成小康社会、加快推进社会主义现代化、实现中华民族伟大复兴的必由之路。"

我体会，这段重要论述旗帜鲜明地向世人表明，我们中国共产党人必须毫不动摇地坚持和发展中国特色社会主义，必须坚定地走中国特色社会主义道路。回顾中国近代历史，从太平天国起义、洋务运动、

Movement, from the Hundred Days' Reform to the Xinhai Revolution, farmers, enlightened feudal landlords, bourgeois reformists, and national bourgeoisie went on the stage of history one after another. However, due to the limitation of their classes, these movements, reforms and revolutions failed to make China strong. The same reason also applies to western capitalism, which didn't fit in with China's context and would eventually lead to a dead end. Mao Zedong, a major figure of the Communist Party of China, and all Party members creatively used Marxism to solve China's problems, looked deeper into China's national conditions and the characteristics of the Chinese revolution, created a path from new-democratic revolution to socialist revolution, and realized national independence and liberation. After a long and arduous journey of exploration, the CPC led the people of all ethnic groups in China to the path of socialist construction, reform and opening up, while upholding and developing socialism with Chinese characteristics. History and practice have fully proved that this path is the only correct one. It is the result of the long and arduous exploration of the CPC and the historical choice of the people. It is the road to national rejuvenation, the path to national prosperity, and the path to people's happiness.

戊戌变法到辛亥革命，农民、封建地主阶级开明派、资产阶级改良派和民族资产阶级纷纷登上历史舞台，但由于历史和阶级的局限性，这些运动、变法和革命都没有能使中国走上富强之路。同样，照搬西方资本主义的道路也不适合中国国情，也走不通。以毛泽东同志为主要代表的中国共产党人创造性地运用马克思主义解决中国的问题，深入研究中国国情和中国革命的特点，开创了一条由新民主主义通向社会主义的革命道路，实现了民族独立和人民解放。在长期艰辛的探索中，中国共产党带领全国各族人民终于走上了社会主义建设、改革开放、坚持和发展中国特色社会主义的道路。历史和实践都充分证明，这条道路是唯一正确的道路。它是中国共产党长期艰辛探索的结果，是人民的历史选择，是实现民族复兴之路、国家富强之路、人民幸福之路。因此，在道路问题上我们必须旗帜鲜明、毫不动摇、引领未来。

Therefore, regarding the question of which path to take, we must stand firm and be unwavering when moving forward.

Under no circumstances will the Party waver in the slightest degree in standing firm in support of the ideals of the Party and holding Marxism as our guiding philosophy. General Secretary Xi Jinping pointed out, "The guiding philosophy is the spiritual beacon of a party. Over the past 95 years, the CPC has accomplished so many tasks which were thought to be impossible by other political forces. The reason for this has been precisely attributed to upholding Marxism as our guide of action, while the theories of Marxism have then been further developed." This incisive deliberation fully appreciates the guiding position of Marxism in our Party's undertakings, namely, the fundamental guiding thought for the establishment of our Party and our country. At the same time, it also emphasizes that Marxism does not put a lid on truth but opens a path to truth. Just as Engels put it, "Marx's whole way of thinking is not so much a doctrine as a method. It provides, not so much ready-made dogmas, as aids to further investigation and the method for such investigation."

For instance, after the 18th CPC National Congress, responding to the call of the times

坚定共产党人的理想、坚持马克思主义的指导地位，是我们党在任何时候、任何情况下都不能有丝毫动摇的。习近平总书记曾指出，“指导思想是一个政党的精神旗帜。95年来，中国共产党之所以能够完成近代以来各种政治力量不可能完成的艰巨任务，就在于始终把马克思主义这一科学理论作为自己的行动指南，并坚持在实践中不断丰富和发展马克思主义。”我认为，这一精辟论述充分肯定了马克思主义在我们党事业中的指导地位，也就是说它是我们立党立国的根本指导思想。与此同时，它也强调了马克思主义并没有结束真理，而是开辟了通向真理的道路。正如恩格斯曾说过的，“马克思的整个世界观不是教义，而是方法。它提供的不是现成的教条，而是进一步研究的出发点和供这种研究使用的方法。”

比如，党的十八大以来，习近平总书记顺应时代和实践

and new requirements of development, General Secretary Xi Jinping stressed that we must continue the commitment to our people-centered development philosophy and pursue the new development concepts firmly: "innovative, coordinated, green, open, shared development", and brought historic changes to China's overall development. These thoughts and theories are elaborated in detail in the first and second volume of *Xi Jinping: The Governance of China*. In "Guide Development with New Concepts", General Secretary Xi underlined that "Innovative development focuses on the drivers of growth", "Coordinated development aims to solve the imbalance in development", "Green development highlights the harmony between humanity and nature", "Open development prioritizes interactions between China and the international community", "Shared development underpins social equality and justice". This is a close combination of the universal truth of Marxism and the practice of building socialism with Chinese characteristics into the new era. These concepts answer the questions of the Times and solve the specific problems in practice. They embody the profound insight and scientific grasp of our Party on basic features of the new stage of development. It is also testimony to the new understanding by our Party of laws of

发展的新要求，坚持以人民为中心的发展思想，鲜明提出要坚定不移贯彻“创新、协调、绿色、开放、共享”的新发展理念，引领了我国发展全局发生历史性变革。这些重要的思想在《习近平谈治国理政》第一卷和第二卷的相关文章中都有详尽的阐述。在《以新的发展理念引领发展》一文中，特别强调“创新发展注重的是解决发展动力问题”“协调发展注重的是解决发展不平衡问题”“绿色发展注重的是解决人与自然和谐问题”“开放发展注重的是解决发展内外联动问题”“共享发展注重的是解决社会公平正义问题”，这就把马克思主义的普遍真理同中国特色社会主义建设进入新时代的实践紧密地结合起来，很好地回答时代之问、解决实践中的具体问题。这一新发展理念集中体现了我们党对新的发展阶段基本特征的深刻洞察和科学把握，也标志着我们党对经济社会发展规律的认识达到了新的高度。因此，习近平新时代中国特色社会主义思想，是我们当前一切工作的实践指

economic and social development. Therefore, the Xi Jinping Thought on Socialism with Chinese Characteristics for a New Era is the guidance of our work in all areas. Only by upholding and developing Marxism at the same time can we really solve the problems in China and walk down a wider path of socialism with Chinese characteristics.

引。只有始终把坚持马克思主义和发展马克思主义有机统一起来，切实解决中国当前面临的实际问题，我们在中国特色社会主义的道路上才能越走越宽。

2. Remain true to our original aspiration and keep our mission firmly in mind.

（二）不忘初心，牢记使命。

To realize the great rejuvenation of the Chinese nation and high ideals of communism, following the right path, we must also remain true to our original aspiration, keep our mission firmly in mind, uphold our faith, and continue the hard work. What is our original aspiration? Simply put, it means to maintain a pure heart towards the people. It is also the oath taken by the CPC when it was founded: Serve the people heart and soul, do not hesitate to sacrifice everything of the individual, strive for the realization of communism for life. What is our faith? It is the high ideals of communism, the adherence to Marxism, and the firm conviction that the Party is rooted in the people and its strength comes from the people.

要实现中华民族的伟大复兴和共产主义远大理想，我们走在正确的道路上，还必须不忘初心、牢记使命、坚守信念、继续奋斗。初心是什么？简言之，就是对人民的赤子之心。也就是我们党一成立时立下的誓言，即必须全心全意为人民服务，不惜牺牲个人的一切，为实现共产主义奋斗终生。信念是什么？就是共产主义的崇高理想、坚持马克思主义真理、坚信党的根基在人民、党的力量在人民。

General Secretary Xi time and again required the whole Party to “remain true to our original aspiration and keep our mission firmly in mind”. The second volume of *Xi*

习近平总书记一再告诫全党：“不忘初心，牢记使命。”在《习近平谈治国理政》第二卷中，特别是节选自

Jinping: The Governance of China includes part of General Secretary Xi's speech at the ceremony marking the 95th anniversary of the founding of the CPC, titled "Remain True to Our Original Aspiration and Continue Marching Forward". The profound meaning of "remaining true to our original aspiration" was elaborated on at the outset. He stressed, "Looking at the mirror we know about ourselves; reflecting on the past we know what to do now.' Today we review our history not to take comfort in our successes, and not to look for excuses for evading the difficulties we currently face, but for the purpose of summing up experience, learning the laws of history, and giving ourselves the power and courage to move forward." This requires us to remain true to our original aspiration towards the ultimate destination. Only if one consistently upholds the original conviction and exerts all his energy, can he achieve the final success in his undertaking.

习近平总书记在庆祝中国共产党成立95周年大会上的重要讲话《不忘初心，继续前进》一文中，开篇就道出了“不忘初心”的深刻含义。习近平总书记强调，“‘明镜所以照形，古事所以知今。’今天，我们回顾历史，不是为了从成功中寻求慰藉，更不是为了躺在功劳簿上、为避免今天面临的困难寻找借口，而是为了总结历史经验、把握历史规律，增强开拓前进的勇气和力量”。这就是说“不忘初心，方得始终”。一个人做任何事，只有始终如一地保持当初的那种信念，竭尽努力，最后才能获得成功。

We should take history as a mirror and draw upon lessons from the past. All the prosperous rises and instant falls of dynasties in history can be explained by the easiness of possessing an aspiration and the hardness of sticking to it to the end. The famous dialogue between Huang Yanpei and Mao Zedong in a Yan'an cave house was about how to break

以史为鉴，殷鉴不远。历史上多少王朝更迭，其兴也勃焉，其亡也忽焉。究其原因，就是初心易得，始终难守。当年黄炎培与毛泽东在延安留下著名的“窑洞对”，就是要探讨如何打破这种兴亡更迭的历史周期律。我们党在全国执政

this kind of historic cycle of rise and fall. Since coming to power, our Party has effectively answered the question of historic cycle via such measures of reform and opening-up, law-based governance, democratic supervision and Party self-discipline. Looking ahead, we still need to further consolidate the long-term foundation for our Party's governance, uphold the purpose of "serving the people" all along, and always adhere to the development thought centered on the people. Those who win popular support can rule the world. Abandoning the original aspiration, we will lose the support of our people.

以来，通过改革开放、依法治国、实行人民民主监督、全面从严治党等措施，有效回答了周期律之问。面向未来，我们还需要不断巩固党的长期执政基础，需要始终恪守为人民服务的宗旨，始终坚持以人民为中心的发展思想。得民心者得天下，丢了初心，就失了民心。

When speaking at the press conference by members of the Standing Committee of the Political Bureau of the 18th CPC Central Committee on November 15, 2012, General Secretary Xi Jinping said, "The people's wish for a good life is our goal." Reading into this sentence, I find profound meaning of the original aspiration and mission of the Communist Party of China, i.e. we will work for the happiness of the Chinese people, for the rejuvenation of the Chinese nation and for the liberation of all mankind. The original aspiration and mission are the fundamental motivation for the continuous progress of the CPC. The people are the root of our Party, the foundation of its governance, and the source of

2012年11月15日，习近平总书记在十八届中央政治局常委同中外记者见面时的讲话中指出，"人民对美好生活的向往，就是我们奋斗的目标。"我体会，这句意味深刻的话道出了中国共产党人的初心和使命，即为中国人民谋幸福，为中华民族谋复兴，为全人类的解放事业作贡献。这个初心和使命是激励中国共产党人不断前进的根本动力。人民群众是我们党的立党之本、执政之基、力量之源。只有让人民群众过上美好幸福生活，才能体现社会主义制度的优越性，才

its strength. Only by giving the people a happy life, can strength of our socialist system be self-evident, can the Party reinforce our class foundation and public support for governance, can boundless strength be gathered to realize the Chinese dream of the great rejuvenation of the Chinese nation.

能夯实党执政的阶级基础和群众基础，才能凝聚实现中华民族伟大复兴中国梦的磅礴力量。

Socialism with Chinese characteristics has entered a new era. Nearing the center of the world stage, we have never been so close as now to reaching the goal of the great rejuvenation of the Chinese nation. There is no doubt that we will usher in a period of opportunity with bright prospects. But we should not feel complacent at this moment. The great rejuvenation of the Chinese nation cannot be achieved easily. We must be prepared for resolving major challenges, risks, resistances and contradictions, and fighting great battles with many new historical features, such as "making solid efforts to advance reform", targeted poverty alleviation and reduction, reining in financial risks. We also have to fight a series of new battles: the battle in the ideological area, the battle in protecting the environment and national security, the battle against corruption, etc. To win these battles, we have to remain true to our original aspiration, keep our mission firmly in mind, keep fighting and continue to move forward.

当前，中国特色社会主义进入了新时代，我们日益走近世界舞台的中央，日益接近中华民族伟大复兴的目标。毫无疑问，我们将迎来一个大有可为的历史机遇期。但越是如此，越不能沾沾自喜。中华民族的伟大复兴不是轻轻松松、敲锣打鼓就能实现的。我们必须时刻准备应对重大挑战、抵御重大风险、克服重大阻力、解决重大矛盾，必须时刻准备进行具有许多新的历史特点的伟大斗争，比如"真枪真刀推进改革"、精准扶贫和脱贫、防控金融风险等。又如意识形态领域的斗争、保护生态环境的斗争、维护国家安全的斗争、反腐败斗争，等等，这些都是具有新的历史特点的伟大斗争。要赢得这些斗争的胜利，就必须不忘初心、牢记使命、不懈奋斗、继续前进。

3. Innovative theories come from practice, glorious thoughts guide reforms.

The most important theoretical outcome of the 19th CPC National Congress was the establishment of the Xi Jinping Thought on Socialism with Chinese Characteristics for a New Era, which is of great significance and provides clear systematic answers to the questions concerning the kind of socialism with Chinese characteristics we should uphold and build, and the approach we should adopt to reach this goal in the new era.

"New realities inspire new thoughts and practice is the source of new theories." New concepts, new thoughts, new strategies of the governance by the Party are formed based upon the correct understanding of the trend of the times, the answers to addressing practical requirements and people's needs by the CPC Central Committee with Comrade Xi Jinping at its core. When studying the books, I deeply felt that the establishment of the Xi Jinping Thought on Socialism with Chinese Characteristics for a New Era has two main distinct features: On the one hand, all the theoretical innovations are made on the basis of the basic principles of Marxism. This is the necessary prerequisite and guarantee for refraining from taking the wrong path, because departing from or abandoning Marxism, the

（三）创新的理论源于实践，光辉的思想引领改革。

党的十九大创立了习近平新时代中国特色社会主义思想，系统地回答了新时代坚持和发展什么样的中国特色社会主义、怎样坚持和发展中国特色社会主义。

"时代是思想之母，实践是理论之源。"我党治国理政的新理念、新思想、新战略是以习近平同志为核心的党中央在把握时代大趋势，回答实践新要求，顺应人民新期待的实践中形成的。在学习中，我深深地体会到，习近平新时代中国特色社会主义思想的创立具有两个鲜明的特征：一是始终坚持在马克思主义基本原理基础上进行理论创新，这是防止走歪路或邪路的必要前提和保障，因为任何背离或放弃马克思主义，我们党就会失去灵魂、迷失方向。二是始终结合新的时代特征和实践发展要求，在实践基础上进行理论创

Party would lose its soul and direction. On the other, it always keeps pace with the new characteristics and trends of the times, and makes theoretical innovations based upon practice, so as to avoid the ossification or alienation of thinking as well as metaphysics.

新，防止思想僵化、异化或受到形而上学的影响。

On February 17, 2014, at a provincial-level official' seminar on studying and implementing the decisions of the Third Plenary Session of the 18th CPC Central Committee on continuing reform, General Secretary Xi Jinping stressed that "The Third Plenary Session of the 18th CPC Central Committee pointed out that the overall goal of continuing the reform to a deeper level is to develop the socialist system with Chinese characteristics and modernize our national governance system and capability. This is a prerequisite for upholding and developing socialism with Chinese characteristics and for realizing socialist modernization."

习近平总书记在2014年2月17日省部级主要领导干部学习贯彻十八届三中全会精神全面深化改革专题研讨班上强调，“党的十八届三中全会提出的全面深化改革的总目标，就是完善和发展中国特色社会主义制度、推进国家治理体系和治理能力现代化。这是坚持和发展中国特色社会主义的必然要求，也是实现社会主义现代化的应有之义”。

As a Party official, I must earnestly study the Xi Jinping Thought on Socialism with Chinese Characteristics for a New Era, strive for a more thorough understanding of the spiritual essence of Marxism and its sinicization. Only when we keep clear-minded, can we remain firm politically, and maintain sharp vigilance against and resolutely oppose to the incorrect understanding and

我作为一名党的领导干部，必须下功夫深刻学习领会习近平新时代中国特色社会主义思想，深刻理解把握马克思主义及其中国化理论的精神实质。只有理论上清醒，才能做到政治上坚定，从而时刻警惕和坚决反对社会思想领域在对待马克思主义上存在的各种错

attitudes towards Marxism in social thoughts. We should make a firm stand against deliberate distortion and hostile dissipation of Marxism, and we should not adopt a narrow understanding or resort to dogmatism. We should earnestly study, understand and believe in these theories and put them into practice so that our work in all areas can be guided by the Xi Jinping Thought on Socialism with Chinese Characteristics for a New Era.

误认识和态度，既要坚决反对刻意歪曲、力图消解，又不能狭隘理解、机械教条，真正做到真学真懂真信真用，用习近平新时代中国特色社会主义思想指导我们各项工作。

4. Keep up with the Times and Strive Forward

（四）与时俱进，砥砺前行。

The last leg of a journey marks the halfway point. Upholding and developing socialism with Chinese characteristics is a long-term and arduous historical task. We must follow General Secretary Xi's requirements, be confident in our path, theory, system and culture, and always maintain the Party's striving spirit and the commitment to the people in its earliest days. We should not rest on our laurels but be prepared for adversity and danger even in times of prosperity and peace, and face up to and try to resolve today's various difficulties and problems with the spirit and integrity of the revolutionaries. We should constantly review historic experience, grasp the laws of history and step up our courage and strength to forge ahead.

行百里者半九十。坚持和发展中国特色社会主义是一项长期而艰巨的历史任务，我们必须按照习总书记提出的要求，坚定道路自信、理论自信、制度自信和文化自信，永远保持建党时中国共产党人的奋斗精神，永远保持对人民的赤子之心。我们不能躺在先辈们的功劳簿上睡大觉，必须增强忧患意识，继续以革命者的精神和气节，积极面对并努力解决今天面临的各种困难和问题，不断总结历史经验，把握历史规律，增强开拓前进的勇气和力量。

As socialism with Chinese characteristics enters a new era, the major contradiction in

随着中国特色社会主义进入新时代，中国社会主要矛

Chinese society has been transformed into the contradiction between the people's growing need for a better life and the unbalanced and inadequate development. China's reform and opening-up will face new problems and opportunities at home and abroad. Customs will also face a series of new contradictions and challenges. For instance, traditional customs management concepts and supervision methods are not adequate to meet the requirements of China's further opening-up, deepening reform and innovative development in the new era; customs capability of supervision and services is not adequate to meet the needs of enterprises and people for customs clearance facilitation; relatively limited regulatory resources and regulatory tools are not adequate to meet the ever-growing and more diversified business needs, etc. All of these have put forward higher requirements for customs' own governance capability.

盾已经转化为人民日益增长的美好生活需要和不平衡不充分的发展之间的矛盾。中国的改革开放将面临国内外各种新问题、新机遇。海关工作也将同样面临一系列的新矛盾、新挑战。比如，传统的海关管理理念和监管方式还不够适应新时代新形势下国家进一步扩大开放、深化改革、创新发展的要求；海关把关服务水平还不够适应企业和人民对海关通关便利化的实际需求；相对有限的监管资源和监管手段还不够适应空前快速增长的、更加多元化的业务需求；等等。这都对海关自身的治理能力提出了更高更新的要求。

In order to fulfill our duty of guarding the border and providing services at entry-exit ports, we must always be firm in our belief, remain true to our original aspiration,and advance our undertaking with the times.

要履行好进出境把关服务职能，中国海关必须始终坚定理想信念，不忘初心、与时代同步、继续奋斗。

Regarding political direction, we must maintain political integrity, think in terms of the big picture, follow the leadership core, and keep in alignment with the central Party

在政治方向上，要切实增强“四个意识”，坚定“四个自信”，自觉地在思想上、政治上和行动上同以习近平同

leadership. We must enhance confidence in our path, theory, system and culture, consciously maintain a high degree of alignment in thought, political direction and action with the CPC Central Committee with Comrade Xi Jinping at its core. We should arm ourselves with the Xi Jinping Thought on Socialism with Chinese Characteristics for a New Era, vigorously carry forward the fine style of study of combining theory with practice, think in terms of solving problems, carry out in-depth investigation, and earnestly implement the decisions of the CPC Central Committee and the State Council.

志为核心的党中央保持高度一致。要以习近平新时代中国特色社会主义思想武装头脑，大力弘扬理论联系实际的优良学风，强化问题意识，深入调查研究，认真地贯彻落实好党中央国务院的各项决策部署。

With regard to reform and innovation, we should carry out the tasks of reform put forward by the CPC Central Committee and the State Council, and we should be problem-oriented, keep up with the high standards of international rules and systems, actively think and boldly innovate. More importantly, we should pursue a fine result of reforms and create a business environment that is fair, transparent, safe and facilitated. We have to make breakthroughs in key "points" during the reform by prioritizing the building of Pilot Free Trade Zones and Free Trade Ports and making supportive policies for the opening-up on a higher level. We have to enhance interactions along the "line" by building the "Single Window", the Risk Management Center, the

在改革创新上，既要落实党中央国务院制定的改革任务，又要坚持问题导向、对标国际、主动思考、勇于创新，更要追求改革实效，营造公平透明、安全便利的营商环境。改革要在“点”上取得突破，以自贸试验区、自贸港建设为重点制定政策支持更高水平的对外开放；改革要在“线”上实现联动，通过“单一窗口”、风险防控中心和税收征管中心及其配套信息化系统的建设，梳理、整合、优化海关各个业务线条；改革要在“面”上实现统筹发展，同步推进全国通关一体化、“三

Duty Collection Center and their computerized systems so as to sort, integrate and improve all lines of customs operations. We have to achieve coordinated development across the "board" by simultaneously advancing important reforms such as national customs clearance integration, the 3Ms cooperation in clearance (i.e. mutual exchange of information, mutual recognition of control, and mutual assistance in enforcement), "Double random inspections and prompt release of results" (the new model of oversight combining randomly selected inspectors who inspect randomly selected entities and the prompt release of results), and the optimization and integration of customs special control areas so that we can make further contribution to creating new ground in pursuing opening-up on all fronts.

互大通关”“双随机、一公开”、海关特殊监管区域整合优化等重点改革项目，为全面开放新格局做出更大的贡献。

As for customs law enforcement, we should place the people at the center of our work and enforce the law for the people, while striking a fine balance between enhancing supervision and improving services. We should always forestall risks and stay true to our principles. We should adopt a legal approach in both thinking and action to comprehensively fulfill the duties of imports and exports supervision, tax collection, combating smuggling, compiling customs statistics, etc. We should focus both on the entities and procedures of law enforcement, and

在海关执法上，要牢固树立以人民为中心的思想和执法为民的理念，处理好强化监管和优化服务的辩证关系。既要具备风险意识和底线思维，以法治思维和法治方式来全面履行海关对进出境监管、征税、打私、统计等把关服务职责，注重执法实体和执法程序，又要充分运用科技手段简化通关手续，改进执法方式，提高执法效率，提升执法效果。

use technological tools to streamline clearance procedures, improve means of enforcement so as to enhance enforcement efficiency and effect.

Concerning self–discipline and conduct, we should follow the requirements of full and rigorous governance over the Party, adopt a two-pronged approach and a dual-investigation scheme (carry out investigations into smuggling activities and violations of Party discipline and the law by customs officers simultaneously). We should further strengthen the building of a paramilitary disciplined customs force, improve supervision and monitoring of the exercise of power, tighten disciplines, step up internal control over the positions and links highly prone to corruption, and request and encourage officials to take on responsibilities, in order to nurture a politically-minded and discipline-abiding customs force with robust conduct, professional proficiency, integrity and dedication, and honor the sacred duty endowed by the Party and the people.

在纪律作风上，要按照全面从严治党的要求，坚持“两手抓”和“一案双查”，不断强化海关准军事化纪律部队建设，加强对权力运行的监督监控，严明纪律，紧盯高风险岗位和高风险环节，加强内控管理，强化责任担当意识，打造一支讲政治、守纪律、作风硬、业务强、重廉洁、肯奉献的海关队伍，以更好地完成党和人民赋予海关的神圣职责。

不忘初心、牢记使命，积极发挥海关把关服务作用

——学习贯彻党的十九大精神体会

2017年12月5日

Remain True to Our Original Aspiration and Keep Our Mission Firmly in Mind to Improve Customs Supervision and Services

—— Studying and Implementing the Spirit of the 19th CPC National Congress

December 15, 2017

Currently, the whole country is thoroughly studying and implementing the guiding principles of the 19th CPC National Congress. The aim to "remain true to our original aspiration and keep our mission firmly in mind, hold high the banner of socialism with Chinese characteristics and work tirelessly to realize the Chinese Dream of national rejuvenation" has become the new historic mission for CPC members in the new era. Part V of the report to the 19th CPC National Congress "Applying a New Vision of Development and Developing a Modernized Economic System" elaborates the goals and tasks of "making new ground in pursuing opening-up on all fronts", which is a major strategic decision

当前，全国上下正在深入学习贯彻党的十九大精神。"不忘初心、牢记使命、高举旗帜、不懈奋斗"，已成为新时代中国共产党人新的历史使命。党的十九大报告第五部分提出了"贯彻新发展理念，建设现代化经济体系"的要求，这是以习近平同志为核心的党中央适应经济全球化新趋势、准确判断国际形势新变化、深刻把握国内改革发展新要求而作出的重大战略部署。

by the CPC Central Committee with Comrade Xi Jinping at the core, responding to the new trends in economic globalization, accurately identifying the new changes of international situations, and profoundly grasp the new requirements from China's domestic reform and development.

Since reform and opening-up began, China has made remarkable achievements in foreign trade and socioeconomic development. Especially in recent years, the country's GDP and total export-import volume, including outbound investment, rank No.2 globally, and export tops the world. The building of the Belt and Road has also received fruitful results. While in comparison, we still have a long way to go in development mode, structural optimization and core competitiveness. For instance, compared with manufacturing, our service industry lags behind on its path towards opening-up to the outside world, and its market access and business environment are still to be improved. At the same time, as China's economy enters "a new normal", labor costs keep growing, resource constraints are tightening, bearing capacity of the environment is nearing its upper limit, our traditional competitive advantages of open economy are weakened, and the conventional development model has hit a bottleneck as well. Furthermore, rising anti-globalization and protectionism cast a shadow over the world's economic and trade

改革开放以来，我国对外贸易和经济社会发展都取得了举世瞩目的成就，尤其是近年来，我国GDP、进出口总量、包括对外投资均位居世界第二，出口位居全球第一，"一带一路"建设也取得丰硕成果。但相比之下，我们在发展方式、结构优化和核心竞争力上，还有进一步提升的空间。比如，相对于制造业，我国服务业的对外开放还相对滞后，准入开放和营商环境还存在一定差距。与此同时，随着我国经济发展进入新常态，劳动力成本持续攀升，资源约束日益趋紧，环境承载能力接近上限，开放型经济传统竞争优势受到削弱，传统发展模式遭遇瓶颈。另外，反全球化思潮涌动，保护主义倾向抬头，给世界经济贸易发展蒙上了阴影。这些

development. All these require us to further expand opening-up through creating new ground in pursuing opening-up on all fronts, in order to provide foundation and guarantee for developing a modernized economy and delivering the two centenary goals.

就要求我们必须通过构建全面开放新格局，进一步扩大开放，为建设现代化经济体系、实现“两个一百年”奋斗目标提供基础和保障。

The path of opening-up is the only path to a country's prosperity and development. General Secretary Xi emphasized that “Openness brings progress, while self-seclusion leaves one behind. China will not close its door to the world; we will only become more and more open”. This sonorous and forceful pledge gives the whole world China's strongest voice on its adherence to reform and opening-up. It is of major importance to make new ground in pursuing opening-up on all fronts. It will help address the contradiction between unbalanced and inadequate development and the people's ever-growing needs for a better life as socialism with Chinese characteristics enters a new era. It will deepen the practice of law-based governance, formulate and improve relevant laws and regulations, ensure law-based government administration by regulators, and protect enterprises' legitimate rights and interests, and “all businesses registered in China will be treated equally”. It will further deepen reforms, facilitate the full use of both overseas and domestic markets and both international and domestic resources, and enhance China's

开放是国家繁荣发展的必由之路。习近平总书记强调，“开放带来进步，封闭必然落后。中国开放的大门不会关闭，只会越开越大。”这一铿锵有力的示言，向全世界发出了中国始终坚持改革开放的最强音。构建全面开放新格局意义十分重大，它有利于中国特色社会主义进入新时代更好地解决人民日益增长的美好生活需要和不平衡不充分发展之间的矛盾；有利于深化依法治国实践，完善制定相关法律法规，规范政府监管部门依法行政，保护企业的合法权益，“凡是在我国境内注册的企业，都要一视同仁、平等对待”；有利于进一步深化改革，充分利用“两个市场”“两种资源”，全面提升我国开放型经济水平；有利于为世界经

open economy in an all-round way. It will inject new momentum into the growth of the world economy, and make economic globalization more open, inclusive, and balanced so that its benefits are shared by all.

济增长提供新的动能，推动经济全球化朝着更加开放、包容、普惠、平衡、共赢的方向发展。

Customs is a country's supervisory and administrative agency of its entry-exit affairs. It is the priority political task for China Customs to thoroughly study and implement the guiding principles of the 19th CPC National Congress for now and in the near future. We should conscientiously study and understand the Xi Jinping Thought on Socialism with Chinese Characteristics for a New Era, all-roundly implement the major plans, strategies and decisions made at the 19th CPC National Congress, carefully consider Customs work, and put all the tasks set by the 19th CPC National Congress into practice. To this end, it is important to pay particular attention to the following areas during customs supervision and services:

海关是国家进出境监督管理机关，深入学习贯彻党的十九大精神是当前和今后一个时期全国海关首要的政治任务。我们要认真学习领会习近平新时代中国特色社会主义思想，全面贯彻党的十九大作出的一系列重大部署、重大战略、重大决策，紧密结合海关工作，把党的十九大提出的各项任务各项要求落到实处。为此，海关在更好地发挥把关服务作用上应重点加强以下几个方面：

1. We should better arm ourselves with theories.

（一）理论武装要有新境界。

The theory reveals the rules, gives directions and opens the minds. It is a prerequisite for providing better Customs service that officials and officers of China Customs are armed with Marxism and its theoretical achievements in adapting Marxism to the Chinese context. We often say that when we study political theories,

理论揭示规律、指引方向、启发思想。用马克思主义及中国化理论成果武装海关系统广大干部群众，是做好海关把关服务工作的必要前提。我们常说，学习政治理论要学深学透、融会贯

we should study them thoroughly and completely, digest comprehensively and achieve mastery, and bear it in mind and in heart. Party members of China Customs, particularly officials at all levels, should spare no efforts in their theory study, thoroughly study and understand the Xi Jinping Thought on Socialism with Chinese Characteristics for a New Era, "remain true to our original aspiration, keep our mission firmly in mind", strengthen our consciousness of the need to maintain political integrity, think in big-picture terms, follow the leadership core, and keep in alignment, always closely follow the Central Committee with Comrade Xi Jinping at the core in terms of our thinking, political orientation, and actions, uphold the authority and centralized, unified leadership of the Central Committee, and conscientiously oppose and resist the erroneous anti-Marxism mindset of all forms, such as "distortion in understanding", "equivocal and noncommittal attitude", "narrow and dogmatic interpretation", and so on. During our study, we should always firmly uphold the Party's political line, link theories with practice, integrate our study with thinking, practice and understanding, and elevate our theoretical learning to a new level that is self-conscious, confident, and natural.

通、入脑入心。作为海关党员干部，特别是各级领导干部学理论要下真功夫，要深入学习领会习近平新时代中国特色社会主义思想，“不忘初心、牢记使命”，切实增强“四个意识”，始终在思想上政治上行动上同以习近平同志为核心的党中央保持高度一致，确保党中央权威和集中统一领导，自觉抵制“歪曲理解”“态度暧昧”“狭隘教条”等各种形式的反马克思主义错误思想倾向。在学习过程中，要始终坚定政治立场，要做到理论联系实际、学思践悟，使理论武装达到自觉自信自然的新境界。

In deepening reform and opening-up, we should pursue the vision of innovative, coordinated, green, and open development

联系到我国进一步对外开放和深化改革，我们就要用“创新、协调、绿色、开

that is for everyone, review and identify the new situations and new challenges. Let's take "turning China into a strong trader" for example. After nearly four decades since the reform and opening-up, China's foreign trade has achieved historic development, yet the problem of "large but not strong" still stands out, mainly reflected in a relatively weak innovative capability, and a relatively poor quality and low added value of export products. The report at the 19th CPC National Congress pointed out that "We will expand foreign trade, develop new models and new forms of trade, and turn China into a trader of quality". This requests us to use the Xi Jinping Thought on Socialism with Chinese Characteristics for a New Era to guide our work. To be specific, we should achieve "three transformations": accelerate the transformation of foreign trade development mode, namely from focusing on trade in goods to a coordinated development of trade in goods and services; from depending on scale and speed to improving quality efficiency and innovation; from relying on maximized imports and exports and minimized costs and prices to a comprehensive competitive advantage of optimized imports and exports with technology, standard, brand, quality and services as the core, so as to keep a firm hold on the priority of our country's opening-up endeavor. Based upon the above-said transformations,

放、共享"新的发展理念来审视和判断当前的新形势、新情况和新挑战。比如，加快贸易强国建设问题。改革开放近40年来，我国对外贸易实现了历史性跨越，但大而不强的问题较为突出，主要是创新能力较弱，出口产品质量、档次和附加值还不高。十九大报告提出，要"拓展对外贸易，培育贸易新业态新模式，推进贸易强国建设。"这就需要我们用习近平新时代中国特色社会主义思想指导我们的工作。具体来说，就要加快转变外贸发展方式，实现"三个转变"，即以货物贸易为主向货物和服务贸易协调发展转变，从依靠规模速度向依靠质量效益、创新创造转变，从大进大出、依靠成本、价格优势为主向优进优出、以技术、标准、品牌、质量、服务为核心的综合竞争优势转变，从而牢牢把握好我国对外开放工作的主攻方向。在海关把关服务工作上，根据这一系列的转变，对进出口监管的思路、对策、方式

we should make changes and adjustments to Customs services accordingly in terms of the thinking, countermeasures and approaches of import and export administration, and relevant work measures should also be formulated and implemented as soon as possible. The process of arming ourselves with theories is the process of elevating our ability of understanding, analyzing and solving problems, as well as the process of using theories to guide practice and achieve new results.

也要随之转变和调整，相关的工作措施也需要尽快制定和跟进。理论武装要有新境界，就是提升认识问题、分析问题和解决问题能力的过程，就是理论指导实践出新成果的过程。

2. We should improve our work performance with due diligence.

（二）忠诚履职要有新水平。

中国海关忠诚履职，把关服务。

China Customs, protecting the border and providing services with due diligence.

The basic missions of Customs include supervision and administration, tariff collection, combating smuggling, compilation of statistics, etc. Its fundamental goal is to promote the

海关的基本任务是监督管理、征收关税、打击走私、编制海关统计及办理其他业务，其根本目的就是为

country's opening-up and a stable and sound socioeconomic development and safeguard the country's and the people's interests. In my view, in order to decide whether Customs officers have diligently performed their duty, we should primarily ask whether they have firmly established a correct political direction and guiding thought in work; whether they have conducted work by law and provided just, civilized and quality services; whether they can solve problems properly in the face of new situations, new challenges or emergencies while sticking to the principles, and whether they can pursue exploration and innovation and advance with times while taking responsibility and maintaining honesty and self-discipline. Under the new circumstances of creating new ground in pursuing opening-up on all fronts, we should step up efforts to improve our work performance with due diligence.

了促进国家的对外开放和经济社会平稳健康发展、维护国家和人民的利益。我体会，衡量一名海关工作人员是否做到了忠诚履职，关键看是否牢固确立了正确的政治方向和工作指导思想；是否做到了依法把关、公正文明、优质服务；是否能在新情况、新挑战或突发事件的情况下，既坚持原则又得体地妥处相关问题，既开拓创新、与时俱进又勇于担当、廉洁自律。在当前构建全面开放新格局的新形势下，我们更应不断提高自身忠诚履职的新水平。

Specifically, on the one hand, as law enforcers, we should firm up and further build the awareness of rule of law and think and act in terms of the rule of law so as to perform Customs duty in all respects. On the other hand, we should firmly hold the thinking of enforcing the law in the interests of the people, streamline administration and delegate power to lower levels, and cut down on complexity, in order to facilitate import and export clearance and

具体来说，一方面，作为执法者要牢固树立法治观念，运用法治思维和法治方式全面履行海关把关职责；另一方面，要牢固树立执法为民的思想，放管服结合，去繁就简、便利进出口通关、提升把关服务效益。在监管工作中，要做到法定职责必须为、法无授权不可

increase the effectiveness of Customs service. In supervision, we must fulfill our mandates by the law, and cannot act without the authorization of the law; and bear in mind that our work should be in accordance with the law, and inspection and release should be efficient. In tax collection and management, we should levy the tax for the country according to law while avoid excessive or repeated taxation. In corporate administration, we should facilitate those who abide by the law while punish those who violate the law and create a good port and business environment. In anti-smuggling work, we should clamp down on unlawful acts in a just and civilized way. In force management, we should accord with the requirements of full and rigorous governance over the Party, focus on both customs operations and force management, and practice strict Customs self-governance, etc. All these seem daily routine, yet we still need to further improve our work quality and level to perform our duty well.

为，工作于法有据、验放讲究效率；在税收征管中，既要为国家依法征税，做到应收尽收，又不能征过头税；在企业管理中，要落实守法便利、违法惩戒的措施，营造良好的口岸和营商环境；在打击走私中，既要依法严厉打击，又要注重执法公正、文明办案；在队伍管理中，按照全面从严治党要求，坚持“两手抓”，从严治关，等等。这些看似都是我们日常的工作，但要真正做好，还需要不断提升我们的工作质量和水平。

3. We should make new breakthroughs in reform and innovation.

（三）改革创新要有新突破。

In recent years, under the unified deployment of the CPC Central Committee and the State Council, the General Administration of China Customs has been proactively pushing forward such reforming measures as customs clearance based on the 3Ms principle (i.e. mutual recognition of control, mutual exchange of

近年来，海关总署按照党中央国务院的统一部署，积极推进“三互大通关”、国际贸易“单一窗口”、全国通关一体化、“两个中心”建设、海关特殊监管区域整合优化、“双随机、一

information, mutual assistance in enforcement), "Single Window" in international trade, "Two Centers" (i.e. the Center of Risk Control and the Center of Duty Collection) in national customs integration, integration and optimization of special customs control areas, an oversight model of "random-inspection and public release across the board (i.e. inspections of randomly-selected entities by randomly-selected inspectors and the public release of inspection results)", etc., which have secured good results. According to the new requirement by the 19th CPC National Congress of "making new ground in pursuing opening-up on all fronts", we need to make more innovations and breakthroughs in our work.

公开"等改革举措，收到了好的效果。按照十九大提出的"推进形成全面开放新格局"要求，我们还有很多的工作需要创新和突破。

For instance, General Secretary Xi Jinping's report at the 19th CPC National Congress specified that "We will adopt policies to promote high-standard liberalization and facilitation of trade and investment", and "We will grant more powers to pilot free trade zones to conduct reform and explore the opening of free trade ports". This has put forward a new challenge on reform and innovation. Approved by the State Council, the Shanghai Pilot Free Trade Zone (PFTZ) was officially launched in 2013, the first of its kind in China. And there are 11 PFTZs across the country so far, from which we have seen first-mover effects. Stepping forward, we should further improve the development quality of PFTZs,

比如，习近平总书记在党的十九大报告中明确提出，要"实行高水平的贸易和投资自由化便利化政策"，"赋予自由贸易试验区更大改革自主权，探索建设自由贸易港"，这就给我们提出了改革创新的新课题。我国自由贸易试验区是2013年经国务院批准在上海首个启动建设的，目前已有11个，取得了先发效应。下一步要在做好做优的基础上，根据我国海岸线长、离岛资源丰富、经济基础和口

and leverage the advantages of long coastlines, abundant offshore resources, good economic and port infrastructures to explore the building of free trade ports with Chinese characteristics, so as to build new heights with a higher level of opening-up, better business environment and bigger influence on surrounding areas.

岸功能健全等特点，积极探索建设具有中国特色的自由贸易港，打造开放层次更高、营商环境更优、辐射作用更强的开放新高地。

4. We should achieve new results in coordinated and win-win cooperation.

（四）协作共赢要有新成果。

For the time being, we are confronted with a sluggish global economic recovery, a lingering financial crisis, and the spread of such unconventional threats as terrorism, refugee crisis, major contagious diseases, climate change, etc. As globalization develops, Customs should follow the tasks and goals set by the 19th CPC National Congress, fully play its role in foreign exchanges, create new ground in pursuing opening-up on all fronts, and make incessant efforts for the development of a community with a shared future for mankind through closer Customs international cooperation.

当前，世界经济增长乏力，金融危机阴云不散，恐怖主义、难民危机、重大传染性疾病、气候变化等非传统安全威胁持续蔓延。随着全球化不断发展，海关要按照十九大提出的任务和目标，充分发挥自身在对外交往中的作用，通过加强海关国际合作，有力助推形成全面开放新格局，为构建人类命运共同体而不懈努力。

First, we should prioritize the building of the "Belt and Road", and actively engage in the "big picture" of the country's diplomacy and foreign trade. In recent years, with China Customs' efforts and support from international organizations including the World Customs Organization, cooperation between customs administrations has blossomed, greatly

第一，要以"一带一路"建设为重点，主动融入国家外交、外经贸大局。近年来，在中国海关的自身努力和世界海关组织等国际组织的支持下，各国海关部门间的合作蓬勃发展，极大促进了商品、人员、货币和信

facilitating the effective and convenient cross-border movement of goods, people, currency and information, and helping ensure border security and trade safety. In the future, we need to further enhance the facilitation of trade and investment between countries along the routes, establish and improve cooperative mechanisms in all areas and at all levels with customs administrations of each country and each region, respect each other, trust each other and support each other, and make due contributions to the development of world trade and regional economic integration.

息有效和便利的跨境流动，积极协助维护了边境和贸易安全，未来我们需要进一步推动沿线国家贸易和投资便利化，与各国、各区域海关建立完善海关各领域、各层级的合作机制，相互尊重、相互信任和相互支持，为世界贸易和区域经济一体化的发展做出应尽的贡献。

Second, we should strengthen policy communication and increase unimpeded trade. a) We should leverage such mechanisms and platforms as the "Belt and Road" initiative and BRICS, strengthen policy communication and reach consensus over major policy affairs of the international customs community. b) We should conduct exchanges on national development strategies, laws and regulations, customs procedures and modernization reforms, and share each other's achievements and experience in the modernization innovation and reform of Customs. c) We should jointly carry out researches on cross-border e-commerce and other types of emerging industries and try to explore from them new growth points for our country's economic development. d) We should firmly oppose trade protectionism, jointly increase customs clearance

第二，要加强政策沟通，提升贸易畅通。一是应借助“一带一路”、金砖国家等合作机制平台，围绕国际海关界重大政策性事务加强政策沟通，凝聚共识。二是应就国家发展战略、法律法规、海关手续和现代化改革等领域开展交流，互通互享各国在海关现代化改革创新中的成果和经验。三是应共同开展对跨境电子商务等新业态的研究，促使新业态为本国经济发展创造新的增长点。四是应坚决反对贸易保护主义，通过简化通关手续，建立海关数据交换、服务和共享的平台等具体措

efficiency via simpler procedures and platforms for Customs data exchange, service and sharing among other measures, and help more enterprises to enjoy concrete convenience.

施，共同提升海关通关效率，帮助更多的企业享受到实实在在的通关便利。

Third, we should provide mutual assistance in enforcement. Customs administrations of all countries should mutually support and engage in the joint enforcement activities proposed on multilateral platforms by any of them, carry out cooperation in key areas such as countering the smuggling of endangered flora and fauna, drugs, guns and ammunition, and hazardous waste, as well as counterterrorism and safety through intelligence exchange, experience sharing and joint studies. Besides, we should conduct cooperation in enforcement by the customs, compliance of the companies, and promulgation of the law among the public, aimed at fostering compliance in the business sector, help companies better understand customs laws and regulations, and guide them to abide by the law in import and export activities, so as to guarantee the safety and efficiency at ports.

第三，促进执法互助。各国海关应相互支持和参与各自在多边领域倡议的联合执法行动，开展打击濒危动植物、毒品、枪支弹药、洋垃圾等走私、反恐与安全等重点领域的合作，积极开展情报交流、经验分享、联合研究，同时围绕提升企业守法水平开展执法、守法、普法合作，帮助企业更好地了解海关的法律、法规，引导企业在进出口活动中遵纪守法，切实保障口岸的安全与便利。

Fourth, we should expand capacity building cooperation. We should make better use of existing resources, launch capacity building exercises at WCO Training Center in the Asia-Pacific Region, expand cooperative areas by means of expert exchanges, themed researches and on-site attachment programs

第四，拓展能力建设。应积极利用现有资源，在世界海关组织亚太地区培训中心创办能力建设活动，通过世界海关组织中国基金赞助、选派专家、专题研讨、现场跟班等形式拓展合作领

under the auspices of WCO Capacity Building Fund established by China Customs. We should learn from each other and help each other to improve Customs officers' morality, enforcement performance, as well as administration and coordination capability, so as to provide good human resources and talent reserves for the development of the open economy.

域，相互学习、相互借鉴、相互帮助，不断提升海关关员的道德品行、执法水准、管理和协调能力，为开放型经济发展提供优质的人力资源和人才储备。

In short, we should take the Xi Jinping Thought on Socialism with Chinese Characteristics for a New Era as our guide, earnestly implement the spirit of the 19th CPC National Congress, stick to the basic state policy of opening-up, and apply the new vision of development. We must take a clear political stand in customs work, improve customs with reforms, exercise law-based supervision, vitalize customs with technology, and govern the customs force with strict discipline. And we must work harder with a pragmatic and innovative spirit to secure concrete progress and make greater contributions to the country's modern economic system and the Two Centenary Goals.

总之，我们要以习近平新时代中国特色社会主义思想为指导，认真贯彻落实党的十九大精神，坚持对外开放的基本国策，遵循新发展理念，坚持“政治建关、改革强关、依法把关、科技兴关、从严治关”，加倍努力，务实进取，为建设我国现代化经济体系、实现“两个一百年”奋斗目标作出海关新的更大的贡献。

辑一

海关专业

Customs Affairs

关于推动我国外经贸高质量发展的建议

——在全国政协第十三届一次会议经济界联组讨论会上的发言

2018年3月6日

Suggestions on Promoting High-quality Development of Foreign Trade and Economic Cooperation

—— Remarks at a joint discussion of the economic sector during the First Session of the 13th CPPCC

March 6, 2018

Currently, the socialism with Chinese characteristics has entered a new era, and so has economic development, whose essential feature is that the country's economy has shifted from a high-speed growth phase to a high-quality growth phase. It ushers in a time of opportunities for foreign trade and economic development, yet it also poses new challenges and brings new problems.

当前，中国特色社会主义进入了新时代，我国对外经贸发展也进入了新时代，其基本特征正由高速增长阶段转向高质量发展阶段。这为我国对外经贸发展迎来了新的机遇期，同时也面临新的挑战和带来新的问题。

I. From a global perspective

一、从国际看

The world is undergoing drastic development, transformation and adjustment. Firstly, in spite of the increasing new industries, new technologies and new forms of business, the world economic growth is still sluggish, and it is

当前，世界正处于大发展大变革大调整时期。一是新产业、新技术、新业态层出不穷，但世界经济尚未走出亚健康和弱增长的调整

still difficult to achieve high-speed foreign trade development. Secondly, economic adjustments are divergent in different regions. The policy changes of the major economies and their spillover effects create uncertainty. And there are many other factors that bring instability and uncertainty. Thirdly, protectionism is mounting, and geopolitical risks are on the ascent. The Trump administration for instance, issued the new Tax Cuts and Jobs Act, and had brought up the border tax adjustment, sparking a new round of competition and adjustment. The US and the EU in particular, have been launching frequent anti-dumping and countervailing duty investigations against Chinese products, refuse to carry out responsibilities as WTO members, and refuse to recognize China as a "market economy" under the global trade rules, which will put on more pressure on China's foreign trade and economic development.

期，国际贸易快速增长仍有难度。二是世界经济分化调整，主要经济体政策调整及其外溢效应带来变数，有很多不确定和不稳定。三是贸易保护主义加剧，地缘政治风险上升。比如特朗普政府出台美国减税和就业法案以及此前曾提出实施的边境调节税，出现新的竞争和调整。尤其是，一直以来美国、欧盟等频繁对华产品发起“双反”，不履行 WTO 成员义务，拒绝中国在全球贸易规则下获得“市场经济”待遇的要求，对我国外贸发展不利影响加剧。

II. From a domestic perspective

Since the 18th National Party Congress, the CPC Central Committee with Comrade Xi Jinping as its core has been reviewing the general trends, crafting overall plans and carrying out practical work, and successfully steered the country's development in all areas. China has maintained the biggest exporter and the second biggest importer in international trade in goods for 8 consecutive years. According to

二、从国内看

党的十八大以来，以习近平同志为核心的党中央总揽全局，确立开放发展新理念，观大势、谋全局、干实事，各项工作取得了可喜成绩。我国已经连续八年保持全球货物贸易第一大出口国和第二大进口国。据中国海关统计，2017年我国进出口

China Customs statistics, in 2017, China had the world's largest import and export volume of 27.79 trillion RMB yuan, increased by 14.2%, an equivalent to 4104.48 billion US dollars and up by 11.4%. According to U.S. statistics, U.S. import and export came in second with 3956.25 billion dollars trade in goods, increased by 6.9%. It is worth mentioning that global market share of Chinese products increased from 10.4% in 2011 to 13.2% in 2016. Besides, the models and structure of trade continue to be improved, and outbound investment of Chinese companies is growing. Meanwhile, although China's foreign trade volume is big, it is not strong enough. Its structure still needs further improvement, and we still need to open up more to the outside world. We have yet to form new competitive advantages that center on technology, brand, quality, standard, and services. In addition, as the country's labor cost increases, the traditional path of growth has come to a bottleneck. There're more constraints on the environment and resources, and we are still faced with challenges in terms of innovative development, and transformation and upgrading. Therefore, it is a long and arduous way ahead for us to build a strong trading nation.

贸易总额达27.79万亿元人民币，同比增长14.2%；按美元计算41044.75亿美元，增长11.4%，成为世界第一。据美国统计，美国货物进出口总值39562.48亿美元，同比增长6.9%，世界第二。值得一提的是，我国出口国际市场份额从2011年的10.4%升至2016年的13.2%，贸易方式进一步改进，进出口结构持续优化，中国企业“走出去”投资的规模不断扩大。但同时，贸易大而不强的问题、结构不合理、开放度不够的问题等客观存在，尚未形成以技术、品牌、质量、标准、服务为核心的对外竞争新优势。另外，我国劳动力成本优势渐减，传统发展模式、环境资源受到约束，创新发展和转型升级方面仍面临挑战。因此，加快贸易强国建设任重道远。

The report of the 19th CPC Congress said that we would make new ground in pursuing opening up on all fronts. The report on the work of the government this year said that we would

按照党的十九大报告提出的推动形成全面开放新格局和这次政府工作报告提出的加大改革开放力度，以高

step up the effort in reform and opening-up and use high-standard opening-up to generate high-quality development. In order to accomplish these new tasks and meet the new requirements, we must follow the guidance of Xi Jinping Thought on Socialism with Chinese Characteristics for a New Era and carry out our own responsibilities. To this end, I have the following suggestions:

水平开放推动高质量发展的新任务和新要求，我们要以习近平新时代中国特色社会主义思想为指导，积极做好自身的相关工作。为此，建议：

1. Strengthen trade and economic cooperation with countries and regions along "the Belt and Road."

（一）加强"一带一路"沿线国家和地区经贸合作。

The building of the Belt and Road is a significant and strategic endeavor to deepen China's opening-up. In 2017, trade with countries along the Belt and Road stood at 7.37 trillion yuan, increased by 17.8%, which was 3.6 percentage points higher than China's foreign trade growth, accounting for 26.5% of China's total trade volume. Import was 2.17 trillion yuan, up by 30.8%. 399.96 billion yuan of tax and duty was collected, up by 28.4%, which means there is massive potential to the trade and economic cooperation with these countries. I suggest that we negotiate for more preferential trade arrangements and investment agreements with the Belt and Road countries and regions, and carry out full-fledged cooperation in customs, quarantine, transport and logistics, e-commerce, and so on. We need to increase clearance efficiency for cargos by streamlining

"一带一路"建设是我国扩大对外开放的重大战略举措。2017年我国对"一带一路"沿线国家进出口7.37万亿元，同比增长17.8%，高于我国整体外贸增速3.6个百分点，占我国外贸总值的26.5%。其中，进口商品2.17万亿元，增长30.8%；税收3999.6亿元，增长28.4%，可见"一带一路"沿线相关国家经贸合作潜力巨大。**建议：**进一步加强与"一带一路"沿线相关国家和地区商谈优惠贸易安排和投资保护协定，全面加强海关、检验检疫、运输物流、电子商务等领域合作，通过简化通关手续，通关时间在已减半

customs procedures, which means having already cut clearance time by half, we should shave another third off, and building a platform for data exchange, services and information sharing. We need to jointly study new trade modes such as cross-border e-commerce and form new competitive advantages as soon as possible. We also need to diversify export destinations, import origins, and investment partners to better adapt to new situations and changes.

的基础上再压缩三分之一，建立数据交换、服务和共享的平台等具体措施，共同提升货物通关效率。同时，共同开展对跨境电子商务等新业态的研究，加快培育外经贸竞争新优势，努力实现出口市场多元化、进口来源多元化、投资合作伙伴关系多元化，更好地适应新的形势和变化。

2. Deepen multilateral and bilateral opening-up and promote trade and investment liberalization and facilitation.

Economic globalization is unstoppable. I suggest first, we should advocate for multilateral trade systems, and fully implement the WTO *Trade Facilitation Agreement*. We should step up facilitation for all of China's major trading partners, promote China's export, and create a facilitated clearance environment. Meanwhile, we should call for trade disputes to be settled through discussion as equals, oppose trade protectionism, and resolutely safeguard our lawful rights. Second, we should deepen opening-up on the bilateral level by advancing the strategy of free trade zones, fully implement and negotiate for more high-standard investment agreements and various preferential trade arrangements. Up till now, we have signed 16 agreements, 15 of which

（二）坚持多双边开放，提升贸易自由化便利化水平。

经济全球化是个势不可当的潮流。**建议：**一是要支持多边贸易体制，落实世贸组织《贸易便利化协定》实施，普遍提高我国与主要贸易伙伴的贸易便利化水平，促进我国产品出口并营造便捷的通关环境。同时，我们也主张通过平等协商解决贸易争端，反对贸易保护主义，坚决捍卫自身合法权益。二是要提高双边开放水平，积极推进自贸区战略，落实并积极促成高水平的投资协定以及各种形式的优惠贸易安排。目前，已签

are already in effect, exempting 90% of the goods from customs duty, covering 23 countries and regions, and over 8000 categories. In 2017, 420.7 billion dollars' worth of goods were traded under the said agreements, and 227.9 billion yuan of duty was reduced. Third, laws, regulations and policies related to foreign capital need to be further reviewed and improved; a negative list for market access needs to be instituted; intellectual property rights need to be protected and any infringement of IPR should be strictly punished. Lawful rights of domestic and foreign companies should be guarded, so that they can trade and do business in a healthy and stable environment.

3. Proactively advance the building of Pilot Free Trade Zones and Free Trade Ports.

The report on the work of government said that "We will spread the use of practices developed in free trade zones all over the country, and explore opening free trade ports, working toward new heights in reform and opening-up." China has a long coastline, and an abundant storage of offshore resources. It is of the utmost strategic importance to build new heights that are more open, can provide better business environment and have a bigger impact on surrounding regions. I suggest: 1. we should grant local governments more decision-making power to embolden them to take on trials and independent endeavors. We need to aim

协定16个，15个已生效，零关税占90%，涉及23个国家和地区，涵盖8000多种进出口商品，2017年协定项下享惠4207亿美元，减税2279亿元。三是要进一步清理完善涉及外资的法律法规和政策文件，推进负面清单管理制度建设，加强知识产权保护，严厉打击侵权假冒违法犯罪活动，保障内外资企业的合法权益，营造健康稳定的对外经贸营商环境和良好的进出口秩序。

（三）积极推进自贸试验区和自由贸易港建设。

政府工作报告中提出，要“全面复制推广自贸试验区经验，探索建设自由贸易港，打造改革开放新高地”。我国海岸线长，离岛资源丰富，打造开放层次更高、营商环境更优、辐射作用更强的开放新高地，战略意义十分重大。**建议**：一是在赋予自贸试验区更大改革自主权上，鼓励地方大胆试、大胆闯、自主改，对标国际、弥补短板，努力提升建设质量。二是继续创

for international standards, strengthen areas of weakness and enhance the quality of our work. 2. We need to keep innovating the current system through the systematic integration of reform measures and policies so as to generate synergy. 3. We need to improve laws and regulations to make sure that all business activities can be governed by law. 4. We need to spread useful experience. 25 innovative customs policies have already been implemented across the country. Our free trade ports should be the special economic zones with the highest standard of opening-up in the world. They should allow the free flow of cargo, capital and people, exempt most goods from customs duty and exercise bonded supervision. From the customs perspective, based upon the free trade port's feature of "within the national territory and outside the customs territory", we should form a new supervision model of "minimum control on the border of the national territory with free trade inside the zone; strict control at the border of customs territory with coordinated control". Except that relevant laws, regulations or international conventions explicitly impose a ban (restriction) on entry and exit, overseas goods can go into or out of the free trade port freely. Customs will conduct risk analysis and control with the help from logistics information shared from the "Single Window" in international trade, and companies inside the zone can do business

新制度，强化改革措施系统集成，形成合力。三是完善相关法规，确保依法有据。四是复制推广有益经验。海关已有25项创新制度在全国推广。探索建设自由贸易港，应该是目前全球开放水平最高的特殊经济功能区，货物、资金、人员进出自由，绝大数商品免征关税并实施保税监管。从海关来说，按“境内关外”的特点，构架“一线放开、区内自由、二线管住、协同共管”的口岸监管新模式。除相关法律法规或国际公约明确禁止或限制外，境外货物可自由进出自由贸易港区，进出境监管管理部门依托国际贸易“单一窗口”共享的物流信息开展风险分析和监管，区内企业可以自由开展业务。对自贸港区与境内区外之间进出的货物，依法照章监管和征税，完善相关法律法规，各部门按职责分工依法按规承担相关管理责任。

freely. For goods moving between the free trade port and areas within the national territory while outside the zone, Customs should carry out supervision and tax collection based on law as well as improve relevant laws and regulations. And each department will undertake their obligations according to its own responsibility.

4. Improve the layout and structure of industrial and regional opening-up.

My suggestions are as follows. First, we need to improve and upgrade the trade in goods to build a big and strong trading nation by enhancing innovation capacity, increase the quality, grade and added value of export goods, encourage the export of new technologies, equipment, and branded products, while at the same time importing more advanced machineries, key components and high-quality consumer products, and hosting the first China International Import Expo for balanced development of import and export. Second, we need to guide the transformation and upgrading of processing trade, encourage the export of services, including culture, tourism, architecture design, software development, research and design, and so on. We should also support new forms of business such as cross-border e-commerce, trade through market purchase, and integrated services of international trade. Third, we should greatly liberalize market access, open up the manufacturing sector as well

（四）优化产业与区域的开放结构和布局。

建议：一是加快货物贸易优化升级解决大而不强问题，加强创新能力，提高出口产品质量、档次和附加值，鼓励高新技术、装备制造、品牌产品出口，同时扩大先进技术设备、关键零部件和优质消费品等进口，办好首届中国国际进口博览会，促进进出口平衡。二是引导加工贸易转型升级，鼓励文化、旅游、建筑、软件、研发设计等服务出口，支持跨境电子商务、市场采购贸易、外贸综合服务等新兴业态发展。三是大幅放开市场准入，在深化制造业开放的同时，积极扩大服务业对外开放，重点推进金融、教育、文化、医疗等服务业领域的有序开放。四是支持

as the service sector, and focus on the step-by-step opening-up of finance, education, culture and medical services. Fourth, we should support the green development of processing trade, and the development of new strategic industries and new models of trade in coastal regions in Eastern China; promote the development of the western region, apply more flexible policies, and encourage processing trade to shift to the central and western regions.

东部沿海地区加工贸易绿色发展和战略性新兴产业及新型贸易业态发展；加大西部边疆开放力度，实施更加灵活的政策，引导和支持中西部地区承接加工贸易产业梯度转移。

5. Enhance risk prevention and control during the high-quality development of foreign trade and economic cooperation.

（五）加强外经贸高质量发展过程中的风险防控。

First of all, port management authorities must keep a sharp lookout for risks during the high-quality development by enhancing the identification, analysis, disposal and monitoring of smuggling risks in the flow of cargo, capital, people and information that might pose a danger for national and people's interests, firmly crackdown on smuggling of endangered species, drugs, guns and ammunition, hazardous waste, and so on, and carry out international cooperation to tackle terrorism and safety issues so as to ensure security, facilitation and efficiency at the ports.

建议：首先，从口岸来说，要围绕进出境货物流、资金流、人员流、信息流等加强对可能危害国家和人民利益的走私违法风险的监控、识别、分析和处置，坚决打击濒危动植物、毒品、枪支弹药、洋垃圾等走私活动，加强反恐与安全等重点领域的国际合作，确保口岸的安全便利高效。

Secondly, concerning statistics analytics, we need to explore new ways to compile statistics regarding emerging industries and new models of trade, monitor import, export, and the

其次，从统计分析来说，要探索新产业、新业态的贸易统计方法，动态监测进出口情况和贸易走势，完

trend of foreign trade in real time, improve the Export Leading Index, and pay more attention to increasing the quality of export and the value added to it. We should also step up the trade statistics analysis of overproduced coal, steel, as well as other bulk commodities that are under macro-control of the Central Government, and strictly deter fake trade.

善外贸出口先导指数，更加注重提升出口质量和附加值，加大对诸如煤炭、钢材等国内产能过剩和中央实施宏观调控的大宗商品进出口的统计分析力度，依法依规严厉管控虚假贸易。

Finally, as for the implementation of policies, government agencies should strengthen the study on import and export policies and follow up on their implementation, do their best to find a balance between “bringing in” and “going global”. We should pay close attention to the issues related to the quality and efficiency of high-quality development that might be caused by the expansion of import and the duty reduction of some import commodities.

最后，从政策实施来说，国家相关部门应加强对进出口相关政策研究和政策实施跟踪，密切关注“引进来与走出去”更好的结合点，以及积极扩大进口、下调部分产品进口关税所涉及的外经贸发展质量和效益问题。

解放思想　勇于创新　不断深化全国通关一体化改革

2018年4月

Free Our Mind and Take Innovations to Deepen the Reform of National Cutoms Integration

April, 2018

In recent years, the General Administration of China Customs (GACC) has been carrying out the requirements of the CPC Central Committee on reforms in all areas, freed its mind, and taken bold innovations and rolled out a list of reforms for customs operations. The reform of national clearance integration for instance, has been deepened, and has shown more results and given importers and exporters a greater sense of gain through trade facilitation.

近年来，国家海关总署按照中央全面深化改革的要求，解放思想，勇于创新，推出了一系列业务改革举措。其中，全国通关一体化改革正在向纵深发展，成效越来越明显，广大进出口企业通关便利的获得感也越来越强。

The primary objective of the reform of national clearance integration is to carry out the reform of customs control systems required by the Third Plenary Session of the 18th Central Committee of the Communist Party of China.

全国海关通关一体化改革，主要目的是为贯彻落实党的十八届三中全会关于“改革海关监管管理体制”的要求，进一步优化营商环

It aims to improve business environment and promote healthy development of foreign trade. The GACC put forth the *Overall Plan to Deepen Customs Reforms in all Areas*, and the *Framework for the Reform of National Clearance Integration*, which focused on a structure supported by the "Two Centers and Three Systems" that aimed to apply consistency to key enforcement activities, and exercise centralized management and coordinated control, in order to make breakthroughs and pave the way for future reforms. These two documents also laid down plans to rebuild current customs procedures, restructure the organization, and implement a clearance system that requires declaration only once and allows the fast release of goods before step-by-step supervision measures. They highlighted the objective to improve customs control and services through reforms and innovation.

境、促进外经贸健康发展。海关总署制定了《海关全面深化改革总体方案》和《全国通关一体化改革框架方案》。以“两中心三制度”为结构支撑，实现全国海关关键业务的统一执法、集中指挥以及各方协同监管，充分发挥深化改革的突破性和先导性作用；以流程再造和机构重组为主要路径，实施货物通关“一次申报、分步处置”，着力突出改革创新，提升把关服务效能。

First of all, we have set up the Two Centers: Risk Management Center and the Duty Collection Center. The Risk Management Center controls the security risks of goods, personal items, and means of transportation using risk parameters, gives orders for physical checks and audits, enhances the control of the GACC at ports, and complements a management system where customs across the country work as one.

第一，建立了“两个中心”。一个是风险防控中心，一个是税收征管中心。风险防控中心侧重于开展货物、物品和运输工具的安全准入风险防控，加载风险参数，统一下达布控查验指令和自主下达稽（核）查指令，强化总署对现场的直接指挥，支撑建立海关全国通关一体化管理格局。

The Duty Collection Center takes a centralized and targeted approach to manage duty related elements and risks based on different categories of goods and industries with the help of information technology. It standardizes operation procedures and encourages the voluntary declaration and duty payment to ensure both easy payment and revenue security.

税收征管中心以信息技术为支撑，突出集约化和专业化，按商品和行业分类对税收征管要素实施管理和风险防控，规范征管作业流程，推动企业自主申报自行缴税，实现纳税便利与税收安全的有机统一。

Meanwhile, we will take a step-by-step approach to redesign the functions of local customs houses. Through the building of the Two Centers, we will put all the operations including risk management and duty collection that used to be scattered around different customs districts and ports on the national level. In a centralized and intelligent way, customs will efficiently relocate resources before, during and after clearance, and make the links of supervision complementary and interconnected to each other. From the traders' perspective, all customs supervision policies and requirements will be consistent throughout the country, and all customs in the country will serve them as a unity. These new measures will also ensure the safety of cargo and tax revenue, and make the reform of clearance integration more efficient and coordinated

同时，有序推进全国隶属海关功能化建设。通过这两个中心的建设，把原来分散在各个关区、各个口岸的海关作业集中到全国这个层面来，包括风险防控和税收征管等业务。海关将通过集中统一的智能化处置，实现事前、事中、事后监管力量的合理分工和联动互补。对广大企业来说，在不同海关面对的将是统一的海关监管政策和要求，真正做到了全国海关是一家，全国是一关；同时也实现了货物安全与税收安全双强化，形成集约高效、协调统一的一体化通关管理格局。

Secondly, China Customs has introduced a clearance system that requires declaration only once and allows the fast release of goods before customs supervision measures. It

第二，采取“一次申报、分步处置”的通关管理模式。“一次申报、分步处置”，改变了海关现行接受

changes the "series connection" of declaration, document examination, physical inspection, tax collection and release. With the help of pre-arrival manifests and the Two Centers, customs has redesigned the workflow to pre-identify risks from manifests and declarations forms and exercise supervision after release. Goods can be released once they have met the basic requirements by law, and they are subject to other customs procedures afterwards. This new model of supervision has significantly reduced the time of release at ports.

申报、审单、查验、征税、放行的"串联式"作业流程，基于舱单提前传输，通过风险防控中心、税收征管中心将舱单、报关单的风险甄别和业务现场的处置作业环节前推后移。凡符合合法性基本要求以后，货物就可以放行了，其他有关手续可以在货物放行后再来完成。通过这种分步处置，大大压缩了在口岸环节的通关时间。

Thirdly, China Customs is reinventing the way of revenue collection. We are building new relations between duty collection and payment starting with voluntary declaration and voluntary payment. We are creating a risk prevention and control system with multiple layers and aspects that include the management of taxpayers based upon the locations of their registrations, selective examination of elements, specialized supervision, and performance assessments. We are reshaping the means of duty collection through new forms of guarantees for duty payment and paperless operations. We are also shifting the focus from document and physical inspections to post-clearance so as to let goods flow more quickly at ports, save time and reduce cost for businesses.

第三，改革了税收征管方式。以企业自报、自缴税款为切入点，建立新型税收征纳关系；通过属地纳税人管理、要素抽核、专业监控和评估考核等方式，建立涵盖商品、企业和行业等多维度、立体式的税收风险防控体系；创新税收担保形式，逐步实现征管作业无纸化，改革纳税方式；将海关抽查审核的重点放在后续的审查和处理上，有效压缩货物在口岸的滞留时间，节省通关时间，降低企业通关成本。

Fourthly, China Customs has created a new coordinated supervision system. Within the organization, we divide the country's customs houses into two categories based on their different locations and main responsibilities: Port Customs and Management Customs. Port customs deals with cargo supervision and clearance at ports, while Management Customs is mainly in charge of post-clearance audit and the credit management of enterprises. Although each of the two categories has its own staff and organization structures and carries different responsibilities, they collaborate with each other and act together, therefore excising control and providing service as a whole. Outside of the organization, we promote the mutual exchange of information, mutual recognition of control and mutual assistance in enforcement with other enforcement authorities. We excise joint inspection to eliminate redundant inspections on the same company and the same goods by different agencies. For instance, the declaration procedures of customs and quarantine have changed from "series connection" to "parallel connection". And we are actively exploring for an integrated and flat port management model.

Since the above reforms started, China Customs has cut human intervention during the import and export clearance process by over 50%, and 85% of declarations were instantly released

第四，创新协同监管制度。对内，按照不同海关在业务布局中所处的不同位置和承担的不同功能，将全国各现场海关区分为口岸型和属地型海关，口岸型海关主要负责对货物进行通关现场监管，属地型海关主要是对企业进行后续的稽查和信用管理，不同海关配不同的机构与人力，承担不同的职责，协同联动，使得全国海关作为一个整体提供执法监管和服务。对外，推进口岸相关执法部门"信息互换、监管互认、执法互助"；实施跨部门一次性联合检查，即对同一个企业、同一个商品，不同的执法部门要避免多次检查、重复执法。比如，将现行货物报关和报检"串联"流程改为"并联"，探索多环节合一、扁平化管理的口岸管理新模式。

以上改革措施实施以来，海关对进、出口事中人工处置率降幅超 50%，直接放行报关单量占 85% 以上。

upon arrival. In 2017, the average time of clearance for import was 15.87 hours, reduced by 36.85% compared to that of last year; the average time of clearance for export was 1.11 hours, reduced by 38.24%. With the expansion of the deferred duty payment scheme, the management of taxpayers based upon the locations of their registrations, and customs information services related to duty payment such as valuation, classification and laboratory test, China Customs is now able to facilitate traders at a much higher level. For businesses, the benefit is three-fold. First, they can choose the location for shipment and declaration as they like since they can file for clearance at any customs in the country. Second, customs enforcement has become more consistent, transparent and standardized. Third, the redesigned customs procedures have significantly reduced time of clearance at ports, leaving more space for supervision, cutting costs of trade and creating a better balance between control and facilitation.

2017 年，全国海关进口平均通关时间为 15.87 小时，同比缩短 36.85%，出口平均通关时间为 1.11 小时，同比缩短 38.24%。推进企业“自报自缴”后，绝大部分涉税风险处置在货物放行后批量实施。海关通过扩大汇总征税制度，同步实施属地纳税人管理制度，以及提供与征税相关的诸如估价、归类、化验等咨询服务，极大地便利了企业。而对企业来说，一是可以任意选择通关或者报关的地点和口岸，在全国任何一个海关都可以办理相关手续；二是海关的执法更加统一，更加透明，更加规范；三是通关效率随着海关监管前推后移大大提升，口岸通关时间缩短了，监管空间扩展了，贸易成本降低了，海关也能够更有效地处理好“管得住”与“通得快”的关系。

Following the coordinated plans of the CPC Central Committee and the State Council, China Customs is earnestly implementing the *Plan on Deepening Reform of Party and State Institutions* and advancing the work on the smooth

按照党中央、国务院的统一部署，海关总署认真贯彻执行《深化党和国家机构改革方案》，推进出入境检验检疫管理职责和队伍划入

transition of duties and personnel of the quarantine administration to the General Administration of Customs. Starting from April 20th, customs and quarantine officers have all been working under the same name of customs for baggage control and cargo inspection. Quarantine officers now wear customs uniforms and have joined the customs ranking system. China Customs is now merging quarantine operations with the reform of national clearance integration. Security risks of quarantine at ports, for instance public health, animals and plants, import and export goods, and food, are incorporated in the security risk management system, with a clear focus on centralized risk control and the support of an information system. Meanwhile, China Customs is diligently improving procedures, providing more services, and deepening the reform of national clearance integration, so that declaration documents, operation systems, risk management, operation command and field enforcement can all be integrated.

Looking ahead, China Customs will continue to free its mind, make more innovations, and further deepen the reform of national clearance integration. We will improve the Single Window for international trade, and spare no effort to roll out more reforms to enhance the mutual exchange of information, mutual assistance in enforcement and mutual recognition of control. We will keep building on our information system and

海关总署的工作平稳顺利实施。4月20日，已实现了原出入境检验检疫系统统一以海关名义对外开展工作，口岸一线旅检、查验和窗口岗位统一上岗，统一着海关制服，统一佩戴关衔。目前，海关正在将检验检疫作业全面融入通关一体化，将检验检疫涉及的口岸公共卫生、动植物、进出口商品和食品安全等风险，统一纳入安全准入风险实施管理，突出风险集中统一防控和信息系统一体化支撑。同时，海关将进一步优化作业流程，拓宽监管服务，深化全国通关一体化，实现“统一申报单证、统一作业系统、统一风险研判、统一指令下达、统一现场执法”。

下一步，海关总署将继续解放思想，勇于创新，更加积极地将全国通关一体化改革引向深入；加强国际贸易“单一窗口”建设，全力推进“三互”大通关改革；不断提高信息化建设水平，全面推进无纸化作业；加快通关作业装备自动化进程；

advance our paperless transformation. We will be equipped with more automatic inspection tools and an optimized structure of human resource. And we will build systems for the public release, supervision and evaluation of time of clearance, so that customs operations can be transparent to companies and people of all walks of life so as to promote the healthy and steady development of foreign trade and economic cooperation.

优化人力资源的配置，提高作业效率；建立通关时间公开、监督和评估制度，自觉接受企业和社会各界的监督，促进我国对外经济贸易的健康稳定发展。

中华人民共和国海关总署

The General Administration of Customs of the People's Republic of China

世界海关组织与中国海关

——建立更紧密的合作伙伴关系 推动全球海关共同发展

2017 年 7 月

WCO and China Customs

—— Building Closer Cooperative Partnership Advancing Common Development of Customs around the World

July, 2017

The World Customs Organization is the only international intergovernmental organization governing global customs affairs. It plays a significant role in standardizing and coordinating policies of its members, promoting international customs cooperation, and ensuring the safety and facilitation of international trade. The WCO is headquartered in Brussels Belgium, and its 180 members manage over 98% of the global trade. Every year, the WCO holds a council session, where customs administrations of countries and regions discuss issues of mutual concern, plan for the future of global customs community, and settle disputes through consultation.

"世界海关组织"（World Customs Organization，WCO）是当今世界范围内唯一负责海关事务的政府间国际组织。它在规范和协调各成员海关制度、促进国际海关事务合作、保障国际贸易的安全与便利等方面发挥着重要作用。该组织总部位于比利时布鲁塞尔，现有成员180个，覆盖全球98%以上的国际贸易。每年世界海关组织在比利时布鲁塞尔总部召开一次理事会会议，各国各地区海关就共同关注的问题进行讨论，商议国际海关未来发展方向，就合作分歧进行磋商并达成共识。

2011年6月，比利时，在WCO与欧盟、英、法、德、意、荷、比海关署长共同签署中欧安智贸第二阶段共识。

June 2011, Belgium, Signing the Agreement on the Second Phase of the SSTL with the heads of EU, UK, France, Germany, Italy, Holland and Belgium Customs at the WCO.

I still remember vividly that 7 years ago, at the approval of the State Council, I lead a China Customs delegation to attend the 115/116 WCO Council Session for the first time. On the day of the opening session, my colleagues and I left the Hilton Hotel and walked down Rue des Croisades. In less than 10 minutes, we arrived at the WCO Headquarters, a European-style building decorated by a sea of flags of the conference at the gate and along the pathway winding through the courtyard, and a photography exhibition of Customs

记得七年前，经国务院批准，我第一次率中国海关代表团参加WCO第115/116届理事会年会，当时的情景仍记忆犹新。开幕式那天，我和我的同事从下榻的希尔顿酒店，步行穿过Rue des Croisades街道，十分钟就来到了WCO总部大楼。欧式建筑大门口和院内走道旁彩旗招展，各国海关执法和工作摄影展一旁陪衬，显示出年会召开的隆重性和亲切

enforcement and operation. Ceremonious, yet cordial. After the report of Mr. Kunio Mikuriya, General Secretary of the WCO, I shared some of China Customs' insights on compliance and facilitation, combating drug smuggling, building networked global customs and capacity building. During the Council Session, I also had friendly bilateral talks with Mr. Kunio Mikuriya, Mr. Robert Verrue, Director General of Directorate-General for Taxation and Customs Union of the European Commission (EU TAXUD), and heads of customs administrations of the US, Russia, South Africa, China Hong Kong and China Macau.

感。在听取WCO秘书长御厨邦雄先生的工作报告后，我就守法便利、打击贩毒、建设全球网络化海关和能力建设等问题作了回应并代表中国海关发表了意见。会议期间，我还与WCO秘书长御厨邦雄先生、欧盟税务与海关同盟总司司长韦吕先生以及美国、俄罗斯、南非、中国香港、中国澳门等海关负责人进行友好会晤。

In June 2017, the WCO held the 129/130 Council Session again in Brussels. An important agenda of this meeting was to discuss how to promote effective border management using information technologies. China Customs Delegation presented the Session and shared some important notes on Customs control and service of cross-border e-commerce, reviewed the recent development of cross-border e-commerce in China, and China Customs' efforts in improving control and service. China Customs also proposed that, when faced with challenges from the emerging industry, Customs should support inclusive development, control with prudence, step up reform and innovation, and manage e-commerce

2017年6月，WCO第129/130届理事会年会又在布鲁塞尔召开。这次大会的一项重要内容是关于信息技术如何推动海关有效实施边境管理。中国海关代表团在会上就“跨境电子商务海关监管与服务”发表了重要的意见，既回顾总结跨境电商近年来在中国的发展和中国海关为提升监管服务效能所做的工作，又提出海关在面对新型业态监管的挑战时要坚持包容发展、审慎监管、改革创新和协同共管的理念。

with coordinated and joined efforts.

The cooperation between China Customs and the WCO has been very fruitful over the past years. Since its establishment in 1952, the WCO has been essential in guiding global customs operations. It provides measures to streamlining and harmonizing Customs schemes, draws up and interprets international conventions and instruments on Customs matters, and supports member Customs through guidelines and capacity building activities. Through its various working bodies: the Council, Committees, Secretariat, regional intelligence liaison offices and regional capacity building centers, the WCO is promoting and coordinating the cooperation and development of Customs administrations regarding border management, trade facilitation, rules of origin, classification, valuation, enforcement, mutual administrative assistance, modernization, capacity building, anti-corruption, and so on.

The last few years have seen profound changes in global politics, economy and trade. Faced with new issues, new problems and new challenges such as cross border e-commerce, regional economic integration, terrorism, new means of tax evasion, epidemics, and natural calamities, the WCO has been actively deepening reform and development, enhancing the research and application of new technology,

回顾中国海关与世界海关组织的合作，这些年取得的成果是十分明显的。世界海关组织自1952年成立以来，一直指导着全球海关业务的发展。它致力于研究提出推动海关制度简化与协调的措施，起草并解释涉及海关事务的国际公约与文件，向成员海关提供建议以及能力建设方面的支持，在指导全球海关事务上发挥了关键作用。它通过下设的理事会、专委会、秘书处以及地区情报中心和能力建设中心推动并协调着国际海关在边境管理、贸易便利化、原产地、归类、海关估价、海关执法、行政互助、海关现代化、能力建设、反腐败等各个业务领域的合作与发展。

近年来，世界政治、经济和贸易形势经历了深刻的调整和变化。面对跨境电子商务、地区经济一体化以及恐怖主义、新形式税收瞒骗、流行病和自然灾害等新形势、新问题和新挑战，世界海关组织积极深化改革和发展，加强学术研究和技术应用，增强与利益

cementing its relations with stake holders, and playing a more important part in supporting global economic and trade growth, safeguarding public health and safety. 2017 marks the 70th anniversary of WCO's establishment, and the 35th year of China Customs' membership of the organization. I had the privilege to take part in the making of important decisions concerning the international Customs community, witness the reform and innovation of international customs modernization, and see how much China Customs and the WCO have achieved working together.

相关方的联系和配合，在促进全球经济和贸易发展，维护公众健康和安全方面正扮演着越来越重要的角色。2017年是WCO成立65周年，也恰逢中国海关正式成为WCO成员的第35个年头。我有幸深度参与国际海关界重要决策的形成，经历国际海关现代化进程中的改革与创新，也同时见证了中国海关与世界海关组织合作蓬勃发展的成果。

China Custom officially became a member of the WCO on July 18th, 1983. For the past 35 years, China Customs has actively participated in the making of rules and decisions regarding WCO and international Customs affairs, held important conferences and activities, and enhanced the communication and cooperation between Customs administrations. It's worth mentioning that during the course of the past decade, China Customs were actively engaged in dialogues with Secretary General of the WCO and senior officials from member Customs, actively advanced bilateral, multilateral and regional Customs cooperation following the objective and principle of "Mutual recognition of control, Mutual exchange of information, Mutual assistance in enforcement". China

中国海关于1983年7月18日正式成为WCO成员。35年来，中国海关积极参与WCO国际海关事务决策和规则制定，承办重要会议和活动，加强国际海关间的交流与合作。特别是近十年来，积极与世界海关组织秘书长及成员海关高层开展对话、以"监管互认、信息互换、执法互助"为目标和原则，积极推动和深化多双边和区域海关的合作，在国际场合和多边、区域框架下中国海关的影响力不断提升，取得了许多令人瞩目的成果。目前，中国海关已与159个国家和地区的海关开展了合作，签

Customs gained increasing influence in the international arena, as well as under bilateral and multilateral frameworks, and made a number of outstanding achievements. Up till now, China Customs has established cooperative relations with Customs Administrations from 159 countries and regions, signed 191 cooperation agreements, carried out nearly 200 cooperative projects, covering customs control, port cooperation, enforcement, clearance, supply chain security, anti-terrorism, anti-riot, trade facilitation, trade statistics, IPR border protection, capacity building and so on.

署了191个合作协议，开展国际合作项目近200个，合作领域包括海关监管、口岸合作、执法、通关、供应链安全、反恐防暴、贸易便利化、贸易统计、知识产权边境保护、能力建设等。

Contribution to Decision Making

China Customs has been the WCO Asia-Pacific Vice-Chair, member of the Policy Commission and the Finance Committee several times and has shared "China's perspective" on the development of global Customs. We played an active role during the drafting of the *Revised Kyoto Convention, Nairobi Convention, International Convention on the Harmonized Commodity Description and Coding System, SAFE Framework of Standards*, held conferences to propose *Customs and Trade Joint Communiqué on Sharing Knowledge for Trade Development and Economic Prosperity (the Guangzhou Communiqué*) and the *Xi'an Statement on Strengthening of Connectivity by Customs Administrations along the Belt and*

决策制定贡献智慧

中国海关多次担任WCO亚太地区副主席、政策委员会和财政委员会成员，积极为世界海关的发展提供“中国方案”。我们参与了《经修订的京都公约》《内罗毕公约》《协调制度公约》《全球贸易安全与便利标准框架》等文件的完善工作，借主办会议之契机提出《海关与商界共享知识，共促贸易发展和经济繁荣的联合宣言》（广州宣言）和《世界海关组织运用技术工具支持“一带一路”海关加强“互联互通”建设的西安声明》（西安声明），倡议开展

Road Supported by WCO Instruments and Tools. We initiated the first and second phase of "Skynet Operation" (against drugs and chemical precursor via parcels and express packages), Phase 3 of Demeter Operation (against illicit trade of hazardous waste from Europe to the Asia- Pacific region), making a worldwide impact in the Customs community.

了第一、二期"天网行动"（打击通过邮件和快递渠道走私毒品和易制毒化学品的行为）和第三期"大地女神行动"（打击从欧洲等废物生产国向亚太地区走私有害废物的不法行为），在国际海关界取得了巨大反响。

Leading the Reform and Innovation

Riding the tide of modernization, China Customs has carried out a list of reform and innovation regarding paperless customs, classified management of enterprises, technology and equipment, online services, and the remake of clearance procedures. On July 1, 2017, we rolled out the national customs integration reform. It eliminates the boundary between Customs districts, improves consistency in law enforcement, significantly increases efficiency at port, and is more streamlined than existing integration procedures adopted by Customs in developed countries.

改革创新走在前列

中国海关积极引领世界海关现代化改革的潮流，在通关无纸化、企业分类管理、技术装备、"互联网+海关"以及通关流程再造等领域进行了革新。2017年7月1日起，海关通关一体化在全国实施。此次改革与许多发达国家已实施的一体化改革相比，流程更加简洁，消除了申报的关区限制，促进了海关执法统一，大大提高了口岸通关效率。

Following the *SAFE Framework of Standards*, China Customs is also actively promoting the cooperation in supply chain security and facilitation with the EU, the United States and other countries and regions. For instance, China Customs and the EU Customs conducted a 3-phase plan called the Smart and Secure Trade Lane Project (SSTL). Through

中国海关以WCO《全球贸易安全与便利标准框架》为基础，积极推进与欧盟、美国以及其他国家和地区的供应链安全与便利合作。比如，中国与欧盟海关先后开展了三个阶段的安全智能贸易航线试点计划（简称"安智贸"）。中欧

data exchange, mutual recognition of control, electronic seals, and common risk rules, 27 port Customs from 10 countries and regions cooperate for effective control over inbound and outward cargo via specific trade lanes between China and Europe. Another example is that China Customs and U.S. Department of Homeland Security have carried out a joint validation program called Customs-Trade Partnership Against Terrorism (C-TPAT), which grants authorized companies lower inspection rate and top-of-the-list clearance. We have also worked with U.S. Department of Energy under the Megaports Initiative to tackle illicit transit of nuclear and other radioactive materials by means of technical cooperation and training programs. I would also like to stress the successful cooperation in AEO mutual recognition and information sharing with Kazakhstan Customs to establish a "Green Channel" for agricultural produce. In the opening remarks at the recent Belt and Road Forum for International Cooperation in Beijing, President Xi Jinping underlined that for Kazakhstan and other Central Asian countries alone, customs clearance time for agricultural produce exporting to China was cut by 90%.

十个国家和地区的27个口岸海关通过数据交换、监管结果互认、电子封志、统一的风险规则等实现海关对中欧特定运输线路进出境货物的全程有效监管。又如，中国海关与美国国土安全部开展了“海关与商界反恐伙伴计划”（C-TPAT）联合验证，使双方共同认可的“信得过”企业享受较低查验率、优先通关等便利措施;与美国能源部开展了“特大型港口计划”，通过技术合作和人员培训有效防范核及其他放射性物质的非法贩运。再如，中国与哈萨克斯坦海关通过 AEO互认和信息互换建立了农产品快速通关“绿色通道”，推动贸易便利化成效显著。习近平主席前不久在北京召开的“一带一路”国际合作高峰论坛开幕式主旨演讲中专门提到，仅哈萨克斯坦等中亚国家农产品到达中国市场的通关时间就缩短了90%。

Breakthroughs in High-level Official Elections

高官竞选取得突破

As China's influence on the world grows,

随着我国国际影响力的不

China's Customs officials are also going global. After intense competition, China's candidate was elected Director for Compliance and Facilitation Directorate in 2010, the first Chinese official taking this position in WCO history. In 2015, another China's candidate won the election for Director for Tariff and Trade Affairs Directorate. Up to now, China Customs has successively sent high-level representatives to 2 out of the 3 major directorates in the Secretariat of the WCO. Even today, I can still recall the overwhelming challenges when planning and organizing the two campaigns, the arduous journey when campaigning for China's candidates, the anxiety and expectation when waiting for the outcomes, and the thrill and pride after the victories. Now there are 7 China Customs officers deployed in the WCO Secretariat and its regional offices for intelligence and capacity building.

Support for Capacity Building

China Customs sponsored the WCO Asia-Pacific Regional Training Center at the Shanghai Customs College, and the Asia-Pacific Regional Dog Training Center to provide training for regional Customs officers. And our own officers were certified by the WCO as experts to provide technical aids. Moreover, on July 1st, 2014, China Customs set up a 5-year capacity building fund in the

断提升，中国海关的优秀官员也在逐步走向世界。经过激烈角逐，中国海关候选人于2010年成功当选守法与便利司司长，成为该组织历史上首位中国籍高官。2015年，中国海关候选人又成功当选关税与贸易事务司司长。至此，中国海关已先后在世界海关组织秘书处内设的三个业务部门中担任了两任高级官员职务。我至今仍然清晰地记得在组织领导两次竞选过程中筹划竞选方案时的巨大挑战，宣传中国候选人时的辗转奔波，等待投票结果时的焦虑与期待，以及胜选后的欣喜与自豪。目前，中国海关已派驻七名人员在WCO秘书处及其亚太地区情报联络中心、亚太地区能力建设办公室工作。

能力建设提供支持

中国海关承办了世界海关组织亚太地区培训中心（上海海关学院）和亚太地区训犬中心，为本地区海关关员举办能力建设活动，派员参加了世界海关组织专家认证，为成员海关提供技术援助。此外，自2014年7月1日起，中国海关在WCO设立为期五年的能力

WCO, a 600-thousand-EUR （about 850 thousand USD） annual funding which has already been used to support a dozen programs for over 400 officers from the Asia-Pacific, African and European regions.

建设合作基金，每年提供60万欧元（约合85万美元）资金支持。迄今已利用中国基金资助举办十余个项目，涉及亚太、非洲、欧洲等地区，受益学员400余人。

The ancient Chinese believed that, “one should be good at finding the laws of things and solving problems”. Customs modernization faces new opportunities and challenges, and it will provide us with a broader stage for international cooperation. During the dialogue with the international business leaders at the Summer Davos this year, Premier Li Keqiang emphasized that China will continue to establish "single window" service centers, shorten the time needed for customs clearance, enhance cooperation with other countries, and advance trade facilitation. These are the common objectives for Customs from all the countries and regions. As China Customs moves ahead with its modernization reform, we will keep on advancing the strategic development of the WCO, step up our efforts in reform and innovation, more actively provide support in terms of schemes, talents, expertise and funding, and more resolutely advocate and serve for economic globalization, in order to maintain and promote the security and facilitation of international trade.

中国古人说：“善学者尽其理，善行者究其难。”海关现代化的建设正面临新的机遇与挑战，也为我们深化海关国际合作提供了更广阔的舞台和空间。李克强总理在今年夏季达沃斯论坛同国际工商界代表举行的对话会期间强调，中国将继续推动单一窗口，缩短通关时间，加强国际合作，加快推进贸易便利化，这就是我们下一步努力的方向。随着中国海关现代化改革的不断深入，我们将继续致力于推动世界海关组织的战略发展，更努力地参与其改革和创新，更积极地提供制度、人才、智力和资金支持，更坚定地维护和支持经济全球化，维护和促进国际贸易的安全与便利。

在世界海关组织年会上的讲话

2013年7月5日

Speaking at the Annual Conference of the WCO

July 5, 2013

In late June this year, I headed the China Customs delegation to attend the 121/122 annual Council Session of the World Customs Organization (WCO) in Brussels, Belgium. On the first day of the meeting, after a simple opening ceremony, Mr. Kunio Mikuriya, Secretary General of the WCO, delivered a working report. During the discussion of the report I spoke on some common concerns of the international customs community on behalf of China Customs.

今年6月下旬，我率中国海关代表团出席了在比利时布鲁塞尔举行的世界海关组织第121/122届理事会大会。开会第一天，在简短的开幕式后，世界海关组织秘书长御厨先生作了工作报告。在对工作报告进行评议时段，我代表中国海关就国际海关界共同关注的议题发表了讲话。

First, I appreciated Secretary General Mr. Kunio Mikuriya for his comprehensive and informative working report. Last year saw a slow recovery of the world economy and

首先，我对御厨秘书长所作的全面详尽的工作报告给予了肯定。过去的一年，世界经济复苏缓慢，公共安全事件

frequent public security issues and terrorism activities. Under the guidance and coordination of the WCO, members have worked diligently with each other and achieved fruitful outcomes in facilitating trade, promoting economic development and maintaining global supply chain security.

和恐怖主义行为频繁发生。在世界海关组织的指导和协调下，各成员积极努力工作、相互配合，竭尽全力地支持和促进贸易便利化和经济发展，有效保障了全球供应链安全，成果丰硕。

Then I elaborated on the work of China Customs. In the past year, China Customs had continued in-depth cooperation with the WCO and its members, and taken some active and effective initiatives. For the first time, we proposed and launched the Operation Skynet, which turned out to be a great success thanks to the coordination of the WCO Secretariat and the active participation of all members. We began the building of the first Regional Dog Training Center (RDTC) in the Asia-Pacific region and held the inaugural ceremony of its foundation in Beijing on June 18th. For the first time, we sponsored the WCO Fellowship Program. Participants in the Program would be welcomed to join the study tour in China starting the second half of the year. By taking part in relevant cooperation programs, we had made tangible contribution to the international Customs affairs, and reciprocally, we could accumulate precious experience for our own development.

紧接着，我阐述了中国海关工作。在过去的一年里，中国海关一直与世界海关组织和其他成员海关深度合作，采取一些积极有效的措施。我们第一次提出并启动了打击走私的“天网行动”。有赖于世界海关组织秘书处的大力协调和很多成员海关的积极参与，行动取得了巨大的成效。我们成立了亚太地区首个缉私犬培训中心（RDTC），并于6月18日在北京举行了奠基仪式。我们首次资助了世界海关组织的跟班学习项目。项目参与者能够在未来半年内赴中国进行实地考察和学习。通过参与相关合作项目，我们为国际海关事务做出了实实在在的贡献，也为中国海关未来的发展积累了宝贵的经验。

I also pointed out that China Customs would join the effort of the WCO to initiate the Operation Demeter III this year so as to crack down upon hazardous waste smuggling and protect people's health. At the meeting, I sincerely invited all member Customs administrations and international organizations to participate in the operation.

When sharing my view on deepening the cooperation among WCO members, I underlined the importance of the co-operation among all members of customs administrations. The IMF had indicated that in 2013 world economy would grow slowly at the speed of 3.6% and the UN had estimated the speed as low as 2.4%. Meanwhile, the tension in some regions hadn't been eased, and terrorism, organized crime and cybercrime had gravely hampered and affected the development of trade. Against this backdrop, how to reach a balance between trade security and facilitation has become a common challenge for the world Customs community. Innovation should be the theme of the WCO in 2013. China Customs will carry out more exploration and innovation on the subject to significantly enhance security and facilitation of global supply chain and improve customs enforcement and administration. I also called on the members to further strengthen

我在讲话中明确指出中国海关将于今年与世界海关组织联合发起第三期大地女神行动，共同打击有害固体废物走私，保障公共健康安全。借此次会议机会，我向所有成员海关和国际组织发出了参与行动的邀请。

在谈到深化世界海关组织成员海关合作时，我特别强调了成员海关合作的重要性。据国际货币基金组织称，2013年世界经济将继续保持3.6%的低速增长。联合国预计增速将低至2.4%。同时，部分地区的紧张局势仍未缓和，恐怖主义、有组织犯罪和网络犯罪极大地阻碍和影响了贸易的增长。在此背景下，国际海关界亟须找到贸易安全与便利化的平衡点。创新应是2013年世界海关日的主题。中国海关将继续努力进行更多的探索和创新，切实提升国际供应链安全与便利，不断完善海关执法与管理。同时，我也呼吁各个成员海关进一步深化合作，充分利用先进科技开展进出境风险分析和管理，相互交换情报和监管信息，积极开展执法互助，

cooperation, leverage new technology for risk analysis and risk management on the border, exchange intelligence and information, actively engage in enforcement assistance, step up border protection, and focus on research of customs modernization and the actualization of its outcomes, in order to improve customs enforcement and secure the stable growth of the world's economy and trade.

加强边境保护和海关现代化管理研究，并将研究成果进行应用转化，以提升海关执法能力和水平，助推国际经济与贸易的稳定发展。

My speech was well received by the representatives. During meetings with WCO General Secretary, heads of U.S., EU, Russia, and African customs administrations on the sidelines of the Council Session, I learned that they all agreed to the ideas and proposals of China Customs and they all looked forward to a greater role of China Customs in the WCO.

我的讲话得到了与会代表的共鸣。在会议期间我与世界海关组织秘书长和美国、欧盟、俄罗斯、非洲等成员海关负责人会晤，大家一致赞同中国海关的意见和建议，纷纷表示希望中国海关在世界海关组织中能发挥更大的作用。

On the last day of the meeting, a special ceremony was held by China Customs and the EU Customs to welcome new members of the Smart and Secure Trade Lane Pilot Project （SSTL）. SSTL was initiated by China and EU Customs in 2006 in order to fully implement the WCO *SAFE Framework of Standards to Secure and Facilitate Global Trade* （*SAFE Framework*）. And it has promoted trade between the Asia and Europe continents. This pilot project adopted the core elements of *SAFE Framework* and introduced such new concepts and approaches as supply

大会的最后一天，中国海关与欧盟海关共同举办了一个特殊的仪式，欢迎新成员海关加入安全智能贸易航线试点计划（简称“安智贸”）。“安智贸”项目是2006年中欧海关共同商议启动的，旨在全面落实2005年世界海关组织制定的全球贸易安全与便利标准框架，对畅通欧亚大陆的贸易往来起到了积极的推动作用。该试点计划充分参照了《标准框架》的核心要素，引入了供应

chain security, mutual recognition of customs control, AEO mutual recognition and Unique Consignment Reference (UCR) promoted by the WCO.

链安全、监管互认、经认证的经营者互认和货运唯一识别代码等新理念、新措施。

The first phase of the program included 3 ports in China, the Netherlands and the UK. Later on, the number of participants increased to 13 ports in 8 countries including China, the Netherlands, the UK, Belgium, France, Germany, Italy and Poland. And the number of pilot trade lanes had grown from 3 to 39. China-EU SSTL has now become an exemplary program of the *SAFE*, which on the one hand proved the *SAFE*'s effective guidance on the security and facilitation of global supply chain, and on the other hand enriched and improved the *SAFE* itself.

项目第一阶段合作包括中国、荷兰和英国的三个港口。其后参与方逐步发展至包括中国、荷兰、英国、比利时、法国、德国、意大利和波兰在内的8国13港。试点航线数量从3条增加至39条。如今，中欧安智贸已成为《标准框架》的示范性项目，不仅体现了《标准框架》对国际供应链安全与便利的有效指导作用，也使《标准框架》自身得到了完善。

During the conference, I extended our welcome on behalf of China Customs to China Hong Kong and Spanish Customs to join the program. Mr. Heinz Zourek, Director General of Directorate General of Taxation and Customs Union (DG TAXUD) of the European Commission, and I handed over the official letters to the new members and took a group photo to mark the occasion. All delegates of the conference witnessed another new beginning of international customs cooperation.

这次年会上，我代表中国海关专门致辞，向中国香港和西班牙海关加入项目表示诚挚欢迎。随后，欧盟税务与海关同盟总司司长佐利克先生与我一起将批准加入的文件授予了上述成员海关，并合影留念。与会代表共同见证了海关国际合作又一新的进程开始。

世界海关组织竞选再获胜

2015年6月14日

Another Successful Election of the WCO

June 14, 2015

The 125th / 126th annual session of the WCO Council was held during June 11-14, 2015, in Brussels, Belgium. Apart from the routine process and items of the session, such as the report delivered by the secretary general, the working report on rules of Origin, Evaluation and Harmonized System, enhancing coordination and cooperation on Multi-lateral Affairs, discussing the customs measures to implement the Trade Facilitation Agreement of the WTO and improve the new type of trade models of e-commerce as well as releasing the amendments in SAFE revision, one of the most important issues was the elections of the new three directors of the Directorates

世界海关组织（WCO）第125 / 126届理事会年会于2015年6月11日至14日在比利时布鲁塞尔举行。我率中国海关代表团参加了大会。大会首先听取了秘书长所作的年度工作报告，接着听取了原产地、估价和协调制度、多边事务加强协调合作、实施世贸组织贸易便利化协定海关措施、促进电子商务新兴贸易业态报告和公布贸易便利与安全标准框架协定修订案。除了例行会议议程和会议项目外，一个十分重要的议题是关于选举WCO秘

of Compliance and Facilitation, Tariff and Trade Affairs and Capacity Building of the WCO secretariat. So, there were many more members of the WCO attending the session this time than ever before. 165 members from the total 180 attended the meeting.

China Customs nominated Liu Ping, Senior Customs Representative at the Permanent Mission of China to the WTO, to represent China Customs to run for the post of Director of Tariff and Trade Affairs Directorate of the WCO.

Liu has his major advantages for the Candidate of the WCO High-Official Election. **Firstly,** he is a veteran in tariff and trade affairs with over 30 years of working experience. He used to be the Acting Deputy Director in Tariff and Trade Affairs Directorate of the WCO and had been Chair of the Technical Committee of Rules of Origin (TCRO) for 7 consecutive years. **Secondly,** he is very familiar with the tariff and trade affairs under the framework of the WCO. He directly attended the market-access negotiations of China's accession to the WTO, and the WTO Trade Facilitation Agreement. In this April, he was elected as the chairman of the Committee on Customs Valuation in the WTO. **Thirdly,** Liu is a WCO-accredited expert in rules of origin, customs valuation and capacity building, and

书处3位新的司长，即守法与便利司、税收与贸易司和能力建设司的司长。因此，参加这次年会的成员海关代表比以往都多。180个成员海关有163个派代表出席大会。

中国海关推荐的刘平，是中国海关派驻中国常驻世贸组织代表团的高级海关专员。他代表中国海关竞选世界海关组织税收与贸易司的司长。

刘平参加WCO的高官竞选有其主要的优势：**首先，**他在海关关税和贸易领域具有30多年的丰富经验，曾经担任WCO税贸司执行副司长，并连续7年担任WCO原产地技术委员会主席。**其次，**他非常熟悉WCO框架下税收和贸易的业务，直接参与过中国加入世贸的市场准入谈判和WTO贸易便利化协定谈判。今年4月，他被选为WTO估价委员会主席。**最后，**他是WCO经认证的原产地、海关估价、能力建设专家，对WCO 60多个国家海关提供过技术支持。他的竞选理念是：保障海关税收，支持贸易增长。这符

has provided technical assistance to more than 60 WCO member administrations. His election vision was "Secure Revenue, Support Trade Growth". This was in the best interests of all WCO members.

合WCO所有成员海关的最佳利益。

Therefore, we believed that Liu, with both extensive operational experience and strong management capabilities, was the best candidate for running the post of Director of Tariff and Trade Affairs Directorate of the WCO.

因此，我们相信刘平既具有广泛的实践经验，也具有较强的管理能力，是竞选WCO税收与贸易司司长的最佳人选。

But the competition of the election was fierce. The other two candidates for running this post were from Denmark customs and the South Korea customs. They both had extensive operational experiences of customs and were the strong candidates to Liu Ping.

但是，竞争很激烈。另外两位竞选这个职位的分别来自丹麦海关和韩国海关。他们也同样具有丰富的海关实务经验，是刘平的强劲竞选对手。

From the beginning of the year, we startedseveral activities for the election. Mr. Yu Guangzhou, Minister of China Customs sent his personal recommendation letter to the heads of member customs of the WCO: "Thanks to his extensive tariff and trade-related working experience at both the WCO and the WTO, Liu is capable of viewing the relationship between trade growth and revenue collection from the perspective of global trade. With 'Secure Revenue, Support Trade' being his vision, he has come up with a practical approach to ensure an indispensable role of

从年初开始，我们为刘平竞选开展了一系列积极的活动。中国海关总署署长于广洲给世界海关组织所有成员海关的负责人写了推荐信："鉴于刘平先生在世界海关组织和世界贸易组织中具有广泛的税收和贸易相关工作经验，他能从全球贸易的角度，来看待贸易增长和税收征收。'保障海关税收，支持贸易增长'是他的竞选理念，他提出了切实可行的方法，以缓解2008年以来全

Customs in helping the world mitigate the impact of the global financial crisis in 2008."

球金融危机带来的影响，确保发挥海关不可替代的作用。"

According to the revised rules of the election, there would be two rounds of voting, the winner should get more than half votes. And the results of the election for three directors wouldn't be opened one by one in turn, but at the end of the election together.

根据本次修改后的新的竞选规则，选举共经历两轮投票，过半者获胜，三个司长竞选结果非依次逐一公开，而是到最后一次性公开。

In the first round of voting for the director of TTA, none of the three got more than half votes, so the Danish candidate with the least number of votes was out. Then the second round of voting continued. Finally, Chinese candidate Liu Ping successfully beat the South Korean candidate by 88 votes to 75 votes. Liu Ping won the election as the new director of the Tariff and Trade Affairs Directorate of the WCO.

在税贸司长竞选中，第一轮投票后，三位候选人因得票均未过半，故得票最少的丹麦候选人被淘汰，继续第二轮投票。在第二轮投票中，我候选人刘平终以88票对75票击败韩国候选人胜出。

This is our second success to keep the place in the WCO high officials after Mr. Zhu Gaozhang was elected as the director of Compliance and Facilitation Directorate five years ago. The other two candidates from the United States and Brazil Customs were also separately elected as the directors of Compliance and Facilitation Directorate and Capacity Building Directorate of the WCO.

这是我们继朱高章先生竞选成为WCO守法便利司司长五年后，第二次成功保证了我在WCO高官中持续占有一席之地。另外，美国和巴西海关候选人也分别当选WCO守法便利司司长和能力建设司司长。

It's really worth celebrating. Let's sum up the election work. In addition to Liu Ping's own advantages and his hard work, the other main reasons for the success were:

这是非常值得庆贺的。如果要对这次竞选工作做一总结，除了刘平自身条件和工作外，主要原因还应归功于：

Firstly, China's comprehensive strength and influence are increasing. For example, in politics, China is one of the five permanent members of the United Nations Security Council; in economy, China is the world's second largest economy and its import and export trade is among the biggest in the world; in diplomatic affairs, work on the bilateral, multilateral and regional levels has seen significant results. Our influence on the world is increasing and China now has a bigger say in the international community.

一、我国综合实力和影响力不断上升。如政治上，中国是联合国安理会五个常任理事国之一；经济上，中国是全球第二大经济体，进出口贸易量居全球前列；外交上，这几年多双边、区域等外交工作成效明显，影响扩大、话语权增强。

Secondly, we've attached great importance to establishing good multilateral and bilateral relations. This time Liu won 88 votes in the election, many votes were from the traditional friendly countries and some countries with strategic partnership, such as from African, Asian, Oceanian countries and regions. And some European and American countries supported us in the crucial second round of voting.

二、我们高度重视广泛建立良好的多双边关系。这次我候选人获得88票中，很多选票来自传统友好国家和具有战略伙伴关系的国家。如非洲、亚洲、大洋洲国家居多，部分欧美国家在第二轮投票关键时刻也对我们给予了支持。

Thirdly, China customs has been actively and intensively participating in WCO affairs, such as leading some professional committees, joining the law enforcement operations and providing the capacity training under the WCO CCF, China as well as exchanging information and experience in customs practices, which have all seen positive outcomes.

三、中国海关多年来积极和深度参与WCO事务，担任各专业委员会的负责人，多次倡议并广泛开展联合执法行动，设立中国海关能力建设基金为成员国海关提供培训，交换信息并交流海关实践经验，收到了良好效果。

Fourthly, the Ministry of Foreign Affairs and other departments gave full support to us. Especially our embassies and consulates kept good communication with the local governments and customs administrations to support Liu's election. Furthermore, the campaign team played a positive role in planning, organizing, laying down strategies and gaining wide support.

四、外交部等部门给予了全力支持，尤其是我驻外使领馆加强与各当地政府和海关部门沟通联系，发挥积极的促进作用。竞选团队精心谋划、统筹组织、注重策略，争取了广泛支持。

As a leader of the election, I am very pleased to have participated in and witnessed the whole process of the election and have the successful result. I am full of confidence for China Customs to play a bigger role in WCO affairs in the future. I believe Liu Ping will, as he has promised, work closely with all the WCO member administrations and try his utmost to turn the WCO Tariff and Trade Affairs Directorate into a more forward-looking, dynamic and member-driven directorate. China Customs will continue to join hands with all the WCO member administrations to support world trade growth by facilitating legitimate cross border movement of goods and ensure security and facilitation of global supply chain.

作为这次竞选的负责人，我参与和见证了竞选的全过程，对取胜感到十分欣慰，对中国海关在今后世界海关组织中发挥更好的作用充满信心。我确信，刘平将会兑现他作出的承诺，与世界海关组织所有成员海关紧密合作，尽自己的最大努力把世界海关组织税收和贸易司转变成更具前瞻性、充满活力、为成员海关服务的部门。中国海关将继续与WCO所有成员共同努力，通过促进合法货物跨境流动、确保全球供应链安全和便利，支持全球贸易健康发展。

推动国际海关互联互通　促进“一带一路”繁荣发展

2017 年 6 月

Advance Customs Connectivity to Promote Prosperity and Development along the “Belt and Road”

June, 2017

In this lovely season of early summer when every living thing is full of energy, China successfully held “the Belt and Road” Forum for International Cooperation on May 14th and 15th. 29 heads of state and government, and the UN Secretary-General among other heads of major international organizations, attended the Forum, as well as over 1500 distinguished guests from 130 countries and 70 international organizations around the world. 68 countries and international organizations reached cooperative agreements in over 270 different areas. During the Forum, 29 heads of state adopted the *Joint Communiqué of the Leaders Roundtable of the Belt and Road Forum for International Cooperation*, which sets

“孟夏之日，万物并秀”。在这美好的时节，中国于5月14日至15日成功举办了“一带一路”国际合作高峰论坛。29位外国元首、政府首脑及联合国秘书长等重要国际组织负责人出席论坛，共来自130个国家和70个国际组织的1500多位中外嘉宾参会。68个国家和国际组织在270多个领域达成了合作协议与共识，29国领导人在论坛期间发布了《“一带一路”国际合作高峰论坛圆桌峰会联合公报》，从时

forth the direction and focus of "the Belt and Road" cooperation through the general context, cooperation objectives, cooperation principles, cooperation measures, and the vision for the future. The Forum has reviewed the progress of "the Belt and Road" cooperation, built consensus, and sent out a strong message that all parties were willing to build a cooperative platform, seek new driving force for global economic growth and inject confidence in economic globalization.

代背景、合作目标、合作原则、合作举措和愿景展望等五个方面阐述并明确了"带一路"未来合作的方向和重点。这次论坛总结了"一带一路"合作进展，凝聚了各方共识，传递出各方打造合作平台，为世界经济增长谋求动力，为经济全球化发展提振信心的强有力信号。

I was honored to have participated in the Opening Ceremony and the Thematic Session on "Promoting Unimpeded Trade" and listened to President Xi Jinping and other world leaders about their visions and plans for international cooperation along the Belt and Road. President XI delivered a keynote speech - "Work Together to Build the Silk Road Economic Belt and the 21st Century Maritime Silk Road". He reflected on the achievements of policy, infrastructure, trade, financial and people-to- people connectivity since the Belt and Road Initiative was proposed 4 years ago. He pointed out that the Belt and Road Initiative responds to the trend of the times, conforms to the law of development, meets the people's interests, and has broad prospects. He called on all parties to build on the sound momentum generated to steer the Belt and Road Initiative toward greater success and

我十分有幸参加了这次高峰论坛开幕式以及"推动贸易畅通"平行主题会议等一系列活动，聆听了习近平主席以及沿线国家和国际组织领导人对于"一带一路"建设国际合作的愿景和设想。习主席在论坛开幕式发表了题为《携手推进"一带一路"建设》的主旨演讲，从政策沟通、设施连通、贸易畅通、资金融通、民心相通等五个方面回顾了"一带一路"倡议提出4年来取得的丰硕成果，指出"一带一路"倡议顺应时代潮流，适应发展规律，符合各国人民利益，具有广阔前景，各国要乘势而上、顺势而为，将

build the Belt and Road into a road for peace, a road of prosperity, a road of opening up, a road of innovation, and a road connecting different civilizations as well. At the end of his speech, President XI stressed that "the Belt and Road Initiative is rooted in the ancient Silk Road and focuses on the Asian, European and African continents, but is also open to all other countries"; and "the pursuit of this initiative is based on extensive consultation and its benefits will be shared by us all".

In history, the silk roads over land and at sea were not only passageways connecting countries and regions along the routes, but also bridges linking China, Central Asia, West Asia, South Asia, and the Mediterranean for commercial, cultural, people-to-people and information exchanges. For over 2000 years, the Silk Road spirit of peace and cooperation, openness and inclusiveness, mutual learning and mutual benefit has been fostered. As time goes forward, unimpeded trade along the Belt and Road continues to bring economic prosperity and social development to the countries and regions along the routes. Statistics showed that in 2016 the trade volume between China and countries along the routes reached 6.25 trillion RMB yuan, up by 0.6% year-on-year. That of the first 4 months this year topped 2.27 trillion RMB yuan, increased by 25.1%.

“一带一路”建成和平之路、繁荣之路、开放之路、创新之路、文明之路。习主席最后强调，“一带一路”建设植根于丝绸之路的历史土壤，重点面向亚欧非大陆，同时向所有朋友开放，“一带一路”建设将由大家共同商量，建设成果将由大家共同分享。

历史上，陆路和海上的丝绸之路不仅是连接沿线国家和地区的通道，更是中国与中亚、西亚、南亚，直至地中海地区进行商贸、文化、人员和信息交流的纽带，两千多年来积淀了以和平合作、开放包容、互学互鉴、互利共赢为核心的丝路精神。随着时代的进步，“一带一路”上的贸易畅通仍在为沿线国家和地区带来经济繁荣和社会发展。据统计，2016年，中国与沿线国家贸易额达6.25万亿元人民币，同比增长0.6%；今年前四个月为2.27万亿元人民币，增长25.1%。

As a key sector in the global supply chain, Customs has long been an important driving force for unimpeded trade. Since President XI Jinping put forward the Belt and Road Initiative in September and October 2013, China Customs has been committed to the facilitation of trade and carried out comprehensive cooperation with customs administrations along the routes focusing on "mutual exchange of information, mutual recognition of control and mutual assistance in enforcement". On May 27th and 28th 2015, we held the Forum for Heads of Customs Administrations along the Belt and Road under the theme of "Connectivity and Win-win Development", attended by over 400 delegates, including heads and representatives from 63 customs administrations, 8 international organizations and over 100 participants from the business community. The Forum was a complete success. Three outcome papers were released, where customs administrations of countries, regions and international organizations reached consensus on promoting connectivity along the routes. Vice Premier WANG Yang gave a keynote speech at the Forum, in which he stressed, "As the indispensable link of the global supply chain, customs administrations are playing a crucial role in maintaining trade security and facilitating regional economic cooperation. In recent years, with the efforts of China Customs and under the

海关作为全球贸易供应链上的关键一环，一直以来都是推动贸易畅通的重要力量。自习近平主席于2013年9月和10月提出“一带一路”倡议以来，中国海关一直以促进“一带一路”贸易畅通为己任，围绕“信息互换、监管互认、执法互助”与沿线海关开展大通关合作。记得2015年5月27日至28日，我们在西安举行了“一带一路”海关高层论坛。海关论坛以“互联互通，共赢发展”为主题，邀请了包括63个国家和地区的海关、8个国际组织的负责人和代表，以及100多名商界代表在内共400余人参加。会议开得非常成功，发布了沿线国家与地区海关以及国际组织共同推动互联互通的三份成果文件。当时，汪洋副总理出席论坛并发表了重要讲话。他强调：“作为全球供应链上必不可少的环节，海关在维护贸易安全与便利，促进区域经济合作方面起着至关重要的作用。近年来，在中国海关的自身

support of international organizations such as the World Customs Organization, cooperation among customs administrations of all countries is booming. It has promoted effective and convenient cross-border flow of commodities, personnel, currency and information while, at the same time, helped in safeguarding border and trade security thus making a significant contribution to the development of world trade and regional economic integration"

努力和世界海关组织等国际组织的支持下，各国海关部门间的合作蓬勃发展，有效促进了商品、人员、货币和信息有效和便利的跨境流动，积极协助维护了边境和贸易安全，为世界贸易和区域经济一体化的发展做出了重大贡献。"

In recent years, China Customs has stepped up its efforts to promote facilitation for trade and investment. So far, it has carried out mutual exchange of information with customs of 89 countries and regions, realized mutual recognition of control with customs of 40 countries and regions, and has been engaged in assistance in enforcement with customs of 71 countries and regions. For Kazakhstan and other Central Asian countries alone, customs clearance time for agricultural produce exporting to China has been cut by 90%. Building on these inspiring achievements, China Customs will keep on advancing the reform of national clearance integration and make customs service accessible in a far greater area.

近年来，中国海关大力推动贸易和投资便利化，目前已与89个国家和地区海关开展了信息互换，与40个国家和地区海关开展了监管互认，与71个国家和地区海关开展了执法互助。仅哈萨克斯坦等中亚国家农产品到达中国市场的通关时间就缩短了90%。这是十分令人鼓舞的成果。下一步，中国海关将深入推进全国通关一体化改革，为"关通天下"奠定坚实基础。

At the Thematic Session on "Promoting Unimpeded Trade" under the Belt and Road Forum, Mr. YU Guangzhou, Minister of the General Administration of China Customs,

在这次高峰论坛举办的"推动贸易畅通"平行主题会议上，海关总署于广洲署长回顾了沿线国家海关

reflected on the outcomes of the Belt and Road cooperation among customs administrations along the routes and further raised five cooperation proposals, including the docking of mechanisms, innovation of customs control, exchange of information, trade security, and capacity building, which were widely welcomed by the participants. During the Forum, China Customs also invited heads of customs administrations from 12 countries and international organizations, held bilateral talks with them, signed 4 cooperative agreements, and reached extensive consensus on jointly promoting customs connectivity and cooperation.

共建“一带一路”的合作成果，再次提出了深化机制衔接、监管创新、信息共享、贸易安全、能力建设等五个方面的合作倡议，得到了与会各方的一致赞同。此外，中国海关还邀请了12个国家海关和国际组织负责人来华参会，并分别举行了双边会谈，签署了四份合作文件，就共同推进海关互联互通，加强海关合作达成了广泛共识。

The Belt and Road Forum for International Cooperation provides a broader platform for international cooperation of customs. There is an old saying in China, “A single flower does not make a blooming spring.” I believe that as the cooperation between China Customs, customs administrations around the world and international organizations continues to grow, Customs will make more contributions to trade security and facilitation and bring greater economic prosperity and development to countries and regions along the Belt and Road.

“一带一路”国际合作高峰论坛为海关国际合作提供了更广阔的平台。中国有句老话：“一花独放不是春，万紫千红春满园。”我相信，随着中国海关与世界各国海关和国际组织合作的逐渐深入，海关将为推动“一带一路”沿线各国和地区贸易安全与便利，促进沿线国家和地区经贸繁荣与发展作出更大贡献！

谱写金砖海关合作新篇章

——首届金砖国家海关署长会议召开

2013年3月17日

New Chapter for BRICS Customs Cooperation

——The First Meeting of Heads of BRICS Customs

March 17, 2013

From March 7 to 8, The First BRICS Heads of Customs Meeting was held in the beautiful Zebula Lodge, a private wild park near Pretoria, South Africa.

3月7日至8日，首届金砖国家海关署长会议在南非召开。会议在美丽的比勒陀利亚附近的私人野生动物园——Zebula酒店举行。

On behalf of China Customs, I attended the meeting and delivered a keynote speech there. At the opening ceremony, Vice Finance Minister of South Africa Mr. Nhlanhla Musa Nene, Commissioner of SARS (the South Africa Revenue Service) Mr. Oupa G. Magashula and the leaders from Brazil, Russia, and India customs participated in the meeting and made speeches as well.

我代表中国海关出席了会议并发表了讲话。开幕式上，南非财政部副部长恩兰拉・穆萨・内内，南非税务与海关署署长玛甘舒拉以及巴西、俄罗斯和印度海关的负责人也参加了会议并致辞。

2013年3月，南非，出席首届金砖国家海关署长会议（从左到右：巴西、俄罗斯、印度、中国、南非海关负责人）。

March 2013, South Africa, the First BRICS Heads of Customs Meeting (left to right: heads of Brazil, Russia, India、China and South Africa Customs)

It was of milestone significance to the customs cooperation among BRICS countries.

BRICS countries are now the major engine for the global economic development. According to the statistics, the population of BRICS countries accounts for 42% of the world total; in 2012, the GDP of BRICS countries, measured by purchasing power parity, represented 26% of the world total, and the contribution of BRICS countries to the world economic growth accounted for 50%. The drive of BRICS countries for the global economic development can be seen clearly. Trade growth among BRICS countries has also become the locomotive for our economic

这次会议堪称金砖国家海关合作的里程碑。

金砖五国现已成为全球经济发展的主要引擎。据统计，金砖国家的人口占世界总数的42%；2012年，金砖五国的国内生产总值按购买力平价计算占世界总额的26%，而金砖五国对世界经济增长的贡献占到了50%。可见，金砖五国对全球经济发展起到了显著的推动作用。金砖国家之间的贸易增长也已成为带动经济增长的火车头。我们都知道，经济的发展离不开贸易的增长。2012

development. As we all know, economic development cannot do without the growth of trade. In 2012, the trade volume among BRICS countries reached 340 billion USD, accounting for 15% of the world total. The trade volume has increased by 10 times in the last decade, becoming the major impetus for the economic development of the five countries.

年，金砖国家之间的贸易额达到3400亿美元，占世界总量的15%。贸易额在过去的十年中增加了10倍，成为金砖五国经济发展的主要动力。

BRICS customs cooperation plays a unique and irreplaceable role in promoting trade among BRICS countries. Different from other border management authorities, customs has a direct influence on import and export trade cost in terms of time spent on customs clearance. Therefore, the international organizations, such as the WTO, WCO, UNECE, UNCTAD and APEC, all define simplifying customs procedure and reducing paper documents as the core content of trade facilitation. In the *Global Enabling Trade Report 2012*, the World Economic Forum presented a table of Enabling Trade Index 2012 Rankings, analyzing the trade performance of various countries, based on the import tariff, efficiency of import-export procedures, availability and quality of transport services, regulatory environment, and physical security. In this table, China Customs is ranked as the 56th. (India 100th, Brazil 84th, Russia 112th).

金砖国家的海关合作在促进金砖国家贸易方面发挥了独特的、不可替代的作用。不同于其他边境管理部门，海关的通关时间直接影响着进出口贸易成本。因此，国际组织（世贸组织、世界海关组织、联合国贸发会议和亚太经合组织等）都把简化海关手续，减少文件材料需求作为提升贸易便利化的核心内容。在《2012年全球促进贸易报告》中，世界经济论坛以表格的方式呈现了2012年促进贸易指标排名，基于进口关税、进出口程序的效率、运输服务的有效性和质量、监管环境和安全等因素对不同国家的贸易进行了分析。在这个表中，中国海关排名第56位（印度第100位，巴西第84位，俄罗斯第112位）。

China Customs has established friendly cooperation with the customs of South Africa, Brazil, Russia and India. With the SARS, working groups have been set up for specific cooperation in the areas of anti-smuggling, trade statistics, compliance and facilitation, and customs valuation, so as to foster the trade environment of fairness, compliance and facilitation. With Brazil Customs, customs cooperation has been incorporated into the intergovernmental ten-year cooperation program. With Russia Customs, cooperation has been promoted intensively and extensively through the China-Russia Customs Cooperation Sub-committee, in terms of standardizing customs clearance procedures, promoting bilateral trade, and improving customs control and services. With India Customs, heads of both customs have reached a series of agreements, including exchange of intelligence, assistance in enforcement mutual and training of officials.

中国海关与南非、巴西、俄罗斯和印度海关建立了友好的合作关系。其中，我们与南非海关建立了工作组，旨在共同打击特定领域的走私，开展贸易统计、守法与便利化和海关估价等领域的合作，营造公平、守法、便利的贸易环境。我们与巴西海关的合作已纳入两国政府间的十年合作计划。我们与俄罗斯海关通过中俄海关合作委员会机制深入和广泛地推动了通关流程标准化，促进双边贸易和改进海关监管和服务。与印度海关在领导层面也达成了一系列合作协议，包括情报交换、执法互助和官员培训等。

During the past 2 days of the meeting, the customs counterparts from the 5 countries gathered there, exchanging opinions, communicating experience and reaching agreements on common concerns, such as exchanging information, strengthening administrative mutual assistance, practicing AEO, facilitating trade, fighting against smuggling and commercial fraud as well as

在这次为期两天的首届金砖国家海关署长会议期间，来自五个国家的海关同事聚集一堂，就信息交换、行政互助、经认证的经营者、贸易便利化、打击走私和商业瞒骗以及保障关税收入等各方共同关注的问题交流意见、分享经验、达成共识。许多的介绍和演讲

protecting customs revenue. Many introductions and speeches were inspiring to all participants and were of great value to designing the prospect of customs cooperation among BRICS countries. Most important of all, this meeting endorsed the joint communiqué, which mapped out the direction of BRICS customs cooperation, specified the working mechanism, and put forward the priorities of cooperation. I believe, this communiqué will be an important guide for our future customs work of BRICS countries.

对各方参会者都具有启发意义，也对规划金砖国家海关合作的前景具有重要价值。最重要的是，这次会议发表了一份联合公报，指明了金砖国家海关合作的方向，建立了工作机制，并明确了合作重点。相信这一联合公报将成为未来金砖国家海关合作的重要行动指南。

As we all know, state leaders of BRICS countries will meet in Durban, South Africa at the end of March. The Durban Declaration and its action plan, as the important achievements of the Summit, will include the content of customs cooperation. So, this time we initialed the joint communiqué which indicated the closer cooperation of BRICS customs in the future.

金砖五国的国家领导人将于3月底在南非德班举行峰会。作为此次峰会的重要成果，德班宣言及其行动计划将涵盖海关合作的内容。所以此次我们对有关金砖国家海关合作的文本进行了草签。

This time, I met many old friends of mine and also made more new friends. Customs counterparts gathered at the exotic Zebula Lodge to build our friendship. This is truly a beautiful and amazing place. Arranged by South Africa customs, we had a field trip in the wild park. There was the famous BIG FIVE of Africa, such as elephant, buffalo, lion, rhino and leopard. And you could easily see some wild animals everywhere like giraffe,

会议期间，我遇见了很多老朋友，也结识了不少新朋友。海关的同事们齐聚在独具非洲风情的Zebula酒店畅抒友情，这真是个美丽又神奇的地方。南非海关安排我们在酒店所在的野生动物园进行了参观。我们看到了著名的非洲“五大兽”：大象、野牛、狮子、犀牛和豹。早上或傍晚散

antelopes, buck, goat, jackal, eagle, wild boar and zebra if you just took a walk in the morning or in the evening.

步时，也能经常看到许多野生动物，如长颈鹿、羚羊、鹿、山羊、豺狼、老鹰、野猪和斑马等等。

The fresh air, clean water, blue sky, vast grassland and amazing landscape deeply impressed me. It is the place where landscapes drift into distant horizons, where mountains are waiting for you to explore. It's vibrant, alive and filled with African traditional culture and zest. It's the embodiment of the harmony of between human and nature.

新鲜的空气，清澈的水，湛蓝的天空，辽阔的草原和令人叹为观止的景色给我留下了深刻的印象。这里的风景绵延至遥远的地平线，这里的山脉等待着你去探索，这里充满了动感和活力，充满了非洲传统文化和热情，这里象征了人与自然的和谐。

There is a great saying in South Africa: Go fast, go alone; go far, go together! I should say, today, we have opened the gate of BRICS customs cooperation; tomorrow, we shall compose a new chapter of BRICS customs cooperation with our wisdom, just like the harmonious and spectacular landscape!

在南非有一句名言：要走得快，独自走；要走得远，一起走！我相信，今天我们为金砖国家海关合作打开了一扇大门；明天，我们将用共同的智慧为金砖国家海关合作谱写出犹如这和谐而壮美的风景一般的新篇章！

继往开来　开创金砖海关合作新的“金色十年”

2017 年 9 月

Usher in a New “Golden Decade” of BRICS Customs Cooperation

September, 2017

The 2017 BRICS Summit was successfully concluded on 4 September 2017 in Xiamen, China. Under the theme of “Stronger BRICS Partnership for a Brighter Future”, leaders of the five countries reviewed the BRICS cooperation during the past ten years, conducted in-depth exchange of views on the current international situation, global economic governance, BRICS cooperation, and other global and regional hotspot issues, and reached wide-ranged consensus. The BRICS Leaders *Xiamen Declaration* was adopted afterwards, which mapped out the blueprint and pointed out the direction for the future development of BRICS cooperation. On the sidelines of the Summit, China hosted the

2017年9月4日，金砖国家领导人第九次会晤在中国厦门成功闭幕。金砖五国领导人围绕“深化金砖伙伴关系，开辟更加光明未来”这一主题，回顾了金砖合作十年历程，就当前国际形势、全球经济治理、金砖合作、国际和地区热点问题等深入交换看法，达成一系列共识，并于会后通过了金砖国家领导人《厦门宣言》，为金砖国家合作未来发展规划了蓝图，指明了方向。此次会晤期间，中方还举办

Dialogue of Emerging Market and Developing Countries, creating a "BRICS+" cooperation model, establishing a widespread network of development partners, initiating a shared path of innovative, coordinated, green open and mutually-beneficial sustainable development, and providing bright prospects for deepening South-South cooperation and global development collaboration.

了新兴市场国家与发展中国家对话会，开拓性地打造"金砖+"合作模式，建立广泛发展伙伴关系，共走一条"创新、协调、绿色、开放、共享"的可持续发展之路，为深化南南合作和全球发展合作提供了广阔的前景。

BRICS countries come from Asia, Africa, Europe, and South America. The total area, GNP and population of the five countries account for 26.5%, 22.5% and 42.6% of the world, respectively, leading in emerging market countries and developing countries. Since BRICS cooperation was launched 10 years ago, the five countries' economic aggregate has grown by 179%, and urbanized population by 28%, making outstanding contributions to the recovery of the world economy. In 2017, the economic and trade cooperation among BRICS countries continues to enjoy sound growth. During the first 7 months of this year, China's bilateral trade with other BRICS countries all grew by over 20%, reaching a total volume of $167.07 billion, 26% higher than the same period last year.

金砖国家跨越亚洲、非洲、欧洲和南美洲。五国的总面积、国民生产总值、总人口分别占全世界的26.5%、22.5%和42.6%，是新兴市场国家和发展中国家的领头羊。金砖合作启动十年来，五国经济总量增长179%，城镇化人口增长28%，为世界经济企稳复苏做出了突出贡献。2017年，金砖国家经贸合作保持了良好发展势头。今年前七个月，我国与其他金砖国家双边贸易增长均在20%以上，总值达到1670.7亿美元，比去年同期增长26%。

As a crucial link in foreign trade, customs cooperation among BRICS countries is also boosting BRICS economic development. In the *Xiamen Declaration*, BRICS leaders speak highly

作为推动进出口贸易的关键一环，中国海关与金砖国家海关一道为五国经贸发展做出了重要贡献。五国领

of the progress made by Customs Administrations in their cooperation on trade facilitation, security and enforcement, capacity building and other issues of mutual interest, and set out new goals for future collaboration. I still recall that back in 2013, I led the China Customs delegation to the First Meeting of BRICS Heads of Customs in South Africa. During my speech at the Meeting, I highlighted the importance of customs ties in BRICS cooperation, and proposed to hold ministerial and working-level discussions on a regular or irregular basis, where discussions of major multilateral issues could be made, and practical cooperation in administrative assistance, law enforcement and trade facilitation could be conducted. The proposal received a warm welcome from all participating parties, and the BRICS Customs Cooperation Mechanism was officially established. In 2015, when attending the Annual Conference of the World Customs Organization in Brussels, Belgium, I took part in the Second Meeting of BRICS Heads of Customs. After thorough study and arduous consultation, the five countries reached agreement on the *Rules of Procedure of the BRICS Customs Cooperation Committee* brought up by Russian Customs and pushed forward the negotiations of the *Agreement on BRICS Customs Cooperation and Mutual Assistance*. Since then, I have had a number of bilateral talks and mutual visits with BRICS

导人在《厦门宣言》中对海关在贸易便利化、安全与执法、能力建设等方面取得的合作进展给予了高度评价，并为未来合作指明了方向。记得2013年，我曾代表中国海关率团参加了在南非举行的首届金砖国家海关署长会议。会上，我强调海关合作对于金砖国家合作的重要意义，提议召开署级或工作层面的定期和不定期会晤，就重大多边问题交换看法，并在行政互助、海关执法、贸易便利化等领域开展务实合作，得到了与会各方的一致认同，并通过会议成果文件形式正式确立了金砖国家海关合作机制。2015年，我在比利时布鲁塞尔参加WCO年会期间，再次参加了金砖国家海关署长会议。经反复研究，与多方协调，就俄罗斯海关提出的《金砖国家海关合作委员会章程》达成一致意见，推动了《金砖国家海关合作与互助协定》的磋商。此后，我多次与金砖国家海关负责人进行双边会谈与互访，增进相互了解，推

Customs Administrations, during which we have enhanced mutual understanding, promoted joint programs, and discussed development routes, laying a solid foundation for the rapid development of BRICS customs cooperation.

动合作项目实施，商讨合作发展路线，为金砖国家海关合作快速发展奠定了基础。

After the Xiamen BRICS Summit, witnessed by the leaders of the five countries, Minister of the GACC signed the *Strategic Framework of BRICS Customs Cooperation* with heads of other BRICS customs administrations. This is a strategic and instructive document, embodying the fruit of broad consultation and joint contribution among BRICS Customs. It will play as a guideline for the customs cooperation between BRICS countries in a period to come and its outcomes will be shared among them all.

此次金砖国家领导人会晤后，在五国元首的共同见证下，中国海关总署署长与金砖国家海关负责人正式签署了《金砖国家海关合作战略框架》。这份具有战略性、指南性的文件，是金砖国家海关共商共建的结晶，将为金砖海关未来一个时期合作提供指导，其成果将为五国海关所共享。

In his speech at the Opening Ceremony of BRICS Business Forum on 3 September, President Xi Jinping stressed that BRICS countries should help each other and made concerted efforts, jointly ushering in the second "Golden Decade" of BRICS cooperation, in order to deliver more benefits to the peoples of the five countries and the world. BRICS Customs should also leverage this opportunity and stride forward. Based upon the principles of openness and inclusiveness, equality and solidarity, mutual understanding and mutual benefits, we should further strengthen communications, build consensus and deepen cooperation, setting up

习近平主席9月3日在金砖工商论坛开幕式致辞中强调金砖国家要守望相助、携手同行，努力开创金砖合作第二个“金色十年”，造福五国人民，惠及世界各国人民。金砖国家海关也应以此为契机，借力前行，在开放包容、平等团结、相互理解、互利合作等原则指导下，继续加强沟通、凝聚共识、深化合作，为全球发展中国家和新兴市场国家海关

an example for customs cooperation among developing countries and emerging market countries.

合作树立典范。

Looking ahead, I believe there are five aspects that we ought to focus on in future BRICS customs cooperation:

我想，下一步金砖海关国际合作的重点应围绕以下五个方面展开：

First，we should increase mutual respect and mutual trust. In the past decade，we have cultivated a BRICS spirit of mutual respect and mutual understanding. And BRICS Customs have also developed a close relationship since 2013，with ever growing cooperation speed and cooperative areas. None of these would have been possible without the precondition of mutual respect，mutual trust and mutual support. “A single arrow is easily broken，yet ten put together become strong.” BRICS Customs should base themselves upon the signing of the *Strategic Framework*，set up and improve customs cooperation mechanisms in different domains and on various levels，maintained institutionalized and frequent dialogues and mutual visits，and pool strength，seek common ground while respecting the difference，and pursue substantial results through joint programs.

第一，增进互尊互信。金砖十年培育出了互尊互谅、平等相待、团结互助、开放包容、互惠互利的金砖精神。从2013年至今，金砖国家海关也越走越近，越走越亲，合作速度加快，合作内容丰富，这前提就在于相互尊重、相互信任和相互支持。“一箭易断，十箭难折”。五国海关应以此次《金砖国家海关合作战略框架》的签署为契机，建立和完善海关各领域、各层级的合作机制，保持机制性、经常性的对话与互访，在推进合作项目的过程中凝心聚力、求同存异、求实求效。

Second, we should enhance policy communication. We should utilize the BRICS Customs Cooperation Committee among other platforms, build consensus over major policy issues in the international customs arena, and

第二，加强政策沟通。一是应借助金砖国家海关合作委员会等机制平台，围绕国际海关界重大政策性事务凝聚共识，加强在世界海

promote communication and coordination within multilateral frameworks such as the WCO, in order to safeguard the common interests of customs in BRICS countries and all developing member states. We should carry out exchanges in national development strategies, laws and regulations, customs procedures and modernization reforms, share each other's outcomes and experience in the reform and innovation of customs modernization. We should conduct joint researches on cross-border e-commerce and other new business models and create new growth points for BRICS economic development and the "Belt and Road" construction.

Third, we should facilitate unimpeded trade. China is the largest trade partner of South Africa and Russia; and South Africa and Brazil are China's largest trade partners in Africa and Latin America respectively. In the past decade, the bilateral trade volume among BRICS countries grew by 94%, opening up a broader stage and also raising higher requirements for BRICS customs cooperation. BRICS countries should stand firmly against trade protectionism, adhere to and develop an open world economy. We should further simplify customs formalities, promote AEO mutual recognition, introduce a series of measures such as customs data exchange, service and sharing, based on mutual recognition of control and mutual exchange of information, with a view to increasing customs clearance

关组织等多边合作框架下的立场沟通与协调，维护金砖国家和广大发展中成员海关的共同利益。二是应就国家发展战略、法律法规、海关手续和现代化改革等领域开展交流，互通互享各国在海关现代化改革创新中的成果和经验。三是应共同开展对跨境电子商务等新业态的研究，促使新业态为五国经济发展和“一带一路”建设创造新的增长点。

第三，提升贸易畅通。中国是南非和俄罗斯的最大贸易伙伴国，南非和巴西是中国在非洲和拉美地区的最大贸易伙伴国。过去十年间，金砖五国双边贸易总额增长了94%。这为五国海关合作开辟了更广阔的舞台，也提出了更高的要求。金砖国家海关应坚决反对贸易保护主义，维护和发展开放型世界经济，通过简化通关手续，推动“经认证的经营者”（AEO）互认，建立海关数据交换、服务和共享的平台等一系列以监管互认和信息互换为基础的具体

efficiency together. We should also step up efforts in the implementation of the *Trade Facilitation Agreement* (TFA), and help more enterprises enjoy facilitated customs clearance.

措施，共同提升海关通关效率，推动世界贸易组织《贸易便利化协定》（TFA）的实施，帮助更多的企业享受到实实在在的通关便利。

Fourth, we should promote mutual assistance in enforcement. BRICS Customs should support and engage in the joint enforcement activities proposed on multilateral platforms by any member, carry out cooperation in key areas such as fighting against trafficking in endangered flora and fauna, drugs, guns and ammunitions, and hazardous waste, as well as counterterrorism and safety, and so on through intelligence exchange, experience sharing and joint studies. Besides, we should conduct cooperation in enforcement by the customs, compliance of the companies and promulgation of the law among the public, aim at fostering compliance in the business sector, help companies better understanding customs laws and regulations, guide them to abide by the law in export and import activities, so as to guarantee the safety and efficiency at ports.

第四，促进执法互助。五国海关应相互支持和参与各自在多边领域倡议的联合执法行动，开展打击濒危动植物、毒品、枪支弹药、洋垃圾等走私、反恐与安全等重点领域的合作，积极开展情报交流、经验分享、联合研究。同时，围绕提升企业守法水平开展执法、守法、普法合作，帮助企业更好地了解海关的法律、法规，引导企业在进出口活动中遵纪守法，切实保障口岸的安全与便利。

Fifth，we should expand capacity building cooperation. We should make better use existing resources，launch capacity building exercises at BRICS Customs Training Center、WCO Training Center in the Asia-Pacific Region，and WCO Dog Training Center in the Asia-Pacific Region，expand cooperative areas by means of

第五，拓展能力建设。应积极利用现有资源，在金砖国家海关培训中心、世界海关组织亚太地区培训中心、世界海关组织亚太地区训犬中心创办能力建设活动，通过世界海关组织中国

expert exchanges, themed researches and on-site courses under the auspices of WCO Capacity Building Fund established by China Customs, and learn from each other and help each other in the planning of training programs, research and faculty development.

As an old Chinese saying goes, "Nothing can separate people with common goals and ideals, not even mountains and seas." After ten years' development, BRICS cooperation has been further deepened, economic and trade ties strengthened and people better connected and integrated. We have proved with our actions that "BRICS countries do not just seek our own development but work for the common development of all countries around the world". The "BRICS+" model proposed by China will facilitate the dialogue and cooperation among BRICS countries and other emerging market countries and developing countries, create a wider-ranged partnership and promote common development and prosperity to a broader extent. I am convinced that as BRICS cooperation grows, BRICS Customs will also ride the wave, and usher in the second "Golden Decade" of cooperation with even greater vitality and outcomes.

基金赞助、选派专家、专题研讨、现场跟班等形式拓展合作领域，并在培训项目规划、业务研究、师资运用等方面相互学习、相互借鉴、相互帮助。

“志和者，不以山海为远”。历经十年发展，金砖国家的合作进一步深化，经贸进一步畅通，民心进一步相融，也以实际行动证明了“金砖国家合作不是独善其身，而是致力于同世界各国共同发展”。中国提出的“金砖+”思路，将进一步加强金砖国家同其他新兴市场和发展中国家的对话合作，推动建立更为广泛的伙伴关系，促进更大范围的共同发展繁荣。相信随着金砖国家合作的不断深化，金砖五国海关也将顺势而为，共同开创海关合作新的更富活力和成效的“金色十年”。

APEC海关合作推动区域贸易便利化

2014 年 8 月 15 日

APEC Customs Cooperation for Regional Trade Facilitation

August 15, 2014

On August 12 and 13, two important meetings had been held in Beijing. One was ACBD （the APEC Customs and Business Dialogue 2014） and the other was SCCP （the APEC Sub-Committee on Customs Procedures）. As the host and chair of the meetings, I attended the meetings and delivered two speeches.

8月12日和13日，有两个重要的会议在北京举行。一个是APEC2014年海关与商界对话会(ACBD)，另一个是海关手续分委会(SCCP)。作为东道主和会议的主席，我出席了这两个会议并发表了演讲。

In 2001, China Customs hosted the ACBD for the first time in Shanghai. 13 years later, facing new economic and trade situations, we met in Beijing and discussed the development of a new partnership between Customs and the business in pursuit of comprehensive connectivity and economic

回想2001年，中国海关在上海举办了首次海关与商界对话会。13年后，面对新的经济和贸易形势，我们在北京聚会，讨论海关和商界新的伙伴发展关系，以实现亚太地区全方位的互联互通和经济繁荣。

prosperity in the Asia-Pacific region. The dialogue had profound significance. It not only pursued the APEC vision of liberalization and facilitation of regional investment and trade but also followed the trend of innovative and sustainable growth in the APEC region.

Over the past 20 years since its establishment, SCCP has always been committed to promoting the cooperation among member Customs as well as between Customs and the business. To push forward trade facilitation in the APEC region, SCCP has launched 18 collective action plans to simplify and harmonize Customs procedures and has identified the long-term strategy for Customs and business partnership. ACBD and SCCP have always been supportive of each other. They work closely on a series of hot issues within APEC. These issues include supply chain connectivity, single window, e-commerce, intellectual property rights, risk management and others. The close cooperation between the two has been playing a critical role in advancing regional trade facilitation and economic development. In order to strengthen routine communication between Customs and the business, the SCCP Virtual Working Group (VWG) was established last year for supporting the work of ACBD. Today, ACBD, as a pragmatic platform with APEC style, has been well recognized by high-level APEC mechanisms and private sectors.

对话会具有深远的意义，它不仅追求亚太经合组织区域投资和贸易自由化便利化的愿景，也紧随亚太经合组织地区创新和可持续增长的趋势。

海关手续分委会自成立以来20年里，一直致力于推动海关与海关、海关与商界的合作。为推动亚太经合组织区域贸易便利化， 海关手续分委会推出了18项集体行动计划，简化和协调海关程序，并确定了海关和企业的长期战略伙伴关系。海关与商界对话会和海关手续分委会一直相互支持。他们在亚太经合组织内一系列热点议题上密切合作。这些议题包括供应链连接、单一窗口，电子商务、知识产权、风险管理等等。两者之间的良好合作一直在推进区域贸易便利化和经济发展中发挥着重要作用。为了加强海关和商界之间日常的沟通，去年海关手续分委会成立了虚拟工作组以支持海关与商界对话会的工作。今天，海关与商界对话会作为亚太经合组织一个务实的平台，已得到APEC高层和私企行业的赞同。

Cooperation with other APEC member Customs and communication with the business have long been important agenda items of China Customs. In recent years, we have taken actions to enhance information transparency, field research, Customs business dialogue, policy explanation as well as lecture and training. Through these measures, we have maintained a good channel to seek comments and suggestions from the business, helped them with their difficulties in Customs clearance and improved their understanding of Customs procedures.

与亚太经合组织其他成员海关合作和与商界的沟通，一直是中国海关的一个重要议题。近年来，我们已经采取信息透明，实地调研、海关与商界对话、政策解释以及讲座和培训等行动。通过这些措施，我们保持一个好的渠道寻求商界的意见和建议，帮助他们解决通关中的困难、更好地理解海关执法程序。

Moreover, we have signed memorandums of understanding with private sectors and business administration departments in order to make a concerted effort to promote compliance and self-discipline in business, combat illicit trade and protect enterprises' legal interests. The above-mentioned practices reveal that Customs work would not go on without support from the business while the development of business would not be possible without the support of Customs. The sustainable development of economy and trade would be a joint effort of us both. To that end, our dialogue in the meetings served as just such a platform for us to better understand one another and learn from each other.

此外，我们与私企行业和工商管理部门签署了合作谅解备忘录，为的是共同努力促进企业的合规和自律，打击非法贸易和保护企业的合法利益。上述实践显示，海关没有商界的支持，就不能很好地开展工作；而企业没有海关的支持，也不可能有好的发展。为促进经济和贸易的发展我们必须精诚合作，彼此理解，互相学习。

Now the world economy is still experiencing

现在世界经济在后金融危

a profound adjustment in the post-financial crisis era, and the overall situation admits of no optimism. We come to realize that we have no choice but deepen the cooperation between Customs and the business, continuously build consensus and create a better trade environment. Only by doing so, can we finally achieve APEC connectivity and the Bogor Goals, and can the private sectors really enjoy the benefits of APEC trade facilitation and economic integration.

机时期仍经历着深刻的调整，整体形势不容乐观。我们意识到，海关与商界只有加强合作，凝聚共识，营造更好的贸易环境，别无其他选择。只有这样，我们才能实现亚太经合组织互联互通和茂物目标，私营企业才能享受亚太经合组织带来的贸易便利化和经济一体化的红利。

To that end, we hope that all member Customs and all business elite work hand in hand under the 2014 APEC theme "Shaping the Future through Asia-Pacific Partnership" and strive shoulder to shoulder to promote "mutual exchange of information, mutual recognition of control and mutual assistance in enforcement" among Customs for the improvement of connectivity between Customs and the business. I am convinced that our joint efforts will further advance the partnership between Customs and the business and inject fresh momentum into the rapid economic and trade recovery in the APEC region.

为此，我们希望所有成员海关和商界精英，按照2014年亚太经合组织提出的"共建面向未来的亚太伙伴关系"的主题，携手合作，并肩努力，促进海关之间"监管互认、执法互助、信息互换"，加强海关与商界的互联互通。我相信，我们的共同努力将会进一步推进海关和商界之间的合作伙伴关系，为亚太经合组织区域经济和贸易快速复苏注入新的动力。

中国—东盟互联互通为海关合作带来新机遇

2015年9月20日

China-ASEAN Connectivity Brings New Opportunities for Customs Cooperation

September 20, 2015

On September 18, 2015, I led a China customs delegation to attend the China-ASEAN seminar on customs cooperation in connectivity during the China-ASEAN Expo in the city of Nanning, Guangxi.

As we all know, 2015 is the China-ASEAN Maritime Cooperation Year. This time, the China-ASEAN Expo, which is co-sponsored by the Ministries of Commerce & Industry of China and the 10 ASEAN member states as well as the ASEAN Secretariat, takes on the theme of "Together Building the 21st Century Maritime Silk Road and Creating Beautiful Prospects in Maritime Cooperation". It aims to promote innovation in multi-tiered

2015年9月18日，我率领中国海关代表团前往广西南宁参加中国—东盟博览会，并出席期间召开的中国—东盟海关互联互通合作研讨会。

众所周知，2015年是中国—东盟海上合作年。这次，中国—东盟博览会是由中国商务部、工信部、10个东盟成员国以及东盟秘书处共同举办的。博览会的主题是“携手共建21世纪海上丝绸之路，共创中国—东盟海上合作美好未来”，旨在促进中国和东盟以及其他国家在不同领域多层级

exchange and cooperation between China and ASEAN as well as other countries in different aspects, which will open a new chapter in cooperation and development. Under the theme of "Connectivity across China and ASEAN—Together Building the Grand Passageway of Connectivity along the 21st Maritime Silk Road", our Workshop focused on connectivity, trade facilitation and win-win cooperation.

交流合作创新，开启合作发展的新篇章。以“中国—东盟互联互通，共同打造21世纪海上丝绸之路大通道”为主题，我们海关的研讨会重点讨论互联互通、贸易便利和双赢合作。

Since the China-ASEAN FTA came into effect in 2010, remarkable achievements of bilateral trade have been made. Two-way investment and trade have continued to expand. In the first 8 months of this year, two-way trade has reached 302.8 billion US dollars, increased by 0.6%. China's main exports to ASEAN were: mechanical and electrical products, textile, and steel. China's main imports from ASEAN were: mechanical and electrical products, resource products, and agricultural products. China continues to be ASEAN's largest trade partner. In this regard, customs administrations have been playing a vital role in boosting regional economic growth, people's exchange and mutual development.

自2010年中国—东盟自贸协定生效实施以来，双边贸易取得丰硕成果，双边投资和贸易继续扩大。今年前八个月，双边贸易达到3028亿美元，同比增长0.6%。中国主要出口东盟国家的产品包括机械和电子产品、纺织品、钢铁；而中国从东盟国家进口的商品包括机械和电子产品、能源产品、农产品。中国依然是东盟最大贸易伙伴国。为此，海关在促进区域经济增长、人员往来和相互发展中发挥着重要作用。

In 2013, President Xi Jinping proposed the "Belt and Road" initiative, and as connectivity is the primary area of the 21st Century Maritime Silk Road. China Customs

2013年，习近平主席提出“一带一路”倡议，互联互通是21世纪海上丝绸之路的主要内容。中国海关一直积极参与

has been actively participating in international cooperation to improve measures and projects with ASEAN customs administrations by means of fora, dialogue mechanism, joint enforcement etc., in order to enhance connectivity and trade facilitation.

国际合作，完善措施，和东盟国家海关一起开展合作项目，通过论坛、对话、联合执法行动等渠道加强互联互通，促进贸易便利化。

Currently, the performance of major economies in the world is divergent, growth is generally sluggish, international trade lacks impetus, global economic recovery is slow, and countries and businesses along the Belt and Road are faced with severe challenges. Hence, to help businesses out of difficulties and serve sustainable development, customs must cooperate to promote connectivity and trade facilitation.

当前，世界主要经济体表现差异大，增长缓慢，国际贸易缺乏动力，全球经济复苏迟缓，“一带一路”沿线国家和贸易面临严重挑战。为此，要帮助企业走出困境，服务可持续性发展，海关必须通过合作促进互联互通和贸易便利化。

The 21st Century Maritime Silk Road opens new historical opportunities for coordinated national and regional development. It requires that customs promote connectivity in all dimensions through international cooperation in mutual recognition of supervision，mutual assistance in enforcement and mutual exchange in information. To this end, customs administrations in the region should pool their efforts in the following areas:

21世纪海上丝绸之路为协同的国家和地区发展开启了历史机遇。它要求海关通过“信息互换、监管互认、执法互助”国际合作全方位加强互联互通。为此，区域内海关应在如下领域共同努力：

Ⅰ. **Promote trade facilitation cooperation.** We should devise policies that keep abreast with regional economic integration,

一、促进贸易便利化合作。我们应制定政策，与区域经济一体化保持同步发展，履

do our duty to safeguard trade security and handle trade frictions. With simple and coordinated procedures as the goal, we need to explore clearance models that recognize the inspection of other parties and raise clearance efficiency. We should promote AEO mutual recognition, explore, improve and innovate emerging business models such as cross-border e-commerce, strengthen cooperation with international and regional organizations, and forge win-win partnerships with the business.

职保障贸易安全，解决贸易摩擦。以简化和协调的通关手续为目标，探索监管互认的通关模式，提高通关效率。我们应该促进AEO互认，探索完善创新跨境电子商务新兴业态，加强与国际和区域机构合作，与企业建立双赢合作关系。

Ⅱ. **Promote cooperation in information sharing.** Science leads innovation in the internet era. We should strengthen information exchange among customs, the WCO and other organizations for the Maritime Silk Road to improve smart supervision of customs. Especially, customs should share information such as laws and regulations, foreign trade policy adjustment, trade statistics, credibility of enterprises and a major change in administration patterns, promote online verification of certificates of origin, and provide information for enforcement and administration. We should also strengthen the communication of risk information, raise the capacity of identifying high-risk goods and safeguard international trade safety.

二、推动信息共享合作。网络时代科技带动创新。我们应加强海关和世界海关组织以及其他组织之间就海上丝绸之路开展信息交换，提高海关智能监管。特别是，海关交换的信息应包括法律法规、对外贸易政策调整、贸易统计、企业诚信等级以及管理模式方面的重大变化，促进网上原产地证明审核，提供执法和行政信息。我们还应加强风险信息沟通、提高甄别高风险货物的能力，保障国际贸易安全。

Ⅲ. **Promote enforcement mutual assistance and cooperation.** We should reinforce cooperation in preventing terrorist attacks, anti-smuggling, combating tax fraud and preventing the entry and exit of unsafe and counterfeit goods to create an orderly and safe international trade environment. We should step up regional enforcement assistance, undertake when appropriate joint enforcement operations to safeguard border security and stability. We should enhance intelligence swap and sharing and raise the effectiveness and timeliness of customs enforcement.

三、促进执法互助合作。我们应加强合作，防止恐怖袭击、打击走私和税务瞒骗，防止不安全的、侵权货物进出境，共同营造有序且安全的国际贸易环境。我们应加强地区执法互助，适时开展联合执法行动，保障边境安全和稳定。我们应加强情报交换和共享，提高海关执法时效性。

Ⅳ. **Promote capacity building cooperation.** Customs in the region should establish a more comprehensive education and training platform to raise the administration, supervision and enforcement capacity of customs officers. We should promote international exchange between customs colleges, provide expert support, communicate on matters of mutual interest and design capacity building projects under the Maritime Silk Road initiative.

四、加强能力建设合作。区域海关应搭建更为全面的教育和培训平台，提高海关关员管理、监管和执法能力。我们应加强海关学院之间的国际交流，提供专家支持，就共同关心的事务进行沟通，并在海上丝绸之路倡议下设计能力建设项目。

Ⅴ. **Promote integration mechanisms.** We should integrate connectivity into the framework of the WCO, the Sub-Committee on Customs Procedures of APEC, meetings with heads of ASEAN Customs and other

五、促进一体化机制。我们应将互联互通纳入世界海关组织框架、亚太地区经济合作组织的海关手续分委会、中国—东盟会议框架下的署长碰

multilateral mechanisms and identify it as a priority. We should also promote the application of international conventions and customs in goods categorization, rules of origin, risk management, corporate administration and supervision and inspection, communicate and cooperate on systems, procedures and measures.

头会以及其他多边机制下，并将此作为重点工作内容。我们也应推动使用国际公约、商品归类、原产地、风险管理、企业管理以及监管查验，并就制度、手续和措施加强沟通合作。

During the seminar, I also had the bilateral meetings with the heads of Cambodia, Vietnam, Laos Customs administrations. We reached great consensus on the customs cooperation in connectivity.

研讨会期间，我还和缅甸、越南、老挝海关署长举行了双边会谈。我们就海关在互联互通领域合作方面达成了一致意见。

Connectivity has always been the aspiration of all mankind. Enhancing connectivity among countries and regions along the 21st Century Maritime Silk Road has significant implications and broad prospects. China Customs will strengthen pragmatic and win-win cooperation in all aspects with all parties to make further contribution to trade and investment liberalization and facilitation, the Maritime Silk Road as well as peace, stability and prosperity in countries and regions within the area.

互联互通一直是全世界共同的愿望。提高21世纪海上丝绸之路沿线国家和地区的互联互通有着深远的意义和广阔的前景。中国海关将与所有相关方全面加强务实双赢合作，为贸易和投资自由化、便利化、海上丝绸之路以及沿线国家和地区的和平稳定和繁荣发展作出应有的贡献。

善用科技创新　打造智慧海关

——写在 2017 年国际海关日

2017 年 1 月 17 日

Build Smart Customs Through Technology and Innovation

—— On the 2017 International Customs Day

January 17, 2017

The International Customs Day is here again. The theme for this year is "Data Analysis for Effective Border Management". I attended the reception of the International Customs Day hosted by China Customs and had very friendly talks with Customs Attachés and representatives from different countries.

Today, the world is witnessing growing exchanges. New technologies such as big data, cloud computing and artificial intelligence are emerging. E-commerce is becoming a part of our daily life as a new business model, bringing a significant impact on global trade. These changes have created new economic growth and brought about great opportunities

每年的国际海关日又到了。今年的主题是"数据分析：实现有效边境管理"。我参加了中国海关为庆祝国际海关日举办的招待会，与各国海关驻华专员和代表进行了友好交流。

当今，全球各国各地区交往日益频繁，大数据、云计算、人工智能等新技术相继涌现，电子商务作为一种新业态也逐渐走入各国百姓家庭，对国际贸易方式产生了深远影响。这些变化创造了新的经济增长点，给各国带来了新的发

for development. At the same time, the explosive growth of information and data have added to the complexity of global trade environment, bringing new challenges to the international Customs community.

Under such circumstances, the WCO decided that 2017 International Customs Day would be devoted to the theme of "Data Analysis for Effective Border Management", which emphasizes innovation and technology, as well as the role of data collection and data analysis in Customs modernization. We share the same vision with the WCO, and believe that only through timely and efficient collection, selection, comparison and analysis of a large amount of data can we guarantee fast clearance and supply chain security based on risk management. Communication and cooperation must also be strengthened and information shared among Customs, and between Customs and other border enforcement agencies so that concerted efforts can be made for effective border management against the increasingly complicated trade environment.

In 2016, China remained the second largest economy in the world. Its import and export totaled 24.33 trillion RMB yuan, equivalent to about 3.69 trillion US dollars, with a year-on-year increase of 0.9%. Tax and duty collected by customs stood at 1.54 trillion

展机遇。同时，信息和数据的爆炸式增长也使得全球贸易环境越发复杂，为国际海关界带来了新的挑战。

在此背景下，世界海关组织(WCO)将2017年国际海关日的主题定为"数据分析：实现有效边境管理"，强调国际海关界需要创新手段，善用科技，进一步发挥数据收集和数据分析在海关现代化进程中的重要作用。中国海关对此表示深深赞同。我们认为，各国海关需要及时高效地对大量甚至杂乱的数据进行收集、筛选、比对和分析，才能够有效依托风险管理确保通关便捷和供应链安全。同时，各国海关之间、海关与其他边境执法机构之间必须加强交流与合作，共享信息与数据，形成边境管理的合力，更好地应对复杂的贸易环境。

2016年，中国保持世界第二大经济体地位，进出口总值达24.33万亿元人民币，约合3.69万亿美元，同比下降0.9%。海关税收入库约1.54万亿元人民币，同比增长2.6%，

yuan, increased by 2.6%. We have investigated 2633 criminal smuggling cases and detained 52.9 billion yuan's worth of smuggled goods. In order to efficiently manage such vast amount of international trade, China Customs has always been committed to developing towards a smart Customs with big data as the key technology, as well as an interconnected Customs with IT as the cornerstone.

侦办2633起走私违法刑事案件，查扣走私货物价值529亿元人民币。为了更好应对如此庞大的贸易量，中国海关一向致力打造以大数据技术为核心的智慧海关和以通信技术为基础的互联互通海关。

In 2016, new progress has been made. Domestically, we finished building 7 new IT projects, continued pushing forward Phase II of the Golden Customs Project, and established the Customs information and data exchange platform to support our national reform of Customs clearance integration. We equipped our field officers with mobile devices connected to 3G and 4G networks for physical checks, inspection of Customs control areas and auditing of enterprises, thus increasing the mobility of Customs operations.

2016年，我们取得了新的成绩。国内来说，中国海关完成了7个科技项目的建设，继续深化金关工程二期建设，建立起海关信息资源共享服务平台，满足全国通关一体化数据共享需要；利用3G、4G通信技术，实现现场关员通过移动设备完成查验、巡视和稽查等业务，极大地提高了海关各现场作业的机动性和灵活性。

We fully support the growth of cross-border E-commerce and have established a cross-border E-commerce interface for data exchange among Customs, other relevant government agencies and businesses. As a result, the compliance of e-vendors has been greatly improved. More “Single Window” have been set up in 11 coastal ports in Tianjin, Fujian and Guangdong to improve the flow

我们大力支持跨境电子商务发展，逐步建立起跨境电商公共服务体系，促进海关、其他监管部门以及企业之间的数据共享，大大提升了跨境电商守法水平；在天津、福建、广东等11个沿海地区口岸建成并启用“单一窗口”，提升信息数据的使用效率；统筹使用监

of information. Through the overall planning and deployment of control facilities, we provide one-stop service for businesses. The Customs-quarantine cooperation featuring "one declaration, joint inspection and single release" now covers all Customs districts and quarantine offices nationwide, which greatly enhances coordinated border management.

管设施资源，逐步推进"一站式作业"，并将关检合作"三个一"，即"一次申报、一次查验、一次放行"推广到全国所有直属海关和检验检疫部门，全面提升协调边境管理水平。

Internationally, we highly value cooperation and communication with other Customs administrations. At the bilateral level, we have signed 22 inter-governmental or Customs to Customs cooperation documents with 18 countries and regions concerning administrative assistance, clearance facilitation, mutual recognition of control, law enforcement, and so on. Through our active engagement in AEO mutual recognition arrangement, we have helped over 3000 AEOs in China receive preferential treatment of Customs clearance in the EU, U.S. and other countries and regions. At the regional level, we have been building the Customs cooperation network along the Belt and Road and facilitating trade in this region. We have been exploring the possibility of data exchange and mutual recognition of control among Customs along the Belt and Road by using a new type of e-lock.

在国际上，中国海关高度重视与其他海关的合作与交流。在双边层面，与18个国家签署了22份政府间或海关间合作文件，涉及海关合作与行政互助、通关便利、监管结果互认、执法等多个领域；积极推进经认证的经营者(AEO)互认，帮助国内3000多家AEO企业在欧盟、美国等相关国家和地区享受到通关便利。在区域层面，构建"一带一路"海关合作网络，并探索依托安全智能锁开展中欧班列沿线海关数据交换和监管互认方案，全力提升"一带一路"沿线国家贸易便利化水平。

We opened "green channel" for

积极推进农产品快速通

agricultural products to assure minimum delay, upgraded the Safe and Secure Trade Lanes Pilot Project and successfully initiated Operation Irene in the Asia Pacific region to combat the smuggling of arms and ammunition. At the multilateral level, we signed the first *Regulation on the Customs Cooperation Committee of the BRICS* with our BRICS partners under the witness of the national Leaders, put "Combating Illegal Financial Flows" into the outcome of G20 Summit along with the WCO, made "mutual exchange of information, mutual recognition of control and mutual assistance in enforcement" (3Ms), "Customs control of cross-border E-commerce" and "sharing of practices and experience in *Trade Facilitation Agreement* (TFA) implementation" part of the *2016 APEC Joint Ministerial Statement*, initiated the discussion of TFA implementation under the framework of ASEM, acceded to the TIR Convention and accepted two more Annexes of the *Revised Kyoto Convention*.

关"绿色通道"、安全智能贸易航线等合作，并在亚太地区成功发起打击走私武器弹药的"和平女神"联合执法行动；在多边层面，会同其他金砖国家海关领导人在金砖五国元首的见证下首次签署了《金砖国家海关合作委员会章程》；成功与WCO合作将海关应对"非法资金流"纳入G20峰会成果；积极推动将"三互"理念和"跨境电子商务海关监管""世界贸易组织《贸易便利化协定》(TFA)实施经验交流"等国际海关界的关注热点纳入《2016年APEC部长级联合声明》；牵头开展了亚欧会议下(ASEM)TFA实施经验的交流；正式加入联合国《国际公路运输公约》(TIR公约)，新接受了《经修订的京都公约》两个附约。

Sponsored by CCF-China, we hosted 11 training programs and workshops that involved more than 400 participants from 20 countries, thus contributing to the capacity building efforts of the international Customs community. As the Host and Secretariat of the Customs Attaché Club, we assisted the Chairs

利用WCO中国海关能力建设合作基金举办各类项目11个，涉及来自20个国家的400余人，为推进国际海关界能力建设做出了积极努力。作为驻华海关专员俱乐部的东道主和秘书处，我们协助各季度轮值

in hosting seminars on Customs Technology and Innovation, Customs Information Source and Management, and made the Club an excellent platform for exchange of views and best practices.

You can do anything you set your mind to. China Customs has always cherished the intensive cooperation with its partners, and it will keep on building a more comprehensive, systematic and coordinated framework for better international Customs cooperation based on the 3Ms principle. Our understanding of international Customs cooperation fits in very well with the theme of this year's International Customs Day, showing the common aspiration to share ideas, enhance mutual trust and achieve efficient border management. Hopefully, 3Ms will help customs administrations in different countries and regions better exchange and use each other's data and information, and bring about more efficient, more integrated and more deepened Customs cooperation for common development.

主席成功举办了“海关科技与创新”“海关数据收集与应用”等多个专题研讨会，积极搭建各海关间分享先进理念与最佳实践的交流平台。

世上无难事，只怕有心人。中国海关一向高度重视与各国海关的紧密合作，将继续以“信息互换、监管互认、执法互助”(“三互”)为理念，努力构建一个更为全面、系统和协调的国际海关间合作框架。中国海关的这一国际海关合作理念与今年“国际海关日”的主题不谋而合，体现了国际海关界互通有无、增进互信、实现高效边境管理的共同愿望。我们希望通过“三互”理念推动各国各地区海关加强信息与数据的交换与互认，提高我们的合作效率，整合我们的合作内容，深化我们的合作关系，实现我们的共同发展。

出席国务院新闻办新闻发布会

2016年10月20日

Press Conference of the State Council Information Office

October 20, 2016

At 3 o'clock in the afternoon, October 20, 2016, I attended a press conference of the State Council Information Office with some of the Director Generals and colleagues from the General Administration of China Customs (GACC).

10月20日下午3时，我和海关总署的部分司局长及相关同事出席了由国务院新闻办组织的新闻发布会。

The press conference was held at the media hall of the SCIO. The theme is to disclose information on promoting innovative growth of processing trade and upgrading customs special control areas, and answer questions of the media. Head of the Information Bureau of the SCIO moderated the press conference.

此次新闻发布会在国务院新闻办新闻发布厅举行，主要内容是围绕海关促进加工贸易创新发展和海关特殊监管区域整合优化情况向媒体进行发布，并回答记者提问。国务院新闻办新闻局负责人主持了新闻发布会。

I started off by extending the gratitude to

一开场，我首先代表

our friends from the media and the people for their care, understanding and support for China Customs over the years. Then I briefed them of customs' operations on the control of processing trade and bonded goods, and spoke about our efforts in deepening reform, improving service and control, and promoting innovative growth of processing trade and upgrading customs special control areas according to the decisions and plans of the CPC Central Committee and the State Council.

In my opening remarks, I pointed out that China's economy is now growing steadily, with its structure being optimized, and is expected to maintain the increase, which was encouraging. Yet new circumstances and problems continue to emerge for the economy, and China's foreign trade, processing trade in particular, faces challenges and new uncertainties. Customs statistics showed that in the first nine months of this year, China's import and export were registered at 17.53 trillion yuan, a decrease of 1.9% year-on-year. Over the same period, inward and outward processing trade reached 5.16 trillion yuan, down by 7% compared to the previous year, wider than the decreases of foreign trade, and accounting for 29.4% of China's foreign trade. As an important platform for processing trade, customs special control areas witnessed

海关总署向新闻媒体朋友和社会各界长期以来给予海关工作的关心支持表示衷心感谢。紧接着，我简要地介绍了近年来全国加工贸易和保税监管业务方面发展情况，海关总署按照党中央、国务院的决策部署全面深化改革、优化监管服务、有效促进加工贸易转型升级创新发展和海关特殊监管区域整合优化所做的工作。

我在介绍中指出，当前我国经济运行总体平稳。据国家统计局发布的经济指标，我国经济运行稳中有进、稳中提质、预期向好，这是十分令人鼓舞的。但与此同时，我们也要看到在经济运行中也面临着一些新情况、新问题。比如，我国外贸特别是加工贸易正面临挑战和新的不确定因素。据海关统计，今年1至9月，我国进出口总值17.53万亿元人民币，同比下降1.9%。其中加工贸易进出口5.16万亿元，同比下降7%，下降的幅度比外贸整体要大，加工贸易占我国外贸总值的29.4%。海

2.78 trillion yuan worth of cross-border goods in the first 9 months, a minor decline of 0.4%. It is worth mentioning that in the third quarter of this year China's total export and import have increased by 1.1%, 0.4% and 2.1%, respectively, showing signs of recovery. Take August for an example, import and export stood at 2.2 trillion yuan, up by 7.8%, among which processing trade totaled 654.25 billion yuan and up by 2.3%. It is an encouraging and hard-won achievement:

关特殊监管区域作为加工贸易的重要载体，今年1-9月实现进出口2.78万亿元，同比略降0.4%。但值得关注的是，今年第三季度我国外贸出现回稳向好的迹象，第三季度进出口、出口和进口分别增长1.1%、0.4%和2.1%。比如8月份进出口总值2.2万亿人民币，同比增长7.8%，其中加工贸易是6542.5亿元人民币，同比增长2.3%，回稳向好的迹象十分可喜，也非常来之不易。

Then I explained the causes of the stabilization and growth: firstly, policies and measures adopted by the CPC Central Committee and the State Council in promoting steady growth, restructuring the economy and improving people's livelihood have started to prove effective in driving domestic demand. As a result, the actual quantity of imported goods in the first three quarters increased by 3.2%, in contrast to a decrease of 1.8% last year. Secondly, narrowing of drop in import price has resulted in higher import value. In the first three quarters, China's monthly import price decreased by 5.3%, 6.3 percentage points lower than the previous year. Thirdly, recovery of foreign demand has contributed to growth in

随后，我对出现这种回稳向好的迹象的主要原因作了分析：一是党中央、国务院出台的一系列稳增长、调结构、促改革、惠民生的政策措施成效逐步显现，国内需求增加，前三季度我国实际进口货物数量同比增长3.2%，去年全年则为减少1.8%；二是进口商品价格跌幅收窄提高了进口总值，前三季度我国月度进口价格下跌5.3%，较去年全年收窄6.3个百分点；三是外需转暖也带动了出口增长，8月份美国咨商会公布的消费者信心

export. According to the US Conference Board, the Consumer Confidence Index（CCI）reached 101.1 in August, the highest since September last year. We are looking forward to even better results in the fourth quarter.

指数为101.1，为去年9月以来的最优表现。我们期待第四季度外贸有更好的表现。

There were a lot of questions from reporters during the Q&A session, and I answered them one by one candidly. The first question was from a lady with China National Radio. She asked about customs special control areas: "The Government rolled out policies and measures to address uneven development among different customs special control areas. Could you give up more information on that? What are the plans and policies looking forward?"

在开场介绍后的提问环节，记者们纷纷踊跃提问，我也坦诚地逐一进行了解答。记得第一个提问的是中央人民广播电台女记者。她提的问题是关于海关特殊监管区域的问题。她问："为解决海关特殊监管区域发展不平衡的问题，国家出台了整合优化的政策和措施，请问这方面的发展现状是怎么样的？下一步我们的具体工作思路和支持措施是什么？"

This question was right to the point, I said, "The GACC leads the work with 10 ministries and committees in reviewing the applications for building customs special control areas, and reporting to the State Council for final approval. Currently, there are 129 customs special control areas in the country. Some have made extraordinary progress and become the window and beacon of China's open economy. Most are average, while some are underdeveloped. There is indeed the problem of unbalanced and inadequate

我认为这个问题还是切中要害的。我回答："设立海关特殊监管区域是国务院事权，由海关总署牵头会同十个部委共同审核报批，地方建设。目前全国共有129个海关特殊监管区域。从已设立运作的海关特殊监管区域看，好的特别好，发挥了开放型经济窗口和桥头堡的作用。但中等居多，差的

development, hence a list of supporting policies." Plans of the Customs are:

也有。确实存在发展不平衡不充分的问题。为此，国家出台了一系列支持促进发展措施。”海关下一步的考虑：

Firstly, we will work to contribute to the implementation of national strategies. We will focus on optimizing geographical deployment of customs special control areas to meet the needs of national strategies including the Belt and Road initiative, synergetic development of Beijing, Tianjin municipalities and Hebei province, as well as building the Yangtze River economic belt. So far, 116 customs special control areas have been set up in provinces and cities key to the strategies, accounting for 89.9% of the country's total. Meanwhile, there will be more newly-built areas in the central, western and northeastern regions.

一是服务国家战略。海关总署将紧紧围绕“一带一路”、京津冀协同发展、长江经济带等国家发展战略要求，不断优化海关特殊监管区域布局。在这三大战略的省市区域，共有海关特殊监管区116个，占全国总数的89.9%。同时，新设海关特殊监管区域向中西部地区和东北地区重点倾斜。

Secondly, we will expand the functions of customs special control areas. We play an active role in developing new pilot services, such as to grant businesses in the areas the VAT general taxpayer status, to allow businesses in the areas to decide if their domestically-sold processed goods are to be taken as raw material, semi-finished products or finished products when duty is levied, and to exercise differentiated controls over goods by status, i.e. goods in bond or non-bonded goods, so as to give businesses in the areas a

二是拓展区域功能。积极探索赋予区内企业增值税一般纳税人资格、内销货物选择性征收关税、货物按状态分类监管等试点，创造有利于区内企业对接国内国际市场，延伸产业链价值链，培育外贸竞争新优势的发展环境。

better access to domestic market, help them move up the value chain and foster an enabling environment for businesses to grow increasingly competitive in foreign trade.

Thirdly, we will support the growth of new forms of trade, including display and trading of goods in bond, and financial leasing. We guide the special control areas to upgrade their functions to accommodate high-end manufacturing, logistics, research and development, maintenance, sales and settlement, so as to create new drive for foreign trade growth.

Fourthly, we will focus on the quality of development. Following the instructions from the State Council to integrate and optimize customs special control areas, we have set up mechanisms for the approval, assessment and revoking starting 2010.. Since 2015, we have asked 41 special control areas to make rectifications where the land use rate failed to meet the standard, shifting the focus of development of special customs control areas from quantity growth to quality improvement.

A reporter with *Economic Daily* followed up with another question on how to improve industrial structure through the reform of supply-side structural reforms during customs supervision over processing trade.

It was also an important question. As

三是促进新型业态发展。积极支持保税展示交易、融资租赁等新型贸易业态发展，引导海关特殊监管区域向高端制造、物流、研发、维修、销售、结算等方向转型，形成新的外贸增长点。

四是注重发展质量。2010年以来，我们按照国务院整合优化的要求，严格设立审核考核评估和实施退出管理，特别是去年以来，先后对土地利用率不达标的41个特殊监管区域进行通报整改，引导区域从量的增长向质的提升转变。

紧接着，来自《经济日报》社的记者提的问题是关于海关在加工贸易监管上是如何结合实施供给侧结构性改革、采取举措促进产业结构不断优化。

我认为这个问题也很

processing trade is an important part of China's open economy, promoting processing trade and improving customs special control areas have been among the priorities for the work of both the CPC Central Committee and the State Council. In recent years, the State Council has issued *Guidelines on Promoting Sound Development of Customs Special Control Areas, Plan for Accelerating the Integration and Optimization of Customs Special Control Areas, Opinions on Advancing Innovative Growth of Processing Trade, and Opinions for the Steady Recovery of Foreign Trade by the State Council.* The General Administration of China Customs will earnestly implement the decisions of the central government, continue to streamline administration and delegate power to lower levels, strike a balance between liberalizing and controlling, and further improve its services, so as to ensure effective implementation of the policies and innovative measures.

重要。加工贸易是我国开放型经济的重要组成部分，党中央、国务院高度重视加工贸易发展。近年来，国务院先后印发了《关于促进海关特殊监管区域科学发展的指导意见》《加快海关特殊监管区域整合优化方案》《关于促进加工贸易创新发展的若干意见》和《国务院关于促进外贸回稳向好的若干意见》。海关总署坚决贯彻落实中央决策部署，以推进简政放权、放管结合、优化服务为抓手，推动各项政策措施和创新制度落地见效。

For instance, regarding optimizing the industrial structure, we have worked with related authorities in making adjustments to nearly 2000 items on the processing trade negative list to phase out high energy-consuming, highly polluting and resources-dependent industries. The first three quarters have seen processing trade of high and new tech products reach 2.66 trillion yuan, which accounts for 51.6% of the total

比如，在促进产业结构不断优化方面，我们积极落实供给侧结构性改革部署，联合有关部门调整加工贸易禁止类目录近2000项，淘汰“两高一资”落后产能。今年前三季度，加工贸易高新技术产品进出口值达到2.66万亿元，占加工贸易进出口

processing trade volume. The value-added ratio of processing trade has surged from 35% in 1996 to 80% in 2015.

总值的51.6%。加工贸易增值率由1996年的35%上升为2015年的80%。

We are also helping China's processing trade further move up the value chain. By introducing new supervision and control models over bonded processing, bonded logistics and the service sector, we are playing our part in boosting the growth of emerging industries with strategic importance and new trade types. For example, in the first three quarters of this year, 112 million shipments of online-purchased goods were imported under bonded operations, with a total value of 17.31 billion yuan, giving customers access to fast-delivered quality goods at a reasonable price.

又如，在引导产业链向高端延伸方面，我们通过创新保税加工、保税物流、保税服务等加工贸易保税监管模式，支持战略性新兴产业和新型贸易业态发展。比如，今年前三季度，全国跨境电子商务网购保税进口1.12亿票，进口总额达173.1亿元，为消费者提供质优价廉配送快的新选择。

In addition, we are facilitating the transfer of processing trade to central and western China, in particular, 44 locations in the inland and border frontier areas. Statistics showed that in the first nine months of 2016, processing trade in central and western China increased by 0.8% over the same period last year, and its share in the national total rose from 4.4% in 2010 to 15.4%, up by 11 percentage points.

与此同时，我们积极推动加工贸易向中西部转移。积极推动加工贸易向内陆和沿边地区44个重点承接地梯度转移，2016年前三季度，中、西部地区加工贸易进出口同比增长0.8%，占全国的比重从2010年的4.4%上升到15.4%，提高11个百分点。

When we were about to close the press conference, a reporter with *China Daily* insisted asking one last question: "There are 4 Pilot Free Trade Zones in Guangdong, Shanghai, Tianjin and Fujian. What new measures will be

新闻发布会快结束时，《中国新闻社》的一位记者抢着提问，"目前广东、上海、天津、福建设立了四个自贸试验区，海关在支持自

introduced by customs in the Pilot Free Trade Zones?"

In response to that question, I answered, the State Council decided to set up three new Pilot Free Trade Zones (PFTZs) in Tianjin, Fujian, Guangdong after the establishment of Shanghai PFTZ. During earlier development of the PFTZs, **firstly, we made innovations in customs supervision systems**. Taking the initiative in aligning our measures with high standards of international economic and trade rules, we have introduced 187 innovative customs supervision measures which aim at delivering benefits and facilitation to businesses, including "entry first, declaration later", "self-arranged transportation within the PFTZ", "fast release at smart checkpoints", "centralized collection of aggregate duty payments" and "AEO mutual recognition", among others. The *China Business Climate Survey Report* published by the American Chamber of Commerce in Shanghai showed that the new measure of "entry first, declaration later" claimed a satisfaction rate of 87.8% among businesses. Recently, the Central Government decided again to set up 7 new PFTZs in Liaoning and other provinces. We are now developing customs measures to support the operations of the newly set-up PFTZs based on the principles of giving the PFTZs the right positioning, leveraging their distinctive features, fostering innovation-driven

贸试验区有何新的措施？”

针对这位记者朋友的提问，我回答道，自上海自贸试验区成立以后，国家又批准了天津、福建、广东设立自贸试验区。在前期自贸试验区的实践过程中，海关**一是创新海关监管制度**。主动对标高标准国际经贸规则，先后推出了一批给企业带来实惠和便利的海关监管创新制度。比如“先入区，后报关”“区内企业自行运输”“智能化卡口验放”“集中汇总征税”等等，涉及四个区域，共七个直属海关，创新制度总数187项。据上海美国商会发布的《贸易环境满意度调查报告》显示，“先入区后报关”创新制度企业认可度达87.8%。前不久，中央又决定在辽宁等省市新设七个自贸试验区，海关正按照“围绕定位、注重特色，创新引领、分类施策，先行先试、复制推广”的原则，研究制定海关支持措施。

growth, accommodating different conditions, launching pilots to implement new measures and applying proven practices to the entire country.

Secondly, we have stepped up efforts in replicating the proven practices in places outside the PFTZs. Since 2014, the GACC has introduced 25 innovative supervision measures adopted in the PFTZs to other customs supervision areas.

二是加大复制推广力度。2014年以来，海关总署先后在全国海关复制推广了自贸试验区25项海关监管创新制度。

Thirdly, we are now working on measures to support the reforms of delegating power, streamlining administration and improving government services. A change in administration philosophy has been made, with administrative approval power removed or delegated to lower levels, restrictions lifted and the list of power and responsibilities put in place. Facilitative measures including "Internet plus administrative approval", smart checkpoints and paperless clearance have been introduced. Schemes of AEO mutual recognition and the disclosure of business credit ratings have been adopted, in a bid to form a new model of customs control featuring business self-discipline and coordinated administration by multiple authorities, and strive to create an open, well-regulated and enabling business environment.

三是推进"放管服"改革。转变监管理念，取消、下放、放开审批事权和限制，公布权力责任清单；全面推行"互联网+行政审批"、智能化卡口、通关无纸化等便利措施；实施"海关AEO国际互认、企业信用信息公开"等制度，逐步建立企业自律、多方共管的新型监管模式，努力营造法治化、国际化、便利化营商环境。

The press conference was only a bit more than an hour, but I was impressed by how much importance the media put to the country's

这次新闻发布会虽只有一个多小时，但媒体记者对我国对外开放和进出口形

opening-up and foreign trade. News media help us promote the country’s policies, regulations and measures, and oversee customs work on supervision and services. We have to work even more diligently and make greater achievements to be worthy of the attention and trust of the society and the media.

势关注的程度以及提问的热情，给我留下了深刻的印象。新闻媒体既帮助我们宣传国家的政策、法规和工作措施，也是对我们履行海关把关服务职责的监督。我们唯有加倍努力工作，做出成绩，才能更好地回报社会和新闻媒体的关心和信任。

支持自贸试验区建设　中国海关在路上

2017 年 10 月

China Customs on the Road to Support the PFTZs

October, 10

It is a strategic measure adopted by the CPC Central Committee and the State Council of China to build the Pilot Free Trade Zone (PFTZ) so as to comprehensively deepen reforms and expand opening-up under new circumstances. In September 2013, the Shanghai PFTZ was officially launched. At the end of 2014, the State Council approved the expansion of Shanghai PFTZ, as well as the construction of PFTZs in Guangdong, Tianjin and Fujian. Over the past 4 years, following the decisions and plans of the CPC Central Committee and the State Council, China Customs among other government administrations explored courageously and made remarkable progress in the supervision and innovation of trade and investment

建设自由贸易试验区是党中央、国务院在新形势下全面深化改革和扩大开放的一项战略举措。2013年9月，上海自贸试验区挂牌。2014年底国务院批准上海自贸试验区扩区，批复同意设立广东、天津、福建三个自贸试验区。四年来，海关等部门按照党中央、国务院决策部署，在国务院自由贸易试验区工作部际联席会议统筹推进下，在贸易投资自由化和便利化监管创新领域进行了大胆探索，取得了重大

liberalization and facilitation under the holistic plan by the Inter-ministerial Conference of Work on PFTZ of the State Council. These efforts have brought valuable experience for comprehensively deepening reforms and promoting the country's high-standard opening-up. Statistics showed that 46,157 companies registered with the customs in the four PFTZs in Shanghai, Guangdong, Tianjin and Fujian in 2016, attracting 87.96 billion RMB yuan of foreign investment, and achieving an export-import volume of 2.65 trillion yuan, which accounted for over 10% of the country's total. With a view to conducting reforming and innovative practices and explorations in a wider area and building more "test fields" of reform and opening up, at the end of August, 2016, the CPC Central Committee and the State Council approved 7 more PFTZs, respectively in Liaoning, Zhejiang, Henan, Hubei, Chongqing, Sichuan and Shaanxi. Up till now, a total of 11 PFTZs cover an area of 1,314 square kilometers in China.

进展，为全面深化改革、推动我国高水平对外开放积累了宝贵经验。据统计，2016年，上海、广东、天津、福建4个自贸试验区内海关注册企业共计46157家，实际吸收外资879.6亿元人民币，实现进出口总值2.65万亿元，占比超过全国同期进出口总值的10%。为了在更大范围进行改革创新实践和探索，建设更多改革开放“试验田”，2016年8月底，党中央、国务院决定，在辽宁、浙江、河南、湖北、重庆、四川、陕西等省市再设立7个新的自贸试验区。截至目前，11个自贸试验区面积总计约1314平方公里。

自贸试验区中的海关监管现场。

Customs control in PFTZs.

The PFTZ is different from the Free Trade Area and the Free Zone. The Free Trade Area is a specific region where countries and countries, or countries and regions render preferential treatments in taxation, open market and services, and realize trade and investment liberalization through the signing of a free trade agreement, or simply put, a mutually beneficial agreement between countries or between countries and separate customs territories. In this sense, Free Trade Area essentially means Free Trade Agreement, the fundamental idea of which is to render mutually preferential treatments to promote the liberalization and facilitation of trade and investment.

自由贸易试验区，与我们以前熟知的自由贸易区和自由贸易园区是有区别的。自由贸易区是国与国或国家与地区之间通过自由贸易协定所给予的相关税收、市场开放、服务的优惠，形成贸易投资自由化的一种特定区域，简单说是国与国之间或者国家与单独关境区域之间的互惠协议。从这个意义上说，自由贸易区讲的就是自由贸易协定，它的实质是以协定的形式相互给予优惠，以促进贸易和投资自由化便利化。

China's special customs control area is an example of the Free Zone with Chinese characteristics, which is, according to the Specific Annex D2 Free Zones to the *Kyoto Convention*, a part of the territory of a country where any goods introduced will be granted preferential treatments in taxation and clearance.

我国的海关特殊监管区域是具有中国特色的自由贸易园区，参照《京都公约》“自由区附约”，即在一个国家领土里面划出一小块地，给予税收优惠及特殊监管通关便利。

The Pingtan Comprehensive Experimental Area in Fujian Province and the Hengqin New Area in Guangdong Province are evolved from customs special control areas. Established in 2009, the two areas implemented the general development plans set forth by the State Council, and their development was included in the 12th Five-year

广东横琴新区和福建平潭综合实验区就是在海关特殊监管区基础上发展形成的。横琴新区和平潭综合试验区均始建于2009年，先后经国务院批准实施了总体发展规划，并于

Plan. Based up the development of customs special control areas, they are the result of the country's effort in exploring new ways to deepen reform and expand opening-up in the new era, and forming new forms of cooperation between Guangdong and Hong Kong, Guangdong and Macau, and across the Taiwan Strait. On June 21, 2012, GACC and Fujian Provincial Government held a press conference in Beijing, where GACC issued 27 measures in 10 aspects to support the development and opening-up of the Pingtan Area. Some of these facilitation measures were the first ones in the country and were only implemented in Pingtan and Hengqin at the time.

2011年写入了"十二五"发展规划纲要。这是国家在海关特殊监管区域基础之上的新探索，旨在开辟新时期深化改革和扩大开放的新路径，形成粤港澳合作和两岸合作的新模式。2012年6月21日，海关总署与福建省人民政府在北京召开新闻发布会，公布了海关支持平潭综合试验区开放发展的10个方面共27条措施。其中的部分优惠便利措施在全国范围内是首次实施，且仅在横琴和平潭两地实施。

In my opinion, the PFTZ in China is a special area that combines the functions of special customs control areas that facilitate the trade in goods and areas that focus on expanding investment, finance and trade in services. It carries the features of both the Free Zone in international terms and the Free Trade Area and features such supervision modes as pre-establishment national treatment and the negative list management. Therefore, China's PFTZ is a unique innovation in the country's restructuring of the economic system, expansion of opening-up and transformation of the government functions. As an experimental field of reform and a test area

我国创设自由贸易试验区，我个人认为，是一种以货物贸易便利化为主的海关特殊监管区域和以扩大投资、金融、服务贸易开放为主相结合的特定区域。既有国际上自由贸易园区的性质，又有自由贸易区的特征，还体现了实施准入前国民待遇和负面清单管理等模式。因此，我国自由贸易试验区是我国加快经济体制改革、扩大开放和转变政府职能过程中特有的创新产物，

of opening-up, the PFTZ is playing a leading and demonstrating role.

作为一个改革的试验田，开放的测试区，起着引领和示范的作用。

Since 2013, following the CPC Central Committee's instructions and centered on the core task of institutional innovation, China Customs has conducted bold trials and independent endeavors, and actively engaged itself in the building of the PFTZs, thus seeing notable results and winning recognition of the CPC Central Committee, the State Council, the business sector and the general public. Our work prioritizes the following five aspects:

2013年以来，中国海关按照中央的统一部署，紧扣制度创新这一核心任务，大胆试、自主闯，积极参与自贸试验区建设，取得了显著成效，得到了党中央、国务院以及广大企业和社会的认可。主要体现在以下几个方面：

Firstly, we innovated control models to facilitate trade. Guided by the new idea of innovative, coordinated, green, open and shared development, we actively promoted the institutional innovations such as "entry First, declaration Later", "Single Window", "centralized collection of aggregate duty payments", "single declaration, joint inspection and single release" with quarantine authorities, and differentiated control over goods, etc. At present, over 50 out of the 60 core measures for trade facilitation in world-class free trade agreements are up and running in PFTZs in Shanghai and other provinces, shortening average clearance time for imported goods by 41.3%, and that for exported goods by 36.8%.

一是创新监管模式，促进贸易便利。以"创新、协调、绿色、开放、共享"的新发展理念为引领，积极推进"先入区后报关"、国际贸易"单一窗口"、集中汇总征税、关检合作"三个一"（一次申报、一次查验、一次放行）、货物按状态分类监管等制度创新。目前全球高水平自由贸易协定中的60条贸易便利化核心措施，已有50多条在上海等自贸试验区实施，进口货物平均通关时间比区外缩短41.3%，出口货物平均通关时间比区外缩短36.8%。

Secondly, we transformed our vision for control and strengthened control during and after. We proactively streamlined administration, delegated more powers to lower-level government and society, improved regulation and optimized services. A total of 22 pre-approval items or restrictions have been canceled, delegated, alienated or relieved. At the same time, reforms in smart checkpoints, video inspection, centralized image inspection, auditing, individual inspection equipment have been making steady progress. New measures such as voluntary disclosure and third-party auditing have increased the effective rate of customs auditing from 50% to 72%.

二是转变监管理念，加强事中事后监管。积极推进"放管服"改革，共取消、下放、让渡、放开22项前道审批事权或限制，同步推进了智能卡口、视频化查验、机检集中审像、稽查、查验单兵作业等改革，并实施企业主动披露、引入中介机构协助开展企业稽查核查，稽查有效率从50%提升到72%。

Thirdly, we conformed to development needs and encourage new trade models. We integrated the foreign and domestic markets, formulated customs bonded control regulations, supported bonded repair and maintenance operations, bonded exhibition and trading, bonded operations for cross-border e-commerce retail sales, futures bonded delivery business, bonded financing lease business, bonded trading for cultural industries, thus expending functions of the PFTZs, and advancing the structural transformation and upgrade of industries.

三是适应发展需求，促进新型贸易业态发展。统筹国际国内两个市场，制定相应的海关保税监管制度，支持自贸试验区境内外保税维修检测、保税展示交易、跨境电子商务保税网购、期货保税交割、保税融资租赁、文化保税交易等新兴贸易业态发展，不断深化功能拓展，促进了产业结构转型升级。

Fourthly, we drew upon and spread successful experience. So far, China Customs has introduced 187 new control schemes in support of the development of the PFTZs, among which

四是不断总结经验，及时复制推广。目前，海关共推出了187项支持自贸试验区发展的监管创新制度，其

25 have been adopted all over the country. At the end of last year, the State Council put forward 19 more schemes to be extended across the country and tasked Customs with 13 of them (11 are spearheaded and coordinated by Customs), and all those have been put in place as required.

中25项已在全国复制推广。去年底，国务院布置的下一步在全国复制推广19项制度中，海关13项（其中牵头11项）任务也已按要求完成到位。

Fifthly, we stuck to the bottom line and strengthened supervision. China Customs held fast to our duty in guarding and providing service, and stepped efforts in companies' credit system and the supervision of exports and imports. Via technological innovations, we highlighted early risk warning, and maintained a firm hand on combating smuggling, aimed at striking a balance between lifting restrictions and improving regulations.

五是守住风险底线，加强实际监管。海关认真履行把关服务职责，着力加强企业信用体系和进出口实际监管，依托科技创新，强化风险预警，始终保持打击走私高压态势，努力打造"放得开、管得住"的监管格局。

As times change, China's PFTZs will usher in new opportunities for development. Customs shoulders the task of reform and is still on the road in supporting the construction of the PFTZs. Following the arrangement of the CPC Central Committee and the State Council, we should focus on the following tasks:

随着新形势的发展，我国自贸试验区将迎来新的发展契机。海关肩负改革重任，在支持自贸试验区建设中仍在路上。下一步，按照党中央、国务院的统一部署，重点考虑做好以下几个方面的工作：

1. Follow high standards and improve weak links to further optimize customs control models.

（一）对高标补短板，进一步优化监管模式。

First, we should strengthen the systematic research on the high standards of international trade rules and systems, especially on the trade models in the United States, the European Union,

一是要加强对国际高标准贸易规则体系的系统性研究，尤其是对美国、欧盟、中国香港、新加坡及新兴经

China Hong Kong, Singapore and emerging economies, choose and follow the ones that are good basing on China's situation. Second, we should manage customs control in its entirety, and cut down on complexity. China is obliged to implement 40 WTO trade facilitation measures. Other than the 4 measures among Category B commitments for the transitional period, 36 Category A commitments are to be implemented this year. This requires us to accelerate the reform of national customs integration, increase the performance and efficiency of the "Two Centers" (the Center for Risk Control and the Center for Duty Collection), optimize work models, streamline procedures, provide better services and strike a balance between lifting restrictions and improving control. Third, we should, jointly with the relevant ministries, actively advance pilot reforms such as differentiated control over different kinds of goods, granting general VAT taxpayer status to companies in pilot zones, and selective collection of customs duty. Fourth, we should promote the building of the Belt and Road, support new modes of trade, turn successful management models and experience of China Customs into norms for the international customs community, and actively participate in making international rules and standards to support Chinese market entities going global.

济体经贸运行模式的深入研究，立足国情，择善而从。二是要着眼整体、精简去繁，我国承诺的WTO贸易便利化措施共40项，除B类4项过渡措施外，其余36项A类承诺今年开始实施，这就要加快全国海关通关一体化改革，提高“两个中心”（风控和税管）运行质量和效率，优化模式、简化流程、放管服结合。三是会同有关部委积极推进诸如货物分类监管、赋予区内企业增值税一般纳税人资格、选择性征收关税等改革试点，早出成效。四是服务“一带一路”建设，适应新型贸易业态发展，将我国海关已经比较成熟的管理模式、管理经验尽可能转换为国际海关通行规则，并积极参与相关国际规则和标准制定，推动市场主体“走出去”。

2. Give full play to the advantages of the

（二）发挥试验优势，

pilot zones and explore the establishment of a system to evaluate the result of trade facilitation.

PFTZ is a powerhouse of reforms instead of just a place for favorable policies. The advantages of the PFTZ should be directed to innovation driven, exploration and replicable practices, which should be identified by a scientific evaluation system. With the reform of the PFTZ, local customs carried out an evaluation in different ways, and third-party organizations were employed in some cases. Recently, the Sub-Administration of China Customs in Guangdong Province formulated the 'Index System for the Evaluation of Trade Facilitation Performance of the Guangdong PFTZ'. The system includes 25 indices in 3 layers and will help with our future exploration in this area. I suggest dedicating more resources to assess the level of trade facilitation and take into account other indicators that help fostering a sound environment for trade, for instance the transformation of functions of trade, and the driving effect of trade, in order to establish a comprehensive and quantifiable evaluation system for innovative practices in the PFTZ.

3. Step up technological innovation to further improve control and services.

The trade facilitation reform in the PFTZ needs technological innovation. Top-level design of the system should rely on new technologies such as big data, cloud computing, smart

探索建立贸易便利化评估体系。

自贸试验区不是政策洼地，而是创新高地，其试验的优势要集聚在创新驱动、经验探索和可复制推广上，这就需要有一套科学的评估机制来鉴定。随着自贸试验区改革的推进，各相关海关均通过不同方式开展了评估工作，也有的聘请第三方机构来做评估。前期广东分署研究提出了“广东自贸试验区贸易便利化绩效评估指标体系”，列出了3级共25个评估项目，这是十分有益的探索。建议继续组织力量，以评估贸易便利化水平为主，兼顾贸易功能转型、辐射带动效应等营商环境的其他指标，建立多维度、可量化的自贸试验区创新制度评估体系。

（三）推动科技创新，进一步优化监管服务。

推进自贸试验区贸易便利化改革，必须以科技创新为支撑。在顶层设计方面，要充分依托大数据、云计

equipment, and mobile terminals. An integrated data base of customs information should be built in order to coordinate management systems and data from customs control, and to put all operational 'pieces' together along the line including risk management, clearance, logistics control, duty collection, auditing, statistics and anti-smuggling, etc. We should promote the building of 'Internet + Customs', set up a comprehensive service and information platform for all function modules such as declaration, real-time query, clearance status, tax withholding application, automatic release and so on. We should also enhance the share of information at port, promote the overall development of 'Single Window' for international trade, so as to bring a sense of gain for all enterprises and the public.

4. Fend off risks and improve supervision and control.

Customs should assume effective control, and at the same time accelerate the flow of goods. First, we should resolutely uphold policies and regulations, i.e., reforms must have a legal basis, but local customs should nonetheless push forward innovation, brave the challenges and take responsibility to timely report to and ask approval from the General Administration of China Customs according to regulations and procedures, as long as the innovation is in line

算、智能装备、移动终端等新技术，搭建统一的海关信息化数据库，加强管理系统与监管数据的整合应用，彻底打通风险、通关、物控、税管、稽核、统计、缉私等各个业务条线、各个监管环节之间的阻隔，防止“碎片化”。要推进“互联网+海关”的建设，逐步建立集成申报录入、实时查询、通关状态、发送税费预扣申请、自动放行等所有功能模块的综合信息服务平台，并加强口岸信息共享，统筹推进国际贸易“单一窗口”建设，让广大企业和社会有实实在在的获得感。

（四）强化风险防范，提高监管水平。

要处理好“管得住”与“通得快”的关系，一是要守住政策红线，即改革要于法有据，但同时只要对符合市场经济规律，有利于企业发展，有助于提高监管效能的需求和举措，各海关要勇于创新，敢于担当，并按规程及时向海关总署请示汇报。二是要守住安全底线，

with the rules of market economy, conducive to business development and the efficiency of supervision. Second, we should defend the bottom line of security. Unnecessary restrictions should be lifted while risks should be contained. We should always keep in mind that deepening reforms goes hand in hand with fending off risks, especially when it comes to people's lives and property, environmental safety, as well as security on the ideological sphere. Risk management should be reinforced and constantly perfected. Third, we should improve rules and regulations. We should promote reform and innovation using legal thinking and legal methods. Improving regulations should be on top of the agenda during the reform and innovation in the PFTZ, so that not only could laws be enforced with a consistent standard, successful results of the reform and innovation could also be passed on as regulations. Operation mechanism of power should also be improved to mitigate risks in customs enforcement and administration, and to deter corruption, so as to improve customs control and services.

改革既要做到最大限度的“放开”，又要确保最有效的“管住”。要把深化改革与防控风险有机统一起来，特别是对于改革中涉及的人民生命财产安全、国家环境安全、意识形态领域安全等重点问题，始终绷紧这根弦，加强防范，并不断修正完善。三是完善规章制度。要运用法治思维和法治方式推进改革创新。在自贸试验区监管制度创新过程中，切不可忘了完善相关的规章制度。既以此统一执法标准，规范执法行为，又以规章制度固定改革创新成果，并健全权力运行机制，防范海关执法、管理和廉政风险，不断提高海关监管服务水平。

创新海关税收征管制度　推进供给侧结构性改革

2017 年 11 月

Innovate Customs Duty Collection to Promote the Supply-side Structural Reform

November, 2017

Promoting the supply-side structural reform is a significant decision made by the Central Committee of the Communist Party of China （CPC） based upon a comprehensive analysis of the world's economy and the new normal of China's economic development.

推进供给侧结构性改革，是党中央在综合研判世界经济形势和我国经济发展进入新常态的基础上作出的一项重大决策。

In his report to the 19th CPC National Congress，General Secretary Xi Jinping pointed out that "we must put quality first and give priority to performance，take supply-side structural reform as the main task，make more efforts for better quality，higher efficiency，and more robust drivers of economic growth，and raise total factor productivity" in order to achieve the "Two Centenary Goals"，realize the

习近平总书记在中国共产党第十九次全国代表大会上的报告中指出，实现“两个一百年”奋斗目标、实现中华民族伟大复兴的中国梦、不断提高人民生活水平，“必须坚持质量第一、效益优先，以供给侧结构性改革为主线，推动经济发展

Chinese dream of great national rejuvenation, and constantly improve people's living standards.

Premier Li Keqiang also stressed in this year's *Report on the Work of the Government* that "we must give priority to improving supply-side structure; we should streamline administration, reduce taxes, further expand market access, and encourage innovation; and we should keep micro entities energized, reduce ineffective supply while expanding effective supply, and better adapt to and guide demand".

At the present, socialism with Chinese characteristics has entered a new era, and the principal contradiction facing Chinese society has shifted to the one between the people's ever-growing needs for a better life and unbalanced and inadequate development. In economy and trade, as China's economic development enters a new normal, challenges arise on both the supply and demand sides, but the contradiction mainly lies in the supply side. In terms of the **fundamental objective,** supply-side structural reform aims to meet the demand through quality supply, so that the supply satisfies the increasing needs of the people for a better life; as for the **main direction,** the current priority of supply-side structural reform comprises of the five major tasks of cutting overcapacity, destocking, de-leveraging, lowering costs and improving weak links; with regard to the **essential attribute,**

质量变革、效率变革、动力变革，提高全要素生产率"。

李克强总理在今年的政府工作报告中也强调："必须把改善供给侧结构作为主攻方向，通过简政减税、放宽准入、鼓励创新，持续激发微观主体活力，减少无效供给、扩大有效供给，更好适应和引导需求。"

当前，中国特色社会主义进入新时代，我国社会主要矛盾已经转化为人民日益增长的美好生活需要和不平衡不充分的发展之间的矛盾。在经贸领域，随着我国经济发展进入新常态，面临的问题，供给和需求两侧都有，但矛盾的主要方面在供给侧。**从根本目的看，**供给侧结构性改革是为了提高供给质量满足需要，使供给能力更好满足人民群众日益增长的美好生活需求。**从主攻方向看，**供给侧结构性改革当前重点是推进去产能、去库存、去杠杆、降成本、补短板五大任务。**从本质属性看，**供给侧结构性改革本质

supply-side structural reform aims at structural adjustment through reform, and stimulate internal impetus and nurture sound external environment for quality supply. In terms of **main participants,** we should ensure that the market plays the decisive role in resource allocation, and motivate all parties involved and make use of the enthusiasm, initiative and creativity of innovative talents, officials and the people.

Tax and duty policy is an essential link on the supply-side structural reform. Tax and duty collected by China Customs is a major component of the country's revenue, as well as one important instrument in its macro-economic management and supply-side structural reform. In the last 5 years, customs revenue submitted to the national treasury reached 8198.1 billion RMB, 50.1% more than that of the previous 5 years, accounting for 25.4% of the total revenue collected by the Central Government. In recent years, China Customs has been proactively conducting policy research into supply-side structural reform, carrying forward the country's Free Trade Area (FTA) strategy, implementing various import tax and duty reduction policies, and continuously pushing on domestic industrial structural reform and technical advancement to meet the demand for the upgrade of domestic consumption. In 2016 alone, China Customs granted 50.2 billion RMB worth of tax and duty reduction and exemption,

是要用改革的办法推进结构调整，为提高供给质量激发内生动力、营造良好的外部环境。**从参与主体看，**要使市场在资源配置中起决定性作用，调动各方面积极性，充分发挥创新人才和广大干部群众的积极性、主动性、创造性。

税收政策是供给侧结构性改革的关键一环。中国海关税收是国家财政收入的重要组成部分，也是国家实行宏观经济调控、推进供给侧结构性改革的重要工具。近5年，海关实现税收净入库总计达81981亿元，较上一个五年增长50.1%，约占中央本级财政收入的25.4%。近年来，海关积极开展供给侧结构性改革政策研究，推进国家自由贸易区战略，落实各项进口税收优惠政策，不断推动国内产业结构调整、技术进步和满足国内消费升级需求。仅2016年，海关减免进出口税款502亿元，已实施的17个优惠贸易安排项下进口货物优惠税款490.5亿元，增长15.1%。

and 49.05 billion RMB of preferential tax and duty was reduced under 17 existing preferential trade agreements, up by 15.1%. In the same year, 787 commodities enjoyed lower preferential tariff rate, with an average rate of 2.2%, which was 54% lower than the most-favored-nation tariff rate, and 43.86 billion RMB worth of preferential tax and duty was granted, up by 2.6%. Altogether, the abovementioned policies led to 163.91 billion RMB worth of tax and duty reduction and exemption, with a year-on-year increase of 13.74 billion RMB.

2016年有787项商品实行较低的进口暂定税率，平均关税税率为2.2%，较最惠国税率低54%，优惠税款438.6亿元，增长2.6%。上述政策实施合计优惠或减免税款1639.1亿元，规模较上年同期增加137.4亿元。

Take China's major technical equipment manufacturing for instance, given that some key components and raw materials are not available at home, preferential import tax and duty policies for major equipment enable domestic manufacturers to reduce their expenditure on imports, ensure the quality of their products and an effective cost control, and lay a solid foundation for the strong competitiveness of homemade equipment. According to statistics, an average of around 8.8 million RMB worth of tax and duty reduction and exemption was granted to each of the 174 manufacturers that enjoyed preferential import tax and duty policies for major technical equipment in 2016. And remarkable effects on output were produced through tax and duty reduction and exemption for key components and raw materials.

以我国重大技术装备制造领域为例，在部分关键零部件、原材料国内仍无法提供的背景下，重装进口税收优惠政策为重装制造企业降低了进口的资金支出，使企业制造的重大技术装备品质得到了保证，成本有效控制，为装备的竞争力提升打下良好基础。据测算，2016年度享受重大技术装备进口税收政策的174家制造企业平均减免税款约为880万元，通过关键零部件、原材料税收减免带动产出效果明显。

Another example is that China Customs had been engaged in negotiations on the China-Australia Free Trade Agreement （FTA） for 9 years, which officially took effect on 20 December 2015. Since then, 3 rounds of tax and duty reduction have been conducted. In 2016, over 85% of the two countries' trade in goods benefited from the tariff reduction and exemption as provided. Australian formula milk, beef and lamb, red wine, etc., which are popular among Chinese consumers, will see their tariff, originally at 10% - 25%, canceled in 4 to 10 years. All these reflect the significant role of customs import and export tax and duty policies in adjusting foreign trade development, alleviating companies' burden, increasing effective supply and improving people's livelihood.

又如，海关参与的中国—澳大利亚自由贸易协定谈判历经9年，于2015年12月20日正式生效。协定生效至今，已实施了3次降税。2016年两国超过85%的货物贸易受益于协定规定的关税优惠减免。中国消费者热衷的澳大利亚配方奶粉、牛羊肉、红酒等商品原需缴纳的10%至25%的关税将在4到10年的时间内取消。这都充分说明了海关进出口税收政策在调节外贸导向、减轻企业负担、提高有效供给以及改善人民生活水平方面的重要作用。

The Central Government's plan for supply-side structural reform raises newer and higher requirements for our endeavor in enabling the market to play the decisive role in resource allocation and giving better play to the role of government. General Secretary Xi Jinping said in his report to the 19th CPC National Congress that "we must prioritize the development of the real economy, focus on increasing quality supply, and enhance China's economic advantage in quality so as to build a modernized economic system" China Customs, as the government agency engaged in formulating and

中央关于推进供给侧结构性改革的部署，对使市场在资源配置中起决定性作用和更好发挥政府作用提出了更新更高的要求。习近平总书记在十九大报告中专门指出："建设现代化经济体系，必须把发展经济的着力点放在实体经济上，把提高供给体系质量作为主攻方向，显著增强我国经济质量优势。"海关作为进出口税收政策的参与制定和执

implementing import and export tax and duty policies, should also pay more attention to the quality of the reform of its tax and duty policies and duty collection, and should closely relate ourselves with the actual requirements of the country's economic and trade development in the new era, earnestly carry out the work plans of the CPC Central Committee and the State Council to "maintain steady growth, promote reform, make structural adjustments, improve living standards and guard against risks", and promote the supply-side structural reform through customs duty collection reform and institutional innovation in the following areas:

行部门，也应更加关注税收政策改革和税收征管工作的质量，应紧密联系新时代国家经贸发展的实际需求，认真落实党中央和国务院关于"稳增长、促改革、调结构、惠民生、防风险"的各项工作部署，通过海关税收征管改革和制度创新的措施来积极推进供给侧结构性改革。具体可从以下几方面入手：

1. We should materialize national macro-level policy and support structural tax and duty reduction.

（一）落实国家宏观政策，服务结构性减税。

Tariff reduction and exemption in line with adjustments to national macro-economic policies can effectively bolster industrial transformation and upgrading as well as enterprises' independent innovation, improve public utilities and people's livelihood, and boost the development of strategic emerging industries. Currently, there are still imbalance and underdevelopment in different industries and regions. Quality and efficiency of the development need to be improved. And more dividends from structural tax and duty reduction are still to be released. For one, we should perfect our supporting implementation measures

关税减免政策配合国家宏观经济政策的调整，能够有效支持产业转型升级和企业自主创新，改善公共事业与民生，支持战略性新兴产业的发展。当前，行业、地区发展不平衡不充分的情况仍然存在，发展质量和效益还不高，结构性减税的政策红利仍有待进一步释放。鉴此，一方面应完善税收优惠政策的海关配套实施措施及管理规定，确保政策落实到位，并结合振兴东北老工业

and administrative regulations for preferential tax and duty policies to ensure that they are fully implemented, and align ourselves with the strategies of Northeast Area Revitalization, Coordinated Development of Beijing-Tianjin-Hebei, Western China Development, etc. to reinforce policy publicity and help companies make full and good use of those preferential policies. For another, we should attach greater importance to industrial survey, strengthen policy research into structural tax and duty reduction, streamlining trade control, financing costs reduction for the business that are aimed at expanding import and export demands, proactively put forward policy proposals that support increased imports of advanced technical equipment and key components, which are conducive to the development of domestic high-end equipment manufacturing and, ultimately, supply-side structural reform.

基地、京津冀协同发展、西部大开发等战略，加强政策宣传力度，帮助企业用足用好税收优惠政策。另一方面应注重行业调研，加强对结构性减税、简化贸易管制、降低企业融资成本等扩大进出口需求的政策研究，积极提出支持扩大先进技术设备、关键零部件进口等有助于提高国内高端装备制造业水平，有利于推动供给侧结构性改革的政策建议。

2. We should intensify innovative thinking and promote duty collecting reform.

Cost is the life line for an enterprise and even an economy. We must not lose sight of the challenges China faces: the internal forces driving economic growth need to be strengthened, some enterprises face difficulties in their production and operations, and government imposed transaction costs for businesses need further reduction. To this end, we should pilot institutional innovations

（二）强化创新思维，推进税收征管改革。

成本是企业乃至经济发展的生命线。我们应当清醒地看到目前国内经济增长内生动力仍需增强，一些企业生产经营困难较多，企业的制度性交易成本仍有待进一步降低。为此，应以重点领域试点推动机制创新，充分

in major areas, allow full play to the guiding role of duty collection policies, and build a friendly customs clearance environment as well as institutional environment for import and export. We should start with the effectiveness analysis of China's tariff policy to solve the problems such as the small dispersion index of tariff rates, and unclear boundaries of different layers of tariff rates, continue to optimize the structure of tariff rates, and make well tailored and effective tariff policies. We should further expand the pilot of the nationwide reform of customs clearance integration, expedite the construction of "Risk Management Centers" and "Duty Collection Centers", and encourage importers and exporters to maximize the customs clearance and taxation convenience via honest and lawful operations, so as to achieve "effective control" and "fast clearance" at the same time.

发挥税收征管政策的导向作用，为推动供给侧结构性改革营造便捷的进出口通关环境和制度环境。应以自由贸易背景下我国关税政策有效性分析为切入点，研究解决关税税率离散系数过小、税率设置层次不明显等问题，不断优化关税结构，提升关税政策的针对性和有效性。应进一步扩大全国海关通关一体化改革试点范围，加快风险防控中心和税收征管中心建设，引导进出口企业以诚信守法赢得最大的通关和纳税便利，实现“管得住”与“通得快”相统一。

3. We should take advantage of the bonded policy and advance industrial transformation and upgrading.

（三）发挥保税政策优势，推动产业转型升级。

The bonded policy, an innovation and flexible application of the tariff policy, better exercises the tariff policy's function of serving foreign trade development. With its focus on industrial structural adjustment and technical advancement, the bonded policy plays an active part in accelerating the transformation and upgrading of processing trade and the gradient

保税政策是对关税政策的创新和活用，更多体现关税服务于对外经贸发展的功能。保税政策重点在产业结构调整、推动技术进步，促进加工贸易的转型升级，促进加工贸易企业向中西部梯度转移等方面发挥积极作

transfer of processing trade enterprises to central and western China. First, we should maintain a stable market share for conventional products of processing trade. We should encourage companies to speed up the upgrade of their equipment, introduce new technology and new equipment, and increase labor productivity by means of adjusting the bonded system. We should put in place supervision and control rules adaptive to product research and development, examination and after-sales maintenance services of companies, in order to help them product quality, level up their maintenance services, and consolidate the market share. Second, we should optimize the policy function of the special customs control area. We should consider advancing pilot reform to grant general VAT taxpayer status in qualified special customs control areas, as well as the launch of differentiated control over goods. In special customs control areas in central and western China, we should actively promote the pilot of a selective collection of customs duties for goods sold in the domestic market, and create a favorable policy environment for companies' development in the home market. Third, we should push forward the early and pilot implementation of policies in the Pilot Free Trade Zones in a holistic approach. We should support the development of the new batch of PFTZs, and guide processing trade companies to utilize preferential bonded policies for their

用。一是稳定加工贸易传统产品市场份额。通过调整保税制度鼓励企业加快设备的更新换代，引进新技术新设备，提高劳动生产率。建立与企业开展产品研发、检测和售后维修服务相适应的监管办法，促进企业提高产品质量，提升产品售后服务水平，巩固市场份额。二是完善海关特殊监管区域政策功能。研究在符合条件的海关特殊监管区域推广赋予企业增值税一般纳税人资格试点，积极探索开展货物按状态分类监管；在中西部地区的海关特殊监管区域积极推进内销货物选择性征收关税政策先行先试，创造有利于区内企业开拓国内市场的政策环境。三是统筹推进自贸试验区先行先试。支持新一批自贸试验区建设，引导加工贸易企业利用自贸试验区的优惠保税政策进行转型升级，化解产能过剩。

transformation and upgrading in order to address overcapacity.

4. We should implement the FTA strategy and better engage in its negotiations.

Facing the challenge from trade protectionism, we need to focus on the building of the "Belt and Road", resolutely advance the liberalization and facilitation of international trade, promote global economic cooperation, and play an active part in bilateral and multilateral trade negotiations. First, we should, on the one hand, carry out the concluded FTAs in good faith and on the other, continue to engage in the negotiations on such FTAs and preferential trade arrangements as the *Regional Comprehensive Economic Partnership* (RCEP). Second, we should facilitate e-certificate of origin and paperless customs clearance, step up efforts in the assessment and analysis of Free Trade Areas, and encourage more companies to make good use of the FTAs. Third, we should explore ways and channels for Chinese enterprises to safeguard their legitimate rights and interests in FTA partner countries and improve cooperative mechanisms with foreign customs.

（四）落实自贸区战略，继续做好谈判磋商。

面对贸易保护主义的挑战，我们要以"一带一路"建设为重点，坚定不移推进国际贸易自由化便利化，推动全球经济合作，积极参与双多边贸易谈判。一是在落实好现有自贸协定的同时，继续积极参与《区域全面经济伙伴关系》（RCEP）等自贸协定和优惠贸易安排的谈判；二是推进原产地证书的电子化和无纸化通关，加大自贸区评估分析力度，提升企业的自贸协定利用率；三是探索建立我国企业在自贸协定伙伴国维护合法权益的方式和渠道，完善与伙伴国海关的合作机制。

关于降低我国关税总水平的建议

2018年5月16日

Suggestions on Lowering China's Overall Tariff Rate

May 16, 2018

Customs tariff rate is a kind of turnover tax collected by customs on inbound and outbound cargos and items according to national tariff policy, laws and regulations. It is a symbol of state sovereignty. Tariff collection is governed by the *Customs Law*, *Regulations on Import and Export Duties*, *Customs Import and Export Tariff*, while tariff rate is an essential element of tariff collection.

There are 8549 HS codes in *China Customs Import and Export Tariff*. Arithmetic average of most favored nation (MFN) tariff rates is 9.8%. Although China fulfilled its commitment to the WTO in 2010 by lowering tariff rate to 10%, China's tariff rate is still

关税，是海关按照国家制定的关税政策、法律、法规对进出境货物、物品征收的一种流转税。关税象征国家主权，征收关税以《海关法》《进出口关税条例》和《海关进出口税则》为主要依据，而税率（计算税额的比例系数）是其中的重要组成部分。

目前，按现行《税则》对8549种税号商品最惠国关税税率的算术平均值计算，我国关税现总水平为9.8%。应该说，我国2010年已实现了加入世贸组织前承诺的约束关

higher than most of the major developed countries (US 3.4%, Japan 4%, EU 5.2%, Canada 4.5%, Australia 2.5%). It is generally lower than most developing countries (Brazil 13.6%、India 12.9%、Thailand 11%、Russia 10.5%、Vietnam 9.6%). According to the World Customs Organization, average tariff rate of the world is 9.34%, which means China's rate is still 0.46 percentage points higher than the world's average.

税须降至10%的任务，但关税水平仍远高于主要发达国家（现美国3.4%、日本4%、欧盟5.2%、加拿大4.5%）；总体低于大多数发展中国家关税水平（巴西13.6%、印度12.9%、泰国11%、俄罗斯10.5%、越南9.6%）。另据世界海关组织统计，现全球的平均关税水平为9.34%。可见，我国的关税总水平仍高于全球平均关税水平0.46%。

As the country's economic and foreign trade growth gains speed, and its competitiveness and market share increases, it is imminent to lower the overall tariff rate. According to China Customs, foreign trade volume in 2015, 2016 and 2017 stood at 10.44 trillion RMB yuan, 10.49 trillion yuan and 12.46 trillion yuan, while import tax and duty collected by the customs was 1.51 trillion yuan, 1.54 trillion yuan and 1.90 trillion yuan. The actual tariff rate for import goods was 3.6%, 3.6% and 3.3%, and was reduced to 3.1% in the first 4 months this year, which indicates that our nominal tariff rate is much higher than the actual tariff rate. If we take into account the trade structure, weighted average of tariff rate is 4.4%, which is closing up to the level in developed countries (US 2.4%, EU 3%),

随着我国综合经济和对外贸易的快速发展，国际竞争力和市场占有力明显增强，降低关税总水平迫在眉睫。据近3年海关的统计，2015年、2016年、2017年我国外贸进口总值分别为10.44万亿元（人民币，下同）、10.49万亿元、12.46万亿元，海关征收的进口税收分别为15094.1亿元、15388.1亿元和18967.8亿元，而应税进口商品实际关税税率水平则分别为3.6%、3.6%和3.3%，今年1—4月进一步降为3.1%。这表明，名义关税税率大大高于实际关税税率。如果考虑到贸易结构的因素，我国实际外贸加权平均关税税率为4.4%，这一

but still more than 50% lower than the 9.8%. Therefore, the overall tariff rate is too high, and the nominal tariff rate is unreasonably higher than the actual rate.

状况已非常接近发达国家水平（美国贸易加权的实际进口关税是2.4%，欧盟是3%），但距9.8%的关税总水平仍相差一倍多。因此，目前我国关税总水平过高，且名不副实。

In recent years, the CPC Central Committee and the State Council have been advancing the supply-side structural reform and working toward opening-up on a higher level. A list of tariff reduction was implemented and has seen significant results. In order to promote reform and opening-up, and inject new growth drivers to an open economy, it is necessary to further lower our tariff rate.

近年来，党中央、国务院着眼于推进供给侧结构性改革和高水平对外开放，先后研究并实施了一系列自主降税的举措，收到了十分明显的成效。为确保我国改革开放进一步深入，为开放型经济发展注入新动能，有必要进一步加大关税总水平的降幅力度。

First, regarding the level of tariff protection. Tariff is a trade protection measure legally recognized by WTO's rules. Before China's accession to the WTO, it was critical for us to use protective tariff to secure the growth of national industry and economy. In recent years, the Chinese economy is growing at a faster speed, comprehensive strength of the nations is increasing, and the country is establishing a more important position in the international community. Overall tariff rate should be in line with the volume of China's economy, the share of its products on the world's market, the level of its participation

第一，从关税的保护程度看。关税是世贸组织规则可以合法使用的贸易保护措施。入世前，为保护国家民族工业和促进我国经济发展，我们采取了保护关税政策，这是十分必要的。但入世后，尤其是近年来随着我国经济的快速发展、产业结构稳步调整、综合国力日益增强、国际地位明显提升，关税的总水平应与我国经济总量、占国际贸易份额、参与经济全球化程度及国家对外开放形象相一致，必须实施有

in economic globalization, and the image of its opening-up. And an effective tariff policy should be carried out. Lowering the overall tariff rate will promote transformation and upgrading, and advance high-quality development under the new normal of our economy. It will eliminate overprotection in some of the industries or areas by introducing more competition. It will bring high nominal tariff rate closer to the actual rate so as to expand import. It will also show China is committed to opening more to the outside world, and against trade protectionism. So, I suggest lowering tariff rates of the industrial products in areas where we already have enough advantages on the global market (by about 50% on average).

效的关税政策。因此，从这一点上看，降低关税总水平有利于我国在新的经济常态下，更好地转型升级推进经济高质量发展；有利于解决部分行业或部分领域存在过度保护问题，鼓励竞争；有利于去掉过高的名义关税税率，与实际征税水平相吻合，扩大进口；也有利于向世界表明，中国将以更加积极的姿态进一步扩大开放，反对贸易保护主义。为此，建议下调已具备国际市场竞争优势的工业产品税率（平均降幅应在50%左右）。

Second, when it comes to the imbalance between supply and demand. After the accession to the WTO, the tariff rates of resource products, parts, semi-finished products and finished products maintained a pyramid structure from the bottom to the top. It has effectively promoted the development of domestic industries and maintained a sound trade order. But the focus of previous tariff rates was on promoting manufacturing instead of benefiting consumers. The report of the 19th CPC National Congress pointed out that “What we now face is the contradiction between

第二，从供需矛盾看。入世以来，我国关税基本维持了资源性产品、零部件、半成品、制成品关税税率由低至高的阶梯型税率结构，总体上有效地促进了国内产业发展、维持了正常贸易秩序。但以往较多地侧重于满足生产需求，对消费者利益考虑少些。党的十九大报告指出，进入新时代，我国社会主要矛盾已经转化为人民日益增长的美好生活需要和不平衡不充分的发展

unbalanced and inadequate development and the people's ever-growing needs for a better life." Therefore on the one hand, we need to leverage tariff to promote the work in the five priority tasks of cutting overcapacity, reducing excess inventory, deleveraging, lowering costs, and strengthening areas of weakness, increasing the quality of manufacturing and supply, as well as keep pace with the development of manufacturing. On the other, we have to think more about customer demands, and make sure that supply can meet people's ever-growing needs for a better life. I suggest further shaving off tariff rates of consumer products, especially cars, home appliances, daily necessities, and medical and health care products (by about 50%-60%). MFN tariff rates of some of the consumer products should be the same with their provisional rates, which were already lowered.

之间的矛盾。为此，一方面要借助关税为推进“三去一降一补”、提高生产供给质量、满足生产发展需求服好务；另一方面，要充分考虑消费者需求，使现有供给能力更好满足人民群众日益增长的美好生活需要。建议进一步大幅降低各类进口消费品的关税税率，尤其是汽车、家电、日化、医药保健类等相关进口消费品（平均降幅应在50%—60%）。已作暂定税率降税的部分消费品和药品，建议直接转为最惠国税率。

Third, concerning high-quality development. The global competitiveness of a country's industry is ultimately reflected by the market share of its products. Over the past few years, China's foreign trade has grown steadily, reinforcing China's leading position in international trade. China has been the largest exporter and the second largest importer for eight consecutive years. Its market share continues to increase. However, we need to

第三，从高质量发展看。一个国家的产业国际竞争力大小，最终表现在该产业的产品在国际市场上的占有率。近年来，我国外贸稳步发展，货物贸易大国地位不断巩固，已经连续八年保持全球货物贸易第一大出口国和第二大进口国，出口国际市场份额不断提升。但同时我们也要清醒地看到，

be keenly aware of the fact that some medium or low-end products are overproduced, while some high-end products are in short supply, and we are still relying on foreign products when it comes to core components and technology. I suggest that based on the national plan of Made in China 2025, we should lower tariff rates for some machinery so as to promote the structural adjustment and upgrading of industry. And we should keep the preferential tariff treatments for key components that cannot be produced domestically to cut cost, enhance quality, encourage innovation, and strengthen the manufacturing of high-end equipment. Besides, in order to achieve the sustainable development of economy, society and environment, we need to lower the rates for resource products in pursuing green development.

我国部分低端产品过剩和中高端产品供给不足并存，一些关键核心技术还受制于人。在经济全球化的大趋势下，我们要做好市场竞争的长期准备。建议围绕“中国制造2025”计划，降低有助于产业结构调整升级的部分机电产品的税率。重装制造领域部分关键零部件、原材料国内仍无法提供的，进口税收优惠政策仍需保持，以降低成本，提升品质，支持企业自主创新，不断提高我国高端装备制造业水平。此外，为实现经济、社会和环境可持续发展目标，建议降低与绿色发展理念一致的资源性产品税率。

Fourth, as for tariff structure. Tariff rates of 93% HS codes are 20% or below, while only 7% are over 20%. There are a total of 52 levels of import tariff, ranging from 0 to 65%, meaning there are too many levels and the dispersion of different rates are too small, which will create confusion for declaration and customs enforcement. So, I suggest that we simplify tariff levels, widen the gap between different levels, and apply the same rate to the same or similar products. It will help

第四，从税率结构看。目前我国关税税率在20%及以下的税目占比达93%，税率高于20%的只占7%。进口关税税率共设52级，从0至65%不等，税级过多，税目过繁，税率离散系数过小，给企业申报和海关执法带来困扰。为此，建议考虑简并税级，加大税级差，原则上对同类或相类似的商品适用相同税率。这样既有利于

businesses declare more easily and correctly, and solve the problem of enforcement consistency regarding classification, which has been bugging the customs for a long time, so that clearance can be faster, and trade can be facilitated.

企业正确报关，也有助于解决海关在归类问题上长期困扰的执法不统一等问题，以更有效地提高通关效率，促进贸易便利化。

Fifth, in terms of the actual effect of tariff reduction. China has voluntarily reduced its import tariff rate several times in recent years. Starting from December 1, 2017, import duty of 187 kinds of commodities has been reduced. From May 1, 2018, import duty of cancer medications has been brought down to zero. These tariff reductions are welcomed by the public, but we also have to think about whether they will cause a decrease of customs revenue, and whether tariff's role of revenue collection and economic adjustment will be diminished. To answer these questions, we need to reduce tariff to a perfect extent where businesses aren't overloaded with heavy duty, and revenue is increased from a larger dutiable foundation. After analyzing the effect of recent tariff reductions, I found out that firstly, tax reductions have a significant effect on the import of consumer products. Since December 1 last year, import of 176 comparable products has increased by 17.4% to 57.54 billion yuan. Import of 125 products has increased, with their number accounting for 71% of the total

第五，从降税实际效能看。我国近年来连续自主降低进口关税，尤其是2017年12月1日起调降187项商品进口关税（平均税率由17.3%降至7.7%）和2018年5月1日起对进口抗癌药品实施进口零关税，深受广大消费者的欢迎。在大幅降税的同时，海关税收收入是否会减少？关税的财政和调节作用是否会受到影响？这些问题需要我们把握好降税的最佳切点，也就是平衡好既减轻过重税负又通过降税扩大税基增加税额的关系。从近期降税后的实际效能分析看，一是降低关税对促进消费品进口效果显著。自去年12月1日降税以来，176项可统计分析降税消费品的一般贸易进口总值达575.4亿元，同比增长17.4%。其中125项消费品进口总值正增长，数量占比达71.0%，金额占比高达95.2%。二是消费

import, and their value accounting for 95.2% of the total. Secondly, tariff income from imported consumer goods is increasing instead of decreasing. During the same period, these 176 products have generated 12.02 billion yuan of tax revenue, up by 1.8%. Moreover, in 2017, Customs collected 392.4 billion yuan from imported consumer goods, which accounted for 20.7% of the total revenue and increased by 13.3%, 8.6 percentage points higher than last year's growth rate. Thirdly, tariff reductions have benefited the people. The above 176 products generated 1.46 billion yuan of tax revenue in general trade, with duty reduction of 2.73 billion yuan, making import goods more affordable for domestic consumers, and providing the people with the personalized, diversified, and different choices that they need.

品进口征税不降反升。同期，上述176项可统计分析降税消费品的进口环节实征税款120.2亿元，同比增长1.8%。此外，2017年海关对进口消费品征税3924亿元，占税收总额的20.7%，增长13.3%，增幅较上年提升8.6个百分点。三是降低关税极大地惠及民生。同期，176项可统计分析降税消费品一般贸易进口实征关税共计14.6亿元，关税减让达27.3亿元，切实有助于减轻百姓的消费负担，并满足了广大人民群众对美好生活个性化、多元化、差异化的需求。

In conclusion, based on these analyses and estimate on tariff reduction, I suggest we further reduce tariff rate, expand the scope of tariff reduction, and lower the overall tariff rate from the current 9.8% to 6%-7%.

基于以上综合分析和降幅的估算，建议进一步下调进口关税税率，扩大降税品种范围，将我国关税的总水平从目前的9.8%降至6%—7%。

自贸区战略对我国外经贸发展的作用

2016 年 4 月 22 日

The Role of FTA Strategy in China's Foreign Trade Development

April 22, 2016

It was a privilege to participate in the workshop of ministerial officials on the construction of the Free Trade Area (FTA) organized by the Ministry of Commerce and learned a lot from it.

很有幸参加了由商务部主办的省部级领导干部自贸区建设专题研讨班学习，收获很大。

By diligently studying the spirit of relevant speeches by General Secretary Xi Jinping with regard to accelerating the implementation of the Free Trade Area strategy, my understanding of the importance and urgency of this undertaking has been deepened, my confidence in building an open economy in China has been strengthened, and my sense of mission and responsibility of developing steady and sound foreign trade has been enhanced.

通过认真学习领会习近平总书记关于加快实施自贸区战略的一系列重要讲话精神，我加深了对加快实施自贸区建设重要性和紧迫性的认识，更坚定了做好我国开放型经济工作的信心，增强了力促外贸回稳向好的使命感和责任感。

During the workshop, we related to the courses as well as the reality, thoroughly shared our opinions, and brought up a lot of good advice and suggestions. For instance, we mentioned the need to speed up the system reform in building FTAs, continue to more areas to the outside world, and reinforce international cooperation in production capacity; when carrying out the "Going Global" strategy, we should not only aim at transforming overcapacity, but can also consider bringing business models to foreign countries and conduct overseas processing, breeding and planting. For another example, in elevating the liberalization level of trade in goods, trade in services and investment and the supervision capability of government bodies, we should focus on both increasing the number of FTAs, but the quality and performance of them as well, in order to effectively improve China's international response ability and competitiveness. And we should also expedite copying and promoting the successful experience in the PFTZs in Shanghai, Tianjin, Fujian and Guangdong, bring in more pilot sites, coordinate policies and improve functions in the zones, expand the range of policy application, make accelerated efforts in realizing the "Single Window" in international trade, optimize the collaboration between various departments, create a more enabling business and legal environment, etc.

在研讨中，我们结合课程、联系实际、畅所欲言，提出了很多意见和建议。比如，加快自贸区建设制度创新，不断扩大开放领域、加强国际产能合作，在实施“走出去”战略中，不仅要考虑过剩产能转化，也可以尝试商业模式“走出去”、搞境外加工和养种植等。又如，不断提高货物贸易、服务贸易及投资等开放的自由化水平和政府监管能力，既要努力扩大自贸区数量，也要注重其质量和效益，切实提高我国际应对能力和竞争力。再如，加快复制推广已建的上海、天津、福建、广东四个自贸试验区的经验，拓宽试点面，在自贸试验区内融通政策、完善功能，扩大政策适用范围，加快推进国际贸易“单一窗口”建设，优化各部门间协作配合，营造更好的营商和法治环境等。

When it comes to customs work, I feel that in recent years, China has secured great results

联系到海关工作，我感到这些年我国加快实施自

in the implementation of the Free Trade Area strategy, which reveals that FTA construction has been playing an active role in boosting foreign trade and economic development.

贸区战略是很有成效的。从自贸区实施情况和实际效果看，自贸区建设已对我国外贸和经济发展起到了积极的作用。

In January, 2014, China's first Free Trade Agreement (FTA), the China-ASEAN FTA entered into force. From then on, 14 FTAs and 3 preferential trade arrangements have been signed and implemented between China and other countries or regions. On the whole, the implementation process of the FTAs has been going smoothly and yielded obvious effects, which are mainly reflected in the following five aspects:

自2004年1月我国第一个自贸协定——中国—东盟自贸协定实施以来，我国已陆续签订并实施14个自贸协定和3个优惠贸易安排。从实施的总体情况看，进展顺利，效果十分明显。具体体现在以下五个方面：

1. Import growth under preferential arrangements remains steady.

（一）协定受惠进口保持稳步增长。

By 2015, imports under FTAs and preferential trade arrangements topped US$436.5 billion, maintaining a double-digit growth rate until 2014, with reduced tariff reaching RMB179.6 billion. Last year, imports under preferential arrangements were worth US$74.2 billion, down by 3%; exempted tariff was RMB36.4 billion, up by 9%. After the China-ROK and China-Australia FTAs took effect at the end of last year, remarkable results were secured in merely 100 days. By March 28 this year, RMB7.76 billion-worth goods were imported under the China-ROK FTA, involving 864 tariff codes, and China's exports to the ROK during

截至2015年，自贸协定和优惠贸易安排项下进口货物总值达4365亿美元，关税优惠金额共计1796亿元人民币。2014年前均保持二位数增长，去年受惠进口货值742亿美元，下降3%；关税优惠364亿元，增长9%。去年底中韩、中澳自贸协定实施后，100天就显成效。截至今年3月28日，中韩自贸协定项下受惠进口77.6亿元人民币，涉及864个税号，同期我国向韩出口货值

the same period reached RMB161.07 billion; RMB7.59 billion-worth goods were imported under the China-Australia FTA, involving 184 tariff codes, and China's exports to Australia during the same period reached RMB65.9 billion. The implementation of the two FTAs is registering good progress.

1610.7亿元人民币；中澳自贸协定项下受惠进口75.9亿元，涉及184个税号，同期我国向澳出口货值659亿元人民币，实施进展十分良好。

1. The utilization of FTAs remains sound.

Calculated by the ratio of imports under preferential arrangements in the taxable value of general trade with a certain trading partner, the average utilization rate of 12 FTAs reached 66% in 2015. Among them, the utilization rate of 7 FTAs neared or exceeded 80%, with that of the FTAs signed between China and Chile, Pakistan and New Zealand respectively surpassing 90%.

（二）协定利用率保持较好水平。

以各自贸协定进口受惠货值占自该贸易伙伴一般贸易进口应税货值比例计算，2015年12个自贸协定平均利用率为66%。其中，利用率接近或超过80%的有7个协定，中国—智利自贸协定、中国—巴基斯坦自贸协定、中国—新西兰自贸协定利用率均超过90%。

3. Imported and exported goods are highly complementary.

In 2015, the four major categories of China's imported goods, e.g. plastic products, mineral products, chemical products and plant products, accounted for over 60% of the total imports under preferential arrangements. The major categories of our exported goods were mechanical and electrical products, textile products, plastic and its products, furniture and lighting, and steel products, taking up over half of the total. These

（三）进出口商品互补性强。

2015年，自贸协定和优惠贸易安排项下进口以塑胶制品、矿产品、化工产品和植物产品四大类为主，合计占受惠进口总值六成以上，我出口以机电产品、纺织品、塑料及制品、家具灯具和钢铁制品等为主，占签约总值五成以上。这些受惠商

imported and exported goods are in great need and highly complementary, which could both boost bilateral trade and economic development, and meet our domestic demands.

品需求性、互补性强，既拉动双边经贸发展，又满足国内需求。

4. The liberalization level of FTAs is rising.

（四）协定自由化程度逐步提高。

In recent years, the liberalization level of trade in goods between China and FTA partners has been greatly enhanced. For example, after the China-ROK Free Trade Area was established, 91% of taxable items will enjoy zero-tariff treatment (20 years of transition period), covering 85% of imports from the ROK; after the China-Australia Free Trade Area was established, 96.8% of taxable items will enjoy zero-tariff treatment (15 years of transition period at the most), covering 97% of imports from Australia, contributing to bilateral trade between China and the ROK, and between China and Australia.

近年来，我国商谈的自贸协定中货物贸易自由化水平（关税减让）已有较大提升。如中韩自贸区建成后，91%的税目将对韩实现零关税（20年过渡期），覆盖自韩国进口额的85%；中澳自贸区建成后，96.8%的税目将对澳实现零关税（最长15年过渡期），覆盖自澳大利亚进口额的97%，这有利于拉动双边贸易额提升。

5. Trade facilitation has been further improved.

（五）贸易便利化水平进一步提升。

As China signed FTAs with developed countries including New Zealand, Switzerland, the ROK, Australia, a series of new administrative ideas and systems that could further facilitate businesses have been incorporated into these agreements. Take the China-Switzerland FTA for example, 87% of export companies conducted self-declaration of origin in order to enjoy preferential duty rates last year. Another

随着我国与新西兰、瑞士、韩国、澳大利亚等发达国家签署自贸协定，一系列更加便利企业的新型管理理念和制度引入自贸协定中。如中瑞自贸协定，使用出口商自主出具原产地声明享受优惠关税，去年已达87%；又如，试点自贸协定海关间

example is, customs authorities that carry out pilot projects of implementing the FTAs have realized the networking of electronic information on country of origin and data sharing, and simplified document requirements for transshipped cargos, so that customs clearance time has been immensely reduced and corporate costs have been cut.

实现原产地电子信息联网、数据共享，简化中转货物运输的单证提交要求，这样大大节约通关时间，降低企业成本。

We can then see that the implementation of the FTA strategy with other countries or regions has been playing a positive role in enhancing China's foreign trade and economic development. At the present time, our country's foreign trade is faced with severe and complex situations. The share of Chinese-made goods in the European Union, the United States, Japan and other developed markets is already nearing the "ceiling", and exports to Russia, Indonesia, Brazil and other emerging markets are decreasing at double-digit rates. With that and taking into consideration that the U.S. used Trans-Pacific Partnership Agreement (TPP) and Transatlantic Trade and Investment Partnership (TTIP) to constrain and suppress China, we have to take comprehensive measures to keep our status as a major trading country, among which, accelerating the implementation of the FTA strategy is a crucial tool in stabilizing growth, adjusting structure, expanding market and maintaining market shares.

从上可见，实施自贸区战略对我国外贸和经济发展起到了积极的拉动作用。当前我国外贸正面临严峻复杂的形势，我在欧盟、美国、日本等发达市场的外贸份额都已逼近“天花板”，对俄罗斯、印尼、巴西等新兴市场的出口分别以两位数速度在下降，加之美国利用“跨太平洋伙伴关系协议（TPP）”和“跨大西洋贸易与投资伙伴协议（TTIP）”对我形成挤压，因此要保住我贸易大国地位，必须综合施策，其中加快实施自贸区战略是稳增长调结构、拓市场保份额的重要手段之一。

To this end, I have come up with the following six proposals.

为此拟提六点建议：

First, we should center on major trading partners and radiate to those along the "Belt and Road", promote the implementation of existing FTAs, expedite the negotiations on newly-added ones, focus on building Free Trade Areas with emerging market countries and extend the range in an orderly way, increase proportion of China's exports in the global total, and stabilize and expand the market.

一是以主要贸易伙伴为重点，辐射“一带一路”，有效推进已签协定的实施，加快新增协定谈签进程，注重与新兴市场国家自贸区建设，有序扩围，提升贸易占比，稳固并拓展市场。

Second, we should accommodate the interests of domestic industries, try to open up the Chinese market for a greater opening-up of foreign countries without touching the bottom line, expand areas and guarantee smooth transition and transformation, promote trade and investment liberalization, and face up to the impacts and influences on China from the TPP and TTIP dominated by the U.S.

二是统筹兼顾国内产业利益，在不触碰底线的前提下，尽可能以“开放换开放”，拓宽领域、过渡转换，不断提升贸易与投资自由化水平，主动应对美主导的TPP、TTIP对我带来的冲击和影响。

Third, as the number of zero-tariff commodities continues to increase, the level of tariffs is becoming lower and lower, thus we should attach more importance to the protection of sensitive commodities by utilizing rules of origin, so as to guarantee the mutual benefit and reciprocity between trading partners and prevent free riding by other parties.

三是随着货物贸易零关税税目增加，关税减让空间缩小，应更加重视运用原产地规则等对我敏感产品的保护，确保成员间互利互惠，避免非成员“搭便车”。

Fourth, we should strengthen international customs cooperation in law enforcement, improve the digital networking among customs authorities of FTA signatories, establish direct communication

四是加强国际海关执法合作，扩大建设自贸区协定方海关电子联网，构建与企业直接沟通机制，实施原产

channels with the business sector, set up a data exchange system of self-declaration of origin, expand the time and space of customs supervision, and optimize customs service, which could on the one hand facilitate business activities, and on the other strengthen inspection and comparison and avoid fraud, so that the implementation quality and utilization rate of FTAs can be effectively improved.

地自主声明电子数据交换系统，拓宽进境监管时空，优化服务，既便利企业，又强化核查比对、防止瞒骗，有利提升自贸协定实施质量和利用率。

Fifth, we should encourage and support companies to "go global", participate in global trade to extend the industrial chain and increase the added value, and resolve relevant overcapacity in certain areas; meanwhile, in the adjustment of the global industrial landscape, we should avoid more processing companies, orders and industries leaving China to foreign countries, and promote the transformation and upgrade of processing trade, in order to create a whole supporting industrial chain at home, and more competitive edges for China's foreign trade.

五是支持企业“走出去”，参与到全球贸易中去拓展产业链，提高附加值，化解我部分领域相对过剩的产能；同时又要在全球产业竞争格局调整中，避免我加工贸易企业外迁、订单转出、产业跨境转移等现象的加速，助推加工贸易转型升级并向我中西部地区转移，形成内源化的国内配套产业链，形成外贸竞争新优势。

Sixth, when enhancing the system innovation of PFTZs and promote successful experience, we should take into account both building more pilot zones and improving policies, as well as supporting and encouraging the independent exploration and innovation at localities, so as to contribute to the steady growth of foreign trade, and provide guidance for the building of more high-standard FTAs in future.

六是在加快推进自贸试验区制度创新和经验复制推广工作中，既要考虑扩围试点，优化政策功能，也要支持鼓励地方自主探索、自主创新，为稳定外贸增长提供助力，为我国建设高标准自贸区提供借鉴。

中国与韩国、澳大利亚自贸协定生效

2015年12月20日

China, South Korea and Australia FTAs Take Effect

December 20, 2015

China - South Korea Free Trade Agreement (FTA) and China - Australia Free Trade Agreement officially entered into force today. According to the agreements, both sides will cut tariffs on certain traded goods. The target is to eventually eliminate all tariffs. Many will be removed for the first time, and more goods tariffs will be cut every year. FTA talks between China and South Korea started in May 2012. It took three years to finalize the deal. The negotiation between China and Australia had lasted for more than 10 years, and the deal was finally inked in June 2015. Both agreements cover various fields, including goods, services and investments.

中国和韩国自由贸易协定、中国和澳大利亚自由贸易协定今天正式生效。根据协议,双方将削减某些贸易商品的关税，最终目标是消除所有关税。许多商品是第一次被降税，以后每年将会有更多的商品关税被削减。中国和韩国之间的自由贸易协定谈判始于2012年5月，历经三年后最终完成协议。中国和澳大利亚之间的谈判超过10年,最终于2015年6月签署。协议涉及各个领域,包括货物、服务和投资。

China Customs, a regulatory authority of the country at the border, what role has it played in the process of setting up a high standard Free Trade Areas? What effects will Free Trade Areas with South Korea and Australia bring to the foreign trade and people's life? And what new measures will be carried out by China Customs to promote the Free Trade Areas? I'd like to make my personal comments on these issues.

海关作为国家的进出境监督管理机关，在建设高标准自由贸易区过程中发挥了什么作用？中韩、中澳自贸区为我国对外贸易和百姓生活带来哪些影响？为推进自贸区建设，海关还将推出哪些新举措？我想就这些问题谈谈我个人的看法。

General Secretary Xi Jinping pointed out that speeding up the implementation of Free Trade Area Strategy is an important part of China's new round of opening up policy. The 13th five-year plan for national economic and social development also mentioned, "by speeding up the implementation of Free Trade Area Strategy, promoting the regional comprehensive economic partnership agreements and pressing ahead with the creation of Asia-Pacific Free Trade Area, we'll try our best to form a high standard network of the global FTAs."

习近平总书记指出，加快实施自由贸易区战略，是我国新一轮对外开放的重要内容。我国国民经济和社会发展第十三个五年规划也进一步提出："加快实施自由贸易区战略，推进区域全面经济伙伴关系协定谈判，推进亚太自由贸易区建设，致力于形成面向全球高标准自由贸易区网络。"

2016年4月，北京，就海关落实中澳自贸协定与澳大利亚边境执法署副署长会谈。

April 2016, meeting to promote implementation of the China—Australia FTA with Deputy Head of Australian Border Force.

Customs is one of the important participants in FTA negotiations and plays a positive role in FTA negotiations. China Customs takes the lead in the negotiations on rules of origin. It aims to make sure that only FTA partners can enjoy tariff concessions and prevent goods from seeking preferential tariff concessions outside of the FTA. Customs also leads the negotiations of Customs procedures and trade facilitation, aiming to simplify Customs procedures and provide efficient and convenient, fair and transparent Customs clearance environment for the import and export goods under Free Trade Agreements.

海关是自贸区谈判的重要部门，在自贸协定谈判中发挥着积极的作用。一方面是牵头原产地规则谈判，保证享受自贸协定项下各项优惠待遇的货物确实属于自贸区原产，防止区外货物冒名搭车。另一方面是牵头海关程序与贸易便利化谈判，承诺简化海关手续，为自贸区协定项下货物进出口提供高效便捷、公正透明的通关环境。

We insist on paying equal attention to import and export, reasonably designing rules of origin and promoting more efficient regional and global value chain as well as enhancing trade facilitation. China Customs is also the main agency who takes charge of implementing the tariff concessions, rules of origin and trade facilitation in the FTA. So far, China has signed 14 free trade agreements, involving 22 countries and regions. China-South Korea and China-Australia Free Trade Agreements are included. 8 free trade agreements are under negotiation, covering 27 countries.

我们坚持进口、出口并重，合理设计原产地规则，推动构建更高效的全球和区域价值链，提升贸易便利化水平。海关同时也是自贸协定实施的主要部门，承担着关税减让、原产地规则及贸易便利化等内容的具体执行落实。迄今，中国已对外签署14个自贸协定，涉及22个国家和地区，其中包括：中国—澳大利亚、中国—韩国。正在谈判的自贸区有8个，涉及27个国家。

As of October 2015, the imported goods with a total value of $405.6 billion under the

截至2015年10月，各自贸协定项下进口货物4056亿美

FTAs enjoyed preferential tariff worth 164.2 billion yuan. In this regard, tariffs on most of the goods under China - South Korea Free Trade Agreement and China - Australia Free Trade Agreement will gradually be removed.

元，享受关税优惠1642亿元人民币。随着中韩、中澳贸易协定的实施，协定项下的绝大多数货物将逐步实现零关税。

Some reporters from the media once asked me what changes to the customs tariffs would be taken place after implementing the FTAs of China and South Korea, China and Australia? And how much impact would tariff reduction impose on the bilateral trade?

一些媒体记者曾问我：中韩、中澳自贸协定实施后关税会有什么变化？关税降低对双边贸易有多大影响？

I admitted that the FTAs between China and South Korea, China and Australia are the ones of the largest trade volume and the highest level of liberalization in trade and investment respectively among all the agreements that we have signed. Since their implementation, 6108 tariff headings of Chinese origin goods and 1649 tariff headings of South Korean origin goods have enjoyed zero tariffs immediately. Likewise, 5662 tariff headings of China origin goods and 2402 tariff headings of Australian goods have also been treated with zero tariffs. On January 1st, 2016, the two agreements will be implemented for the second time tariff reduction. So, tariff-cuts will be further expanded.

我回答，在我国已签署的自贸协定中，中韩、中澳自贸协定分别是涉及国别贸易额最大、贸易投资自由化水平最高的自贸协定。中韩、中澳自贸协定自实施之日起，6108个税号的中国原产货物和1649个税号的韩国原产货物在对方国家进口时，立即享受零关税；5662个税号的中国原产货物和2402个税号的澳大利亚原产货物在对方国家进口时，立即享受零关税。2016年1月1日两个协定将实施第二次降税，关税削减幅度会进一步扩大。

After the transition period, the vast majority of the goods under the above two Free Trade Agreements will achieve zero

在过渡期之后，中韩、中澳贸易项下绝大多数货物将实现零关税。中韩自贸协定的过

tariffs. China-South Korea FTA sets up maximum 20 years of transitional period. South Korea will eliminate tariffs on 92% Chinese origin goods while China will remove tariffs on 91% of goods from South Korea. With regard to China-Australia FTA, Australia will adopt the zero tariffs for all goods from China within five years, and China will remove tariffs on 96.8% Australian origin goods within 15 years.

渡期最长为20年，韩国将对92%的中国原产货物实行零关税，我国将对91%的韩国原产货物实行零关税；中澳自贸协定生效5年内，澳大利亚将对全部中国原产货物实行零关税，中国对96.8%的澳大利亚原产货物将在15年内实行零关税。

Due to the large bilateral trade volume and the effects of trade creation and trade diversion, the preferential trade volumes will be rapidly grown after the two agreements put into effect. Surely, people care more about their benefits from the FTAs. After the implementation of the two agreements, the most direct material benefit is low cost of imported goods. South Korea's small commodity and specialty foods are so popular among Chinese consumers, and Australian lobster, red wine are also much consumed on the dinning-tables in China. With the tariff concessions, tariffs on these popular goods will be gradually reduced to zero. Therefore, Chinese consumers will have more varieties to choose from.

鉴于中韩、中澳双边贸易量大和自贸协定的贸易创造、贸易转移效应，两个自贸协定实施后的优惠贸易量都将得到快速增长。当然，人们更关心的是中韩、中澳自贸协定的实施，究竟能给百姓生活带来哪些实惠？中韩、中澳自贸协定实施后最直接的实惠就是由关税减让带来的进口货物成本降低。韩国的小商品及特色食品等深受中国消费者喜爱，澳大利亚的龙虾、红酒等也备受欢迎，随着中韩、中澳自贸协定实施，上述产品都会逐步降低关税并最终实现零关税，给中国消费者带来更多的选择机会。

In order to give more dividend from FTAs and bilateral trade growth to businesses and

为了让企业和人民享受自贸协定和双边经贸发

the people, China Customs has made great progress in deepening reform, facilitating and securing trade in recent years, for instance the integrated customs clearance reform following the "3Ms" principle, i.e. "mutual exchange of information, mutual recognition of control and mutual assistance in enforcement", paperless clearance and single window; innovative policies and measures that are created in Pilot Free Trade Zones and then adopted across the country, such as "entry first, declaration later", consolidated tax payment, declaration by batch, simplified and standardized entry and exit recordation lists, and smart checkpoints; the mechanism of electronic data exchange on origin of goods. And we have also adopted measures to streamline administration with delegating power to lower levels and implementing the principle of lean at the top and strong at the bottom so as to guarantee more convenient customs clearance for the enterprises and support cross-border e-commerce.

展带来的更大红利，近年来，中国海关在深化改革、促进贸易便利和安全等方面取得了很大进展。比如，在口岸管理部门落实“三互”（“信息互换、监管互认、执法互助”）推进大通关建设，实施“无纸通关”“单一窗口”建设；又如，在自贸试验区推出“先入区，后报关”、汇总征税、批次进出集中申报、简化统一进出境备案清单、智能化卡口验放等海关监管创新制度，并有序向全国复制推广；再如，积极支持跨境电子商务贸易发展，首创原产地电子数据交换机制，并实施简政放权、瘦上强下等，为企业便利通关提供制度保障。

In a word, along with the implementation of the FTAs, a significant increase in preferential trade will boost the economic and trade development, and it will be also more beneficial to the people.

总之，随着中韩、中澳自贸协定的实施，受惠贸易量大增将有效拉动经贸发展，也将更多地惠及广大老百姓。

依法把关　防控进出境风险

2018 年 1 月

Exercise Law-Based Administration and Control Risks in Entry and Exit

January, 2018

China's annual Central Economic Work Conference held in the wake of the 19th CPC National Congress pointed out that since the 18th CPC National Party Congress, we had been reviewing the general trends, crafting overall plans and carrying out practical work, and successfully steered the country's economic development, and the Xi Jinping Thought on Socialist Economy with Chinese Characteristics for a New Era, mainly based on the new development philosophy that is innovation-driven, coordinated, green, open and beneficial to all, had taken shape in practice. Guided by this Thought, and through deepening reform and expanding opening-up, China's economic strength has seen

党的十九大后首次召开的中央经济工作会议明确指出，党的十八大以来，我们坚持观大势、谋全局、干实事，成功驾驭了我国经济发展大局，在实践中形成了以"创新、协调、绿色、开放、共享"新发展理念为主要内容的习近平新时代中国特色社会主义经济思想。在这一思想的指导下，通过深化改革、扩大开放，我国的经济实力再上新台阶，经济年均增长7.1%，国内生产总值从54万亿元增长到80万亿

a new height: the country's GDP rose from 54 trillion RMB to 80 trillion RMB, up by 7.1% annually, retaining the world's second place, and contributing over 30% to the world's economic growth.

元，稳居世界第二，对世界经济增长贡献率超过30%。

The Conference stressed that in the next three years, the country would strive to win three toughest battles in preventing and addressing major risks, taking targeted measures for poverty alleviation, and preventing and controlling pollution, so as to secure the decisive victory in completing the building of a moderately prosperous society in all respects. In 2018, with high-quality development as a fundamental requirement, we should prioritize eight key tasks, including deepening the supply-side structural reform, promoting regional coordinated development, making new ground in pursuing opening-up on all fronts, ensuring and improving people's wellbeing, etc.

会议强调，今后三年要重点抓好决胜全面建成小康社会的防范化解重大风险、精准脱贫、污染防治三大攻坚战。2018年要围绕推动高质量发展，重点做好深化供给侧结构性改革、实施区域协调发展战略、推动形成全面开放新格局、提高保障和改善民生水平等八项工作。

With our goal set, we now have to focus on its realization. In order to accomplish the above-mentioned tasks, we should always uphold the underlying principle of pursuing progress while ensuring stability. "Stability" and "progress" form a dialectal unity. The focus of "stability" lies in stabilizing the economy, ensuring that there are no major fluctuation in economic growth, employment and commodity prices and that there's no systematic risks in the financial

目标在前，关键是抓好落实。要完成好上述各项任务，我们必须按照党的十九大精神，始终把握好稳中求进的工作总基调。"稳"和"进"辩证统一，"稳"的重点要放在稳住经济运行上，确保经济增长、就业、物价不出现大的波动，确保金融等不出现系统性风险；

sector; while that of "progress" is on adjusting the economic structure and deepening reform and opening-up, ensuring new achievements in the transformation of the economic development mode and innovation-driven development. We should be aware that "stability" is the foundation and the prerequisite of "progress" in seeking high-quality economic development. And preventing and addressing all kinds of risks are the fundamental guarantee for "stability" as well as quality and cost-effective "progress". The task of preventing and addressing major risks put forward at this year's Central Economic Work Conference has its priority in preventing and addressing financial risks, yet concerning entry and exit administration by Customs, we also face the challenges of guaranteeing efficient customs clearance, advancing high-quality development of import and export trade, and strengthening the risk prevention and control in entry and exit.

"进"的重点要放在调整经济结构和深化改革开放上，确保转变经济发展方式和创新驱动发展取得新成效。应当指出，要取得经济高质量发展，"稳"是基础，是"进"的前提；而要实现"稳"，确保有质量和效益的"进"，防范和化解各种风险乃是根本保障。这次中央经济工作会议提出的打好防范化解重大风险攻坚战，重点是防控金融风险，但联系到海关对进出境管理，也同样有一个如何确保口岸便捷通关、力促进出口贸易高质量发展和加强防控进出境风险的问题。

Currently, the socialism with Chinese characteristics has entered a new era, and so has economic development, whose essential feature is that the country's economy has shifted from a high-speed growth phase to a high-quality growth phase. We have to understand that in this transition to high-quality development, we will certainly find ourselves in a lot of new situations, encountering new problems, which make preventing and controlling risks a necessary

当前，中国特色社会主义进入了新时代，经济发展也进入了新时代，基本特征就是我国经济已由高速增长阶段转向高质量发展阶段。必须看到，在经济转向高质量发展阶段中，必然会带来一系列新的情况和新的问题，这之中防控风险就成了必要手段。从海关工作来

countermeasure. In Customs work, we are also faced with new challenges and problems both externally and internally.

看，也存在外部和内部面临的新挑战和新问题。

1. External environment.

The volume of customs supervision has sky rocketed in recent years along with the development of China's foreign trade and economic cooperation. During the 12th Five-year Plan period (2011-2015), China Customs supervised 18.2 billion tons of import and export goods worth of 124.88 trillion yuan, an increase of 43.09% and 48.64% respectively over the period of the 11th Five-year Plan (2006-2010). The development of economic and trade globalization calls for more efficient and facilitated customs clearance at ports, and better business environment that provides a level playing field under the rules of law. Customs should promote the quality of import and export with facilitating and efficient service through reform, promote the steady and healthy development of foreign trade and economic cooperation, while at the same time exercise control in accordance with law, and make the best efforts to safeguard national interests and security. Meanwhile, the rapid development of emerging trade forms such as cross-border e-commerce has created challenges where the customs regulatory resource is limited, inbound and outbound environment is complicated, and smuggling and other illegal

（一）从外部环境看。

近年来，海关监管业务量随着我国外经贸发展而呈现爆发式增长。“十二五”期间中国海关共监管进出口货物182.06亿吨、总值124.88万亿元人民币，比“十一五”时期分别增长43.09%和48.64%。经贸全球化的发展对口岸高效便利的通关和公平法治的营商环境提出了更高的要求。海关既要通过改革便捷高效地支持优进优出，促进外经贸平稳健康发展，又要依法把关，全力保障国家利益和安全。与此同时，随着跨境电子商务等新兴贸易业态的飞速发展，在海关监管资源有限、进出境情况复杂、走私违法行为频发的情况下，监管与逃避监管、征税与偷漏税、渗透与反渗透、走私与打击走私等斗争日趋尖锐，海关把关服务的任务和职责更显艰巨和繁重。

behaviors are frequent, putting Customs in a more fierce battle between control and eluding control, taxation and tax evasion, infiltration and anti-infiltration, and smuggling and anti-smuggling. The tasks and responsibilities of Customs to perform supervision and provide service are more arduous and onerous.

2. Customs' internal conditions.

In recent years, China customs has actively promoted the reform to "streamline administration, delegate powers, and improve regulation and services", and has made positive contributions to promoting the development of China's foreign economic and trade development and creating a safe and facilitated trade environment. For example, the average customs clearance time for import goods in November 2017 was 8.96 hours, shortened by 64.4% compared with that of the same period in 2016. The average customs clearance time for export goods was 0.85 hours, cut by 52.7%, which means the goal of "cutting customs clearance time of goods by a third" set by the Central Government has been achieved ahead of schedule. Another example is the customs duty collection reform. We have promoted "voluntary declaration and duty payment" to give import and export traders a massive boost in facilitation. In January and November, 2017, China Customs collected 1728.9 billion yuan of tax revenue, a year-on-year increase of 25.8%,

（二）从海关自身看。

近年来，中国海关积极推行"放管服"改革，为推动我国对外经贸发展，营造安全便利公平的外贸营商环境做出了积极贡献。比如，2017年11月全国海关进口货物平均通关时间为8.96小时，较2016年同期压缩64.4%；出口货物平均海关通关时间为0.85小时，缩短52.7%，提前实现中央确定的"压缩货物通关时间三分之一"的工作目标。又如，加强税管改革，推行税收"自报自缴"，极大地便利了进出口企业。2017年1至11月全国海关征税入库17289亿元，同比增长25.8%，提前完成了年初确定的税收任务。

accomplishing the goal set at the beginning of the year ahead of schedule.

However, we must not lose sight that facing the mounting trade volume, Customs still has a long way to go towards promoting the high-quality development of the country's economy and trade, through setting a clear focus of our work, exercising well targeted control, and providing efficient services. For instance, in order to deepen the supply-side structural reform, and advance "capacity reduction, de-stocking, deleveraging, cost reduction, and improving underdeveloped areas", we must think of the bigger picture and have a clearer priority of customs control, and the control and administration of entry and exit should be further enhanced. We should also lay down more specific measures, implement the measures more effectively, and achieve greater progress to support the "bringing in" and "going global" strategy, advance the coordinated growth of trade in both goods and service, bring more added value to the processing trade and move it higher up in the industrial chain, and carry out the regional coordinated development strategy. In terms of customs internal control, laws and regulations are sometimes not fully enforced or lack of consistency. Risk prevention and control should be more accurate, and we still need more methods to contain the risks. There are still some Customs enforcement officers that have violated

但我们也应清醒地看到，面对日益增长的业务量，海关要做到重点突出、精准监管、高效服务，为促进我国经济贸易高质量发展还有不少的差距。比如，针对深化供给侧结构性改革、推进“三降一去一补”工作，我们的全局思维和监管重心还有待聚焦，进出境管控力度还亟须进一步强化。又如，支持引进来走出去、推进货物贸易和服务贸易协调发展、促进加工贸易产业链向高端延伸、提高附加值、实施区域协调发展战略等方面，举措还不够细化，落实还不够有力，效果还不够明显。此外，从海关内控上来说，执法不统一和执行不到位的情况仍然存在，风险防控准度和管控手段仍然不足，海关执法人员违纪违法现象时有发生，海关执法、管理和廉政风险形势依然严峻复杂。

Party disciplines or laws. Customs enforcement, management and integrity risks are still high.

In order to brave the new challenges and address these issues, meet the requirements of making new ground in pursuing opening-up on all fronts raised in the report of the 19th CPC National Congress, accomplish the tasks to promote the high-quality development of our economy set forth at the recent Central Economic Work Conference, here are some of my suggestions for enhancing inbound and outbound risk management:

为了更好地应对新挑战和解决上述问题，主动适应党的十九大提出的推动形成全面开放新格局的要求，落实好中央经济工作会议明确的推动我国经济高质量发展的任务，拟提几点加强进出境风险防控的工作意见：

1. Think in big-picture terms, keep preventing and controlling risks in mind.

（一）立足全局大势，增强风险防控意识。

China's economic development has entered a "new normal", with its speed changing, its structure improving, and its driving forces shifting. These changes are essentially required during different phases of economic development, and the Chinese economy must go through these changes when transitioning from a phase of rapid growth to a stage of high-quality development. When it comes to opening up and foreign trade, we need to consider and put our work on the same level with the objectives to "pursue development with our doors open wide" and "develop an open economy of higher standards". We should always act in response to the evolution of the principal contradiction in Chinese society, pursue with firmness the new

当前，我国经济发展进入了"新常态"，突出表现为经济发展速度变化、结构优化、动力转换这三个特点。这些变化是经济阶段性发展特征的必然要求，是我国经济由高速增长阶段转向高质量发展阶段的必经过程。反映到对外开放和进出口贸易上，我们就要把海关工作放在"坚持打开国门搞建设""发展更高层次的开放型经济"这个大局上来审视和把握。要紧扣我国社会主要矛盾转化，按照"创新、协调、绿色、开放、共

vision for development that is innovation-driven, coordinated, green, open and beneficial to all, direct our efforts to support the quality of the supply side system, take effective measures to advance the shift of foreign trade and economic cooperation, from factor driven to innovation driven, from relying on scale and speed to quality and effect, from cost and price advantages to comprehensive advantages in technology, standards, brands, quality and service, in order to realize the evolution of quality, evolution of efficiency and evolution of driving force.

享”新发展理念，把服从和服务于提高供给体系质量作为主攻方向，采取有力措施支持外经贸由要素驱动向创新驱动转变，由规模速度型向质量效益型转变，由成本、价格优势为主向以技术、标准、品牌、质量、服务为核心的综合竞争优势转变，从而实现质量变革、效率变革、动力变革。

Due to the transitions and evolutions of economic development, we should strictly keep risks in mind. On the one hand, we must keep a sharp lookout for risks during the high-quality development by enhancing the identification, analysis, disposal and monitoring of smuggling risks in the flow of cargo, capital and information that might pose a danger for the national and people's interests, so as to ensure security, facilitation and efficiency at the ports. On the other hand, we need to explore new ways to compile statistics regarding emerging industries and new models of trade, monitor import, export, and the trend of foreign trade in real time, improve the Export Leading Index, and pay more attention to increasing the quality of export and the value added to it. We should also step up the trade statistics analysis of overproduced coal, steel,

基于上述经贸发展方式转型和变革，我们在推进高质量发展中要切实增强风险防控意识。一方面，要十分关注高质量发展过程中可能出现的各种风险，围绕进出境货物流、资金流、信息流等，加强对可能危害国家和人民利益的走私违法风险的识别、分析、处置和监控，确保口岸的安全便利高效。另一方面，探索新产业、新业态海关统计方法，动态监测进出口情况和贸易走势，完善外贸出口先导指数，更加注重提升出口质量和附加值，加大对诸如煤炭、钢材等国内产能过剩和中央实施

as well as other bulk commodities that are under macro-control of the Central Government, and strictly deter fake trade. Meanwhile, we should strengthen policy study, especially into issues related to the quality and effect of development, such as easing market access, further opening the service sector, expanding import, cutting duties of some import goods, and provide timely suggestions for decision making at the Central Government level.

宏观调控的大宗商品进出口的统计分析力度，依法依规严厉管控虚假贸易。同时，要加强政策研究，尤其是要对放宽市场准入、扩大服务业对外开放、积极扩大进口、下调部分产品进口关税所涉及的发展质量和效益问题，及时提出意见建议，为中央决策提供参考。

2. Establish risk management centers, improve internal control system.

（二）创建风控中心，完善内控机制。

Establishing the two-tier risk management centers is a key project in the customs clearance integration reform. It is the reform of customs itself, and more importantly a significant reform of the country. The first-tier risk management centers focus on systematic risks that are found at ports across the country and affect the whole landscape, give consistent and coordinated orders regarding risk management of all the ports, enhance prediction, early warning and trend analysis of security access risks, and carry out holistic management over security risks within the customs territory. The second-tier risk management centers take the main account for security risks at the ports within its jurisdiction, and operational risks that are specific to the customs districts. In a word, the first tier takes charge and the second tier assists the first, which

建立两级风险防控中心是海关在通关一体化改革中的一项重要任务，这项工作不仅仅是海关自身的改革探索，更已上升为国家的重要改革项目。海关一级风险防控中心主要是针对全国各口岸普遍发生的全局性和系统性风险，对各口岸风险防控发出协同和统一的指令，增强对安全准入风险的预判、预警和态势分析，实施全关境安全风险的统筹防控。二级风险防控中心主要是对关区所辖口岸的安全风险和关区特色业务的业务风险负主责。这样一级管总、二级辅助，既有利于统筹防控、

is good for the coordinated control of risks, and ensures enforcement consistency at the primary level while at the same time harnesses enthusiasm of officers working on the frontline, locate, dispose of and monitor the risks firsthand and in time, so as to safeguard the quality and effect of foreign trade.

规制基层一线的执法，也有利于调动基层积极性，在一线及时发现、处置和监控风险，确保进出口贸易的质量和效益。

Internal control, an integral part of scientific customs administration, and an important way to deter the "three risks", runs through all aspects and sections in customs' internal operations to control inbound and outbound activities. Internal control and risk management centers should be complementary and supportive of each other. Our current task is to improve the internal control system to optimize the integration of internal resources, increase the synergy of for oversight, prioritize the focus of risks, enhance the use of information technology, and so on. We should coordinate our resources. Vertically, the General Administration of China Customs, internal departments, local Customs districts, primary level posts should form a tiered system. Horizontally, we should form a circuit of internal control containing early warning before risks take place, real time monitoring during risk management, and correction and feedback afterwards; we should also integrate the technology platforms for customs internal control, to share data, merge functions of internal control

内部控制是海关科学管理的重要组成部分，也是防范海关"三大风险"的重要手段，它贯穿于海关进出境内部管理活动的各个方面和各个环节，应与风控中心形成呼应和互补。当前，应完善内控机制，有效解决内部资源整合不够优化、监督合力不强、风险重点不够聚焦、信息化技术手段有待提升等问题。要统筹资源，纵向上要完善海关总署、职能部门、直属海关、一线岗位的内控层级体系；横向上要完善事前预警规范、事中实时监控、事后纠偏反馈的内控闭合链条；要整合海关内控的技术平台，实现内控与风险管理的数据共享、功能整合，形成互为支撑、密切协作的有机整体。

and risk management, in order to build them into a mutually supportive, closely cooperative unity.

3. Strengthen frontline control，uphold the bottom line for security.

National security is the most important cornerstone for its development, and the safety net for its people's welfare. Customs is an important force for safeguarding the nation's economic, political, social, cultural, and ecological security at the border and ports. Customs risk management has a direct effect on the interests and safety of the country and the people. There are security access risks and revenue risks, static risks and dynamic risks, major risks and specific risks. It should be noted that as conventional and unconventional threats become more intertwined, the time and space to protect national security during inbound and outbound activities are stretched, and the situation is getting more complicated. For instance, Customs is facing increasing pressure and challenges concerning anti-terrorism and maintaining stability, anti-proliferation, anti-infiltration, keeping out hazardous chemicals, combating drugs, environmental protection, and so on. Take drug and arms smuggling for example, during the 12th Five-year Plan period, Customs investigated in 33.6% and 63.6% more criminal smuggling cases than during the 11th Five-year Plan period.

Therefore, we must not forget "the holistic

（三）加强正面监管，守住安全底线。

国家安全是国家发展的最重要基石、人民美好福祉的最根本保障。海关是在边境和口岸守卫国家经济、政治、社会、文化、生态等安全的重要力量，海关风险防控直接关系着国家和人民的利益与安危。这里既有安全准入风险，也有经济涉税风险；既有静态和动态的风险，也有重大和特定的风险。必须强调，随着传统和非传统安全威胁问题相互交织，进出境国家安全的时空领域更加广阔、形势更加复杂。比如反恐维稳、防扩散、防渗透、防危化、禁毒、环境保护等方面，海关面临的压力和挑战不断加大。仅以毒品和武器弹药走私为例，"十二五"期间海关查办的走私犯罪案件比"十一五"时期分别增长33.6%和63.6%。

对此，我们要牢记习近

approach to national security" raised by General Secretary Xi and its requirements. On the one hand, we should enhance the identification, analysis, prediction and timely disposal of risks during import and export through risk management. On the other, we should strictly carry out supervision on the frontline, strengthen physical inspection, reinforce the verification between documents and goods with H986 container inspection machines, X-ray machines, radiation detection equipment, and hand-hold inspection devices. We should explore to separate the inspections for security access and the inspections for classification, advance "Double random inspections and prompt release of results" (the supervision model comprises inspections of randomly selected entities by randomly selected inspectors and the public release of inspection results in customs enforcement), set a reasonable ratio and frequency for random inspection, apply the result of inspections to the enterprise credit management system, and enable the sharing of information between enforcement agencies. We should keep customs enforcement transparent, and make sure security risks are found and addressed in time to ensure the high-quality growth of foreign trade and economic cooperation.

平总书记提出的"总体国家安全观"的要求,一方面通过风险管理手段加强对进出口风险的识别、分析、预判和及时处置;另一方面也要实施严密的正面监管,强化实货查验,利用H986集装箱检查设备、X光机、辐射探测设备、手持式监管查验设备等加强单货验核,探索建立准入查验与验估查验分类作业模式,深入推进执法领域"双随机、一公开",合理设定随机抽查的比例和频次,实行抽查结果与企业信用管理联动,在执法部门之间实现信息共享共用,促进海关执法公开透明,确保及时发现和处置安全风险,为我国外经贸高质量发展提供有力保障。

4. Give full play to technology, improve the effect of risk management.

The primary objective of Customs risk management is to assume effective control with

(四)发挥科技优势,提升防控效能。

海关风险管理最主要的目标是确保进出口"管

minimum delay of import and export. Thus, Customs should strengthen control and improve service at the same time, and keep risks at bay while stepping up trade facilitation, which requires us to give full play to technological advantages such as risk decision system, big data, cloud computing, and artificial intelligence in order to bring effective results to risk management.

得住”与“放得快”有机统一。因此，海关应推进强化监管和优化服务的“双加强”，在防好风险的同时提升通关便利水平。这就需要我们充分发挥风险决策、大数据、云计算和人工智能等先进科技的优势，提升风险管理工作的效能。

First, we should be highly focused on building the models for risk identification, decision making and assessment, and use mathematical methods and relevant parameters to find out, both in nature and in number, the operational logics and possibility of risks occurring. We can then calculate to optimize the use of customs control resources and lower clearance cost for enterprises based on Multiple Objectives Programming （MOP） and Digraph. Performance should be evaluated afterwards using Balanced Score Card （BSC） or other methods.

第一，要高度重视进出境风险识别、决策、评估等模型的构建，运用数学方法和相关参数定性和定量地推理出风险发生的业务逻辑、概率等，基于多目标规划（MOP）和有向图（Digraph）等方法导出有限的海关监管资源利用率达到较大化、企业通关成本降到较小，并采用平衡计分卡（BSC）等手段作绩效考评。

Second, we should put our efforts in tapping the potential of big data. We should extend the sources of data through field investigations, information exchange and data purchases, carry out comprehensive assessment and analysis on business entities, logistics and cargo, and achieve smart data drilling and automated analysis.

第二，集中力量深挖大数据应用潜力。通过外部调查、信息交换和数据采购等多种渠道，大力拓展独立信息源，对企业主体、物流和货物这三者进行综合评估分析，实现对数据的智能挖掘和自动分析。

Third, we can link Enterprise Resource Planning (ERP) systems with our own in real time, automatically extract data from enterprises, "Single Window" and other external data sources, and realize auto verification, analysis, early warning of risks, so that our control is well targeted and intelligent, and has full coverage.

第三，充分利用ERP（企业资源计划系统）信息资源，通过实时联网，自动提取企业数据、"单一窗口"数据以及其他外围数据源数据，自动开展分析验证、提供风险预警，实现精准监管、全程监管和智能监管。

Fourth, with the advantage of the Internet, we need to think deeper and get a more thorough understanding of cross-border e-commerce, build up our capability and efficiency of risk identification, thus safeguarding the emerging industry towards a higher-quality, more efficient, more sustainable, and fairer direction.

第四，依托互联网优势，对跨境电商开展更深入细致的调研，增强风险识别的能力和时效，确保新兴贸易业态朝着更高质量、更有效率、更加公平、更可持续的方向发展。

5. Develop talent reserves, intensify responsibility awareness.

（五）造就人才队伍，强化责任担当。

People are an important asset in Customs risk management. We should spare no efforts in fostering a politically strong, highly-competent, and reliable Customs risk management team. We should conduct human resource evaluation and equip the two-tiered risk management centers with specialists in risk management, and train and cultivate risk management personnel in the General Administration of China Customs and local Customs at all levels. We should build platforms for professionals to sharpen their skills

人是开展海关风险管理的关键因素。要着力培养一支政治坚定、业务过硬、值得信赖的海关风险管理队伍。要通过人力资源评估，在全国两级风险防控中心配齐配强专门风险管理专家，在总署各相关部门和各层级海关要培养、造就一大批风险管理人员。要从政策研究、课题攻关、技能培训、

and give play to their talent by means of policy study, research projects, skill training, incentive mechanism, foreign exchanges and software and hardware support.

At the same time, we should strengthen Customs self-discipline and intensify responsibility awareness. In team management, we should strengthen our consciousness of the need to maintain political integrity, think in big-picture terms, follow the leadership core, and keep in alignment, and have confidence in the Party's chosen path, guiding theories, political system and culture. According to the requirements of full and rigorous governance over the Party, we must consolidate our ideals and convictions, improve conduct and discipline, and heighten our sense of mission and responsibility. We should always focus on both the building of a clean Customs, as well as operation reform and enforcement administration, make sure Customs operations are recorded, trackable and traceable in the system, pay close attention to high-risk posts and high-risk links. We also need to strengthen the supervision and monitoring of power operation, and provide talent support for Customs' prevention and control of entry and exit risks, and the country's high-quality development of foreign trade and economic cooperation.

激励机制、对外交流和软硬件配套设施等各个方面，为专门人员提升素质、发挥好聪明才智搭建良好的平台。

另一方面，要坚持从严治关，强化责任担当。在队伍管理中，要切实增强“四个意识”，坚定“四个自信”，按照全面从严治党要求，坚定政治信念，加强作风和纪律建设，不断强化使命和责任担当。要始终坚持“两手抓”，注重廉政建设与业务改革、执法管理相结合，推进作业过程“进系统、留痕迹、可追溯”，紧紧盯住高风险岗位和高风险环节，加强对权力运行的监督监控，为海关更好地防控进出境风险，有力促进我国外经贸高质量发展提供人才支持和队伍保障。

深化海关监管和国际合作　有效保护知识产权

2017 年 4 月 25 日

Enhance Customs Control and International Cooperation to Protect Intellectual Property Rights

April 25, 2017

Tomorrow is April 26, the 17th World Intellectual Property Day. This year's theme is "Innovation — Improving Lives." Indeed, innovation is a ceaseless force driving the progress of nations, development of society, and even progress of the human race. In order to act ahead of the time that we live in, we must have creative thinking and take innovative actions. In this sense, to protect IPR is to encourage innovation, support innovation and maintain innovation.

明天是4月26日，世界知识产权日又将到来。今年是第17个世界知识产权日，主题是“创新改变生活”。是的，创新是推动民族振兴、社会发展乃至人类进步的不竭动力。一个民族要想走在时代前列，就一刻也不能没有创新思维，一刻也不能停止各种创新，而有效的知识产权保护，就是鼓励创新、支持创新、保障创新的必要前提。

IPR is the lawful right of citizens, legal entities or other organizations, and it includes intangible creations of the human intellect

知识产权是指公民、法人或者其他组织在科学技术方面或文化艺术方面，对创造性的

in areas of science, technology, culture and art. In 2001, the World Intellectual Property Organization designated April 26 as the World Intellectual Property Day. The purpose of the Day is to foster an environment where intellect, science and IPR are respected and protected, and promote legal support to encourage innovation and protect IPR.

劳动所完成的智力成果依法享有的专有权利。世界知识产权组织于2001年4月26日将当天设为“世界知识产权日”，目的是在世界范围内树立尊重知识、崇尚科学和保护知识产权的意识，营造鼓励知识创新和保护知识产权的法律环境。

Over the years, China Customs has done a lot in IPR protection on the border and has made many commendable achievements that worth our full recognition.

多年来，中国海关在知识产权边境保护上所做的工作和取得的成效是值得我们充分肯定和认真总结的。

Following the plans of the CPC Central Committee and the State Council and taking into account the reality of customs enforcement, the General Administration of China Customs (GACC) focuses its enforcement resources on border supervision, carried out special crackdown operations, bringing targeted, efficient and stringent punishment to serious IPR violations that had a big impact internationally or domestically, therefore effectively protecting international trade order and the business environment based on the rule of law.

中国海关总署根据党中央、国务院部署，结合海关执法实际，集中全国海关执法力量，加强一线实际监管，大力进行专项整治，精准高效严厉地打击危害性强、国际国内反响大的进出口环节侵权行为，保持打击侵权假冒高压态势，有效维护了进出口经贸秩序，营造法治化营商环境。

We have been diligently implementing *IPR protection laws and regulations, issued the IPR Protection Action Plan for Companies* with Foreign Investment with 12 government agencies including the Ministry of Commerce, promoted our policies to the public and

我们认真贯彻落实国家有关知识产权保护的法律法规，会同商务部等12个部门联合印发《外商投资企业知识产权保护行动方案》，加强政策宣传，提高执法的透明度，营造

improved enforcement transparency, and created a level playing field for investment. Meanwhile, we have effectively enhanced customs supervision on the border.

公平竞争的市场投资环境。同时，切实加强了海关一线实际监管。

For instance, we launched the “Longteng Action” to protect the IPR-advantageous export enterprises. Customs districts across the countries have taken this Action as the key mission in promoting the competitiveness of Chinese brands, mobilized all available resources and taken several measures. During the Action, the number of domestic IPR registration increased by over 1400. 78 companies designated about 200 new personnel for IPR protection and invested another 11.57 million yuan in the cause. By enhancing the communication with key enterprises in the Action, local customs investigated 253 cases involving more than 3.11 million pieces of goods, saving over 74 million yuan's losses for businesses. Companies said that without counterfeit products contaminating the market, they had reclaimed the share in the foreign market.

比如，开展出口知识产权优势企业知识产权保护“龙腾”专项行动。全国海关将开展“龙腾”行动作为实施培塑计划的重点内容和主要抓手，广泛发动、多措并举。行动期间新增自主知识产权备案1400余项，78家企业新增专业维权人员约200人、维权资金1157万余元。各地海关加强与“龙腾”行动重点企业的沟通配合，行动期间立案调查涉嫌侵犯自主知识产权案件253起，涉及货物数量311万余件，为企业挽回经济损失7400余万元。企业普遍反映海外市场得到显著净化，市场占有率明显回升。

中国海关查获的手表等侵权商品。

Counterfeit watches and other knockoffs intercepted by China Customs.

We have also been advancing the fight against IPR infringement in online trading. We aim to promote the development of cross-border e-commerce by cracking down on counterfeiting. China Customs is proactively building a long-term mechanism to tackle problems in e-commerce. Hangzhou Customs and Alibaba have established a working mechanism to share information and intelligence and jointly combat IPR infringement, where Customs provides infringement intelligence to the company , while the company verifies the information and close down online shops on its platform. 37 online shops have been closed down and all criminal cases found under the mechanism have already been in the investigation and prosecution process. Guangzhou Customs has also worked closely with e-commerce platforms to detain 632

又如，深入推进互联网领域侵权假冒专项治理。我们以促进跨境电子商务等新兴业态健康发展为目标，加强打击跨境电子商务进出口侵权假冒行为。中国海关积极探索跨境电子商务长效治理机制，杭州海关与阿里巴巴集团建立了“信息共享、线索互通、联合打击”的跨境电商知识产权保护常态化协作机制并向其通报侵权线索，后者从中比对查实并关闭侵权店铺37家，双方合作通报的侵权犯罪案件均已进入刑事程序。广州海关与电商平台密切合作，查获互联网领域侵权邮包632批次，查获涉嫌侵权货物6197件。厦门、大

illegal postal parcels, 6197 pieces of counterfeit goods related to online transactions. Xiamen, Dalian, Jinan, Gongbei, Harbin, Chongqing, and Zhengzhou Customs have also made a large number of seizures.

连、济南、拱北、哈尔滨、重庆、郑州等海关也查获大量侵权货物。

We cooperate with the international community in 3 aspects. Firstly, we have built bilateral cooperative mechanisms with over 130 countries and regions, and signed 190 agreements, including MOUs on IPR enforcement cooperation with the US, the EU, Russia, Japan and Korea among others. Secondly, we have taken part in IPR-related issues under multilateral frameworks such as the WCO, WIPO, Interpol and the Shanghai Cooperation Organization (SCO). Thirdly, we have been communicating with businesses and signed cooperation MOUs with the International Trademark Association (INTA), the Motion Picture Association of America (MPAA), and other business associations and civil groups.

在开展知识产权保护国际合作方面，中国海关开展的国际合作主要分为三个层面：一是与130多个国家和地区海关建立了双边合作机制，签署了190多份合作文件，其中与美国、欧盟、俄罗斯、日本、韩国等国家和地区海关签订了专门的知识产权执法合作备忘录。二是积极参与世界海关组织、世界知识产权组织、国际刑警组织、上海合作组织等主要多边合作框架下的保护知识产权事务。三是注重与业界的沟通合作，与国际商标协会、美国电影协会等国际行业协会、民间团体签订了合作备忘录。

For example, we have carried out two joint operations with US Customs, each for a month, against counterfeit consumer electronics, auto parts, food, medication and sportswear shipped or sent in parcels between the two countries. During the joint operations, Guangzhou Customs detained 615 postal items through the e-commerce

比如，组织开展中美海关知识产权联合执法行动。中国海关与美国海关合作开展了两次各为期一个月的联合执法行动，重点监控通过快件、海运渠道往来美国的侵权消费类电子产品、汽车零配件、食品药品、运动服饰以及通过邮递

channel by risk analysis, including clothing and accessory, luggage bags and handbags, leatherwear. Shanghai, Huangpu, Ningbo, Shenzhen, and Xiamen Customs also detained a significant number of fake products between China and the US.

渠道寄自（往）美国的侵权商品。广州海关通过风险分析在跨境电商渠道查获寄往美国侵权邮包615批次，涉及商品主要为服装鞋帽、箱包及皮革制品。上海、黄埔、宁波、深圳、厦门等海关在行动期间也查获了数量较多的来往美国的侵权货物。

We have also carried out the "Qingfeng Action" to improve the image of Chinese products. The Action aims to fight against IPR infringements and counterfeits related to mechanical and electrical products, cellphones, medical equipment, and medication exported to Africa, the Arab region, Latin America and other countries and regions along the Belt and Road. By stepping up intelligence sharing and mutual assistance in enforcement, we have kept the high pressure on infringements and investigated several major cases. The three-year Action saw the seizure of around 53,300 shipments, 115 million pieces of goods netting 520 million RMB yuan and improved the image of "Made in China".

又如，开展中国制造海外形象维护"清风"行动。行动期间海关以出口至非洲、阿拉伯、拉美和"一带一路"沿线国家和地区的机电产品、手机类电子产品、医疗器械、药品等商品为重点，加强国际海关间的情报交换和执法互助，持续加大对出口侵权货物违法行为的打击力度，查获多起大案要案。在为期三年的行动中，海关系统共查获涉嫌侵权货物5.33万批次，数量1.15亿件，案值5.2亿元，进一步树立"中国制造"良好形象。

China Customs protects innovation with reforms of enforcement. We enforce the law while encourage innovation, and we protect IPR while inspire businesses to create and innovate. By fully implementing

中国海关以执法改革保护创新，坚持依法治理和促进创新相结合，保护知识产权和激发企业创新活力并重，深入实施国家创新驱动发展战略，

the innovation-driven development strategy, we promote the self-governance and compliance of industries, lower the cost for businesses to protect their IPRs, and advance the transformation of the country "from a manufacturer to an innovator, and from Chinese made to Chinese brand." Statistics showed that in 2017, China Customs applied protective measures over 22,500 times, and seized around 19,100 shipments of suspected infringements, including around 41 million pieces of items, greatly contributing to the world's cause of IPR protection.

促进了行业自律管理，企业维权成本持续降低，助推我国实现“从制造大国向创造强国转变、从中国产品向中国品牌转变”。据统计，中国海关2017年采取知识产权保护措施2.25万余次，实际扣留进出境侵权嫌疑货物1.91万余批，涉及货物4094万余件，为有效地保护知识产权作出了杰出贡献。

The achievements of China Customs are recognized and highly appraised. In June 2011, China Customs won the National Public Body Award of the Global Anti-Counterfeiting Network (GACN), the only government agency among the winners that year. In September 2015, China Customs received Interpol's global anti-counterfeiting award and the award for international cooperation on the investigation of IP crimes. In the U.S. Chamber's *2018 International IP Index Report*, China Customs got a perfect score for IP enforcement transparency.

海关打击侵权假冒工作的成绩也得到了外界的高度评价。2011年6月，全球反假冒组织将中国海关评为2011年度“反假冒最佳政府机构”，中国海关是该年度全球唯一获此奖项的政府机构；2015年9月，国际刑警组织为中国海关颁发“国际知识产权犯罪调查合作奖”。美国商会发布的《2018年国际知识产权指数报告》中，对中国海关知识产权执法透明度给予了满分评价。

IPR border protection is an important task for customs. We are still faced with complex situations and the mission to protect IPR on the border is still arduous, which means we have

知识产权边境保护是海关的一项重要职责。当前，我们面临的形势仍然复杂，知识产权海关边境保护的任务仍然艰

to keep enhancing supervision, and working with international customs administrations, governments, businesses and all walks of life to lend more significance to the World Intellectual Property Day, and give it our best for innovation, for the prosperity and of progress the society and mankind.

巨。我们要继续努力，加强实际监管，与世界海关、各级政府、广大企业和社会各界一起携手合作，为世界知识产权日增光添彩，为人类的创新进步和社会的繁荣和谐作出我们更大的贡献。

新形势　新征程　新作为

——新时期中国海关打私工作

2017 年 8 月

New Trend, New Journey and New Actions

——China Customs' endeavor to combat smuggling in the new age

August, 2017

China Customs is the competent antismuggling authority of the Chinese government. Established in 1999, China Customs' anti-smuggling police force is responsible for investigation, detention, execution of arrests and preliminary inquiry on criminal smuggling cases within its jurisdiction to stop smuggling crimes. In recent years, China Customs has rolled out a series of operations, such as "National Shield", "Green Fence" and "National Sword" to tackle smuggling activities concerning key areas, regions and commodities. It has also strengthened international customs cooperation and successfully fought in 5 major campaigns

中国海关是中国政府查缉走私的主管部门。1999年组建的海关缉私警察，依法负责对走私犯罪案件开展侦查、拘留、执行逮捕和预审工作，专司打击走私犯罪违法活动。近年来，中国海关先后开展了"国门之盾""绿篱行动""国门利剑"等一系列专项行动打击走私，并针对重点领域、重点地区、重点商品进出口形势和走私态势，加强国际海关合作，开展了打击农产品、偷逃税、毒品和枪支、"洋垃圾"、象牙等濒危动植

against the smuggling of agricultural produce, drugs and weaponry, hazardous waste, endangered species such as ivory, and tax evasion, making outstanding contribution to political and economic security, social stability and people's interests.

物走私的“五大战役”，取得了丰硕的战果，为保障国家政治和经济安全、维护社会稳定和人民利益做出了突出贡献。

Smuggling is a social and economic phenomenon worldwide, rooted in a country or region's political and economic status — especially its tariff scheme, price differences, as well as trade restrictions and prohibitions. In other words, where there is control over foreign trade or difference in prices in domestic and overseas markets, there is smuggling. According to the *Customs Law of the People's Republic of China*, any act of evading Customs control, payable duties, or control by the State over restricted or prohibited goods is smuggling. China's *Criminal Law* stipulates that an act constitutes a crime of smuggling if units or individuals violate customs laws and regulations, evade supervision and control by the Customs, transport, carry and mail articles, the export of which is forbidden by the State, evade payable duties, transport, carry and mail articles, the export of which is forbidden by the State, and if the amount involved is huge, or if the circumstances are serious. Smuggling crimes can wreak havoc in the socialist market economy, drain national

走私是一种国际性社会和经济现象，它的产生是与一国(区域)政治经济尤其是关税制度、国家（区域）间商品差价和贸易管制的存在相联系的。也就是说只要国家（区域）实施对外经济贸易管理，只要存在国内外市场差价，就会有走私现象的发生。根据《中华人民共和国海关法》规定，凡逃避海关监管，偷逃应纳税款、逃避国家有关进出境的禁止性或者限制性管理的行为都属走私行为。根据我国《刑法》有关规定，单位或者个人违反海关法规，逃避海关监管，运输、携带、邮寄国家禁止进出口货物、物品或者依法应当向国家缴纳税款的货物、物品进出境，数额较大、情节严重的犯罪行为就构成走私罪。走私犯罪是一种严重破坏社会主义市场经济秩序的犯罪行为，它不仅影响国家税收，冲击本国

revenue, damage domestic industry and commerce, diminish national security, foster corruption, and ruin the ethos. Therefore, we should resolutely enforce the law to combat any smuggling activities.

Anti-smuggling is a long-term and hard battle, the dynamics of which is constantly shifting as a country or regions progresses into different phases of economic and trade development. In the 1990s, I was Deputy Director General of Nanning Customs leading the anti-smuggling campaign in Guangxi Zhuang Autonomous Region. Working on the border frontier showed me the severe and complex nature of the fight against smuggling. Guangxi is the only coastal autonomous region in China. It borders Beibu Bay to the south, facing Southeast Asia and neighboring Vietnam, with a coastal border of about 1595 km and a land border of 1082 km, an ideal passage for trade in southwest China. Back in 1991, the State Council had ordered to regulate foreign trade and close down coastal docks set up by the local government for border trade. Yet driven by ill-gotten gains, some of the units or companies were still in the so-called "maritime border trade" business without the approval of the authorities. Some criminals saw the long coastal line, hidden bays and favorable loading conditions as advantages for their smuggling

工商业，而且危害国家安全，损害国家主权和利益，滋生腐败现象，败坏社会风气。对此，我们必须依法予以坚决打击。

打击走私是一场艰巨而持久的战役，它往往伴随着国家（区域）经济贸易的阶段性发展而不断变化。记得20世纪90年代，我担任南宁海关副关长期间曾主管过打私工作，在边境业务一线工作，深深感受到了我国反走私斗争的严峻形势和复杂尖锐。广西是我国唯一一个沿海的少数民族（壮族）自治区，南濒北部湾、面向东南亚，与越南毗邻，大陆海岸线长约1595公里，陆路又有1082公里长的边境线，是我国西南地区最便捷的经贸通道。当时，根据国务院要求，为规范进出口贸易秩序，全区关闭了原地方自行设立的沿海边贸过货码头。但一些单位和企业在利益驱动下仍擅自进行所谓的海上边贸活动，一些不法分子更是利用海岸线长、潜湾隐蔽、集散快捷等自然条件，大肆进行走私违法活动。与此同时，广西陆路边境也处

spree. Meanwhile, Guangxi's land border was also overwhelmed with smuggling because of its easy accessibility, scattered checkpoints, and substandard port management facilities. The most smuggled products included cars, motorcycles, air conditioners, color TV, steel, product oil, rubber, palm oil and so on. Faced with these grave challenges, however, we managed to rise above the pressure with strong confidence under the leadership of the General Administration of China Customs by working closely with local Party Committee, government, and all other enforcement agencies, focusing our strength on major targets to tackle the use of fake approval documents, fake units and fake stamps, and carrying out effective measures to stop smuggling at sea and on land. For instance, we cracked down an attempted smuggling of 798 cars and other serious smuggling activities, established deterrence against smuggling, maintained foreign trade order, and safeguarded the interests of the State and the people.

于渠道多、卡口散、口岸设施尚未完善等状况，边境陆路走私也一度呈猖獗势头。当时走私入境的主要品种是汽车、摩托车、空调、彩电、钢材、成品油、橡胶、棕榈油等。但在严峻的反走私斗争形势面前，我们坚定信心，顶住压力，在海关总署的正确领导下，紧紧依靠自治区党委和政府，协同各有关执法部门，集中力量、突出重点、打“三假”、查海上、堵陆路，采取有力措施严厉打击沿海沿边走私违法活动，查处了诸如“798特大汽车走私案”等大要案，有效地遏制了走私违法的嚣张气焰，维护了正常的进出口秩序，保障了国家和人民的利益。

Global and domestic dynamics over the past decade brought along new threats from smuggling, including conglomerate operations, better equipped with technology, and more networked. In the economic domain for example: while there were no fundamental changes in the supply-demand balance on

十多年来，随着国际国内环境的变化，走私活动出现了集团化、科技化、网络化等新的特点。比如，在经济领域，全球市场的供给与需求总态势没有根本改变，但经济发展仍处低迷，一些不法分子团伙作

the global market, economic growth was still sluggish. Criminals teamed up to frequently attempt to smuggle through land border without customs checkpoints or through marine transport using Internet and high- tech communication; the number of serious cases was high, where goods with fraudulent origin and price were smuggled in due to higher domestic prices of food, frozen goods, product oil and other bulk commodities; the smuggling of commodities that were key revenue sources, fake trades, and tax refund fraud were ubiquitous. In the political and social domain: influenced by the trend of "counter globalization" and "populism", political fragmentation, ideological diversity, and infiltration from hostile forces never stopped, therefore counter-subversion and anti-secession faced many new challenges; we were taking on heavier responsibilities to protect the society, environment and people, as the smuggling of guns and explosives that were related to terrorism and caused instability kept reoccurring, and the smuggling of prohibited items such as drugs, solid waste, ivory and other endangered species remained problematic. Statistics showed that in 2016, anti-smuggling police investigated 2633 smuggling criminal cases, involving 52.93 billion RMB yuan, increased by 17% and 4% respectively, among which there were 1446 tax related cases

案，利用网络、通讯等高科技手段，通过非设关地及海上偷运走私持续多发；国内由于粮食、冻品以及成品油等大宗商品价格相比国外处于高位，货运进口渠道原产地、价格瞒骗走私大要案高发；涉及重点税源商品走私、虚假贸易、骗退税等违法现象也大量出现。又如，在政治社会领域，受“逆全球化”“民粹主义”思潮的影响，政治碎片化、意识形态多样化、敌对势力渗透干扰一直没有停止过，反颠覆反分裂斗争形势严峻；维护社会安全、环境安全、民生安全等任务加重，涉枪、涉爆等涉恐、涉稳走私不断涌现，毒品、固体废物、象牙及其他濒危物种等违禁品走私仍较突出。据统计，2016年，全国海关缉私部门共立案侦办走私犯罪案件2633起，案值529.3亿元，同比增长17%和4%。其中，涉税走私犯罪案件1446起，案值487.9亿元，涉嫌偷逃税款101.4亿元；侦办1187起非涉税走私犯罪案件中，立案侦办走私武器弹药案件216起、走私毒品案件477起、走私濒危物种

involving a total amount of 48.79 billion yuan, and tax evasion of 10.14 billion yuan. In the 1187 non-tax-related cases, 216 were guns and ammunition, 477 were drugs, and 143 were endangered species, increased by 63.6%、33.6%, and decreased by 16.4% respectively。

案件143起，分别比上年增长63.6%、33.6%和下降16.4%。

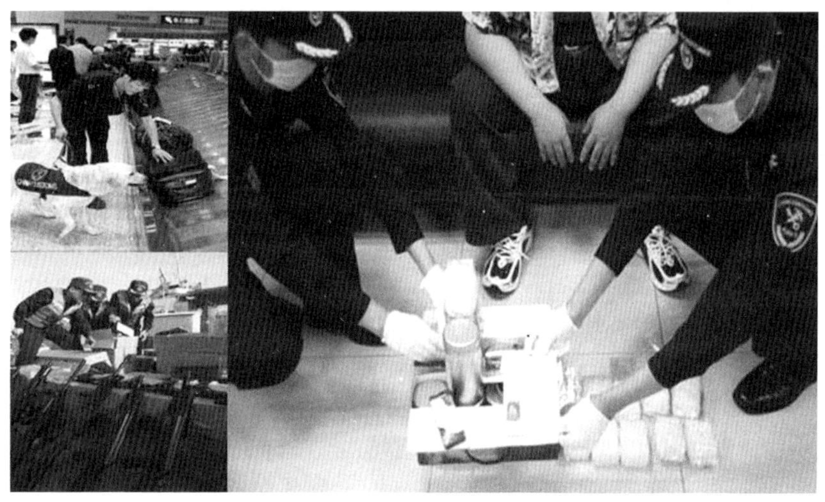

中国海关打击走私，守卫国门。
Combating smuggling and safeguarding the nation.

Countering solid waste smuggling, in particular, has become a substantial part of our job in recent years. The continuous growth of population and economy and urbanization made solid waste a global issue. Every year the world produces proximately 7 to 10 billion tons of solid waste, industrial waste, construction waste and domestic waste mainly from the US, the UK and the EU. Waste plastics, copper slag, waste tires, waste batteries, electronic waste, old clothing, domestic waste and

值得一提的是，近年来我国打击固体废物走私的任务更加紧迫和繁重。随着人口增长、城市化和经济持续发展，固体废物已成为全球性问题。每年全球约产生总量70亿~100亿吨的固体垃圾、工业废料、建筑和生活垃圾等，主要产自美国、英国及欧盟等国家，物品有废塑料、铜矿渣、废轮胎、废电池、电子垃圾、旧服

medical waste to name a few. The disposal of these types of waste will keep damaging the environment for a long time, pose severe risks for public health and security, and even cause social issues. Recently, leaders of the CPC Central Committee and the Central Government attached great importance to these issues. The General Office of the State Council issued a plan to ban the import of hazardous waste and promote the reform of the management system for the import of solid waste.

装、生活和医疗垃圾等危险废物。上述废物走私入境后，其后续处置过程对环境所产生的危害长期难以消除，对我国人民群众健康和公共安全形成严重威胁，极易引发社会问题。近期中央领导同志高度重视此事，国务院办公厅印发《禁止洋垃圾入境推进固体废物进口管理制度改革实施方案》。

The fight against smuggling concerns national security and social stability as well as the order of the market economy and the vital interests of the people. New dynamics, new challenges, and a new journey in history make new missions and new actions of customs anti-smuggling more prominent. It should be noted that full-fledged opening to the outside world will render more responsibility for anti-smuggling, price difference of bulk commodities will put more pressure on anti-smuggling, the deepening reform of streamlining administration and delegating power to lower levels will set a higher standard for anti-smuggling, and the rule of law will lay down more stringent requirements for anti-smuggling. We should combine punishment with prevention, address both the symptoms

打击走私关乎国家安全与社会稳定、事关市场经济秩序、事关人民群众切身利益。新形势、新挑战和新的历史征程更加凸现了海关打私工作的新使命和新作为。我们要清醒地认识到，在全方位对外开放的背景下反走私工作任务更重，在大宗商品价格倒挂的背景下反走私工作压力更大，在“放管服”改革日益深入的背景下反走私工作难度更高，在“依法治国”的背景下反走私工作要求更严。要坚持打防结合，标本兼治，探索建立“多元共治、整体联动、智慧缉私”的打私工作新方式，努力开创打击走私工作新局面。重

and root cause, explore a new work model to coalesce efforts from different authorities, combat as a well- organized unity, and use more smart and efficient methods and technologies, so as to make new progress in the fight against smuggling. We should stick to the following four key points in our work.

点应突出以下“四个坚持”：

First, we should keep curbing smuggling in some of the specific areas. The dire situation in these areas should be dealt with resolutely and swiftly. We will focus on the concerns of the central government, the society and the public, and carry out the joint operation “National Sword 2017”. We will clamp down on the smuggling of hazardous waste, agricultural produce, weapons, drugs, and endangered species, strike hard at smuggling cartels and the masterminds that hide behind the scene, in order to hunt down the most reckless criminals and contain the most serious problems.

一是坚持专项治理。当前要坚决迅速遏制重点领域走私猖獗的势头，紧紧围绕中央关注、社会关切、群众关心的突出走私问题，深入推进“国门利剑2017”联合专项行动。严厉打击“洋垃圾”、农产品、枪支、毒品、濒危物种等走私活动，将打击的锋芒对准幕后走私团伙和首要分子，坚决把冒头的团伙打下去，把突出的问题压制住。

Second, we should join all the efforts. The work of anti-smuggling should be spearheaded by the government, hold all related authorities accountable, and supported by the whole public in order to generate more synergy from all parties. We will enhance control over import and export, step up international customs cooperation following the principle of “mutual exchange

二是坚持综合治理。建立政府统一领导、部门各负其责、群众积极参与的反走私工作机制，推进实施“齐抓共管、开放共治”的打私整治合力。要加强进出口实际监管，以“信息互换、监管互认、执法互助”为抓手，深化海关国际合作，精准狠地打击“海陆

of information, mutual recognition of control and mutual assistance in enforcement" to precisely hit the smuggling via sea, land, air, mail, and the Internet. We will increase publicity of our work so that the people and social environment become the strong backing of anti-smuggling.

空邮网"的走私违法活动。要加强舆论宣传，使人民群众和社会环境成为反走私工作的坚强后盾。

Third, we should deal with and eliminate the root causes of smuggling. On one hand, reform and opening up need to be deepened in order to promote the supply side structural reform and alleviate the contradiction between supply and demand in the domestic market. On the other hand, we should open up more "front doors" while boarding up the "back doors", especially by fostering border trade and leading people in the area out of poverty. Meanwhile, we should enhance communication with neighboring countries to regulate the setting and management of ports and trading places.

三是坚持源头治理。努力消除走私高发多发的诱因。一方面要深化改革开放，为推进供给侧结构性改革助力，努力缓解国内市场供需矛盾；另一方面，在"堵邪门"的同时，积极研究"开正门"，尤其在边境地区积极发展互市贸易，带领边民脱贫致富，稳边固边。同时，还要加强对外交涉，敦促周边邻国规范边境口岸、互市点设置和管理。

Fourth, we should uphold the rule of law. We should speed up the legislative process for the enactment the *Regulations on Anti-smuggling*, so that laws are enforced in a strict, standard, fair and civil manner, administrative law enforcement are better converged with criminal justice, and law enforcement is legally, politically and socially effective. We should build a strong anti-smuggling police force, allocate more manpower to the frontline,

四是坚持依法治理。要加快《反走私工作条例》立法进程，争取尽快出台，严格规范公正文明执法，加强行政执法和刑事司法的衔接，实现法律效果、政治效果和社会效果的有机统一。要切实加强海关缉私队伍建设，充实一线、提升素质，加快推进先进装备应用和信息化平台建设，推行"智

and enhance capacity building. We should also promote advanced equipment and information platform to realize “smart anti-smuggling” and clean customs, while making great efforts in supervision and assessment, in order to comprehensively improve our performance in anti-smuggling.

慧缉私”、廉洁海关，抓好监督考核，全面提高打击走私工作的水平。

打击固体废物走私

2015年4月7日

Combat Smuggling of Solid Waste

April 7，2015

China Customs has recently uncovered 192，000 tons of solid waste illegally imported from abroad，which would have posed a danger to the environment. The figure was more than triple the amount found at the same period in the previous year.

中国海关近期查获了19.2万吨从海外走私入境并将对环境构成危害的固体废物。这个数字是去年同期的三倍以上。

The imported solid waste, which is dubbed "foreign garbage", refers to solid waste produced abroad and smuggled into China. The waste includes electronic, medical and mineral garbage and would severely pollute water, soil and air.

进口的固体废物也称为“洋垃圾”，指的是在国外产生并偷运至中国的固体废物，包括电子产品、医疗和矿物垃圾，将会严重污染水质、土壤和空气。

Since 2012, China customs officers have uncovered 174 cases of waste smuggling involving 385,900 tons of material and

自2012年以来,中国海关查获了174起固废走私案件，涉及38.59万吨走私废料，抓获

captured more than 700 suspects. Many companies disguised prohibited waste as something legal for import.

700多名嫌疑人。许多公司将禁止进口的废料伪装成合法货物走私进入国内。

Imports of many categories of waste are banned, including waste that poses risks to the environment because it contains hazardous substances and waste that is costly to recycle. But some people ignore pollution and even work with overseas organizations to smuggle prohibited waste for high profits.

许多含有害成分，可能会对环境造成威胁，或者回收成本昂贵的废物是禁止进境的。但许多人对污染熟视无睹，甚至与境外组织勾结走私禁止类固体废物以谋取暴利。

According to the law and regulations, customs needs to check the certificates of waste that have been approved by the environmental, commercial and quarantine departments. However, smugglers have found dodging ways that have made our work very difficult.

根据法律法规规定，海关须检查环保、商务、检验检疫部门出具的废物入境许可证。而走私者想尽办法逃避监管，这给我们的执法工作带来了很大的困难。

China customs officers have taken steps to intercept “foreign garbage” that pollutes the environment. They have strengthened their inspections of solid waste through manual inspection of goods that look suspicious in X-ray images and weighing all vehicles transporting waste. Smuggling solid waste should be punished severely and the country should improve its regulations and law on solid waste control. Stringent law enforcement is essential now to prevent smuggling.

中国海关对污染环境的“洋垃圾”走私采取了一系列打击措施，对X光扫描图像存异的货物实施人工查验，并对所有运输废物的车辆进行称重检查。固体废物走私行为应受到严厉惩罚，国家也应不断完善固体废物管控的相关法律法规。目前，严格执法是防止固废走私最重要的手段。

Effective control over solid wastes is critical to national health and safety. Therefore, China Customs has always

对固体废物的有效管控对国民健康安全至关重要。因此，中国海关一直高度重视打

attached great importance to it. In order to enhance customs control over and fight against the illegal trafficking of solid wastes, a ten-month special operation named “Green Fence” was launched from February to November last year, which had detected 600 thousand tons of illegal overseas garbage.

击固废走私。为加强海关监管，有效打击固体废物非法贩运，我们在去年2月至11月开展了为期十个月的“绿篱”行动，查获了60万吨非法入境的固体废物。

中国海关查获的走私固体废物。
Solid waste intercepted by China Customs.

We have also taken measures to control solid waste smuggling from its source. Over the years, we increased the customs international cooperation. For example, we’ve strengthened the cooperation with European customs. The EU is the second largest origin of solid waste that is imported to China. It’s necessary for both of us to reinforce solid waste supervision. It helps maintain environmental safety and public health. According to China Customs statistics, China has imported more than 8 million tons of solid waste from the EU last

近年来，我们积极开展了海关国际合作，从源头上打击固体废物走私。比如，我们加强了与欧盟海关的合作。欧盟是向中国出口固体废物的第二大来源。双方加强固体废物监管有利于保护环境和公共健康安全。据中国海关统计，去年中国自欧盟进口固体废物超过800万吨。因此欧盟海关积极参与了中国海关和世界海关组织共同发起，旨在打击固体废

year. So, EU Customs proactively participated in the "Demeter Ⅲ Operation", which was initiated by China Customs and organized by the WCO to tackle solid waste smuggling. We hope that we can continue to take solid waste control as an important part of our cooperation, especially the cooperation within the newly founded solid waste supervision working group. In the meantime, we should set up a mechanism to exchange information on solid waste repatriation.

物走私的“大地女神第三期”行动。希望中欧双方继续把固体废物监管作为合作的重要内容，特别要加强新成立的固体废物监管工作小组的合作。同时，双方应建立固体废物退运信息的共享机制。

Information exchange is also important to customs enforcement. We are facing serious challenges, not only from the EU, but also from other countries of the western world, such as from the U.S., Canada and Australia etc. A good way to crack down on the illegal transit of solid waste is to return the goods back to its origin (repatriation). So, we have to work together with the original Customs to conduct intelligence exchanges and investigation assistance on such kinds of hazardous wastes and have their feedback to ensure effective control.

信息交换对海关执法非常重要。我们面临的挑战不仅来自于欧盟，也来自于其他西方国家，如美国、加拿大、澳大利亚等。打击固体废物非法贩运的一种措施是对其进行退运。因此我们需要与国外海关合作，开展有害废物领域的情报调查合作，通过来源国的反馈确保对有害废物实施有效的监管。

There is no doubt that fighting against solid waste smuggling is, to the customs, a long-term and arduous task.We must make unremitting and strenuous efforts to firmly safeguard the ecological and environmental security of our country, and protect people's health.

毫无疑问，对于海关来说，打击洋垃圾走私将是一个长期而艰巨的任务。我们必须坚持不懈、全力以赴，坚定维护国家生态环境安全和人民群众身体健康。

零容忍 中国海关严厉打击濒危野生物种走私

2015年6月25日

Zero Tolerance against Smuggling of Endangered Wild Species

June 25, 2015

On May 30, 2015, the Chinese government again destroyed 662kg of confiscated ivory and its products in Beijing Wildlife Rescue and Rehabilitation Center located in Shunyi District.

2015年5月30日，中国政府再次在北京顺义区野生动物救援和康复中心销毁了662公斤的查获没收象牙及制品。

The ivory was crushed in front of foreign diplomats and reporters as a strong demonstration of the stance the country is taking against the illegal wildlife trade and crime.

在外国外交官和记者们的见证下，查获没收的象牙被粉碎销毁，鲜明地显示出我国坚决打击野生动植物非法交易和犯罪行为的立场。

The ivory was normally smuggled from Africa either by travelers who carried it in their luggage or through mail service. The elephant tusks and carved ivory artworks, which were seized by customs over the past year, were

象牙往往通过旅客携带行李或邮件从非洲走私入境。中国海关去年一年没收的象牙和象牙雕刻艺术品都被投入大型粉碎机里进行粉碎，尘粉遮

fed into a large crushing machine that sent clouds of dust and powder into the air. All of them were dumped and ground down by the General Administration of China Customs (GACC) and the State Forestry Administration (SFA). Actually, in January last year, 6.1 tons of confiscated ivory were also destroyed in the southern city of Dongguan, Guangdong Province.

天，弥漫到空中。所有的走私象牙均由中国海关总署和国家林业局实施销毁。事实上，去年1月，已有6.1吨被查没收的象牙在中国南方城市广东东莞被销毁。

Perhaps there are people who don't understand why such precious and valuable articles should be destroyed in the public? Why has the government of China stepped up its efforts to combat the illegal trade in endangered species and wildlife products?

也许有人不明白，为什么这么珍贵和有价值的物品要被当众销毁？为什么中国政府加大了打击濒危物种和野生动植物产品的非法交易的力度？

China is a contracting party of the *Convention on International Trade in Endangered Species* (CITES) and shoulders the responsibility to fight against illegal trade of endangered species. In May 2012, China Customs was rewarded the Certificate of Recognition by the CITES Secretary-General. So far, only 11 Certificates have been granted, which fully affirms customs achievements in endangered wild species enforcement. So, China has been complying with the CITES since joining, and proactively participating in law enforcement with other countries. China is committed to cooperating with the international community in stopping poaching

中国是《濒危野生动植物种国际贸易公约》的缔约方，肩负着打击濒危野生物种非法贸易的责任。2012年5月，中国海关荣获濒危野生动植物种国际贸易公约秘书长颁发的奖励证书。截至目前，总共只颁发了11份奖励证书，这是对我们保护濒危野生物种海关执法的充分肯定。因此，我国自加入上述公约以来，一直遵守国际濒危野生动植物贸易公约，与其他国家一道积极参与执法。中国致力于与国际社会合作阻止偷猎象牙和贸易。在打

and the ivory trade. Beijing has taken a zero-tolerance approach to the illegal ivory trade and made the great efforts in improving related laws and regulations to crack down on wildlife smuggling.

击非法象牙贸易问题上，中国政府已经采取了“零容忍”的态度，努力完善相关法律法规，严厉惩处濒危野生动植物走私违法行为。

The western media has reported unfairly on this issue. American Time's website issued an article on November 1, 2013, entitled "*The ivory trade is out of control, China needs to do more to stop*". The article said that China's demand for ivory, bear bile and other animal products brought disaster to the animals, and the Chinese mainland and Hong Kong's enforcement agencies confiscated smuggled ivory products, never publicly destroyed, but held up for smuggling ivory back into the market.

西方媒体对此事的报道有失偏颇。美国时代网站2013年11月1日发表了题为《象牙贸易失控，中国需要采取更多行动制止》的文章。这篇文章说，中国人对象牙、熊胆和其他动物产品有需求，这给动物带来了灾难。中国大陆和香港的执法机构没收走私象牙制品，但从未公开销毁，反而将走私象牙投放到市场上。

Furthermore, according to the letter on the website of Action for Elephants U.K., "African elephants are dying every year in their tens of thousands to feed the appetite for ivory of consumers in China and elsewhere." Other news claimed, "In 2013, China – a signatory of CITES – was identified as one of eight nations failing to do enough to tackle the illegal ivory trade."

此外，据英国“大象行动”网站称，“每年都有成千上万的非洲大象死亡，以满足中国和其他国家消费者对象牙的需求”。其他报道则称，“2013年，作为《濒危野生动植物种国际贸易公约》的缔约方，中国被认定为八个未能充分解决非法象牙贸易问题的国家之一”。

What is the truth then? China Customs has never stopped fighting against and bringing harsh punishment to the smuggling of ivory and other wildlife products. From 2012 to last

真相如何？中国海关从未停止严厉打击和惩处走私象牙和其他野生动植物制品的行动。自2012年至去年，

year, China Customs had investigated 282 cases involving the smuggling of ivory and products and arrested 458 suspects. There have been 39 cases and 39 arrests so far this year.

中国海关查处了282起涉及走私象牙及其制品的案件，逮捕了458名嫌疑人。今年，39起案件已经立案，39名嫌疑人被逮捕。

中国海关查获的濒危野生物种及其制品。

Endangered wildlife and products intercepted by China Customs.

There is a typical case in September, 2014, when customs officers in Shanghai confiscated 10 pieces of ivory and 345 ivory products, including ivory-made necklaces and chopsticks, from two suspects. The items were valued at 6 million RMB yuan (US$970,000). The suspects flew to Shanghai from Ethiopia and were detained as they passed through customs checks.

2014年9月有一个典型案例：上海海关关员从两名走私嫌疑犯身上查获没收了10件象牙和345件象牙产品，包括象牙制项链和筷子，价值600万元人民币（合97万美元）。他们是从埃塞俄比亚飞往上海的，在通过海关检查时被扣留。

China has taken a series of measures to combat ivory smuggling. New laws were introduced and a number of special operations have been staged to effectively curb the illegal

中国采取了一系列措施来打击象牙走私。我们正在实施新的法律和一些特殊措施，有效遏制了非法捕猎野生动物和

hunting of wildlife and trafficking. During the 23-day "Cobra" campaign that started on May 4，2014，182 suspects were captured in 123 cases involving trafficking and illegal trading of wildlife and endangered animals. Officers seized 10 pieces of raw ivory，292kg of worked ivory items，226kg of pangolin scales and 16.2kg of products made of rhino horn，along with live animals such as turtles and birds.

交易。从2014年5月4日起，中国海关开展了为期23天的“眼镜蛇”专项打击行动，总计查获123起非法交易野生濒危动植物案件，逮捕了182名嫌疑人。关警员们还查获了10块原始象牙，292公斤象牙制品，226公斤的穿山甲和16.2公斤的犀牛角制成品，以及活的海龟和鸟类动物。

This campaign was the third joint law enforcement action, with financial and technical support from Interpol and the World Customs Organization, in which China Customs cooperated with customs authorities from 63 countries, including South Africa, Thailand, France, Germany and the United States, to forcefully fight cross-border trafficking involving Tibetan antelopes, rhinos, redwoods and a variety of other animals and plants.

在此次由国际刑警组织和世界海关组织提供资金和技术支持的第三次联合执法行动中，中国海关在包括南非、泰国、法国、德国和美国等63个国家海关主管部门的配合下，有力地打击藏羚羊、犀牛、红杉和各种其他动物和植物的跨境走私交易。

Therefore, reports by the western media are a distortion of facts with ulterior motives. This time, we crushed the ivory and destroyed its artworks in front of foreign diplomats and reporters to show our firm resolution to protect the environment, conserve wildlife and combat the illegal trade in wildlife and its products. John E. Scanlon, Secretary-General of the CITES, highly appreciated this event. He said,

因此，西方媒体的宣传是夸大事实和别有用心的。我们这次当着外国外交官和记者的面销毁走私象牙及其制品，展示了我们保护环境、保护野生动植物和打击野生动植物及其制品非法交易的坚强决心。濒危野生动植物种国际贸易公约秘书长约翰·斯坎伦高度赞扬

"This action reflects China's resolution to curb illegal trading of ivory."

了我们的行动。他说："这一行动反映了中国遏制非法象牙交易的决心。"

The United States also appreciated China for destroying more than 600 kilograms of ivory and for its commitment to halting the commercial processing and sale of ivory and related products. "China's crush action today, as well as similar events held in the United States, the United Kingdom, France, Chad, Belgium, Kenya, Ethiopia, the United Arab Emirates and the Republic of Congo, sends a powerful message to wildlife poachers and traffickers and to the consumers of illegal wildlife products", said the U.S. State Department in an announcement.

美国也对中国销毁逾600公斤象牙的举措表示赞赏，认为中国此举恪守了停止商业处理和出售象牙及其相关制品的承诺。美国国务院在一份声明中称，"中国今天的销毁行动，以及在美国、英国、法国、乍得、比利时、肯尼亚、埃塞俄比亚、阿拉伯联合酋长国和刚果共和国所采取的类似行动，给野生动物偷猎者、贩运分子和非法野生动物产品的消费者，发出了强有力的警示信号。"

In fact, concrete actions of stopping the poaching, ending wildlife trafficking and securing a ban on the commercial sale of ivory are a critical element in our efforts to protect endangered wild life. It is also the common commitments and agreements made by China and the U.S. at the China-U.S. Strategic and Economic Dialogues. We look forward to continuing our mutual efforts to work together in banning illegal activities and protecting elephants and other wildlife.

事实上，制止偷猎和贩运野生动植物、禁止象牙商业销售的具体行动，是我们努力保护濒危野生动植物种的关键一环。在中美战略与经济对话中，中美双方对此也有共同承诺和合作安排。我们期待继续与美方携手努力，禁止非法活动，保护大象和其他野生动植物。

Meanwhile, it's necessary for us to enhance judicial cooperation with other

与此同时，我们也有必要加强与其他国家的司法合作，

countries, especially some Asian and African countries, so that case information can be shared timely and investigations can be launched to cut off interest chains between the traffickers and the purchasers.

尤其是与一些亚洲和非洲国家的合作，及时共享案件信息，启动调查，切断走私贩与购买者之间的利益链条。

In order to reach these goals, we still have a long way to go, but no matter how difficult the task might be, we will incessantly combat and strictly punish the smuggling of endangered species and wildlife products with "zero tolerance" to protect the safety of the ecosystem and environment and to maintain the harmony between man and the nature.

诚然，要实现上述目标还要走很长的路，但不管任务有多么艰难，我们都将不懈努力，以“零容忍”的态度坚决打击和严厉惩处走私濒危物种和野生动植物及其制品的非法活动，保护生态与环境安全，实现人与自然的和谐发展。

参观缉私犬训练基地

2015 年 7 月 5 日

Visiting the Detector Dog Training Center

July 5, 2015

July 2, 2015 was a lovely day with bright sunshine, blue sky and gentle breeze. Early in the morning, I arrived at the Detector Dog Training Center of Beijing Customs to wait for the Australian Customs delegation.

China Customs enjoys a good relationship and cooperation with Australian Customs. Last month, Mr. Roman Quaedvlieg, CEO of ACBPS, visited China Customs. We had a sound discussion and signed a new cooperation arrangement of the 2015 *Strategic Partnership Plan* in which the three areas of risk management, enforcement cooperation and trade facilitation were identified as the pillars of our bilateral cooperation.

2015年7月2日，天高云淡，惠风和畅。清早我就来到了北京海关的缉私犬训练基地，等待来访的澳大利亚海关代表团。

中国海关与澳大利亚海关拥有良好的合作关系。上个月，澳大利亚海关与边境保护署负责人罗曼·柯德武利格先生访问了中国海关。我们进行了友好交流，并签署了《2015年度战略合作伙伴计划》文件。其中，风险管理、执法合作和贸易便利化被确定为双方合作的三大重点领域。

On July 1, 2015, a new Australian customs organization – the Australian Border Force (ABF) was set up. Mr. Roman Quaedvlieg was just sworn in as the new ABF Commissioner for a five-year term the previous day.

2015年7月1日，澳大利亚成立了新的海关主管机构——澳大利亚边境执法署。前一天，罗曼·柯德武利格先生刚刚宣誓就职，成为边境执法署新任署长，任期五年。

But this time, we would meet with the head of the Australian customs delegation, Ms. Michaela Cash. She is the assistant minister of DIBP and the minister of women affairs in Australia. Because she is in charge of customs affairs, so she is also the boss of Mr. Roman Quaedvlieg.

但这一次，与我会见的将是澳大利亚海关代表团团长米凯拉·凯旭女士。她是澳大利亚移民和边境保护部助理部长、妇女事务部部长。她在澳负责海关事务，因此也是罗曼·柯德武利格先生的上司。

During our meeting, Ms. Michaela Cash highly appreciated the cooperation between China Customs and Australian Customs at first. Then she was focusing on the risk management and the fight against drug smuggling. She expressed her passion for the dog program and how pleasing it was to see the good cooperation between both countries. In response, I also expressed my sincere thanks and gratitude for the ongoing support for Detector Dog breeding and training regimes.

在会谈中，米凯拉·凯旭女士首先对中澳海关合作表示了高度赞赏。她重点提及了风险管理和打击毒品走私两大问题。在缉私犬合作项目上，她显示出浓厚的兴趣，并表示十分高兴看到两国间在此领域已经开展了高水平合作。作为回应，我对澳大利亚海关在缉私犬繁育和训练项目上给予中方的支持表示了感谢。

The Beijing Detector Dog Training Center of the General Administration of China Customs (GACC) is located at the Capital Airport Logistic Park, about 7 km to the north of the airport. The training center has a total area of 67.3 thousand square meters, with

海关总署北京缉私犬训练中心位于首都机场物流园内，机场以北7公里处。该训练中心占地面积达67300平方米，其中建筑面积7800平方米。经过近20年的发展，该中心已经

7800 square meters of floor space. Through nearly 20 years of development, it has become a leading institute for the breeding and training of detector dogs in China. Its facilities include office buildings, training rooms, breeding center, and indoor and outdoor exercise areas. There are 60 rooms for adult dogs and 20 rooms specialized for quarantine and other purposes. The green area is about 50 thousand square meters.

成为国内缉私犬繁育和训练的领先机构。中心的设施包括办公楼、训练房、繁育中心、室内和户外训练场等，有60间成犬犬舍和20间检疫犬及其他工作犬犬舍。绿化面积达到了5万平方米。

In June 2005, the Agreement between China Customs and Australian Customs on Detective Dog Program was signed. Beijing DDC officially kicked off bilateral cooperation program for detective dogs with assistance provided by Australian Customs in both training and gene-based breeding aspects.

2005年6月，中澳海关签署了缉私犬项目合作协议。在澳大利亚海关的协助下，北京缉私犬中心正式启动了双边缉私犬训练和基因繁育合作项目。

The center now has 81 dogs. Among them 15 are detector dogs, 6 breeding dogs, 17 puppies, and the rest of them are dogs to be trained or disqualified. There are 4 main breeds: German Shepherd, Golden Retriever, Labrador, and English Springer Spaniel. Currently Labrador proves the most suitable for the mission of anti-smuggling. Dogs are trained here to be able to detect drugs, explosives, ivories, tobaccos and even cash. Drug detector dogs play a very important role in fulfilling the obligation of Customs.

该中心现有81只犬，其中15只缉私犬，6只种犬，17只幼犬，其余均为即将接受训练或不符要求的犬。犬种方面，主要有四种：德国牧羊犬、金毛寻回犬、拉布拉多犬和英国斯宾格猎犬。目前已经证实，拉布拉多是最适宜执行缉私任务的犬种。在这里，缉私犬接受各种训练，学会搜查毒品、爆炸物、象牙、烟草和现金。缉毒犬在海关履行职责过程中扮演着重要的角色。

From April 23 in 1996, when the training center was officially opened till now, the detector dog teams made 104 seizures of drugs across Beijing Customs region, seizing more than 219 kilograms of heroin, cocaine, cannabis, ice and opium.

自1996年4月23日北京缉私犬中心正式落成以来，缉私犬团队在北京关区共查获104批毒品，包括海洛因、可卡因、大麻、冰毒、鸦片等共计219千克。

Drug detective dogs are capable of identifying more than 6 drugs and their derivatives including cannabis，heroine，ice，opium，ecstasy，and ketamine. Firearms and explosive dogs are able to sniff up plastic explosives，detonation cord，smokeless powder，firearms and chemical products.

缉毒犬能够识别六种毒品及其衍生品，包括大麻、海洛因、冰毒、鸦片、摇头丸、氯胺酮。枪支弹药和爆炸物侦测犬能够识别塑性炸药、雷管、无烟火药、武器、化学产品等。

The priority of the development of the dog center is to enhance K-9 drug detection capabilities and raise dog handlers' level of commitment. The center adheres to the principle of training and practice with the bid to prevent drugs from moving into the border. Using advanced genetic technology，the center also provides high-quality K-9 candidates for regional customs dog units within China.

建立缉私犬中心，最主要的目标是加强犬类的毒品侦测能力，并提升训犬员的专业水平。该中心遵循训练与实战相结合的原则，有效防止毒品流入境内。利用先进的基因技术，该中心为国内地区海关带犬工作小组提供了高质量备用犬。

Last year, Australian experts came and visited the dog training centers in Beijing and Ruili of Yunnan Province. They exchanged views with the Chinese side. Australian Customs also proactively participated in the "Detector dogs Training Seminar for the AP Region" held by China Customs in Ruili.

去年，澳大利亚专家来华访问，参观了北京和云南瑞丽两地的训犬中心。中澳双方专家展开了富有成果的交流。澳大利亚海关还积极参与了中国海关在瑞丽主办的“亚太地区缉私犬训练研讨会”。

From April to June this year, at the invitation of the Australian Customs, we have sent out 3 handlers to Australia for attachment programs. Australian Customs also expressed that a certain number of dogs and frozen sperms would be given to the China Customs.

After a friendly meeting, we visited the training center and enjoyed the performance of detector dogs detecting drugs in the luggage from outside. It was not the producing season for puppies, but I told Ms. Michaela Cash that I would send her some photos of the lovely puppies as soon as they were born 3 months later.

The visit and the meeting were conducted in a pleasant and friendly atmosphere. Towards the end of the visit, I again appreciated the long-term support and assistance from Australian Customs in terms of dog training and breeding for China Customs, and expressed our hope to continue to strengthen our exchange and cooperation in this area.

今年4月至6月，受澳大利亚海关邀请，我们派出了三位训犬员赴澳参加实习课程。澳大利亚海关还许诺，将赠予中国海关一定数量的缉私犬和冷冻精子。

经过友好的会谈交流后，我们共同参观了训犬中心，并观看了缉私犬侦测行李内毒品的表演。由于当时未到工作犬的繁殖期，我向米凯拉·凯旭女士表示，待到3个月后幼犬出生，我一定会给她寄去可爱幼犬的照片。

整个参观和会谈都是在十分愉快友好的氛围中进行的。最后，我再次感谢澳大利亚海关在缉私犬训练和繁育方面长期给予中国海关的支持与协助，并希望双方继续加强该领域的交流与合作。

全面从严治党　打造清正廉洁的准军事化海关纪律部队

2018年2月

Exercise Full and Rigorous Governance over the Party, and Nurture a Paramilitary Disciplined Customs Force with Integrity

February, 2018

To exercise full and rigorous governance over the Party is the most distinctive character of the governance of China by the Party Central Committee with Comrade Xi Jinping as the core. Since the 18th CPC National Congress, with a view to realizing the mission of the Party's governance in the new era, the Party Central Committee has been responding proactively to the new changes in the global, national and intra-Party conditions, and has incorporated strengthening Party discipline into the four-pronged comprehensive strategy. Last October, General Secretary Xi stressed in his report at the 19th CPC National Congress to exercise strict governance over the Party and improve the

全面从严治党，是以习近平同志为核心的党中央治国理政最鲜明的特征。党的十八大以来，党中央着眼实现党在新时代的执政使命，积极应对世情国情党情新变化，把全面从严治党纳入“四个全面”战略布局。去年10月，习总书记在十九大报告中强调，要坚定不移全面从严治党，不断提高党的执政能力和领导水平。2018年1月11日，习总书记在十九届中央纪委二次全会上作了重要讲话，再次深刻阐

Party's ability to govern and lead. On January 11 2018, General Secretary Xi delivered an important speech at the second plenary session of the 19th Central Commission for Discipline Inspection of the CPC, where he once again deeply elaborated on the strategic plans of the 19th CPC National Congress on exercising full and rigorous governance over the Party, conducted an in-depth analysis of the risks and challenges confronting the Party, put forward the general requirements and primary tasks of governing the Party with strict discipline for now and the near future, and identified the direction of Party building to resume our journey forward.

述了党的十九大关于全面从严治党的战略部署，深入分析了党面临的风险和挑战，明确提出了当前和今后一个时期全面从严治党的总体要求和主要任务，为党的建设重整行装再出发明确了方向。

China Customs, a paramilitary disciplined force led by the Party, fulfills its law-based duty of guarding the border and providing services at entry-exit ports. Its nature defines its most essential characteristic as a paramilitary disciplined force following the Party's command, loyal to the Party, servicing the people, impartial in law enforcement and strictly disciplined. China Customs is a national public enforcement force with a majority of nearly 80% CPC members. Therefore, it is of great significance to exercise full and rigorous governance over the Party for the building of the Customs force. Since the 18th CPC National Congress, China Customs has been resolutely carrying out the plans and requirements of the Party Central Committee on

中国海关是党领导下的人民海关，是一支依法履行进出口把关服务职责的准军事化纪律部队。从队伍性质上看，听党指挥、对党忠诚、服务人民、执法公正、纪律严明是人民海关准军事化纪律部队最本质的特征；从队伍结构上看，海关队伍有近80%的中共党员，是一支以党员为主体的国家公务员执法队伍。因此，全面从严治党对海关队伍建设来说具有特别重要的意义。党的十八大以来，中国海关坚决贯彻落实党中央全面从

exercising strict discipline over the Party in light of actual conditions of entry-exit administration and strengthening Customs building, improving Party conduct and enforcing Party discipline, and maintaining a tough stance in the anti-corruption campaign, where new progress and new results have been achieved. The goal of creating a deterrent against corruption has been initially attained; the cage of institutions that prevents corruption has been strengthened; and moral defenses against corruption are in the making. The overall building of the Customs force as a paramilitary disciplined customs force has thus been effectively advanced.

严治党部署和要求，紧密联系进出口管理和全面从严治关工作实际，正风肃纪，高压反腐，全面从严治党取得了新进展新成效。海关队伍"不敢腐"的目标已初步实现，"不能腐"的笼子越扎越紧，"不想腐"的堤坝正在构筑，有效地推进了海关准军事化纪律队伍的整体建设。

However, we must also be fully aware of the severe situation our Party faces in strengthening its self-governance. For the Customs, the environment for entry-exit law enforcement is still complex; the fight between corrosion and anti-corrosion is still intense; and embezzlement and bribe-taking, smuggling and indulgence of smuggling, abuse of power, traffic offence, as well as formalism, bureaucratism, hedonism, and extravagance within the system still happen occasionally. All these demand us to always remain sober as if treading upon thin ice, elevate our political stance, focus on solving problems, maintain political resolve, and ensure strict Party self-governance as the top priority in building the

但同时，我们也要清醒地看到全面从严治党面临的形势仍然严峻。就海关系统而言，进出境执法环境仍然复杂，腐蚀与反腐蚀的斗争依然尖锐，系统内贪污受贿、走私放私、滥用职权、交通肇事及"四风"问题仍时有发生。这些都告诫我们必须时刻保持如履薄冰的警醒，要求我们必须提高政治站位、坚持问题导向、保持政治韧劲，把全面从严治党放在海关队伍建设最突出的位置。在党的十九大会议上，习近平总书记用"三个

Customs force. During the 19th CPC National Congress, General Secretary Xi clearly warned everyone in the Party against such thinking in governing the Party with strict discipline that we should never stop to catch a breath and have a rest when the work is seemingly more or less done; never rest on our laurels after winning a battle; and never end on good note. Practice has proved that ensuring full and strict Party self-governance is a journey to which there is no end.

不能有”明确告诫全党：在全面从严治党这个问题上，我们不能有差不多了，该松口气、歇歇脚的想法；不能有打好一仗就一劳永逸的想法；不能有初见成效就见好就收的想法。实践证明，全面从严治党永远在路上。

In my opinion, under current circumstances, China Customs must base itself upon the unified plans and requirements of the Party Central Committee and resume the journey in order to exercise full and rigorous governance over the Party, and nurture a paramilitary disciplined Customs force with integrity. We should mainly focus on the following five aspects:

我认为，在当前的形势下海关要深入推进全面从严治党，打造清正廉洁的准军事化海关纪律部队，必须按党中央的统一部署和要求，重整行装再出发。重点围绕以下五方面工作：

I. Arm the force with scientific theories

一、以科学的理论武装队伍

The Xi Jinping Thought on Socialism with Chinese Characteristics for a New Era takes root in the great endeavors of upholding and developing socialism with Chinese characteristics, making clear the core contents of building socialism with Chinese characteristics in the new era in 8 aspects and listing 14-point fundamental principles of putting theories into practice. The Thought has rich implications and rigorous logic and constructs a complete system of scientific theories that represent the latest achievement

习近平新时代中国特色社会主义思想根植于坚持和发展中国特色社会主义伟大实践，提出的“八个明确”核心内容和“十四条坚持”实践要求，内涵十分丰富、逻辑十分严密，建构起系统完备的马克思主义中国化最新的科学理论体系。科学理论具有巨大的思想价值

in adapting Marxism to the Chinese context. Scientific theories have tremendous ideological values and power of truth. Party members and officials of China Customs should always keep the Party's original aspiration and mission firmly in mind, and enhance our confidence in the path, theory, system, and culture of socialism with Chinese characteristics. We should arm ourselves with the Xi Jinping Thought on Socialism with Chinese Characteristics for a New Era, remove all kinds of interferences and uphold the right stance and orientation politically, inwardly dispel all kinds of confusion and hold dear the Party's lofty belief and ideals, while in practice stay loyal to the Party, have moral integrity, and demonstrate a keen sense of responsibility and suit our action to our knowledge, in order to resolutely carry out the decisions and plans of the Party Central Committee. As regards the attitude towards work and life, we should guide Customs officers to value ideal over gains, value integrity over reputation, and value contribution over rewards. In particular, fully arming all Customs officers with theories and strengthening their ideals and convictions are not an empty slogan. We should carry them out by loyally fulfilling our duty and improving the quality and effectiveness of our work and services, by achieving progress in the exploration, innovation and modernization reform of Customs, and by making efforts and

和真理力量，海关党员和干部必须始终牢记党的初心和使命，不断增强“四个自信”，以习近平新时代中国特色社会主义思想武装头脑，在政治上排除各种干扰、坚持正确政治立场和方向；在思想上消除各种困惑、坚定党的崇高信仰和目标追求；在行动上做到忠诚干净担当、知行合一地坚决贯彻落实党中央的一系列决策部署；在对待工作和人生的态度上，要引导海关党员和干部努力做到“三重三轻”，即重理想轻利益、重品行轻荣誉、重奉献轻回报。特别需要强调的是，海关党员和干部理论武装和理想信念不是空洞喊口号，而是要落实在忠诚履职、提升把关服务的工作质量和效益上，反映在海关开拓创新、推进现代化改革的成效上，体现在为实现我国经济高质量发展多尽努力多作贡献上。

contributions to making new ground in pursuing opening up on all fronts and realizing the high-quality development of China's economy.

II. Restrain the force with strict disciplines

Full and rigorous Party self-governance and the building of Customs force cannot be ensured without strict disciplines as an underpinning. **First, we should underline the importance of building Customs politically and tighten political disciplines.** Party members and officials should take the lead in conscientiously obeying political discipline and rules, maintain political integrity, think in terms of the big picture, follow the leadership core, and keep in alignment with the central Party leadership, firmly uphold the position of Comrade Xi as the core of the CPC Central Committee and the whole Party, and uphold the authority and centralized, unified leadership of the Central Committee. All Customs and anti-smuggling police officers should think and act in big-picture terms in serving the Party and the whole nation, and fully carry out fundamental principles of the Party Central Committee and the State Council without any reservation. **Second, we should ensure that disciplinary responsibility is fulfilled at each level.** In tightening disciplines, we must focus on oversight over the "key few", clearly define the persons that assume main responsibility in each agency and department,

二、以严明的纪律约束队伍

没有严明纪律作保证，全面从严治党就无从抓起，全面从严治关就会落空。**首先要突出政治建关、严明政治纪律**。海关党员干部要带头自觉遵守政治纪律和政治规矩，牢固树立“四个意识”，坚定维护以习近平同志在党中央、全党的核心地位，坚定维护党中央的权威和集中统一领导。全体关警员要自觉站在党和国家大局上想问题、办事情，把党中央国务院大政方针不折不扣落实到位。**其次要落实纪律的责任**。严明纪律，必须抓好“关键少数”，明确各单位各部门的责任主体，夯实责任内容，确保有权必有责、有责要担当、失责必追究。各级纪检部门要发挥好监督执纪问责的职责。**三要坚持把纪律和规矩挺在前**。充分运用好监督执纪“四种形态”，立足抓早抓小、

concretize the content of responsibility, and ensure that duties always go with power, responsibility always goes with duties, and dereliction of duties always triggers investigation. Disciplinary inspection commissions at all levels should perform their functions of executing accountability for overseeing discipline compliance. **Third, we should give top priority to ensuring compliance with Party discipline and rules.** We should conduct four forms of oversight over discipline compliance, identify problems early and correct them while they are nascent. We should also intensify disciplinary actions and measures. **Fourth, we should develop and raise Party members' awareness and conscientiousness of discipline.** We should reinforce learning of the Party Constitution, Party rules and disciplines and step up warning education, foster a strong atmosphere of no desire to commit acts of corruption. We should nurture Customs Party members and officers' habits and conscientiousness of strict discipline through formation training, on-duty training and skill competition.

防微杜渐，同时要加大惩戒力度。**四要加强纪律教育，形成纪律自觉**。通过加强党章党规党纪学习教育和警示教育，营造“不想腐”的氛围，通过坚持队列训练、岗位练兵、技能竞赛等活动，培养海关党员和干部严明纪律的习惯和自觉。

III. Guide the force with a robust work style

三、以扎实的作风引领队伍

Recently, General Secretary Xi made important instructions on *Caution: New Patterns of Formalism and Bureaucratism*, an article published by the Xinhua News Agency. He pointed out that the seemingly new patterns mentioned in

近期，习近平总书记就新华社一篇《形式主义、官僚主义新表现值得警惕》的文章作出重要批示，指出文章反映的情况看似新表

the article actually reveal old problems, which once again reveal that formalism, bureaucratism, hedonism and extravagance are intractable and recurrent. Improving conduct is a critical way to link the Party with the people and a manifestation of our Party conduct and political conduct, and meets the practical needs of strengthening the competence of officials. To this end, we should firstly adhere to a down-to-earth working style and seek substantial results. The transformation of conduct is not reflected in the number of meetings held, declarations made or official documents issued, but in how many practical problems have been solved, in whether the decisions and plans of the Party Central Committee have been carried out, whether the issues that the people strongly concerned about have been addressed and whether acts that harm the interests of the people have been corrected with a firm hand. We should guide all Customs' Party members, Customs officers and anti-smuggling police officers, especially officials in positions of leadership to proceed from reality in planning their career and work, stay close to the grassroots to conduct research and learn first-hand situations. We should guide them to think about and address outstanding problems systematically, listen to opinions and suggestions of the people extensively, and sum up new experience gained by the people timely. Secondly, we should act resolutely and swiftly,

现，实则老问题，再次表明“四风”问题具有顽固性、反复性。作风建设是党密切联系群众的重要途径，是党风政风的具体体现，是加强干部队伍建设的现实需要。对此，一是要真抓实干，讲求实效。转变作风，主要不是看开了多少会、作了多少表态、发了多少文件，而是要看解决了多少实际问题，中央的决策部署是否真正落实了，群众反映强烈的问题是否切实解决了，损害群众利益的行为是否坚决纠正了。要引导海关系统广大党员、关警员，特别是领导干部大力从实际出发谋划事业和工作，深入基层调查研究、掌握第一手情况，多系统思考和解决存在的突出问题，广泛听取群众意见和建议，及时总结群众创造的新鲜经验。二是要雷厉风行，讲求效率。工作效率是检验工作作风和工作质量的重要标准。要大力提倡“马上就办、真抓实干”的工作精神和作风，讲求工作时效，提高办事效率，克服办事效

and pursue high efficiency. Work efficiency is an important criterion we use to measure the conduct and quality of our work. We should devote major efforts to advocating a straight-away and down-to-earth working spirit and conduct, strive for effectiveness and efficiency, and root out inefficiency and untimely implementation. Thirdly, we should make improving conduct a regular and long-term practice. We should improve conduct in a continuous and intensive manner by establishing a series of mechanisms including learning and education, management by objectives, supervision, checks and balances, cross-department collaboration, rewards and punishments, etc., in order to guide the force towards integrity and efficiency.

率低、工作落实不及时的状况。三是要推进作风建设常态化、长态化。通过构建学习教育、目标管理、监督制约、部门协作、奖励惩处等一系列机制，推动作风建设持续深入，以此引领队伍的正气和工作效能。

IV. Manage the force with improved system

To ensure full and strict Party governance, we should provide better institutional guarantees in the first place. Firstly, we should further integrate the combat against smuggling and that against corruption. Where there is smuggling, there is often corruption. Therefore, we should pay attention to clues of violations of law and disciplines within the Customs system when investigating smuggling cases, explore the source of unlawful acts through smuggling cases, and carry out investigations into smuggling

四、以完善的制度管理队伍

全面从严治党用完善的制度管理队伍是保障。一是要深化打私反腐“一案双查”制度。走私行为往往与腐败行为相伴而生，为此在侦办走私案件的过程中，要注意发现海关内部违法违纪线索，通过走私案件挖掘违法根源，外查走私和内查违纪同步进行。二是要完善执法管理廉政风险的分

and disciplinary violations simultaneously. Secondly, we should improve the analysis and identification mechanism of integrity risks in law enforcement and management. All units should set up working mechanisms accordingly to create a strong synergy, focus on the potential integrity risks in front-line law enforcement including customs control and inspection, duty collection and management, processing trade and customs bonded operation, audit-based control and risk management, anti-smuggling, etc., and conduct analyses on cases, trends and symptoms that are typical of an industry or a region regularly to predict and identify risks. Thirdly, we should strengthen checks and oversight over the exercise of power. We should record enforcement activities into the system and keep them traceable, closely watch high-risk positions and dimensions, step up oversight and monitoring over the exercise of power and reduce human intervention. Meanwhile, we should apply Internet thinking and new media tools to exercising Customs power to increase openness and transparency, and ensure that Customs law enforcement is transparent to the public and under public oversight.

析研判机制。各业务条线应通过建立相应的工作机制形成合力，重点关注监管、征管、加贸、稽查、打私等一线执法领域可能存在的执法管理廉政风险，定期对行业性、区域性的案件、趋势和苗头问题开展分析，提前预判风险。三是要完善权力运行的监督机制。推进执法行为“进系统、留痕迹、可追溯”，紧紧盯住高风险岗位和高风险环节，加强对权力运行的监督监控，减少人为干预。同时运用互联网思维和新媒体手段推进海关权力运行的公开透明，实现海关执法过程对社会公开，受人民监督。

V. Test the force with concrete results

The fundamental goal of building the Customs force is to maintain loyalty to the Party’s cause, improve our capability of guarding

五、以工作的实绩检验队伍

海关队伍建设的根本目的，在于忠诚党的事业、不断提升海关把关服务工作

the border and providing services, and make greater contributions to the realization of the two centenary goals of socialism with Chinese characteristics and the Chinese dream of the great rejuvenation of the Chinese nation. Hence, to fulfiu our new mission and meet the new requirements in the new era, we should deem concrete outcomes of Customs work as the touchstone to measure our force building. At the Annual National Meeting of District Heads of China Customs and Working Conference on Exercising Strict Governance over the Party held in Beijing in January 2018, the Party Leading Group of the General Administration of Customs of China called on us to thoroughly study the spirit of the 19th CPC National Congress and work hard to make new ground in Customs work in the new era. Especially, new and higher requirements have been raised on such fronts as proactively serving the "Belt and Road" initiative, deepening key reforms of Customs, reinforcing control and inspection and optimizing services to promote the steady and sound development of foreign trade, governing the Party with strict discipline, etc. In this regard, we should build and improve a complete set of scientific performance incentive systems and assessment methods, and lay emphasis on the process and more importantly the results. Namely, we should focus on whether we have followed the people-centered

的能力和水平、为实现“两个一百年”奋斗目标和中华民族伟大复兴的中国梦而不懈努力。因此，从新时代新使命新要求上讲，海关工作是否有实绩是检验海关队伍建设成果的试金石。今年1月在京召开的全国海关关长会议和全面从严治党工作会议上，总署党组提出了深入学习党的十九大精神、奋力开创新时代海关工作新局面的任务和要求，尤其对积极服务“一带一路”建设、深化海关重点改革、强化监管优化服务全力促进外贸稳中向好、全面从严治党等方面提出了更新更高的要求。鉴于此，要建立和完善一整套科学的绩效考核制度和评估方法，既要看过程，更要看实效，也就是看海关“以人民为中心”的思想和“执法为民”的理念是否牢固树立了；看海关依法履行把好国门、维护国家和人民根本利益的监管职责是否到位了，打击洋垃圾、象牙及其制品、毒品、涉恐涉爆等走私是否取得了显著成效；

philosophy and the principle of law enforcement for the people; whether our law-based functions and duties of guarding the national border and safeguarding the fundamental interests of the people have been fulfilled; whether satisfying results have been secured in the combat against smuggling hazardous waste, ivory and ivory products, drugs, explosives and items that are related to terrorism; whether duty collection and management has been fully in accordance with the law and no excessive taxation has been levied; whether fairness, openness, impartiality, quality and efficiency have been guaranteed in Customs services for facilitation during the import and export of compliant traders; whether the issues that concern most people have been addressed and the three major risks in force building have been prevented, i.e., risks in integrity, enforcement and management; whether a Customs force that is loyal to the Party, has moral integrity and demonstrates a keen sense of responsibility has been built with both strictness and care; and so on. Therefore, we should not only pursue the positive energy brought by strict Party self-governance to Customs control and development, but also check and assess the results of the building of the paramilitary disciplined Customs force through work performance, so that we could secure more concrete, effective and sustained outcomes in both Customs reforms and

看依法征管是否做到了“应收尽收”，坚决不征“过头税”；看优化服务、便捷通关、维护广大进出口企业合法进出是否做到了公平公开公正和提质增效；看群众普遍关心的问题是否得到了有效解决，海关队伍建设中防范“三大风险”，严管厚爱打造清正廉洁、忠诚干净担当的队伍具体又体现在哪里，等等。因此，我们既要十分注重全面从严治党给海关改革和促进业务发展带来的正能量，又要透过工作的“成绩单”来检验并印证海关准军事化纪律队伍建设的实际效果，从而使“两手抓”“两手都要硬”的工作更具真实性、有效性和持久性。

operations, and the building of the Customs force.

准军事化海关纪律部队
Paramilitary Disciplined Customs Force

国际海关共促廉政　共商反腐

2015年2月26日

Global Customs Administrations Build Integrity and Fight Corruption

February 26, 2015

Two important meetings were held in Melbourne, Australia during February 5-6, 2015. One was the 16th World Customs Organization (WCO) Customs Head Meeting in the Asia-pacific Region; and the other was the Strategic Dialogue of Customs Integrity. I headed the Chinese Customs delegation to attend these two meetings.

2015年2月5日至6日，国际海关界在澳大利亚墨尔本举行了两场重要的会议：第十六届世界海关组织亚太地区署长会议和海关廉政战略对话会。我率领中国海关代表团参加了上述会议。

Customs Head Meeting in the Asia-pacific Region was directly followed by the Strategic Dialogue of Customs Integrity in the Asia-pacific, the first session of which was held at Shanghai Customs College. The theme of the dialogue this time was "How to cope with the risk of integrity by using customs

亚太地区署长会议结束后，紧接着就召开海关廉政战略对话会。记得首届亚太地区海关廉政战略对话会曾是在上海海关学院举行的。本次对话会的主题是"如何利用海关文化和技术应对廉政风险"。中

culture and technology". We actively engaged in the discussion, introduced China Customs best practices to fight against corruption and smuggling, and put forward proposals for international customs cooperation in this regard.

方代表团积极参与会上讨论，介绍了中国海关在反腐和打击走私方面的最佳实践，并提出了在此领域加强海关国际合作的一系列倡议。

During the Dialogue, I talked about the overall situation and our policy of fighting against corruption in China Customs. China Customs has taken integrity as the "permanent theme" and "lifeline" of customs work. The overall policy of fighting against corruption and building integrity is characterized by "one core objective and four consistencies". One core objective is preventing risk in customs enforcement, management and integrity. Four consistencies mean: incorporating integrity policy with customs operations; combining combating corruption with prevention measures; fighting against corruption with anti-smuggling; as well as combining the Chinese Communist Party's discipline on integrity with accountability in administration and law enforcement.

会上，我介绍了中国海关反腐败建设的总体情况和具体政策。中国海关一直将廉政视作海关工作的“永恒主题”和“生命线”。反腐倡廉的总体思路可以用“一个目标，四个坚持”来概括。“一个目标”是指防范海关执法、管理和廉政风险这一核心目标。“四个坚持”则包括：坚持将廉政政策与海关业务运行相结合；坚持将打击腐败与预防措施相结合；坚持将反腐与打击走私相结合；坚持将党的廉政纪律与执法监管责任相结合。

The overall situation and tendency of integrity in China Customs are sound, but pressure on the fight against corruption is still heavy. The key posts of customs inspection, duty collection, processing trade, post-clearance audit (PCA) and anti-smuggling are still vulnerable. Meanwhile, integrity risks in

中国海关廉政方面的工作态势和趋势总体向好，但仍然面临着很大的反腐压力。海关查验、税收征管、加工贸易、稽查和打击走私等关键岗位仍有弱点。同时，海关内部的人事、财务

the non-enforcement departments like human resources, finance and facilities administration can't be underestimated.

和后勤等非执法部门也存在着不容小觑的廉政风险。

In response to the above problems, China Customs has taken a series of countermeasures. For instance, we have established an integrity accountability mechanism. It is required that customs administrators should combine integrity-related work with administration and customs business, and establish an internal control mechanism to enhance the monitoring of administrative power. We also utilize the 24-hour customs hotline of "12360", the China Customs portal website, the *China Customs* magazine and news bulletin, CD, Micro-blog and Wechat (an instant message application) and other platforms for the real-time publication of polices and public monitoring over customs enforcement. Moreover, through education activities by using typical integrity-related cases and role models, we are enhancing the education of the importance of integrity. We are elevating the integrity level by partnering with other border management agencies, legal authorities, the business sector and the general public.

针对上述问题，首先中国海关采取了多项措施予以防范。比如，我们建立了廉政责任制。要求所有海关负责人将廉政工作与海关管理和业务结合起来，并建立内部监控机制，加强行政权力行使监督。又如，通过“12360”24小时海关热线、中国海关门户网站、《中国海关》杂志和通报、光盘、微博、微信等平台，对海关政策规定和执法工作进行实时发布和公开监督。再如，通过典型廉政案例加强廉政教育，并与其他边境管理部门、法律部门、商界和社会大众开展沟通合作，共同推进提升海关廉政水平。

Second, I analyzed the impacts of illegal behaviors on customs integrity, and introduced countermeasures taken by China Customs. Smuggling is always connected with

其次，我着重分析了违法行为对海关廉政的影响，并介绍了中国海关采取的对策。走私始终与腐败紧密相连。违

corruption. Criminals take every means to solicit and spoil customs officers. In response to this problem, China Customs has taken two major measures: on the one hand, we have established and improved a coordination mechanism on fighting against corruption. It is explicitly stipulated that while an anti-smuggling case is under investigation, clues on internal discipline-related misconducts should also be examined, namely "dual investigations". In the past five years, 70% of discipline-breaking and illegal cases in China Customs were disclosed by itself. 30% of the cases were discovered through the coordination mechanism. On the other hand, we have applied information technology, and expanded the use of the "China Customs Enforcement Risk Alerting and Handling System".

法分子采取各种手段拉拢腐蚀海关关员。针对这一问题，中国海关采取了两项主要措施：一方面，我们建立完善了反腐败协调机制，明确规定任何一起缉私案件调查期间，应该同时调查内部相关违纪线索，即“一案双查”。过去五年里，70%的违法违纪案件都是中国海关主动披露的。30%的案件是通过上述协调机制发现的。另一方面，我们充分利用信息技术，并扩大了“中国海关执法风险预警处理系统”的应用范围。

Finally, I put forward some proposals on international customs cooperation in integrity. In the future, China Customs will continue to promote integrity, draw upon our foreign counterparts, and enhance international cooperation and communication in integrity. We will learn from the best practices by other customs administrations and government agencies of foreign countries to enhance the self-discipline of customs officers and their acceptance of and engagement in the integrity initiative. In this regard, we suggest that the

最后，我提出了各国海关在廉政领域开展国际合作的倡议。未来，中国海关将继续推进自身廉政实践并向国外海关学习借鉴，加强国际海关廉政交流与合作。我们将向其他国家的海关主管部门和其他政府部门多取经，分享最佳实践，以促进海关关员自律水平的不断提升，加强他们对廉政建设工作的接受度和参与度。因此，我们倡议，亚太地区廉政

Asia-Pacific Work Group on Integrity should collect the best practices and real cases of customs integrity and encourage mutual sharing of experience, so as to promote the development of the WCO and its members.

Of course, the construction of a clean government and maintenance of customs integrity are long-term and arduous tasks. We should shoot both the "tigers" and the "flies" in the fight against corruption. Anti-corruption is not only an urgent task at present, but also an effective way to strengthen self-building in the long run. In order to implement customs laws and rules strictly and better serve our country and the people, we have to step up our efforts in integrity building and achieve more progress in this regard.

研讨班应当收集各国海关廉政的最佳实践和真实案例，鼓励各方相互分享经验，促进国际海关组织及其成员国的更好发展。

当然，建设廉洁政府、推进海关廉政工作是一项长期艰难的工作。在反腐败斗争中，我们既要打“老虎”，也不能放过“苍蝇”。反腐败不仅是当前的紧急任务，也是加强海关自身建设的有效途径。为了严格实施海关相关法律法规，更好地服务国家和人民，我们应当继续加大工作力度，推动廉政建设工作不断取得新的成绩。

过去、现在、未来：更好地为商界服务

——上海海关在贸易便利化方面的实践

2005 年 9 月 10 日

Past，Present and Future to Serve Business Better

—— Shanghai Customs Practices in Trade Facilitation

September 10, 2005

The APEC Customs-Business Dialogue (ACBD) was held on September 4, 2005 in the city of Gyeongju, South Korean. Gyeongju was the birthplace of the ancient Korean civilization and used to be the capital of the Silla Empire. It is both a world-renowned cultural and tourist city, as well as one known for its important role in Korea's agriculture and fisheries. It has a population of around 300,000. Imperial tombs, stone pagodas, Buddha statues and relics of temples can be found across its mountains and valleys, receiving an annual tourist volume of 9.06 million trips, including 505,000 trips made from foreign countries. It is indeed a tranquil while vigorous city.

2005年9月4日，APEC海关与商界对话会在韩国庆州召开。庆州是韩国古代文明的摇篮，曾是新罗王朝的首都。它是世界著名的文化旅游城市，也是农业和渔业比重较高的城市。现有人口约30万。举凡山地、溪谷，都有王陵、石塔、佛像、寺庙遗址，年游客流量达906万人次，其中外国游客为50.5万人次，是一座十分恬静又充满活力的城市。

It was my first time to Gyeongju, Korea, and I felt honored to attend the 2005 ACBD on behalf of the General Administration of China Customs (GACC). The theme of the event was "Facilitating Freer Global Trade through Effective, Efficient and E-Friendly Customs". I delivered a speech on Shanghai Customs' past and current practices in trade facilitation and probed into how to serve a free global trade through the strengthened ties between customs and the business sector in the future.

我是第一次到韩国庆州。这次能代表海关总署参加2005年APEC海关与商界对话会并作专题演讲，我备感荣幸。这次会议的主题是"以便捷、高效、智能的海关促进更为自由的全球贸易"，我通过介绍上海海关过去和现在在贸易便利化方面的实践，探讨如何通过加强海关与商界合作伙伴关系，更好地在未来为促进自由的全球贸易服务。

As is widely known, dialogue between the public and private sectors has been crucial in the process of trade facilitation. Customs, as a state organ for inbound and outbound supervision, plays an important role in improving business conditions in the region by creating an atmosphere that increases trade opportunities and helps businesses save time and reduce costs.

众所周知，开展政府部门与商界的对话，在促进贸易便利化的过程中愈显重要。海关作为国家进出境监督管理部门，在创造贸易机会，为企业节省时间，降低成本继而改善企业的商业运作环境方面发挥着重要的作用。

In 1999, a pilot initiative called the "Shanghai Model Port Project" was launched, which was brought to fruition through cooperation between the Chinese and U.S. Customs administrations and the private sector. It served not only as a model for cooperative ventures between public and private sectors, but also provided Shanghai Customs with the opportunity to take bold new steps towards trade facilitation. It focused on upgrading

1999年，由中国海关、美国海关以及商界联合倡议发起的"上海示范通关点"计划开始启动。该计划不仅为政府部门与商界合作提供了示范，而且也为上海海关向促进贸易便利化方向迈进提供了新的机遇。在该项计划中，浦东国际机场快件中心的建立和上海海关网站的升级成为项目实施的

activities of the Shanghai Pudong International Express Handling Center and the website of Shanghai Customs, and emphasized the importance of Intellectual Property Rights protection. Since the completion of this project in September 2001, Shanghai Customs has continued in its efforts to achieve world-class standards of efficiency and service in expediting customs clearance.

重点，同时知识产权保护也被作为重点内容加以强调。到2001年9月该项目结束为止，上海海关经过不懈的努力，在快速通关方面达到了效率与服务的世界级标准。

In my speech, I mainly touched upon five underlying concepts which were identified as the effective practices in creating a favorable clearance environment:

会上，我着重从五个方面对创造良好通关环境的有效做法向与会者作了介绍。

First, implement the "Integrated Clearance System" project. In 2001, China Customs established a coordinating mechanism with the quarantine bureau, the port authority, shipping and airfreight agents, and forwarding and warehouse enterprises, which enabled us to implement a one-stop service for enterprises. As a result, customs clearance efficiency and effectiveness were substantially improved. In the context of simplification and optimization of customs procedures and processes, we have fully implemented a new mode of "advance declaration, goods release upon arrival" by setting up a centralized declaration point at the Shanghai International Shipping Center. In February 2002, Shanghai Customs started to implement a system for EDI paperless

一是实施"大通关"工程。2001年，海关与卫生检疫部门、港务局、航运空运代理和货运仓储企业建立协调机制，为企业实施"一站式服务"，海关通关效率得到了极大的提高。我们不断简化和优化各种通关程序和手续，在上海航运交易所设立了集中报关点，全面实施"提前报关、实货放行"的新型通关模式。自2002年2月起，上海海关启动EDI无纸化通关系统。高新技术企业享有很多便捷通关措施，包括打开快速通道，银行担保货物放行、预归类等。此外，快速通关还在诸如保税区

clearance. High-tech enterprises have adopted various facilitative measures including opening express channels, releasing goods under the guarantee of banks, and implementing advance classification. Moreover, fast clearance was granted for particular areas such as free trade zones and export processing zones. To justify whether those actions have paid off, Quanda Computer at one of the export processing zones was selected to solicit feedback on customs practices. We were informed of the fact that the time spent on air cargo movement from landing at the airport to the export processing zone has been significantly slashed from the previous 72 hours to the current 4 hours. Of this period, customs clearance only took up around 10 minutes. Thus, to some extent, this feedback is encouraging for the customs administration. It is also worth mentioning that tariffs and other import and export fees and charges incurred in the process of customs clearance could all be paid through the EDI system. The EDI system is interconnected with seven banks via the electronic platform of the Integrated Clearance System.

和出口加工区等海关特殊监管区域加以实施。为了验证海关的措施是否有效，我们选择出口加工区的达丰电脑公司作为研究对象。通过分析，该企业的空运货物从在机场降落到运往出口加工区所花的时间从以前的72小时，大大缩短为现在的4小时，而海关通关所花时间仅为10分钟左右。这样的海关管理成效十分地令人鼓舞。还值得提及的是，关税和海关通关环节中涉及的进出口费用都可通过EDI系统进行支付。EDI系统已经通过“大通关”体系中的电子平台与七家银行相互连接。

Second, advance China E-Port. On October 25, 2004, the GACC signed an MOU with the Shanghai Municipal government, formally commencing the Shanghai e-Port program. This was an important step in

二是推动中国“电子口岸”建设。2004年10月25日，海关总署和上海市政府签署《关于建设上海电子口岸的合作备忘录》，上海电子口岸

promoting trade facilitation. The network of customs, entry-exit commodity inspection and quarantine administration, industrial and commercial administration and relevant departments engaged in international trade, taxation, foreign exchange and transportation can now be interconnected. Through this network, electronic account based on data pertaining to import and export information flows, capital flows and the flow of goods can all be stored in a public data center. Relevant authorities can conduct cross-department and cross-industry data sharing, exchange, checks and retrieval, while enterprises can carry out online importing and exporting procedures such as customs formalities, quarantine, tax refunding after export, foreign exchange write-offs and online payment.

正式启动，这对推进贸易便利化进程具有十分积极的现实意义。海关、出入境检验检疫局、工商局以及与国际贸易、税务、外汇管理、运输等有关的相关部门进行系统联网。通过“电子口岸”，进出口业务信息流、资金流、货物流等有关电子底账数据能够被集中存放在一个公共数据中心。相关行政管理机关可以进行跨部门、跨行业的数据共享、交换、核查，企业也可以通过互联网方便地办理报关、报检、外汇核销、出口退税、网上支付等一系列手续。

Third, experiment with risk management reform. On February 1 of this year, the Risk Analysis and Supervision Center was established which marked the full implementation of the customs risk management application reform. Based upon analysis of risks to traders, commodities and industries, this approach integrates the risk management and risk assessment programs to allow customs to focus on high-risk goods and the immediate release of other goods according to the principle of “using appropriate customs inspection and then

三是实施风险管理改革试点。2005年2月1日，上海海关成立了风险分析与监控中心，标志着海关风险管理改革的全面启动。该试点在对进出口企业、商品、行业开展科学的风险评估的基础上，对企业大胆探索实行“放、控、管、评”一体化管理模式。2005年6月，上海海关被海关总署选定为全国海关风险管理应用改革试点之一，这项改革将对守法

evaluating the results". In June 2005, Shanghai Customs was selected as one of several pilot sites for the risk management application by the GACC. This reform aims to reduce interference as much as possible in legitimate international trade.

Fourth, enhance enforcement transparency. The website of Shanghai Customs was launched on July 1, 2001, supported by the Shanghai Model Port Project. The website makes a variety of information available to the public and includes sections on "Customs Laws & Regulations", "Announcements", "Biz Guidance" and "Intellectual Property Rights Protection". All administrative rules concerning traders' rights and obligations are made known to the public one month in advance of implementation. In addition, an online publication, public board, and briefings are provided to help traders better understand, master and apply customs rules. We have also taken steps to further strengthen the availability of administrative information. Top customs officials meet businesspeople and customs officers every Thursday to answer their questions. A "satisfaction-guaranteed solution system" has been set up as a rule to facilitate clearance for companies. At present, the customs clearance system has completed its switchover to H2000 from H883. Such major

企业给予最大的通关便利。

四是增强执法透明度。在“上海示范通关点”项目的支持下，2001年7月1日，上海海关外部网站正式开通，其中涵盖了海关法规、公告、企业指导、知识产权保护等一系列与贸易便利化有关的内容。在实施有关涉及管理相对人权利和义务的管理规定时，都提前一个月对外公告。同时，我们还进一步加强了关务公开的力度，确定每周四为“关长接待日”，实行“首问负责制”的做法，方便了企业。目前，海关的通关系统已完成了由H883向H2000的转换，“电子通关”、税费电子支付系统和“大通关”等项目得到大力推广，海关对信息技术的应用达到了一个新的水平。

projects as "electronic clearance", "electronic payment system" and "Integrated Clearance System" have been promoted vigorously. It is fair to say that the application of information technology in customs has been brought to a new level.

Fifth, promote partnership initiative. The international trade and socio-economic environment are dynamic and changing on a global scale. Globalization has accentuated the need for the seamless movement between different economies. As an important gateway linking China and the world, Shanghai Customs has 44 affiliated branch offices with a total staff of 2,940, which comprises merely 6% of the national total; while its import and export volume constitutes nearly 25% nationwide. In this regard, we have to act in a more resource-efficient way. In order to fulfill the customs' complex role in the economy, partnering with the responsible enterprises has been considered the silver bullet for enhancing more liberalized and facilitated global trade. Small- medium- and large-scale customs-business workshops are held on a regular basis in Shanghai. In order to enhance cooperation, the "big four" express companies and 15 other enterprises have signed Memoranda of Understanding with Shanghai Customs. In addition, efficient channels of

五是促进合作伙伴关系。随着国际贸易与社会经济环境在全球范围的迅猛发展与快速变化，全球化更注重各经济体的无缝链接。作为联系国内外的重要门户，上海海关现有44个隶属部门、2940人，以仅占全国海关6%的人员承担着监管全国进出口货物总值25%的工作量。从这一点来说，我们迫切需要提高人力资源利用率。为了完成海关在经济建设中的任务，与商界建立合作伙伴关系便利全球贸易是一良策。因此，大中小型的关企交流会定期在上海召开。为了加强合作，四大快递公司、15家企业已经与上海海关签订了合作谅解备忘录。另外，与行业协会有效的沟通渠道也已建立，如外商投资企业协会品牌保护委员会、上海外经贸企业协会、上海市商标协会等，旨在加强知识产权的保护。

frequent contact and communication with industrial associations, such as the Quality Brand Protection Committee of the National Foreign Investors Association, the Shanghai Association of Foreign Economic and Trade Enterprises, and the Municipal Trademark Association, have been established to reinforce the protection of Intellectual Property Rights.

Shanghai's foreign trade has maintained a momentum of continuous and rapid growth. In 2004, seaborne trade increased to 380 million tons at Shanghai Port. The container throughput soared to 14.55 million TEU, making it one of the biggest ports in the world. From the perspective of international trade supervision and administration, particularly trade through Shanghai Port, security underpins the realization of facilitation. Without security, trade facilitation cannot be achieved in a real sense. Facilitation and security exist as an inseparable whole that none of them can be dispensed with. Looking ahead, we will step up our efforts in the following aspects:

上海的对外贸易一直保持着迅猛增长的发展动力。2004年，上海港货运量达到3.8亿吨，集装箱吞吐量1455万标准箱，已成为世界级大港。从监管国际贸易，尤其是经过上海港的这一角度来看，贸易安全保证了贸易便利化的实现，而贸易便利化又助推了经济的快速发展。便利和安全是不可分割的整体，缺一不可。下一步，我们还将从以下几个方面继续加大力度：

First, promote administrative openness and enhance customs enforcement transparency. We aim to make our requirements more predictable and our public operating procedures more traceable. In addition to a website and other media, we are planning to intensify our training assistance to enterprises,

第一，大力推进政务公开，提高海关执法的透明度。我们的目标是要使企业对海关的管理要求有更大的预见性，公布的作业流程更具操作性。除通过网站和其他媒介进行公告外，将进一步加强对企业的

teaching them how to deal with customs procedures better.

培训，帮助他们更好地办理海关手续。

Second, continue to press ahead with the progress of information-based customs clearance. We will endeavor to promote network data exchange with relevant port authorities and enterprises and improve related functions of the Shanghai E-port. Consequently, the automatic clearance data processing capability will be further upgraded.

第二，继续推进海关通关作业的信息化进程。我们将努力促进与口岸通关相关政府部门和企业的数据联网交换，不断完善上海电子口岸的相关功能，以进一步提高海关通关数据的自动化处理能力。

Third, implement risk management and advance customs modernization. In the next two years, we aim to improve the governance structure of planning, control and execution processes from top to bottom, and improve the operational risk management body, the "Risk Analysis and Supervision Center", with a credit rating system as its core component. Risk management will be composed of four consecutive stages including risk identification, risk analysis, execution and evaluation in an active cycle.

第三，全面实施风险管理，推进海关管理的现代化。接下来的两年，我们的目标是从上到下，改善计划、控制、执行的管理结构，以企业诚信守法管理为核心，完善风险管理的操作实体——"风险分析与监控中心"。通过风险信息的收集、识别、处置和评估四个环节，整体推进风险管理试点。

Fourth, reinforce capacity building in law enforcement. We are attempting to improve management and customize training for customs officers for the purpose of augmenting the uniformity of enforcement and quality of service, and to build a clean customs.

第四，努力加强执法能力建设。我们努力加强对海关关员的管理，并且制定完整的培训计划，保持执法的统一性和提高监管和服务质量，确保队伍清正廉洁。

Shanghai, as one of the most important open cities along the coast, is forging its way

上海作为中国极其重要的沿海开放城市，正在朝着建

towards the ultimate goal of developing into an international economic, finance, trade and shipping center. Shanghai Customs will work resolutely to reinforce its political stance, improve operations and augment its capabilities in the interest of domestic and international development and trade facilitation.

设国际经济、金融、贸易和航运中心的目标迈进。上海海关将坚定不移地加强政治、业务和能力建设，为国内经济的发展、国际贸易的便利化发挥我们应有的作用。

加强关企对话　推动共赢合作

——会晤中国美商会主席

2015年8月15日

Enhance Customs-Business Dialogue and Advance Win-win Cooperation

——Meeting with the President of AmCham China

August 15, 2015

On August 11, 2015, Mr. Mark Duval, the president of the American chamber of commerce in China, headed his delegation to visit the General Administration of China Customs (GACC) again in Beijing. I, accompanied by my customs colleagues, met with them and exchanged views in the meeting room.

2015年8月11日，中国美国商会主席马克·杜凡先生一行再次在京前来拜访海关总署。我和我的同事一起与他们见面并相互交换了意见。

2015年8月，北京，会见中国美国商会会长一行。

August 2015, meeting with President of AmCham China.

The AmCham China is a very important organization which represents more than 3000 U.S. enterprises in China. After having greeted each other, we began to talk about some issues which were both concerned about in the annual *White Paper* 2014 of AmCham. The annual White Paper not only showed AmCham China's attention and support on customs work, but also included problems encountered by businesses that might emerge during customs enforcement and issues that might need further explanation. China Customs always highly values the proposals in the White Paper.

中国美国商会代表了3000多家在华美资企业。双方寒暄之后，我们进入正题，讨论了2014年美商会白皮书中提及的相关问题。白皮书中所涉问题，不仅体现企业对海关工作的关注重点和支持，也包括了企业对海关执法中可能遇到的问题，或需要海关作进一步解释的事项。中国海关一贯非常重视白皮书中的建议。

One year has passed since our last meeting. As far as is known, the members of AmCham China did a good job last year. According to China Customs statistics, the bilateral trade between China and U.S. amounted to USD 555 billion last year, with a year-on-year increase of 6.5%. In the first half of this year, the bilateral number stood at USD 266.72 billion, with an increase of 4%. And foreign-invested enterprises accounted for more than half the proportion of China-U.S. bilateral trade. All this data has shown that our bilateral trade, as the largest two economies in the world, has maintained good momentum. It is even more delightful that those results were achieved against the background of the great downward pressure facing by Chinese economy and foreign trade. We were fully convinced that AmCham

自从上次会面以来已过去一年。据了解，中国美国商会成员去年业绩斐然。根据中国海关统计数据表明，去年中美双边贸易达到5550亿美元，同比增长6.5%。今年上半年，双边贸易量2667.2亿美元，同比增长幅度4%。外资企业在中美双边贸易中占比过半。所有这些数据显示，作为世界上前两大经济体，中美双边贸易保持良好势头。令人欣慰的是，在中国经济和外贸面临双重下滑压力的大背景下，中美双边贸易依然取得良好

China contributed a lot to this engagement. I hope for the great development of both American enterprises doing business in China and Chinese enterprises operating in the U.S. in the future with our sincere cooperation.

成绩。我们相信中国美国商会从中作出了大量的努力。希望通过海关与商界的真诚合作，美国在华企业和中国在美投资企业都能够在未来取得长足发展。

At the end of May this year, China Customs held a Forum for Heads of Customs Administrations along the Belt and Road in Xi'an with the theme of "Connectivity and Win-Win Development". Member companies of AmCham China , such as Dell corporation，also attended relevant activities. It was a good way for us to hear about comments from the enterprises and to exchange views and ideas for further development.

今年5月底，中国海关在西安召开了"一带一路"沿线国家和地区的海关高层论坛，该论坛主题为"互联互通，共赢发展"。中国美国商会企业成员，如戴尔公司等也参加了相关活动。这为我们倾听企业呼声，相互交流意见和建议提供了良好的平台。

In June this year, the seventh round of China-U.S. Strategic and Economic Dialogue was successfully held in Washington DC. China and U.S. Customs have contributed altogether more than 10 outcomes to the dialogue in the economic and strategic tracks. This September, China and U.S. presidents will meet in the U.S. Therefore, the bilateral trade and economic development between the two countries will face new opportunities.

今年6月，第七次中美战略和经济对话成功地在美国华盛顿召开。中美海关在经济和战略双轨道对话中贡献了十大合作成果。今年9月，两国元首还将在美国举行会晤。所以中美双边经贸发展将迎来新的机遇。

Focusing on the White Paper, the U.S. side raised 22 questions related to customs matters last year. Our relevant departments of China Customs gave the written feedbacks to AmCham China after the meeting. This time, the U.S.

去年，美资企业在白皮书中就海关工作提出了22个问题。海关总署相关司局会后书面回复了中国美国商

side put forward 20 specific questions again and followed up with some suggestions related to 7 major aspects, including customs clearance, inspection, classification and valuation, enterprise management, processing trade and bonded supervision, customs legal affairs, customs charges and trade statistics as well. And some of the questions were also involved with science and technology.

会。这次美方又提出了20个具体问题，并从七个方面提出了具体建议。这七个方面包括海关通关、查验、归类估价、企业管理、加工贸易保税监管、海关法规、税费和统计。有些问题也涉及科技。

According to Mr. Mark Duval's remarks, his advocacy was focused on four critical areas: market access, standards, IPR, as well as the rule of law, in terms of credibility, transparency and consistent enforcement of the law. With the good cooperation, we both were able to bring more integration, more consistency, more credibility and more efficiency into the whole import and export process. These were the things that could bring substantial development for the businesses.

根据马克·杜凡先生的介绍，他所谈的主要集中在四个方面：一是市场准入；二是标准化；三是知识产权；四是法制，即在诚信、透明和协调一致的执法方面。通过我们良好的合作，双方真切感受到进出口环节中的业务更为协调、统一、诚信、高效。这些对贸易发展会有实实在在的促进。

The communication was very smooth. President Duval added some points toward the end of the meeting. First, he thanked China customs for giving the great support to U.S. companies operating in China and appreciated the good relationship between China Customs and AmCham China. He invited me to attend the appreciation dinner on December 4th this year and looked forward to listening to my speech there.

这次会晤双方沟通十分顺畅。马克·杜凡主席最后补充了几点，感谢中国海关对美资在华企业所给予的支持，以及中国海关和美国商会之间的良好合作关系。他还邀请我参加今年12月4日举办的答谢晚宴，并期待我在晚宴上的发言。

I then responded to his comments. First, I

highly appreciated our good relationship and the successful work. Then I said, "If a government agency only likes to hear words of praise, rather than critical views or proposals, it is definitely not an open administration. In order to meet the requirements of market development, China Customs has intensified our reforms, especially in terms of a top-level design plan and the operational systems. The reform should be problem-oriented. In the meantime, market economy is run by rules. Everyone is equal before the law."

I continued, "As a government agency supervising on imports and exports, China Customs also needs to transform its functions. We should often listen to the suggestions and proposals from the enterprises and do our best to solve the problems for the business, such as the enforcement consistency, clearance speed, the customs charges which are related to the cost of enterprises and their compliance. "

I concluded with sincerity that the proposals and suggestions that AmCham China raised in the White Paper were inspiring to us, which meant we still had room for improvement. Next, we will give them a closer review as soon as possible and we will discuss the issues with the business to address their concern and find a lawful and appropriate solution.

我对此做了回应。首先，我对双方良好合作关系以及双方所取得的合作成果表示了赞赏。随后，我说，"如果一个政府机关仅是喜欢听好话，而不愿接受批评意见或建议，这绝对不是一个开明的政府。根据市场发展要求，中国海关已加大改革力度，特别是顶层设计和运作体系。改革应是以问题为导向。同时，市场经济是按规则运作的，在法律面前人人平等"。

我继续表明，"作为国家进出境执法监管机构，中国海关也需要转变政府职能。我们应倾听企业的意见和建议，并努力解决企业的难题，例如执法统一问题，通关速度问题以及与企业成本和守法相关的税费问题"。

最后，我真诚表示，中国美国商会在白皮书中所提意见和建议我们会高度重视，这说明我们依然有改进工作空间。下一步我们会尽快研究，与企业共同商量，依法有据、合情合理地解决

Regular exchanges between AmCham China and China Customs benefit both sides. On the one hand, it is a good way for customs to know the requirements of the enterprises clearly and directly, so as to address their problems and help them grow; on the other hand, it is conducive to taking in suggestions of companies and the society to improve our work. Therefore, it is mutually-beneficial and win-win cooperation.

企业关注的实际问题。

中国美国商会和中国海关之间的定期沟通机制让双方受益。一方面，这是海关能真切而直接了解企业需求的好渠道，十分有助于解决企业的实际问题，进一步促进企业的发展；另一方面，也有利于海关倾听企业和社会的意见，改进我们的工作。这是互利共赢的。

访问哈萨克斯坦和俄罗斯海关

2014 年 9 月 25 日

A Visit to Kazakhstan and Russian Customs

September 25, 2014

September 11-17, 2014, I led the Chinese Customs delegation to visit Kazakhstan and Russian Customs.

In Kazakhstan, I met with the Chairman of Kazakhstan Customs in Alma-Ata. We had a meeting on port entry and customs there.

China and Kazakhstan have always been good neighbors that embrace traditional friendship, frequent personnel exchanges, and close economic and trade ties. In September 2013, President Xi Jinping paid a successful visit to Kazakhstan, which brought the bilateral relations and cooperation in various fields to a new height and opened up a new prospect

2014年9月11日至17日，我率中国海关代表团访问了哈萨克斯坦海关和俄罗斯海关。

在哈萨克斯坦阿拉木图，我会见了哈萨克斯坦海关委员会主席。我们举行了双边口岸和海关工作会谈。

中国和哈萨克斯坦是友好邻国，传统友谊深厚，人员交往频繁，经贸关系密切。2013年9月，习近平主席成功访问了哈萨克斯坦，将两国关系和各领域合作上升到了新的高度，打开了全面战略合作伙伴关系新局面。目前，中国是

for our comprehensive strategic partnership. Currently, China is Kazakhstan's largest trading partner, while Kazakhstan is China's largest trading partner in Central Asia, and there exists broad prospect and great potential for our bilateral cooperation.

哈萨克斯坦最大的贸易伙伴国，哈萨克斯坦也是中国最大的中亚贸易伙伴国，两国存在广阔的合作前景和巨大的合作潜力。

In regard to customs cooperation, we have signed three important documents, respectively related to facilitating customs control and clearance, foreign trade statistics methods and information, and a cooperation program in customs and port of entry for 2014-2018. We reached consensus on pushing forward cooperation in joint supervision, information exchange, statistics analysis, Green Channel for fast clearance of agricultural products, AEO mutual recognition, training, etc. We also agreed to maintain the normal operation of border crossings and improve the management on port of entry.

在海关合作方面，中哈两国已经签署了三份重要合作文件，分别关于加强海关监管和通关便利化、对外贸易统计方法和信息以及一份2014—2018年海关和口岸合作计划。我们还就开展联合监管、信息交流、统计分析、农产品快速通关“绿色通道”、AEO互认、培训等领域合作达成了共识，并一致同意确保边境口岸的正常运行，不断提升口岸管理水平。

会见俄罗斯、哈萨克斯坦、乌兹别克斯坦、吉尔吉斯斯坦海关署署长（从左到右）

Meeting Heads of Customs from Russia, Kazakhstan, Uzbekistan, Kyrgyzstan (left to right).

In Russia, I attended the Sixth Meeting of Customs Cooperation Sub-committee which is under the framework of China-Russia Prime Ministers' Regular Meeting Committee. The meeting was held in Sochi where the Winter Olympics were held this year. Facing the Black Sea with mountains covered with red grass in the background, what a beautiful city it is! We enjoyed everything there with our friends from Russian Customs.

在俄罗斯，我参加了中俄总理定期会晤委员会海关合作分委会第六次会议。会议在今年冬季奥运会的举办地索契召开。面对黑海，背靠红山，索契确实是一座美丽的城市。与俄罗斯海关的各位同仁一道，我们在索契度过了愉快而难忘的时光。

At the meeting, we jointly reviewed the achievements of China-Russia customs cooperation:

会上，我们共同回顾了中俄海关合作成果：

1. We had further improved mech-anisms. The number of working groups increased from three to seven under the framework of the Sub-committee, adding to the expert groups affiliated to each working group. The joint meeting of three customs and two bureaus further completed the cooperation mechanism between border customs.

第一，机制进一步完善。分委会框架下的工作组数量从三个增加到了七个，另外还有各工作组项下的专家组。“三关两局”联席会议也进一步完善了边境海关间的合作机制。

2. We had diversified contents of cooperation. Our cooperation had gone beyond the traditional fields such as customs statistics, enforcement and control, and extended to new areas such as IPR customs protection, price information exchange, education and training, risk management, AEO mutual recognition, etc. Almost every aspect of customs operations is now covered.

第二，内容更多元化。我们的合作已经超过了传统的海关统计、执法和监管，扩展到了更多新领域，例如知识产权海关保护、价格信息交流、教育培训、风险管理、AEO互认等，可以说覆盖了海关业务的方方面面。

3. We had made more concrete achie-vements. Based on operations exchange and experience sharing, our cooperation attached more importance to the tangible trade facilitation the enterprises could enjoy, such as mutual recognition of customs control results, information exchange, Green Channel, etc.

第三，成果更务实。在业务交流和经验分享的基础上，我们的合作更加侧重于让企业享受到实实在在的贸易便利，例如海关监管结果互认、信息交换、“绿色通道”等。

4. We had adjusted priority according to actual needs. The prioritized area of our cooperation has transferred from regulating the order of customs control and clearance to promoting trade security and facilitation, so as to strike a balance between effective customs supervision and efficient customs clearance.

第四，按照实际需求调整合作重点。双方的合作优先领域已经从加强海关监管和通关秩序变为促进贸易安全与便利，以平衡有效监管和高效通关间的关系。

China Customs' statistics showed that from January to July 2014, imports and exports between China and Russia valued at US$53 billion, up by 4% percent year-on-year, which contributed 2.2% to China's total foreign trade. As Russia remains China's 9th largest trading partner, the two sides enjoy sound bilateral trade basis and momentum. Since its establishment, the Sub-committee has been playing an increasingly important role. The two sides should seize this historic opportunity and further deepen all-round cooperation, so as to achieve the goal set by our presidents that the bilateral trade volume should reach US$100 billion by 2015.

中国海关统计数据显示，2014年1月至7月，中俄两国进出口总值达到530亿美元，同比增长4%，占中国对外贸易总量的2.2%。随着俄罗斯继续成为中国第九大贸易伙伴，双边贸易拥有着良好的基础和强大动力。自海关合作分委会成立以来，该组织正在发挥越来越重要的作用。双方应抓住这一历史机遇，进一步深化全面合作，努力实现两国元首设定的2015年双边贸易额达到1000亿美元的目标。

Before I flew to Hong Kong, I stopped

在飞赴香港之前，我在

in Moscow for one and a half days. I visited the headquarters of Russian Customs and had a friendly discussion with Mr. Andrey Belyaninov, Russia's Customs Minister.

莫斯科停留了一天半的时间。其间，我访问了俄罗斯海关总部，并与俄罗斯海关署长安德烈·别利亚尼诺夫举行了友好会谈。

To further enhance China-Russia customs cooperation, we reached some important consensus as follows:

为进一步加强中俄海关合作，我们达成了如下重要共识：

1. Promote the integration between the Silk Road Economic Belt and the Eurasian Economic Union. Last fall, President Xi Jinping proposed to build the "Silk Road Economic Belt" and "21st Century Maritime Silk Road", which attracted great attention of the international community. President Putin also expressed on many occasions his support for the construction of the "Silk Road Economic Belt" and infrastructure connectivity, and the co-development with the Eurasian Economic Union (EAEU).

第一，促进"丝绸之路经济带"与欧亚经济联盟间的对接。去年秋天，习近平主席提出了建设"丝绸之路经济带"和"21世纪海上丝绸之路"的倡议，受到了国际社会的广泛关注。普京总统也多次表示支持建设"丝绸之路经济带"，加强基础设施互联互通，并推进与欧亚经济联盟的对接。

2. Promote trade facilitation. Russia Customs is undergoing reforms in electronic customs declaration and risk management, which coincides with China Customs' Paperless Clearance Reform and risk management regime. We should highlight the cooperation in information exchange and develop the Green Channel, in order to make full use and gradually expand the application of the mutual recognition of customs control results.

第二，促进贸易便利化。俄罗斯海关正在推进电子报关和风险管理改革，这与中国海关的无纸化通关改革和风险管理制度不谋而合。我们应该着力开展在信息交流合作，发展"绿色通道"，充分利用并逐步扩大海关监管结果互认的应用范围。

3. Strengthen border customs cooperation. As our two governments put more efforts in developing Northeast China and Russia's Far East and East Siberia, we should seize the strategic opportunity, practically implement the Border Customs Cooperation Program, and make sure the right person delivers right solutions for problems at critical moments.

第三，加强边境海关合作。随着中国政府加大力度振兴东北、俄罗斯政府致力于推进远东和东西伯利亚地区经济发展，我们应该牢牢把握战略机遇，务实开展边境海关合作计划，确保在关键时候办得成事。

4. Coordinate on bilateral and multilateral issues. We should continue to enhance coordination under the framework of the SCO, APEC, BRICS and the WCO, jointly push forward regional customs cooperation, and play a more important role in promoting regional economic and trade security and facilitation.

第四，加强多双边问题协调。我们应该继续在上海合作组织、亚太经合组织、金砖国家和世界海关组织框架下的相互协调，共同推动区域海关合作，在促进区域经济和贸易安全与便利方面扮演更重要的角色。

5. Implement the meeting outcomes. We should formulate feasible working plans in the order of importance and emergency. Targeting the existing challenges, workable solutions should be developed immediately and carried out step by step.

第五，落实会议成果。我们应该根据事项的重要性和紧迫性，制定可行的工作计划，并针对现有挑战，立即着手研究切实可行的解决方案并逐步推进实施。

The visit was a complete success.

此次出访取得了圆满成功。

中美海关共促经贸发展　同享互利共赢

2015年5月6日

China and U.S. Customs: Promoting Trade for Mutual Benefits

May 6, 2015

In 2013, the two heads of states met at Sunnylands, California, and proposed the establishment of a new type of major country relations with "no conflict and no confrontation, mutual respect and win-win cooperation". The heads of states met again in Beijing during the APEC meeting last year and exchanged in-depth views on important issues in our relations.

2013年，两国元首在加州安纳伯格庄园会晤，提出了建立“不冲突、不对抗、相互尊重、合作共赢”的新型大国关系。去年在北京APEC会议期间，两国元首再次见面，就涉及双边关系的一些重要问题深入交换了意见。

According to Chinese Customs statistics, in 2013, the total value of bilateral trade broke the record of 500 billion US dollars, creating a new record of 521 billion US dollars, an increase of 7.5%. It is 200 times as many as the number we had at the beginning of the establishment of

据中国海关统计，2013年，中美双边贸易总额突破了5000亿美元，达到了5210亿美元的新纪录，增长7.5%。这一数字是中美建交时的200倍。从2014年1月

diplomatic relations. From January to October 2014, bilateral trade amounted to 452.92 billion US dollars, an increase of 6.9%. Bilateral cooperation in the area of investment was also fruitful, as China continued to be the major investment destination of U.S. enterprises. China also invested more than 30 billion US dollars in the U.S., covering more than 40 states and creating nearly 30,000 local jobs.

Last month, Mr. Alan D. Bersin, Assistant Secretary and Chief Diplomatic Officer of the U.S. Department of Homeland Security (DHS) visited China for the purpose of co-chairing the Joint Liaison Group (JLG) Meeting in Beijing with the Ministry of Public Security. Meanwhile, according to his schedule, he would visit the GACC and the Supreme People's Court, accompanied by Mr. Thomas S. Winkowski who is now the Acting Director General of the U.S. Immigration and Customs Enforcement (ICE).

Customs cooperation, as the integral part of our bilateral relations and economic cooperation, needed to be deepened and expanded, in order to made new contributions to stabilizing trade growth, providing facilitated environment for compliant traders. In order to further promote China-U.S. customs cooperation and jointly build mutual beneficial economic and trade relationship between the two countries, I met Mr. Bersin, Assistant Secretary of the DHS. During

到10月，双边贸易额已达4529.2亿美元，比上年又增长6.9%。两国在投资领域的合作也是卓有成效。中国继续成为美国企业的主要投资目的地，同时中国也在美国投资300多亿美元，覆盖40多个州，为当地创造近3万个工作就业岗位。

上个月，美国国土安全部的部长助理兼首席外事官艾伦·博森先生访问了中国，并在北京与公安部共同主持了中美执法合作联合联络小组的会议。同时，根据来访行程，他将在美国移民和海关执法局执行局长托马斯·温考斯基的陪同下，访问中国海关总署和最高人民法院。

海关合作，作为我双边关系和经济合作的重要部分，需要继续深化和扩大，为双方守法企业提供便利的通关环境，为稳定贸易增长作出贡献。为进一步推动中美海关合作，共促互利共赢的中美经贸关系，我与美国国土安全部的部长助理博森先生在北京举行了会谈。会晤中，

the meeting, we reviewed the priorities of our cooperation in the following two aspects:

双方共同回顾了我们合作的重点。主要有以下两个方面：

In the first part, we evaluated China–U.S. customs cooperation.

首先，对中美海关合作进行评估。

Over the years, the General Administration of China Customs and the U.S. Department of Homeland Security (DHS), along with the U.S. Customs and Border Protection (CBP) and the U.S. Immigration and Customs Enforcement (ICE) under the DHS have actively served the China-U.S. trade and economic development, promoted China-U.S. supply chain security and facilitation and other pragmatic cooperation and achieved positive progress.

多年以来，中国海关总署和美国国土安全部及其下属的美国海关和边境保护局、美国移民和海关执法局开展了积极合作，有效地促进了中美贸易和经济发展，维护了中美供应链安全和便利，其他一些务实的合作项目也取得了可喜成效。

For example, we established a smooth communication mechanism to participate in high-level China-U.S. Strategic and Economic Dialogue and conducted ministerial-level dialogues with the DHS. We have carried out pragmatic cooperation with the "Container Security Initiative" (CSI), "Customs-Trade Partnership Against Terrorism" (C-TPAT) and "Authorized Economic Operators" (AEO) mutual recognition, and cooperated in the areas of joint training, border enforcement of intellectual property rights and the fight against contraband smuggling.

例如，我们在中美战略与经济对话中建立了一个畅通的沟通机制，与美国国土安全部进行部长级的对话。我们已经在“集装箱安全倡议”（CSI）、“海关商贸反恐计划”（C–TPAT）、“经认证的经营者”（AEO）互认方面开展了务实的合作，并在联合培训、知识产权边境保护和打击走私违法活动等方面开展合作。

In the second part, we exchanged some important views on areas of cooperation. Both sides admitted that GACC and DHS were

其次，我们就合作领域一些重要问题交换了意见。双方承认中国海关总署和美

important agencies for safeguarding China-US supply chain security and facilitation. To implement the strategic consensus of building a new type of major country relations, we should further improve the effectiveness of customs supervision and service and serve bilateral trade better.

国国土安全部都是维护中美供应链安全与便利的重要部门。为实现构建两国战略性的新型大国关系的共识，我们应该进一步改进海关监管和服务效能，更好地为双边贸易服务。

Through in-depth and friendly discussions, we reached consensus on future cooperation in the following aspects:

这一次，经双方深入沟通和友好会晤，我们对下一步加强合作又达成了以下共识：

1）In conjunction with high-level China-U.S. Strategic and Economic Dialogue in 2015, we should further deepen communication at the ministerial level to provide guidance for pragmatic customs cooperation.

第一，围绕2015年中美高层战略与经济对话，应进一步加强部长级层面的沟通交流，就深化海关务实合作提出指导性意见。

2) Move forward the cooperation in CSI, we should accelerate the negotiations on the placement of China Customs officers to U.S. ports and study on expanding the scope of information exchange and extending CSI to new ports so as to enhance the overall effectiveness of the CSI cooperation with the U.S. side for mutual benefits.

第二，积极推进CSI合作，加快中方向美有关港口派驻海关工作人员进程、扩大信息交换和拓展实施CSI新港口范围，以利于强化和做到全面效果，实现互利共赢。

3) Promote the cooperation on C-TPAT joint validation and AEO mutual recognition, we should work together more closely. From 2008 to September 2014, China Customs and CBP conducted 11 rounds of C-TPAT joint validation, through which 361 Chinese suppliers of U.S.

第三，进一步加强合作，促进海关与商界反恐计划项下的联合验证和经认证的经营者互认合作。自2008年至2014年9月，中国海关与美国海关与边境保护局开

enterprises were jointly validated, among which 290 passed the validation and were granted certificates. The passing rate reached 80.3%. The certified enterprises could enjoy clearance facilitation, such as a lower inspection rate, while going through the U.S. Customs procedures.

展了11轮联合验证，对361家美国企业中国供应商进行了验证，其中290家通过验证，通过率达到80.3%。通过验证的企业可以享受美国海关快速通关和更低的查验率。

4) Promote customs enforcement cooperation, we should continue to cooperate in IPR enforcement. Both sides hope to sign the Addendum regarding IPR Enforcement Cooperation with ICE as soon as possible and carry out a joint operation targeting counterfeit auto parts, focusing on drugs concealed in parcels and the smuggling of guns, endangered species and their products, and capitalizing on the platform offered by JLG so as to intensify intelligence exchange and combat smuggling effectively.

第四，继续加强中美海关知识产权执法合作。双方希望通过中国海关与美国移民和海关执法局尽早签署《知识产权执法合作附录》，并开展打击假冒汽车配件联合执法行动，集中打击邮包毒品走私，利用联合工作组平台，加强情报交换，有效打击走私违法。

5) Promote Joint Training Program, we should conduct tailored training for professionals within the available resources and discuss to build a long-term cooperation mechanism as well as share experiences on reforms, including the practices in the fields of risk management, Single Window, paperless clearance, and cross-border e-commerce supervision. We should establish direct communication between colleges and schools, share training experiences and expand communication of trainers.

第五，促进联合培训，在现有资源范围内对专业人员进行量身定制的培训，讨论建立长期的合作机制，分享改革经验，包括风险管理、“单一窗口”、无纸化通关、跨境电子商务监管等实践。我们应该建立院校之间的直接沟通，分享培训经验，扩大培训员的交流。

The China-U.S. Customs Joint Training Program was launched in August 2012. Experts from both sides paid mutual visits and learned each other's inspection systems, clearance procedures and risk management systems. Until May 2014, 5 training courses were held in China and 2 in the U.S., with topics concerning the interception of maritime cargos and air cargos. Over 200 participants benefited from this program.

中美海关联合培训计划在2012年8月启动。来自双方的专家进行了互访，相互学习了监管系统、通关程序和风险管理系统。直到2014年5月，双方在中国完成了五门围绕海上和空运货运拦截的培训课程，在美国完成两门，共有200人参与。

2015年4月，北京，会见美国国土安全部部长助理艾伦·博森。

April 2015, Beijing. with Dr. Alan Bersin, Assistant Secretary of the U.S. DHS

Mutual beneficial relations are at the center of China-U.S. bilateral trade and economic cooperation. I sincerely hope that the China-U.S. customs cooperation could continue on a more substantial and stable course, so as to contribute more to the sound economic and trade development of two countries and the world.

互利共赢是中美经贸关系的本质。衷心希望中美海关合作能够越走越实、越走越稳，为两国乃至全球经贸健康发展作出更大的贡献。

与英国海关签订海关行政互助协定

2015 年 10 月 23 日

The Customs Mutual Administrative Assistance Agreement with UK Customs

October 23, 2015

On Oct. 21, 2015, heads of the General Administration of China Customs (GACC) and Her Majesty's Revenue and Customs (HMRC) signed the *Customs Mutual Administrative Assistance Agreement* (CMAA Agreement) under the witness of the leaders of two states in London.

2015年10月21日，在中英两国领导人的见证下，中国海关总署和英国皇家税务海关署在伦敦签署了两国海关行政互助协定。

Under the *Mutual Administrative Assistance Agreement in Customs Matters* signed by GACC and EU Customs in 2004, and the *China-EU IPR Action Plan*, this was the first legal document of bilateral administrative cooperation with UK customs, mainly focusing on combating the trafficking of illicit and counterfeit tobacco products. Both sides

根据2004年签署的中欧海关行政互助合作协定框架和《中欧知识产权行动计划》，这是我们和英国海关签署的第一份双边行政互助合作的法律文件，主要是针对打击非法、假冒香烟制品走私，开展知识产权边境保护。双方就以下行

reached consensus on the following matter.

动计划达成一致：

I. Purpose of action

一、行动目的

The Agreement supplements the Memorandum of Understanding for cooperation between the GACC and HMRC, acting through its Fiscal Crime Liaison Officer Network in preventing, detecting, suppressing, and investigating infringements and breaches of Customs Legislation. It sets out the Participants' understanding of how to share information, intelligence and feedback related to infringements and breaches of Customs Legislation with a view to ensuring the proper application of Customs Legislation.

该互助协定是中英海关通过打击财政犯罪联络官网络开展行动，防止、甄别、抑制和调查违反海关法律的行为。该协定为参与方界定了针对涉及违反海关法律行为共享信息、情报和反馈的方法，以确保规范海关执法。

II. Areas of action

二、行动范围

This Agreement relates to infringements and breaches of Customs legislation within the Participants' competence at the date of commencement of this Agreement, namely the evasion of revenue, specifically the smuggling, or unlawful handling of cigarettes, tobacco products and other dutiable goods including combating the infringement of intellectual property rights and related conduct.

自签署该协定之日起，双方将共同打击违反海关法律的行为，包括：逃税，特别是走私或非法贩运香烟、烟草制品和其他应税货物、侵犯知识产权等有关行为。

III. Operational and Strategic Information

三、操作层面和战略层面的信息交换

Both sides will share information for the purposes of tackling the infringements. This information may be operational or strategic in nature and both Participants agree to provide

参与方将共享打击侵权货物信息。该信息可以是操作层面的或者战略性的，双方同意反馈共享信息后所取得的成

feedback on the outcome of the information shared. "Operational Information" includes, but is not limited to information which is obtained in the course of any of the Participant's duties where the information may have relevance to another Participant. "Strategic Information" includes, but is not limited to Information about: enforcement actions that might be useful to prevent infringements and, in particular means of addressing conduct which breaches Customs Legislation, risk analysis indicators and new methods used in contravening Customs Legislation as well.

果。操作层面信息包括（但不局限于）任意一方执法时所获取的可能与另一方有关联的信息。战略层面信息包括（但不局限于）有助于防止违法，特别是打击违反海关法行为、风险分析指标以及制止新型违法手段等执法行动。

IV. Feedback of actions

Both sides agreed to monitor intelligence, information and assistance provided in order to exchange regular feedback on outcomes to include, but not limited to: Customs declaration information regarding specific consignments; notification of seizures, detentions or any other action taken as a result of information or intelligence received, either through the identification of directly linked consignments or indirectly through the mutual facilitation of risk analysis; commodity detected, brand and quantity seized or detained.

四、执行结果的反馈

参与方同意对情报、信息和互助行动进行跟进，定期交换所取得的成果。反馈成果包括（但不局限于）：特定货物的海关具体申报信息；查获、扣留信息，或任何因信息或情报以及通过直接货物识别或间接风险分析而采取的行动；查获的货物、品牌和数量。

V. Form of Co-operation

Co-operation and the exchange of Information or feedback under this Agreement may be requested or initiated by either

五、合作形式

协定框架下的合作、信息交换或反馈可以由任意一方通过邮件或信函提出。在该协定

Participant via email or letter. Upon receipt of a request under this Agreement, the requested Participant will issue an acknowledgement within 5 working days or as soon as operationally practicable. The requested Participant will then provide a full, formal response to the requesting Participant within 20 working days of the initial request.

框架下收到有关请求后，被请求方需在五个工作日内或尽快反馈收到信息。在收到请求后20个工作日内，被请求方要向请求方正式回复。

VI. Co-operation content

The cooperation between the two sides may include the following:

(1) spontaneous sharing of Operational and Strategic Information; particularly in relation to trafficking of cigarettes and tobacco products;

(2) development and application of Information provided by any Participant under this Agreement;

(3) the detaining and controlling of cigarette and tobacco shipments which are identified as suspicious, in accordance with national legislation, which are imported, stored, or transited through the territory of the Participants or which are within free or bonded Customs zones in the jurisdiction of the Participants;

(4) Feedback on the outcome of any intelligence, information or assistance provided, including notification of the brand and quantity of tobacco goods seized or

六、具体合作内容

双方合作将包括以下具体内容：

（1）主动分享操作和战略信息，特别是涉及香烟和烟草制品走私的信息。

（2）充分利用任意一方在协定框架下提供的信息。

（3）根据各自国家法律赋予的职权，查获或监控在进口、存储、转关环节，或在自贸园区和保税区中的可疑香烟和烟草。

（4）反馈情报、信息或互助的结果，包括查获烟草的品牌、数量。

detained.

In addition to the above, the Agreement also detailed the national contact points, exchange information, special types of assistance and controlled deliveries and miscellaneous matters as well.

此外，协定还具体规定了国家层面的联络点、所需交换的信息，互助类型、控制下交付和其他各项事宜。

Actually, China Customs had carried out the effective cooperation with UK Customs in 2008. In 2010, the UK Customs seized 6 cases of smuggling cigarette containers with the information offered by China Customs. In May 2015, British customs seized a series of tobacco smuggling cases with more than 21 million cigarettes, 12411 kg of hand-rolling tobacco and 660 kg bulk tobacco, saving 2.2 million pounds of tax losses, assisted by China customs through offering information in time. The British side specially expressed their appreciation to China Customs.

事实上，中国海关自2008年起就已开始和英国海关开展合作。2010年英国海关查获的六起集装箱香烟走私案件，所有信息均来自中国海关。2015年5月，英国海关查获一系列香烟走私案件，共查获2100万条香烟，12411公斤卷烟，660公斤烟草，挽回了220万英镑的税收损失，这些都是通过中国海关及时提供有关信息而使合作方查获的。英方对此表示感谢。

Signing the CMAA Agreement will be conducive to strengthening the cooperation in customs enforcement between China Customs and UK Customs so as to maintain security and facilitation of bilateral supply chain.

这次我们正式签署中英海关行政互助协定将有助于进一步推动加强两国海关执法合作，保障双边贸易供应链的安全和便利。

中美高层对话中的海关合作成果

2016年6月7日

Customs Cooperation in High-level China-U.S. Dialogues

June 7, 2016

The joint opening ceremony of the Eighth Round of China-U.S. Strategic and Economic Dialogues and the Seventh Round of China-U.S. High-Level Consultation on People-to-People Exchange was held in Beijing on June 6. Chinese Vice-Premier Wang Yang and Chinese State Councilor Yang Jiechi co-hosted the Strategic and Economic Dialogue with U.S. Secretary of State John Kerry and U.S. Treasury Secretary Jacob Lew.

第八轮中美战略与经济对话和第七轮中美人文交流高层磋商6月6日在北京举行。中国国务院副总理汪洋和国务委员杨洁篪与美国国务卿约翰·克里和美国财政部长雅各布·卢共同主持战略与经济对话。

At the two-day event — the high-level formal dialogue between the world's top two economies — more than 100 agreements and deals were signed in strategic areas and more than 60 in economic sectors. As a member of

这次为期两天的会议，是世界上最大两个经济体之间高级别的正式对话，会上共签署了100多个战略领域协议以及60多个经济领域协议和合约。

the Chinese Delegation, the GACC proactively participated in the strategic and economic dialogues. After intensive and pragmatic discussions, China Customs and U.S. Customs and Border Protection reached a list of consensus. Among the 120 outcomes in the strategic dialogue, 6 are from China and U.S. Customs. They are:

海关总署作为中方代表团成员单位，积极参与战略和经济轨道的对话。经过紧张而又务实的工作，中美海关取得了一系列合作成果。据统计，在战略对话轨道中，中美双方共达成了120项实质性成果，其中，中国海关与美国海关贡献了六个合作成果，分别是：

1. Customs Cooperation on Supply Chain Security and Facilitation: The General Administration of Customs of the People's Republic of China (GACC) and the U.S. Department of Homeland Security (DHS) decided to sign the *Joint Statement on Global Supply Chain Security and Facilitation* in 2016 to enhance their cooperation mechanism on safeguarding the supply chain security and promoting trade facilitation.

1. **中美海关供应链安全与便利合作：**中国海关总署和美国国土安全部决定2016年内签署《关于全球供应链安全与便利的联合声明》，加强双方在维护供应链安全和促进贸易便利领域的机制化合作。

2.Customs Law Enforcement: The GACC, the Department of Homeland Security's Immigration and Customs Enforcement (DHS/ICE) and the U.S. Drug Enforcement Administration (DEA) decided to continue their regular cooperation in fighting against the smuggling of arms and ammunitions, drugs, endangered species of wild fauna and flora and its product, and solid wastes, cracking down on commercial frauds, establishing a long-term cooperation mechanism and actively carrying

2. **中美海关执法合作：**中国海关总署和美国国土安全部移民与海关执法局、美国司法部禁毒署等执法部门决定继续加强在打击枪支弹药、毒品、濒危野生动植物及其制品、固体废物走私和商业瞒骗等方面的常态化合作，建立长效合作机制，积极开展情报交流、案件协查和联合行动。

out intelligence exchange, investigation assistance, and joint operations.

3. Container Security Initiative: The GACC and the U.S. Department of Homeland Security's Customs and Border Protection (DHS/CBP) decided to strengthen their cooperation on the Container Security Initiative (CSI) program. The two sides intend to sign the *Basic Implementation Procedures for the Declaration of Principle between GACC and DHS/CBP Relating to Bilateral Customs Cooperation at Seaports to Enhance Security Cooperation* in the second quarter of 2016. The two sides intend to expand CSI to address customs violations determined by the two sides, increase the number of CSI inspections, and promote the process of posting GACC officers at the Port of Long Beach in California.

3. **中美海关“集装箱安全倡议”合作：**中国海关总署和美国国土安全部海关与边境保护局决定继续加强“集装箱安全倡议”合作，双方于2016年第二季度签署了《关于在有关港口加强海关双边合作促进安全的原则声明——基本实施程序》。双方有意向将“集装箱安全倡议”扩大至应对双方商定的违反海关规定的行为，提高项目查验数量，推动中国海关总署向美国加利福尼亚长滩港派驻关员工作。

4. Cooperation on Joint Validation and AEO Mutual Recognition: The GACC and the Department of Homeland Security's Customs and Border Protection (DHS/CBP) signed the *Addendum to the Action Plan Implementing the Memorandum of Understanding Concerning Cooperation on Supply Chain Security and Facilitation between GACC and DHS/CBP.* GACC and DHS/CBP have completed joint validations of 437 enterprises in China and seek to conduct additional joint validations in 2016. The two sides plan to conclude

4. **中美海关联合验证与“经认证的经营者”互认合作：**中国海关总署和美国国土安全部海关与边境保护局有意向签署《关于执行〈中华人民共和国海关总署与美国国土安全部海关与边境保护局关于供应链安全与便利合作的谅解备忘录〉的行动计划附录》。中国海关总署和美国国土安全部海关与边境保护局已在中国联合验证了437家企业，并寻求

negotiation of the Authorized Economic Operator (AEO) mutual recognition arrangement (MRA) in 2016 and seek to sign the MRA at an appropriate time.

在2016年开展更多“海关与商界反恐伙伴计划”联合验证。双方计划于2016年内完成“经认证的经营者”互认安排磋商，并择机签署互认安排。

5. Commodity Identification Training (CIT) for Nonproliferation Export Control: The GACC and the U.S. Department of Energy signed the *Statement of Intent for Cooperation in the Field of Commodity Identification Training for Nonproliferation Export Control* in March 2016. The Statement of Intent (SOI) facilitates continued cooperation to develop a Chinese national course for CIT, aimed at combating illicit trafficking of WMD-related materials, equipment, and technology through nuclear and dual-use commodity familiarization and identification.

5. **防扩散出口管制商品识别培训：**2016年3月，中华人民共和国海关总署与美国能源部签署了《关于开展防扩散出口管制商品识别培训合作的意向声明》。该《意向声明》有助于继续合作开发中方商品识别培训课程，旨在通过熟悉和识别核及两用商品，打击与大规模杀伤性武器相关的材料、设备和技术的非法贩运。

6. Combat the Smuggling of Nuclear Materials: The GACC and the U.S. Department of Energy/National Nuclear Security Administration (DOE/NNSA) decided to continue their technical collaboration to mature, expand, and sustain GACC's capacity building efforts in nuclear detection to combat international nuclear smuggling, continue a program on GACC's deployments at the Yangshan Import Lanes, the planned deployment of a radiation detection system at the Port of Tianjin, and the development of a

6. **打击核材料走私：**中华人民共和国海关总署与美国能源部国家核安全署决定继续通过技术合作，完善、扩大和支持中国海关的核探测能力建设，打击核走私，支持中国海关在洋山港进境通道安装设备、在天津港安装辐射探测设备，以及开发用于海关内部培训和演练的流程。

training and exercise process within Customs.

In addition, in the economic dialogue track Chinese customs also contributed three cooperation results. They are:

1.Trade statistics and technical exchange cooperation: the GACC and the U.S. International Trade Commission made commitments to continuing the cooperation in the field of trade statistics exchange.

2.Rules of origin: the GACC and the U.S. Trade Representative Office agreed to communication and exchange in the field of rule of origin.

3.Customs cooperation in IPR: The GACC, DHS/CBP and DHS/ICE decided to further cooperation based on the signed texts, including holding seminars and conducting joint operations.

These outcomes are the results of mutual respect, mutual exchange and mutual collaboration between China and U.S. Customs, They will be the new addition to the efforts in maintaining security and facilitation of global supply chain, promoting China-U. S. trade and advancing global economic development.

在经济对话轨道，中国海关还贡献了三个合作成果，分别是：

1. 贸易统计与技术交流合作：中国海关总署和美国国际贸易委员会同意继续开展贸易数据交换合作。

2. 原产地规则合作：中国海关总署和美国贸易代表办公室承诺将继续就两国原产地规则合作进行沟通与交流。

3．海关知识产权执法合作：中国海关总署和美国海关与边境保护局、移民与海关执法局决定在已签署的知识产权执法合作文本框架下继续深化知识产权执法合作，包括定期召开工作组会议和开展联合行动。

以上合作成果的取得，是中美海关相互尊重、相互交流、相互协作的结果，这必将为保障全球供应链安全与便利、促进中美经贸和世界经济发展作出贡献。

会见瑞士国务秘书

2016年4月8日

Meeting with Swiss State Secretary

April 8, 2016

Ms. Marie-Gabrielle Ineichen-Fleisch, State Secretary for Economic Affairs and head of the State Secretariat, joined the state visit of the President of the Swiss Confederation to China from April 7th to 9th, and had a meeting with me on April 8th.

This was Ms. Ineichen-Fleisch's first visit to China Customs. She mainly wished to talk about the implementation of China-Switzerland FTA and hoped that through the meeting mutual understanding could be further strengthened in a bid to jointly promote sound and steady growth of China-Switzerland trade.

This year marks the 66th anniversary of the establishment of diplomatic relations between

瑞士联邦经济部国务秘书兼经济事务秘书局局长玛丽加布里埃尔·茵艾辛弗莱施女士陪同瑞士联邦主席于4月7日至9日访华。期间，她于4月8日上午来署与我会谈。

此次是国务秘书女士首次访问中国海关。她此次来署拜会主要想就中瑞自贸协定实施等议题进行交流，期待通过此次访问进一步加深双方的相互了解与交流，共同推动中瑞经贸健康稳定发展。

今年正值中瑞建交66周年，近年来中瑞关系保持了良

China and Switzerland. In recent years, it has witnessed the strong momentum in bilateral relations. Switzerland is China's fifth largest trading partner in Europe and China is Switzerland's largest trading partner in Asia. Since the implementation of the *China–Switzerland Free Trade Agreement* (FTA) in July 2014, the FTA has played a significant role in driving economic growth of both countries. According to China Customs statistics, bilateral trade between China and Switzerland in 2015 stood at USD 44.26 billion, with a year-on-year increase of 1.6%. China's exports to Switzerland reached USD 3.17 billion, up by 2.5% and import registered at USD 41.09 billion, with an increase of 1.5%.

好发展势头，瑞士是中国在欧洲的第五大贸易伙伴，中国是瑞士在亚洲最大的贸易伙伴。中瑞自贸协定自2014年7月实施以来对中瑞双方经贸发展起到了积极的推动作用。据中国海关统计，2015年中国与瑞士双边贸易总值为442.6亿美元，比上年增长1.6%。其中，中国对瑞士出口31.7亿美元，增长2.5%；自瑞士进口410.9亿美元，增长1.5%。

In 2015, the total value of imported goods originating in Switzerland under the favorable clause of the FTA reached 1.83 billion US dollars, among which 87% held self-declaration of origin and 13% the held certificate of origin. The top three imported goods under the FTA were clocks and its parts, pharmaceuticals and organic chemicals, altogether accounting for 75% of the total value.

据中国海关统计，2015年《中瑞自贸协定》项下原产于瑞士的货物受惠进口至中国的货值约18.3亿美元，其中使用原产地自主声明申报进口的货值约占受惠进口货物总值的87%，使用原产地证书申报的占13%。受惠进口前三位的钟表及其零件、药品和有机化学品占受惠进口总货值的75%。

Swiss Customs statistics showed that USD 4.77 billion worth of goods originating in China were exported to Switzerland under the FTA, of which 3% hold declaration of

另外，据瑞士海关统计，2015年原产于中国的货物在瑞方受惠进口货值约47.7亿美元，其中使用原产地声明申报

origin and 97% hold certificate of origin. Chinese authorized bodies, including the AQSIQ (General Administration of Quality Supervision, Inspection and Quarantine), Trade Promotion Association and their local branches, issued 155,000 certificates of origin, covering about USD 4 billion worth of goods.

As the global trade has been undergoing tremendous downward pressure, it was quite some achievement that our bilateral trade had registered growth in both import and export, which showed the policy dividends of the FTA. Featuring equity, creativity and mutual benefit, the bilateral cooperation between China and Switzerland has set a good example for friendly cooperation among countries.

Both sides made a good communication about the customs cooperation.

China Customs and Swiss Customs, which is affiliated to the Ministry of Finance, have conducted active and fruitful cooperation since the 1980s. In the past decade, the two sides have held 7 ministerial meetings, conducted close communication at the working level and taken an active part in the cooperation under the framework of China-Switzerland FTA Joint Committee. Key programs are as follows:

进口的货值约占3%，使用原产地证书申报的占97%。中国签证机构，如检验检疫、贸促会及其地方分会等共签发原产地证书15.5万份，货值约40亿美元。

在去年全球贸易增长压力较大的情况下，中瑞贸易进出口均出现“双增长”实属不易，这充分体现了《中瑞自由贸易协定》政策红利释放效果。在平等、创新和共赢的“中瑞精神”的引领下，中瑞合作模式也成为了国家间友好合作的典范。

会谈期间，双方就中瑞海关合作进行了沟通。

自20世纪80年代以来，中国海关与隶属于瑞士联邦财政部的瑞士联邦海关署开展了积极的交往与合作。过去十年间，双方举行了七次署级会晤，开展了密切的工作层面交流，并积极参与了中瑞自贸联委会框架下的合作，有效推动了双边合作发展。目前，双方合作重点主要包括以下方面：

(1) Implementation of China–Switzer-land Free Trade Agreement

Two consultations on origin declaration data exchange and three Customs implementation meetings have been held since the FTA was signed. The two Customs have maintained close contact and have updated each other on a regular basis on the progress of implementation. To ensure proper implementation, a data exchange system for self-declaration of origin was set up and the *MOU on the Data Exchange System on Origin Declaration by Approved Exporters under Article 3.16 of the China–Switzerland Free Trade Agreement* was struck. The system was put into operation on July 1st , 2014, and is running well.

Since maritime cargoes from Switzerland are all loaded at ports of EU member states and therefore no direct consignment documents can be provided, China Customs simplified the document submission procedures for Switzerland and made special arrangements.

(2) AEO mutual recognition nego-tiations

Both sides have adopted the Authorized Economic Operator (AEO) programs in

一、《中瑞自贸协定》实施

《中瑞自贸协定》签署以来，中瑞海关已举行两次原产地声明数据交换磋商和三次海关实施会议。在日常执行中，两国海关联系密切，定时通报协定实施数据，及时沟通实施问题，正确履行核查职责。为确保《协定》的顺利实施，双方建立了原产地自主声明数据交换系统并签署了《中华人民共和国海关总署与瑞士联邦海关署关于中国—瑞士自由贸易协定第3.16条经核准出口商出具原产地声明数据交换系统的谅解备忘录》。该系统于2014年7月1日上线以来，运行情况良好。

针对瑞士海运货物须经欧盟国家的港口装船、难以提交直接运输单证的实际情况，中国海关特别为《协定》项下货物简化了单证提交要求，并在统一简化优惠贸易协定项下为瑞方做出了特别简化规定。

二、“经认证的经营者”（AEO）互认磋商

中瑞海关均已根据世界海关组织《全球贸易安全与便利

accordance with the *WCO SAFE Framework of Standards*. So far, China Customs has signed AEO Mutual Recognition Arrangements (MRAs) with the EU, Singapore, Korea, and Hong Kong Special Administrative Region (SAR), China, and started negotiations with the U.S. AEO cooperation could bring tangible benefits to compliant companies of both countries and hence benefit company development and bilateral trade.

标准框架》实施了"经认证的经营者"（AEO）制度。中国海关已经与欧盟、新加坡、韩国、中国香港等签订了AEO互认合作安排，并与美国海关等进行了AEO互认合作磋商及联合验证等合作。双方开展AEO合作将使彼此守法企业享受到更为优惠的实质性通关便利，对企业的发展和双边贸易有着积极的意义。

China and Swiss Customs started AEO negotiation last year，set up a working group and held 2 meetings in May and November in 2015. So far，comparison of AEO systems has been completed，which turn out to be highly similar to each other，and we have agreed on facilitation measures，MRA document negotiation and related legal affairs. The two sides will stay in close touch and we are hopeful that the MRA will be singed this year.

中瑞海关已于去年启动了AEO互认磋商，成立了专项工作组，并于2015年5月和11月举办了两次会议。目前，中瑞双方已经完成了AEO制度的比对，双方均认为两国海关AEO制度高度兼容一致，在便利措施、互认文本协商及相关法律问题等方面也已达成一致。下一步双方将继续保持积极沟通，有望于年内签署AEO互认安排。

（3） Capacity building

Capacity building started in 2007 and it is a key project for China-Switzerland Customs cooperation. Up to now, 11 training programs have been held, with the Chinese participants amounting to 169. Six training programs have

三、能力建设合作

能力建设是中瑞海关的重点合作项目。合作始于2007年，至今共开展了各类教育培训合作项目11期，中方参训人数达169人。其中，赴瑞培

been held in Switzerland with 30 Chinese participants and 5 training programs held in China, with 13 Swiss experts and 139 Chinese customs officers. The training programs cover a wide range of areas, such as development strategy, tax collection, risk analysis, Customs administration over FTA and e-commerce, enforcement consistency, AEO, cross-border e-commerce and management of training programs. Training programs have become a major platform for communication between the two Customs administrations. In order to consolidate and enhance bilateral cooperation, China Customs provided the draft of *Training Cooperation Arrangement 2016–2018* early this year and so far, both sides have agreed on most of the agreement on the working level.

During the meeting, we also exchanged views regarding the data exchange system for self-declaration of origin during the implementation of the FTA. It is a priority for China Customs to implement the FTA.

Since implementing the FTA is the first time that China Customs implements a commercial document-based origin declaration system, in order to prevent place of origin fraud, China Customs and Swiss Customs built a data transmission system on origin declaration, where Swiss-approved exporters upload scanned copies of origin declarations

训6期，参训人数30人；瑞士专家来华研讨5期，专家人数达13位，中方参加人数达139人。双方交流涵盖多领域，包括：海关发展战略、海关税收征管、风险数据分析、自贸区与电商条件下的海关管理、执法统一、AEO制度、跨境电子商务、培训项目管理等。教育培训合作已成为两国海关重要的交流平台之一。为继续巩固和深化合作，2016年初，中方主动向瑞方提供《中瑞海关2016−2018年教育培训合作安排》文本。目前，双方工作层面已就合作文本内容基本达成一致。

会谈期间，我们还专门就中瑞自贸协定实施过程中原产地电子联网的相关问题交换了意见。这是中国海关实施自贸协定的重点工作。

由于《协定》是中国首次实施基于商业单证的原产地声明制度，为防止原产地瞒骗，中瑞海关建设了原产地声明数据交换系统，由瑞士“经核准出口商”将原产地声明扫描件上传，由瑞士海关发给中国海关。目前该系统运行良好，提

and the copies are then sent to China Customs by Swiss Customs. The system is running well, making clearance at the China end faster by reducing the inspection rate. But the system only allows one-way transmission of scanned copies of origin declarations from Switzerland to China, which means China Customs does not have the data elements needed for a comparison with import declaration forms. And it is impossible for Swiss Customs to know how many cargoes originated from Switzerland have enjoyed preferential treatment in China. So, China Customs proposed on a number of occasions at the Customs implementation meetings and joint committee meetings to upgrade the existing system to an electronic origin data exchange system. The State Secretary expressed that she would be responsible for conveying the information to Switzerland customs and try to reach an agreement as far as possible.

高中方通关效率，降低了核查比例。但该系统仅支持由瑞方向中方单向传输原产地声明扫描件。因此，中国海关缺少与进口报关单对碰的必要数据项，无法满足目前推进无纸化通关和简化单证提交的需求，瑞士海关也无法了解其出口货物在中国海关的实际受惠情况。为此，中方在历次实施会议和联委会上均提出将现有数据交换系统升级为“原产地电子数据交换系统”（简称“电子联网”），国务秘书女士表示，将负责地向瑞士海关转达，尽可能促成达成一致意见。

Finally, I answered some questions, such as long customs procedures for some Switzerland companies and explained the laws and regulations of China Customs. We really had a friendly bilateral talk and reached great consensus on further promoting the development of economic and trade between two countries.

最后，对瑞方提出的一些公司反映通关时间较长等问题，我逐一进行了回应，并阐述了中国海关有关法律规定。双方在十分友好的气氛中进行了双边会晤，为进一步推进双边经贸发展达成了共识。

与美国能源部共同推动核安全行动计划

2016 年 3 月 17 日

Promote the Action Plan for Nuclear Security with U.S. DOE

March 17, 2016

Nuclear security cooperation has become an important part of the building of a new type of major-country relations between the world's largest developing and developed countries. And it must be admitted that our cooperation in nuclear security has become a key part of the cooperation between the two countries. And our cooperation was quoted as one of the outcomes of the Nuclear Security Summit (NSS) and the Strategic and Economic Dialogue on many occasions.

核安全合作已成为世界上最大的发展中国家和最大的发达国家之间建立新型大国关系的一个亮点。中美两国在核安全领域的探索与实践已成为双方合作的重要组成部分。双方的合作内容多次被列为核安全峰会和中美战略与经济对话的重要成果。

In a joint statement released during the Fourth Nuclear Security Summit, leaders of the two countries declared their "commitment to working together to foster a peaceful and

在第四次核安全峰会期间，中美两国元首发表了联合声明，宣布“承诺共同努力营造和平稳定的国际环境，减少

stable international environment by reducing the threat of nuclear terrorism and striving for a more inclusive, coordinated, sustainable and robust global nuclear security architecture for the common benefit and security of all".

核恐怖主义的威胁，争取建立更加包容、协调、可持续和强劲的全球核安全体系，维护共同利益和全球安全"。

Before the Fourth NSS, heads of the General Administration of China Customs (GACC) and the U.S. Department of Energy (DOE) had a friendly exchange on the cooperation in radiation detection and illicit trafficking of nuclear and other radial active materials and signed a cooperative document.

在此次核安全峰会召开之前，中国海关总署与美国能源部负责人再次进行了友好的交流，就加强防辐射探测合作、打击核材料及其他放射性物质非法贩运等议题进行了探讨并签署了合作文件。

After the meeting, the two sides signed a *Statement of Intent in the Field of Commodity Identification Training for Non-proliferation Export Control*, as one of the outcomes for the Nuclear Security Summit. We hope that through closer communication between the top leadership of both sides, we can provide further guidance for our cooperation and play a significant role in anti-terrorism and security.

这次会见后，双方共同签署了《中国海关与美国能源部关于开展防扩散出口管制商品识别培训合作的意向声明》。此《意向声明》也将作为第四届核安全峰会成果之一。我们希望，通过双方高层更加密切的交流，能够更好地指导和促进双方合作，更有效地发挥双方在反恐和安全领域的积极作用。

The relationship between China and the U.S. is one of the most important bilateral relationships in the world. It secured significant progress in 2015, when the two sides reached an agreement on building a new model of major-country relationship. Regarding economic cooperation and trade, China Customs'

中美关系是世界上最重要的双边关系之一。2015年，中美两国就进一步推动构建中美新型大国关系达成新的共识。在经贸领域，据中国海关统计，2015年，中美双边贸易总值达5582.8亿美元，比上年微

statistics showed that China-U.S. bilateral trade in 2015 stood at US$558.28 billion, slightly up by 0.6% from the previous year. The China-U. S. trade is in itself very impressive given the sluggish world economic recovery. The GACC and the U.S. DOE should continue working together to curb terrorism and provide security in order to ensure sustained growth of bilateral trade.

增0.6%。在世界经济复苏乏力的背景下仍保持这样的增长是不容易的。中国海关与美国能源部应继续深化反恐和安全领域合作，为双边贸易持续增长创造更加安全和稳定的外部环境。

Over the years, our partnership has been pragmatic and productive. We have seen frequent ministerial-level exchange of visits between the two countries. For example, in 2011, I made a trip to the U.S., during which I had a talk with the deputy secretary of the DOE and signed cooperative documents. In 2012, I met Daniel Poneman, deputy secretary of DOE, in Beijing. We reached important consensuses on bilateral cooperation. We have maintained frequent exchange visits between experts and professionals nearly on a monthly basis, and the cooperation has been institutionalized. In 2013, we signed the *MOU Concerning Cooperation in Preventing Illicit Trafficking of Nuclear and Other Radioactive Materials*, which has become a significant document in guiding our cooperation.

多年来，中国海关与美国能源部建立了务实、有效的合作关系。双方部级领导互访频繁。比如，2011年我访美时专程与美能源部领导会谈并签署合作文件。2012年，我又在北京会见了美国能源部副部长丹尼尔·彭曼先生，双方达成了重要合作共识。业务专家几乎每月都有访问交流，合作机制逐步完善。2013年，双方共同签署的《中美防范核及其他放射性物质非法贩运合作谅解备忘录》已成为指导双方合作的重要文件。

This time we jointly signed the Statement of Intent, which would be of great importance for our cooperation in commodity identification

这一次我们签署的《意向声明》，对于未来双方开展机制化的出口管制商品识别培训

training (CIT). Our Megaports pilot project and China Customs radiation detection training center have become demonstration projects between the two countries.

合作具有重要意义。中美特大型港口计划和中国海关防辐射探测培训中心合作已成为两国在核安全领域的示范项目。

It has always been a priority for China customs to curb the illicit trafficking of nuclear and other radioactive materials, and guard against the threat of nuclear terrorism in order to secure the global trade supply chain. But we have to admit that nuclear security is a global issue and it calls for the joint efforts of all of us.

中国海关高度重视打击核材料非法贩运，防范核恐怖主义威胁，保障全球贸易供应链的安全。但我们必须承认，核安全是全球性课题，需要各国共同努力。

Both sides agreed to focus future cooperation in the following areas:

未来，双方的合作主要将从以下行动计划着手：

First of all, we should continue to deepen GACC-DOE collaboration, and maintain direct communication between the minister of GACC and the secretary of DOE. Through regular talks and meetings, we can keep informed of each other key issues and programs.

第一，继续加强双方部级交流与合作，保持双方部级领导的直接沟通。通过定期会晤与交流，就重点问题和重要合作事项保持及时沟通与协调。

Secondly, we have to follow up on the signed agreement with action to improve institutionalized cooperation in commodity recognition in non-proliferation export control. The Statement of Intent identifies the key areas for cooperation, the working mechanisms and implementation plans, which will make it possible for us to establish a regular cooperation regime. The signing of the document will be incorporated as an outcome

第二，落实新签署的《意向声明》文件，加强防扩散出口管制商品识别机制化合作。《意向声明》明确了双方开展防扩散出口管制商品识别技术交流与合作的重点领域、工作机制和具体实施方式，为双方推动机制化、常态化合作提供了指导和保障。文件的签署也将成为第四届核安全峰

of the Fourth NSS.

Thirdly, we wish to expand the Megaports pilot project to combat nuclear material smuggling efficiency. The Megaports pilot project was launched at Shanghai Yangshan Port in 2011. By the end of 2015, China Customs had detected 33,500 suspicious vehicles under that framework. We had also interdicted 104 shipments of radioactive contaminants, such as cobalt 60, cesium 137 as well as cargo with an excessively high level of radiation. We had also intercepted cases of explosives concealment. So, our cooperation in the Megaports pilot project has been very successful. Next, we are planning to cover all import lanes at Yangshan Port and also expand it to the ports in Xinjiang and Tianjin. In this process, we wish to get the continued guidance and assistance from the U.S. side, especially in exploring new areas for technical cooperation, image reading and centralized analysis, as well as experts teaching at the training center.

Fourthly, we look forward to more cooperation in the area of security so as to play an important role in safeguarding major international events. We are grateful that our U.S. colleagues have been sharing experience with us and holding training programs for China Customs frontline officers over the years. The U.S. has donated more than 500 sets

会的成果。

第三，拓展“特大型港口计划”合作项目，提升打击核材料走私工作效能。中美“特大型港口计划”试点项目于2011年在上海洋山港启动实施。截至2015年底，中国海关发现可疑处置报警车辆3.35万车次，成功拦截钴60、铯137等放射性污染物或辐射超标货物104批，发现伪报夹藏危险爆炸物案件多起，项目起到了很好的示范效应。下一步中方计划将试点项目推广到洋山港进境通道，以及天津和新疆口岸。希望美方在设备安装、使用和维护方面，尤其是在拓展技术合作新领域、图像读取和集中研判以及派专家来中心授课等方面提供更多的具体指导和支持。

第四，继续开展海关安保合作，发挥海关在保障重大国际活动安全方面的作用。中方感谢美方多年来在重要国际活动安保方面积极分享经验、协助培训中方现场关员，并无偿赠送了500余套手持式、车载式辐射探测设备，助力中方圆

of handheld and mobile detection devices to assist us in completing the security tasks such as the Beijing Olympic Games.

满完成了北京奥运会等多项重要国际活动的海关安保任务。

This year, a number of major events will be held in China including the 8th Round of Strategic and Economic Dialogue and the G20 summit. We hope to exchange experience with the U.S. side on strengthening radiation detection so as to more effectively prevent and curb nuclear terrorism and ensure a success of these events.

今年，第八轮中美战略与经济对话和二十国峰会等重大国际活动将在华举行。希望中美双方继续加强核安全和辐射探测在保障重大国际活动安全方面的经验交流，分享辐射探测领域最新成果、技术及经验，更有效地防范和打击核恐怖主义，保障活动顺利举行。

续写中国—加拿大海关友好合作

2016年6月20日

Renew the Friendly Cooperation with Canadian Customs

June 20, 2016

On the morning of May 30, 2016, I led the Chinese Customs Delegation to visit the Canada Border Services Agency (CBSA) in Ottawa. Ms. Linda Lizotte-MacPherson, the new President of the Canada Border Services Agency met with us in CBSA. Ms. Linda is a kind woman of 50 years old. Both sides highly valued this visit, because it was the first top-level exchange between our two administrations since she took office last July. Vice President Martin Bolduc and other experts from Canadian Customs also participated in the meeting and we had a successful discussion on some key areas of our further cooperation. By exchanging views on a number of important issues of common concern on bilateral

2016年5月30日上午，我率中国海关代表团在渥太华访问加拿大边境服务署。加拿大边境服务署新任署长琳达·李佐蒂·麦克培森女士热情地会见了我们。琳达女士50开外，善意友好。双方高度重视这次访问，因为这是琳达女士去年7月上任以来中加海关首次高层交流。其副手马丁·布多柯和其他加拿大海关专家也参加了会议。双方就一些共同关注的重要问题进行了充分的交流和沟通，体现了中加海

cooperation, we once again confirmed the strong and positive relationship between GACC and CBSA.

关积极而友好的合作关系。

During our meeting, we referred to many highlights in our cooperation, especially the work we had done concerning the *Agreement between the Government of the People's Republic of China and the Government of Canada on Cooperation and Mutual Administrative Assistance in Customs Matters (CMAA)* signed on November 8, 2014, and problems that we face. After discussion, consensus on a wide range of issues has been reached, including to step up negotiations on the *Partnership Agreement between GACC and CBSA*, to quickly form a Joint Customs Cooperation Committee (JCCC) for overseeing the effective implementation of the CMAA, to carry out exchanges on China Customs' AEO and CBSA's Partners in Protection (PIP, a supply chain security program between Customs and business) programs, to strengthen the crack-down on the smuggling of marihuana, NPS (New Psychoactive Substance), narcotics, commercial frauds and IPR infringement, to explore cooperation on capacity building and to share practices of customs supervision over cross-border e-commerce.

会谈呈现了很多合作亮点，尤其是双方回顾了中加海关2014年11月8日签署的行政互助协定以来我们所作的工作及应对共同面临的问题。双方经过讨论就一系列问题达成了广泛共识，包括加快中加海关伙伴关系协议谈判进程，尽快成立联合海关合作委员会，负责有效实施行政互助协定，开展中国海关AEO和加拿大海关PIP项目（海关与商界的供应链安全合作项目）合作，加强打击走私大麻、新精神活性物质和毒品走私、商业瞒骗和知识产权侵权，探索能力建设合作，分享海关监管跨境电子商务实践经验。

This time, we focused on discussing a new Partnership Arrangement between both sides. Based on the Agreement of CMAA, recognizing that the Parties have a unique position in global

我们这次重点讨论了双方新伙伴关系安排。根据行政互助协定，双方认识到在全球供应链方面各自拥有

supply chain and a strengthened partnership would help to secure borders and facilitate trade, we decided to plan and promote cooperation from the strategic height and long-term perspective, to enhance the strategic cooperation through arrangements in the key areas for cooperation, and would endeavor to pursue a broader and closer cooperation which is reciprocally beneficial for the Parties in the future.

独特的地位，加强伙伴关系将有助于确保边境安全、促进贸易，我们决定从战略高度和长远角度规划并促进合作，通过新伙伴关系安排，在重点领域加强战略合作，并努力追求更广泛和紧密的协作，有利于双方未来互利互惠。

We have agreed upon the Partnership Arrangement as follows:

我们的伙伴关系安排主要体现了以下几方面的内容：

I. Principles of cooperation

The Parties will cooperate in order to implement international standards and best practices, with a particular focus on: 1) Mutual recognition of controls, within the framework of CMAA, to reduce duplication and allow better targeting; 2) Mutual administrative assistance, to fight against fraud and protect legitimate trade; 3) Mutual exchange of information, to strengthen risk-management cooperation and improve knowledge on policies and practices, particularly on the application of information technologies in customs procedures.

一、合作原则

双方将通过实施国际标准和最佳实践，遵循以下重点原则展开合作：一是监管互认，在行政互助协定框架下减少重复，以便高效布控；二是行政互助，打击瞒骗，保护合法贸易；三是信息互换，加强风险管理合作，提高政策和实践认知，特别是信息技术在海关手续中的应用。

II. Scope of cooperation

1) Cooperation on Trade Facilitation, experts of the Parties intend to carry out mutual visits and hold seminars to exchange ideas on AEO and PIP programs. By completing the

二、合作范围

一是贸易便利化合作，双方专家互访，召开“AEO”和“PIP”项目研讨会。通过相互比较各自项

comparisons of each other's programs, conducting validation observations, and negotiating mutual recognition arrangement (MRA), the Parties could promote the realization of mutual recognition, so as to grant more customs clearance benefits to the authorized enterprises. **2) Cooperation on Risk Management,** experts of the Parties intend to carry out mutual visits and hold seminars to exchange on each other's risk management systems, risk parameters, and risk analysis methods, so as to lay down a good foundation for further in-depth cooperation. Meanwhile, the Parties intend to enhance the communication and cooperation between each other's national risk targeting centers. **3) Cooperation on anti–smuggling enforcement,** the Parties shall prioritize the document verification requests from each other and exchange views on improving mechanisms for dealing with the requests in order to increase efficiency in this regard. In addition, experts of the Parties intend to carry out mutual visits and hold seminars to share techniques and experience in combating smuggling. The Parties could select areas of common concern, such as the crackdown on marijuana, and to enhance intelligence exchange, investigation assistance and joint enforcement operations, and to establish a regular cooperation mechanism, so as to jointly fight against smuggling. **4) Cooperation on Capacity Building,** the Parties intend to

目，开展验证稽查观摩，磋商互认安排。双方推动互认的实现，以便给予更多认证企业通关便利。**二是风险管理合作，**双方专家通过互访、举办研讨会，在风险管理系统、风险参数和风险分析方法等领域开展交流，为进一步深度合作打下良好基础。同时双方将加强彼此之间在风险布控中心领域的沟通与合作。**三是缉私执法合作，**双方应当优先考虑核查请求并就改善处理请求机制交换意见，以提高协查效率。此外，双方专家拟进行互访，举办研讨会分享在打击走私方面的技术和经验。双方可以选择共同关心的领域，如打击大麻，加强情报交流、调查协助和联合执法行动，并建立定期合作机制，以共同打击走私。**四是能力建设合作，**双方拟选择共同关心的领域，互派专家，举办讲座、培训课程或研讨会。双方拟分享并充分利用不涉及侵犯版权和其他侵权行为的培训材料，并加强双方海关学院和培训机构

select areas of common interests, and conduct personnel exchanges by sending experts to each other's countries for lectures, training courses or seminars. The Parties intend to share and make appropriate use of training materials where copyright infringement and other infringement activities are not involved, and to link each other's customs college and training organizations.

的联络。

III. Mechanism of cooperation

1) High-level exchanges: The Parties intend to draw guidance and make strategic decisions through high-level visits, exchanges and dialogues, for the realization of common objectives. 2) Working group meetings: The Parties intend to set up several working groups, composed of experts in line with areas of trade facilitation, risk management, anti-smuggling enforcement and capacity building, who are responsible for regular communications. Each working group intends to have meetings by rotation, in principle once every year, and will conclude them by minutes, which are expected to be reported to both leadership and to the Joint Customs Cooperation Committee (JCCC) established under the framework of CMAA.

三、合作机制

一是高层交往：双方拟通过高层互访、交流与对话指导并制定战略决策，实现共同目标。二是工作小组会议：双方拟设立几个工作组，组成贸易便利化、风险管理、反走私和能力建设专家组，负责定期联络。每个工作组采用轮流制召开会议，原则上每年一次，会议结束后撰写会议报告，报告提交给双方管理层和联合海关合作委员会。

GACC-CBSA cooperation has great potential. We all look forward to playing our greater role in promoting bilateral trade and safeguarding borders. Finally, I expressed my appreciation to CBSA for its support for our cooperation and

通过访问交流，我们进一步认识到中加海关合作仍有很大潜力。双方都期待着在促进双边贸易和保障边境安全上更好地发挥海关作

sincerely hope to receive the feedbacks to the Partnership Agreement formally from CBSA as soon as possible. I sincerely hope that our new partnership plan could be carried out as soon as possible in an effort to more effectively promote the continuous and healthy development of China-Canada economic cooperation and bilateral trade.

用。最后，我向加方就对深化双边合作所给予的支持和配合表示感谢。真诚希望新伙伴关系安排能得到尽快落实，以更有效地促进两国经济贸易的持续健康发展。

再访美国海关与边境保护局

2016 年 5 月 26 日

Another Visit to U.S. CBP

May 26, 2016

CBP, an abbreviation of Customs and Border Protection of the United States, was newly formed after 9/11. It is an important section of the Department of Homeland Security (DHS) and is also an important cooperative partner of China Customs.

On 24th May, 2016, I led a China Customs Delegation to the U.S. for an official visit. We arrived in Washington DC on the afternoon of 24th May and drove directly to the DHS for a bilateral meeting. According to the plan, Mr. Seth Stodder who is Assistant Secretary of DHS of the United States would talk with me in the meeting room of DHS. After an hour and a half, the meeting was finished with rich

CBP 是美国海关与边境保护局的简称，它是“9・11”事件后新组建的美国国土安全部的重要部门，也是中美海关合作的重要伙伴。

2016年5月24日，我率中国海关代表团访问美国海关。下午飞抵美国华盛顿后，我们就直接从机场驱车前往美国国土安全部进行双边会晤。根据安排，美方由国土安全部助理部长塞斯・斯托德尔先生与我会谈。会晤进行了一个半小时，会谈内容丰富、沟通坦

content, open communication, great consensus as well as productive results in the friendly atmosphere.

诚、共识一致、气氛友好，进行得十分顺利并富有成效。

2016年5月，美国，会见美国国土安全部部长助理赛斯·斯托德、美国海关与边境保护局、美国移民和海关执法局官员。

May 2016, U.S., meeting Mr. Seth Stodder, Assistant Secretary of DHS, officials from CBP and ICE

On the morning of May 25, 2016, I had a discussion with the head of CBP and other U.S. customs colleagues on the issues of customs cooperation.

The GACC and CBP undertake important responsibilities and missions of law enforcement to safeguard the borders and promote trade facilitation. Over the years, both sides have developed pragmatic and efficient cooperation. This time, I met with Mr. Mark Kumas, Assistant Commissioner of CBP, and his team to discuss key issues of bilateral cooperation. I hoped that we could further deepen consensus and set a clear objective for cooperation through the communication, so as to better serve and promote China-U.S. economic and trade development.

At the beginning of the meeting, we made positive comments on bilateral relationship and

2016年5月25日上午，我与美国海关与边境保护局负责人和美国海关同仁再次会面，共商中美海关合作事宜。

中国海关和美国海关与边境保护局都是承担着维护边境安全、促进贸易便利重要职责的执法部门。多年来，双方务实和高效地进行合作发展。这一次，我会见了美国海关与边境保护局助理局长马克·库曼斯先生和他的团队，共同探讨双边合作问题。我希望通过交流沟通，进一步深化合作共识，明确合作目标，更好地服务和促进中美经济和贸易健康发展。

会谈一开始，双方就中美两国关系和海关合作进行了积

Customs cooperation. China and the U.S. have broad converging interests and tremendous potential in business and trade ties. China Customs statistics showed that bilateral trade in 2015 stood at USD558.28 billion, slightly up by 0.6% from the previous year amid sluggish recovery of the world economy, which was not an easy achievement to come by. In the first quarter of 2016, bilateral trade volume reached USD112.72 billion (down by 10.3%), making the U.S. continuously China's largest export destination and 2nd largest trading partner.

极评价。中美两国利益深度交融，经贸合作具有巨大潜力和广阔前景。据中国海关统计，2015年，中美双边贸易总值达5582.8亿美元，比上年微增0.6%，在世界经济复苏乏力的背景下仍保持增长实属不易。2016年前三个月，中美双边贸易额达1127.2亿美元（同比下降10.3%），美国继续保持中国最大的出口市场和第二大贸易伙伴地位。

Over the years, collaboration with CBP has been productive. Remarkable progress has been made in CSI, C-TPAT joint validation, AEO mutual recognition negotiations, IPR joint operations as well as joint training programs.

多年来，中美海关在“集装箱安全倡议”（CSI）、“海关与商界反恐伙伴计划”（C-TPAT）联合验证，“经认证的经营者”（AEO）互认磋商、知识产权保护和联合培训等多个领域开展了广泛、务实的交流与合作，取得了积极成效。

We discussed in a friendly atmosphere. Both sides exchanged views on cooperation.

会谈始终在友好的气氛中进行，双方就有关合作议题交换了意见：

I. Active participate in the 8th Round of Strategic and Economic Dialogue

一、积极参与第八轮中美战略与经济对话

The China-U.S. Strategic and Economic Dialogue (S&ED) is the inter-governmental dialogue platform of the highest level for enhancing mutual trust. In previous rounds,

中美战略与经济对话（S&ED）是两国政府间最高层级的对话机制，是双方增进沟通与互信的重要平台。此

Customs projects were often included in the list of outcomes. In early June, the 8th Round of S&ED is to be held in Beijing. We have agreed on contributing three proposals to the list of outcomes this year, namely expanding CSI cooperation, concluding AEO mutual recognition negotiations, and continuing cooperation on IPR protection. Currently, both sides have reached agreement on these three proposals.

前，中美海关的合作成果多次被列入对话成果清单。今年6月上旬，第八轮S&ED将在北京举行。中美海关拟向本轮对话贡献三项合作成果：扩大CSI合作、完成AEO互认安排磋商和继续加强知识产权保护合作。目前，双方已就这些成果案文达成一致。

II. Comprehensively improve CSI cooperation

二、全面提升CSI合作

The Container Security Initiative (CSI) program is the most pragmatic cooperation project between GACC and CBP in securing supply chain. Since the launching of this program in 2003, CSI has played a positive role in promoting trade supply chain security and facilitation. Over the years, with the help of information exchange through CSI cooperation, GACC and CBP have seized several cases of drugs and antique smuggling, and false declaration.

“集装箱安全倡议”（CSI）是中美海关在维护供应链安全领域最具务实内容的合作项目。CSI项目自2003年正式启动以来，为保障中美贸易供应链的安全与便利发挥了积极作用。近年来，双方还利用CSI合作渠道和资源查获了相关毒品、文物走私和申报不实等案件。

In June 2015, with the joint demands of enhancing cooperation on protecting borders, both sides signed a revised *Declaration of Principles* (DOP) concerning expanding CSI cooperation and agreed to sign the *Basic Implementation Procedures for CSI Cooperation* (BIP), the attachment to DOP as soon as

2015年6月，根据双方扩大边境安全合作的共同需求，双方在华盛顿签署了新的关于加强CSI合作的《原则声明》，并就尽快签署附件《基本实施程序》达成共识。我与助理局长马克·库曼斯先生共

possible. The BIP that I signed with Mr. Mark Kumas, Assistant Commissioner of the CBP, marked a new beginning of our CSI cooperation.

Regarding CSI cooperation, I proposed that:

(1) Implement the newly signed BIP and to build a mutual-beneficial and win-win CSI cooperation.

Comparing with the former BIP signed in 2005, the new one is more comprehensive, practical and operational, especially in which several key points were specified, such as carrying out a two-way CSI officers deployment cooperation mechanism, and expanding the targeting commodities from Weapons of Mass Destruction to commonly recognized high risk goods. In the meantime, explicit provisions are made in the revised BIP regarding the joint analysis of the Non-Intrusive Inspection images, data and information exchanges, and enhancement of coordination between the deployed CSI officers and local Customs officers, which have adequately considered the cooperation needs and concerns of both sides, and will be useful to a more effective CSI cooperation. I hope that both sides would implement the arrangements and make CSI cooperation a model of China-U.S. Customs cooperation.

同签署的《基本实施程序》也标志着中美海关CSI合作将进入新的阶段。

关于深化“集装箱安全倡议”合作我建议：

（一）共同落实好新签署的《基本实施程序》，打造互惠共赢的CSI合作项目。

新的《基本实施程序》与2005年签署的旧版《基本实施程序》相比，内容更加全面务实、更具可操作性，特别是明确了中美CSI合作双向派员的重要内容，并将风险布控对象由“大规模杀伤性武器”扩大到“双方认可的高风险货物”。同时，对双方更为有效的分析机检图像、进行信息数据交换、加大CSI 派驻官员与当地海关现场关员的联系配合做出了明确规定，这些新的规定都充分考虑到了双方的合作需求和关注，能够有效促进CSI合作的开展。希望双方工作层认真落实有关安排，把CSI合作项目打造为中美海关合作的典范。

(2) Support and facilitate China Customs efforts in deploying CSI officers at U.S. ports.

According to the new BIP and the important consensus reached by both Ministers last year, China Customs has started to prepare for sending CSI officers to Long Beach, Los Angeles and are planning to complete the deployment work in 2017. We are very grateful for the support that CBP CSI team and representatives in Beijing had offered regarding the deployment, particularly the professional advice and suggestions. We hope to get continuous support for this engagement.

Regarding the deployment of China Customs officers to the U.S., I proposed that, firstly, both sides designate a liaison officer to conduct direct communication on China Customs deployment of CSI officers. Secondly, we hope to have U.S. assistance with procedures and visa applications for the deployed officers within U.S. capacity. Thirdly, China Customs would like to send a working team to Long Beach before the end of this year to make necessary preparation work before the formal deployment of CSI officers. We hope that CBP could provide facilitation for the team such as arranging field visits at the CSI facilities there and assisting to set up contacts with local

（二）对中方向美派员提供支持和便利。

根据新的《基本实施程序》，以及去年双方部长会谈达成的重要共识，中方启动了向美国洛杉矶长滩港派驻CSI人员的准备工作，并拟于2017年实现对美派员。中方感谢美国海关CSI团队以及驻华海关代表处此前给予中方派员工作的支持，特别是美方为我们派员提出了很好的专业意见和建议，希望美国海关继续支持此项工作。

关于中方向美方派员，我建议：一是请美方就中方CSI派员工作确定联络员，就中方派员具体筹备工作建立直接的沟通渠道；二是希望美国海关根据对等互利的原则，在中方派员的身份、签证等方面给予力所能及的协助；三是中方希于年底前派筹备工作先遣组赴长滩筹备具体工作，并希赴长滩海关业务现场考察，希望美方提供便利，并协助中方筹备组与长滩海关业务现场建立工作联系；四是中方派驻人员实际到位后，希望与美方开展业

CBP CSI officers. Fourthly, we hope that China Customs CSI officers could have discussions with CBP officers after deployment, to define specific coordination measures for conducting CSI cooperation and to learn more about CBP's working protocols and procedures in risk targeting and inspection, in order to cooperate more effectively with the U.S. counterparts. We hope to have the support in this regard as well.

务交流，确定具体的CSI工作配合办法，并深入了解美国海关的风险布控及查验工作制度和流程，便于有效开展工作，请美方给予支持。

(3) Expand CSI cooperation to more ports and the scope of targeting.

（三）扩大实施港口和布控范围。

About expanding CSI to more Chinese ports, I proposed: Over the years, more and more shipments destined for the U.S. have departed from Yangshan Port in Shanghai, and the majority of the inspection requests raised by CBP are containers exported from Yangshan Port. China Customs has done a research on the feasibility of expanding CSI to Yangshan Port. From a technical perspective, we think Yangshan is qualified to be a CSI port since it has been installed with NII (non-intrusive imaging) equipment for inspecting large-scale containers and has a centralized inspection facility. China Customs would like to, based on the principle of mutual benefits, actively discuss with CBP on the participation of Yangshan Port in our CSI cooperation. Meanwhile, since Yangshan port is far away from the current U.S. CSI office at Shanghai

关于扩大CSI在华实施港口，我建议：近年来，越来越多的输美货物经由上海洋山港出口至美国，美方提出的CSI查验请求也更多涉及洋山港。中方已就增加上海洋山港为CSI港口开展了可行性研究。洋山港目前设有集中查验区域，并配备有非侵入式大型集装箱检查设备，已具备加入CSI合作的基本技术条件，中国海关愿本着互惠互利的原则，积极与美方探讨增加洋山港的具体合作。同时，由于洋山港距离美方驻上海CSI办公室距离较远（来回车程约4至5小时），建议美方提早考虑由此可能带来的实际问题。

(a round trip may take a 4-5 hour by drive), we suggest that CBP should consider the possible challenges that may arise because of the long distance.

About expanding the scope of targeting, I pointed out that based on the previous successful practices, China Customs would like to discuss with CBP on expanding CSI targeting scope within each other's responsibilities and to the extent permitted by each other's laws and regulations. We suggest having pilot cooperation on expanding targeting scope to drugs, arms and ammunitions, endangered wild species and their products, and commercial fraud and gradually expand to other areas. Details could be determined by means of signing meeting minutes or memorandum of understanding for future execution.

关于扩大CSI布控范围，我提出：基于以往的成功案例，中方愿意在各自职责范围和法律法规允许范围内，与美方协商扩大风险布控范围。建议首先选取毒品、枪支弹药、濒危野生动植物及其制品走私和商业瞒骗等领域开展试点，并逐步予以完善。双方可以通过会议纪要或备忘录等方式将扩大布控的具体内容确定下来，以便执行。

III. Promote cooperation on C-TPAT joint validation and AEO mutual recognition

三、推进C-TPAT联合验证和AEO互认合作

C-TPAT joint validation is a model of GACC-CBP cooperation. Experts of both sides have created a model of joint validation and maintained close communication and cooperation. Mutual benefits are increasingly demonstrated as validated enterprises are enjoying preferential policies of faster clearance at the U.S. ports. In order to

C-TPAT联合验证是中美海关合作的典范。双方创造性地建立了“联合验证”的模式，两国海关专家保持了密切的沟通与合作，通过验证的企业享受在美口岸便捷通关的优惠政策，合作的互利性日益体现。为扩大中美守法诚信企业

extend the convenience brought by customs cooperation to more compliant enterprises, GACC and CBP launched negotiations of AEO mutual recognition in 2011. As of now, both sides have completed the comparison of each other's AEO systems, observations of each other's validation procedures and the first round of negotiation on the draft AEO Mutual Recognition Arrangements (MRA). Both sides have basically reached consensus on the framework and main contents of the MRA, facilitation measures that could be offered to AEO enterprises, and what data elements to be exchanged and how to exchange them.

In order to promote cooperation in this area, I proposed that, sign the Addendum regarding the *Action Plan* to the *MOU on Cooperation in Supply Chain Security and Facilitation as* soon as possible. Within the Addendum, both sides have made clear commitments of pushing forward C-TPAT joint validations to the next stage and to concluding the AEO mutual recognition negotiations as soon as possible. China Customs has designated Mr. Hu Tianshu, Customs Counselor at the Chinese Embassy to the U.S., to sign the Addendum on behalf of China Customs. We hope that CBP could designate an official as well and to sign the Addendum early this June.

享受海关合作带来便利的受益面，2011年，中美海关启动了“经认证的经营者”（AEO）互认磋商。目前，已完成了制度比对、实地验证观摩和互认安排文本的第一轮磋商，就互认文本的框架和主体内容、便利后给予认证企业的便利措施、相关数据交换的内容和方式等基本达成一致。

对这项合作，我建议：尽快签署《关于执行〈中美海关关于供应链安全与便利合作的谅解备忘录〉行动计划附录》文件。该文件对于推进下一阶段中美海关C-TPAT联合验证和AEO互认作出了明确承诺，中方已确定由驻美使馆海关参赞胡天舒先生代表中国海关签署该文件，希望美方尽快协调有关官员，于今年6月上旬签署《附录》文件。

IV. Explore exchanges and cooperation on risk management

In the context of economic integration at global and regional levels, the security threats at the borders are gradually increasing. And the challenges of risk prevention and control for the safety access are growing accordingly. In addition, with the constant emergence of new types of trade, the international trade rules may have to be reconstructed, which will raise higher demands for customs in executing risk prevention and control. To adapt to this new situation and new challenges, China Customs is now focusing on the establishment of the two-tier (i.e. headquarters and regional customs districts) risk management centers, so as to foster the integrated customs clearance management throughout the nation.

To this end, I proposed to, first conduct risk management expert exchanges. China Customs would like to dispatch a delegation composed of risk management experts to the U.S. this year to discuss and exchange ideas with CBP counterparts, in order to enhance the understanding of each other's risk management systems, parameters and risk analysis etc. which is to lay a better foundation for further in-depth cooperation in this regard. Meanwhile, China Customs also welcome CBP's experts to visit China.

四、研究开展风险管理交流与合作

在全球经济和区域经济一体化发展的背景下，进出境领域的安全威胁正逐步上升，海关安全准入风险防控面临的挑战随之加大。此外，随着新型贸易业态的不断涌现，国际贸易规则面临重构，这些都对海关加强风险防控提出了更高要求。为适应新形势、新挑战，中国海关正在着力建设海关总署和直属海关两级风险防控中心，构建一体化通关管理格局。

对此，我建议：一是开展风险管理业务专家交流。中方希望年内选派业务专家赴美国开展研讨交流，增进对彼此风险管理制度、参数设置、分析方法等内容的了解，为开展更深层次的合作打好基础。同时，中方也欢迎美方派专家来华交流。**二是开展风险防控中心工作交流**。中方希望了解美国国家布控中心的建设和运维经验，为中方建设风险防控

Second, carry out exchanges between both targeting centers. China Customs would like to learn more about CBP's experience in the establishment, operation and maintenance of the National Targeting Center (NTC), which will provide us a useful reference while developing our risk targeting centers. **Third, establish communication channels.** We propose both sides select a contact person from the risk management departments, responsible for coordinating and promoting cooperation in this field, by carrying out regular exchanges of each other's development in risk management so as to enhance mutual understanding and effectively advance our work.

中心提供有益参考。**三是建立联络沟通渠道**。中方建议各自指定一名风险业务联络员，负责协调和推进该领域合作，定期交流彼此业务发展的最新情况，增进了解，有利推进工作。

V. Strengthen cooperation on IPR enforcement

五、继续加强知识产权执法合作

IPR protection is one of the key areas of GACC-CBP cooperation. In accordance with the *Memorandum of Cooperation on Strengthened Cooperation in Border Enforcement of IPR* signed in 2007, both sides have held several working group meetings, finalized cooperation plans and implemented joint IPR operations. From March to April 2013, both customs conducted a joint IPR enforcement operation aiming at curbing counterfeit consumer electronics products smuggling destined for the U.S., during which more than 270,000 counterfeit products were seized and

知识产权保护是中美海关合作的重点内容之一。双方根据2007年签署的《关于加强知识产权边境保护合作的备忘录》，召开了工作组会议，确定了合作计划，并开展了具体的联合行动。2013年3—4月，双方开展的打击输美侵权消费类电子产品联合执法行动，共查获涉嫌侵权的商品27万余件，取得了显著成效。2016年4月，双方开展了针对输美假冒汽车配件等物品的联合执

remarkable results were achieved. In April 2016, both sides conducted a joint operation targeting counterfeit auto spare parts exported from China to the U.S. In the end, 3,600 shipments with a total number of 1.99 million pieces of goods were seized by China Customs.

法行动，中方共查获相关侵权货物约3600批，涉及侵权商品199万余件。

To strictly crack down on IPR infringement and better protect IPR, I proposed to, firstly, draw up the work plan of 2016 as soon as possible. Both sides designate a point of contact to exchange seizure data and cases information in a timely manner, and to resolve the problems emerging in cooperation through discussions at a regular basis by means of conference calls, etc. Secondly, actively publicize the results of joint IPR enforcement operation to expand its social impact. We suggest that both sides jointly avail the results of the joint operation in April on social media including each other's official website, in order to deter the movement and trafficking of illegal goods. Meanwhile, we'd better study lessons learned from previous operations so as to improve effectiveness for future joint operations. Thirdly, explore comprehensive IPR cooperation. Both sides could expand IPR cooperation to discussions on the legislation of IPR protection and IPR filing practices and enhance communications with the business community. Fourthly, hold the third IPR

为严厉打击侵权违法活动和深化知识产权保护，我建议：一是尽快制定2016年度工作计划。指定联系人及时交换查获数据和案件信息，通过电话会议等方式开展经常性的磋商，及时解决合作中出现的问题。二是积极宣传，扩大知识产权执法合作社会影响力。建议双方利用各自官方网站等社交平台加大对4月份联合执法行动成果的宣传，展示行动成效，震慑侵权走私违法行为。同时，注重总结，为未来适时开展更多的联合执法行动提供参考。三是探讨开展全方位的知识产权执法合作。加强在知识产权海关保护的立法、知识产权备案实践、与工商界交流等领域的合作。四是适时召开第三次知识产权工作组会议。评估合作进展，分享合作经验，不断深化中美海关知识产权执法合作。

working group meeting when appropriate. Both sides could evaluate the progress of cooperation and share successful practices so as to gradually deepen GACC-CBP IPR enforcement cooperation.

The intensive discussions during my visit to the U.S. DHS and CBP covered many topics and a wide array of areas. We have worked well together, reached basic consensus, and formed plans and roadmaps to deepen cooperation, laying down a solid foundation for future China-U.S. customs cooperation.

这次访问美国国土安全部及美国海关和边境保护局，讨论的议题很多、范围很广，内容也很深入，双方通过共同努力，基本达成了一致共识，形成了深化合作的工作计划和实施步骤，为下一步有效开展中美海关合作打下了坚实的基础。

访问英国（苏格兰）打击犯罪执法中心

2016年10月

Visiting the Scottish Crime Campus

October, 2016

In September 2016, I led a China Customs delegation to visit the UK. After a friendly and pragmatic discussion and signing a cooperation agreement with Her Majesty's Revenue and Customs (HMRC) and the National Crime Agency (NCA), the delegation paid a field visit to the Scottish Crime Campus (SCC) near Gartcosh, Scotland, where I had a meeting with senior officials deployed to the SCC by HMRC and the NCA, learned the organization structure, objectives, coordination mechanism and intelligence sharing of the SCC. My British colleagues did a presentation on how they tackled cigarette and drug smuggling and money laundering. And we exchanged ideas on

2016年9月，我率中国海关代表团访问英国海关。其间，在与英国皇家税务与海关署和英国国家打击犯罪局进行友好、务实的会谈并签署合作文件后，我们代表团一行实地考察了位于苏格兰盖特科什附近的英国（苏格兰）打击犯罪执法中心（SCC）。在那里，我们与英国皇家税务与海关署、英国国家打击犯罪局派驻执法中心的负责人举行了座谈，详细了解了执法中心组织架构、目标任务、部门间联系配合机制、情报信息共享等工

enhancing China-UK customs cooperation and issues of concern in specific areas.

作情况，听取了英国执法部门打击香烟、毒品走私以及反洗钱执法案例介绍，并就加强中英海关合作和相关专业问题交换了意见。

2016年9月，英国，与英国皇家税务与海关署、英国国家打击犯罪局签署合作文件。

September2016, the UK, signing a cooperation agreement with the HMRC and NCA.

During the meeting, I learned that the purpose of building the SCC was to tackle organized crimes in the region. The SCC brings together a number of crime fighting agencies into a single campus. It provides a focal point and an analysis platform for excellence in intelligence-sharing, operational activity, evidence gathering and forensic science. The strategic aim of the SCC is to improve the efficiency and effectiveness of partner organizations in combating crime. To accommodate current and future needs of operations, the SCC occupies an area of 22,500 square meters. The main building is a four-story structure arranged around a central atrium with transepts and is designed to represent

在交流的过程中，我们了解到英国（苏格兰）打击犯罪执法中心（SCC）是根据近年来打击该地区有组织犯罪的需求而组建的。它是通过将多个打击犯罪部门集中于一处办公，为情报分享、业务开展、证据收集和刑事技术等领域的专家提供了集中交流和分析的机会。该执法中心的战略目标是提升打击犯罪相关部门的效率和效能，以更有力地打击严重的有组织犯罪行为。根据当下和未来的业务发展需求，他们在苏格兰专门建造了一栋占地2.25万平方米、外形设计

human DNA. The budget for the project was 82 million pounds and it belongs to the Scottish Government. It provides accommodation for over 1100 people, including room for growth.

似DNA形状、中间建有交叉走廊天井的4层大型建筑（投资8200万英镑，属苏格兰政府所有），整栋建筑可容纳超过1100人，未来还可视业务需求继续扩充。

There are more than 20 different national and regional agencies working on the campus. For example, the Police Service of Scotland (PSOS). This division comprises a number of departments which are focused on tackling serious organized crime and counter terrorism in Scotland by providing specialist investigative support to each of the 14 local policing divisions across the country. PSOS also houses the Scottish Police Authority Forensic Services (FS), which provides state of the art forensic equipment, cutting edge technology and one of the best modern laboratories in Europe in support of Scotland's fight against crime.

目前共有超过20个国家和地区层级机构在英国（苏格兰）打击犯罪执法中心（SCC）派员办公。比如，苏格兰警察局，该部门下设多个处室，通过向苏格兰14个地方分局提供专业调查建议，打击苏格兰境内严重的有组织犯罪和恐怖主义行为。苏格兰警察局还下设司法鉴定中心，拥有全球一流的刑事技术设备，以及欧洲领先的现代实验室和先进科技，通过尖端刑事技术为打击犯罪提供智力支持。

Another example is the Crown Office and Procurator Fiscal Service (COPFS)-Serious and Organized Crime Division, which focuses on those who are seeking to profit from organized crime by way of involving themselves in, amongst other crimes, drug and people trafficking, money laundering and bootlegging. The division also plays a vital role in counter terrorism operations. There

又如，皇家检察院下属机构打击严重及有组织犯罪司，该司主要负责打击通过参与毒品交易、偷渡、洗钱和走私等犯罪行为牟利的犯罪分子，在反恐领域也发挥着重要作用。再如，英国国家打击犯罪局，这是英国24小时全天候打击犯罪的部门，其员工分散在英国

is also the National Crime Agency (NCA). It is a 24/7 operational crime-fighting agency and its officers are located at a number of hubs situated throughout the UK, including the SCC. NCA offers a number of specialist and unique capabilities, both within the UK and internationally, which can be accessed by Scottish partners to support their serious crime investigations and their fight against emerging crime groups.

的各地，其中也包括在执法中心（SCC）。该局在国内和国际范围内具有一系列专业能力和特殊职权，因此十分有利于苏格兰当地其他执法部门对严重犯罪行为的调查，并重点打击新兴犯罪团伙。

Staff from HMRC located at the SCC comprise of intelligence and criminal investigation officers, in addition to analysts. Using an intelligence driven picture of risk, they focus on those who try to get out of paying their fair share through frontline activity and punishing tax evasion.

英国皇家税务与海关署在执法中心工作的主要是情报和犯罪调查人员和分析人员，他们的主要职责是通过风险智能分析，确保一线执法过程中能够足额征税，惩治故意偷逃税收的行为。

Regarding the management of the SCC, it adopts flexible working hours. The SCC houses investigators, analysts, prosecutors, customs officers and policeman, etc. which provides the opportunity to deal with the threat from its identification through to its mitigation. They could have meetings together, and share resources and expertise anytime they would like. In addition, each agency has its own advanced facility. Working together offers everyone more opportunities to make use of partners' facilities so as to fix the criminals efficiently.

从英国（苏格兰）打击犯罪执法中心（SCC）运行管理看，主要采取特殊的弹性工作制。执法中心员工包括调查员、分析师、公诉人员、海关关员和警察等等，业务涵盖从威胁识别到处置的全程。员工可以在任何时间通过会议分享资源和知识。此外，每个部门都各有不同的先进设备，办公地点集中后，这些设备可得到更加充分的利用，以提高打击

Because there are so many agencies involved, there must be some political competitiveness to bring them together. Therefore, the joint tasking group (JTG) was established, which is composed of senior officers of different agencies. The JTG meets every month. The chair of the group rotates. Once intelligence related to serious and important crime is submitted, the JTG will discuss to identify what crimes are involved and which agency is the appropriate one to deal with it. If it is a multi-tasking, agencies related will work together.

It needs to be pointed out that the SCC has created an open plan working environment, and a new way of work that encourages sharing and collaboration among enforcement agencies. As one of the world's most advanced crime fighting center, it represents the trend of future crime investigation in the world.

Director of Criminal Investigation for HMRC told me, "HMRC's participation in the SCC reflects our commitment to the delivery of the wider law enforcement response to smuggling and organized crime across Scotland and the rest of the UK. The creation of the SCC provides an unprecedented opportunity to take advantage of the strengths,

犯罪的效率。

由于执法中心包括众多执法部门，需要有一个高层机构对各部门进行统筹管理，因此，它选取不同部门的高层官员组成了联合领导小组（JTG）。联合领导小组每月召开一次会议，领导小组组长由成员轮流担任。凡收到有关严重有组织犯罪的情报后，联合领导小组将立即对犯罪的内容、承办部门进行判别。如果案件涉及多个部门，则相关部门将进行联合调查。

值得一提的是，这个执法中心营造了一个全新的开放式的工作环境，倡导了共享的工作方式，加强相关执法部门的协作配合，已成为全球领先的犯罪调查执法中心，这也代表着未来国际犯罪调查的一种最先进的趋势。

英国皇家税务与海关署犯罪调查部门负责人告诉我："皇家税务与海关署在英国（苏格兰）打击犯罪执法中心（SCC）派驻工作人员，说明我们将通过更广泛的部门协作打击苏格兰境内和英国其他地区的走私违法和有组织犯罪行

skills and abilities that each partner will bring to the fight against organized crime."

The prominent realization this visit gave me is that "centralized operations, shared resources, complementary advantages, and enhanced enforcement" are conducive to improving efficiency in fighting various crimes. China Customs is also responsible for import and export supervision, duty collection and anti-smuggling. Customs Anti-smuggling Police, the criminal enforcement arm of China Customs, is responsible for the investigation, detention, arrest and inquiry in a smuggling crime. Faced with a more complex battle against crimes, enforcement agencies have to step up cooperation and collaboration, especially as smuggling of drugs, guns and ammunition, solid waste and endangered wildlife, and crimes related to terrorism and explosives that threaten social stability are increasing. In this sense, SCC could provide valuable experience and offer a possible solution for us to explore for future enforcement cooperation.

为。这个执法中心的成立，为各方相互利用各自人员、技术和职能的优势，打击重大的有组织犯罪活动提供了前所未有的机遇。"

这次实地考察给我留下的一个突出印象就是"集中办公、分享资源、互补优势、强化执法"有利于提高打击各种犯罪活动的效力。中国海关也承担着进出境监督管理、征收关税、打击走私等重任，海关缉私警察依法负责对走私犯罪案件开展侦查、拘留、执行逮捕和预审工作，专司打击走私犯罪违法活动。面对愈发复杂的境内外犯罪形势，尤其是毒品、枪支弹药、固体废物、濒危野生物种等走私及涉恐、涉爆、涉稳等案件不断涌现，更需要各执法部门间加强合作和配合。英国执法打击犯罪执法中心的相关做法，或许能给我们探索未来的执法合作提供一些有益的借鉴。

访美国海关商品分类监管中心

2016 年 5 月 30 日

Visiting the CEE of U.S. Customs

May 30, 2016

I led a Chinese Customs delegation to the United States in the second half of May 2016. During our stay, we visited the Centers of Excellence and Expertise (CEEs) in Houston and Chicago, talked with the officials in charge and learned how these organizations were established and managed.

2016年5月下旬，我率中国海关代表团访问美国。其间，实地考察了美国海关休斯敦、芝加哥商品分类监管中心（CEE），与当地海关和CEE的负责人进行了交谈，了解美国海关建立CEE及其运行的情况。

2016年5月，美国，访美国海关商品分类监管中心及休斯顿港区海关。

May 2016, visiting the U.S. CEE and U.S. Customs in Houston.

The CEEs are industry-specific centers. Since October 2011, the U.S. Customs and Border Protection established 10 CEEs, aiming to secure global supply chain while facilitating trade. All CEEs were up and running before March 3, 2016.

美国海关CEE是按行业进行分工、对不同行业不同商品实施分类监管的专业机构。自2011年10月试点开始，美国海关陆续设立了10个CEE，旨在保证贸易供应链安全的同时，促进贸易便利化。到2016年3月3日，10个CEE已全部正式运作。

I. About CEE

一、美国海关CEE概况

(1) Structure and responsibilities.

（一）CEE的布局及职责分工。

The U.S. Customs and Border Protection chose 10 industry-specific locations with a large volume of import to set up CEEs, i.e. Health & Chemicals CEE in New York; Electronics CEE in Los Angeles; Pharmaceuticals, Automotive & Aerospace CEE in Detroit; Petroleum, Natural Gas & Minerals CEE in Houston; Agriculture & Prepared Products CEE in Miami; Apparel, Footwear & Textiles CEE in San Francisco; Consumer Products & Mass Merchandising CEE in Atlanta; Base Metals CEE in Chicago; Industrial & Manufacturing Materials CEE in Buffalo; and Machinery CEE in Laredo.

美国海关在某些类别商品进口量较大且产业较为集中的10个口岸设立CEE。各中心具体分工为：（1）纽约中心：医药和医疗化工产品；（2）洛杉矶中心：电子产品；（3）底特律中心：制药、汽车、航空航天产品；（4）休斯顿中心：石油、天然气和矿产品；（5）迈阿密中心：农业和农产品；（6）旧金山中心：服装鞋帽、纺织产品；（7）亚特兰大中心：消费品和大宗采购商品；（8）芝加哥中心：贱金属产品；（9）布法罗中心：工业和制造业原材料；（10）拉雷多中心：机械产品。

(2) Objectives.

To secure global supply chain and enhance economic competitiveness, by setting up CEEs, ports of entry are able to more effectively focus resources on high-risk shipments that may pose a danger to national border security, harm health and safety of consumers, and violate trade laws and intellectual property rights. CEEs retain authority to promote legitimate trade and correct errors by dealing with every single industry in every strategic location.

To promote trade facilitation and reduce trade cost, the CEEs serve as resources to trade community and government partners the overall situation of importers and enforcement intelligence, provide trade expertise training, answer questions concerning customs clearance, account management and assist the headquarters in developing comprehensive trade facilitation strategies.

To improve customs expertise and enhance uniformity, by leveraging trade expertise in CEEs and the multidisciplinary teams, the CEEs target high risk shipments more precisely to strengthen customs law enforcement. The CEEs press ahead with uniformity of law enforcement by

（二）设立CEE的预期目标。

为了维护贸易供应链安全，提升贸易竞争力，美国海关通过设立CEE，使口岸海关能够将监管资源更有效地集中于防控准入风险，防范高风险货物对国家边境安全、消费者健康与安全的威胁，打击违反贸易相关法律和侵犯知识产权的行为。CEE通过分析和处置重点地域的特定行业风险，促进合法贸易，纠正违规行为。

为促进贸易便利，降低贸易成本，CEE通过提出企业风险分类及执行建议，为商界和政府部门提供行业全国进口商总体情况、执法情报信息，为企业提供专业知识培训、通关信息咨询、账目审查服务，协助海关总部制定促进贸易便利的综合策略等。

加强海关的专业性，提升执法统一性。通过发挥CEE专业技能优势，利用多学科团队，更精确地定位高风险货物，强化海关执法工作。通过将涉及参与企业的海关业务转移至负责相关商品的

redirecting work involving participating accounts to centralized, industry-specific locations.

某个CEE集中进行审核，推进海关执法统一。

II. Management

二、CEE的管理模式

(1) Administrative management. The CEEs are under the leadership of the Office of Field of the Headquarters of the U.S. Customs. There are 20 local offices of field operation around the whole country which respectively oversee the operations of the CEEs within its administrative region. Directors of the CEEs are at the same level of Directors of ports who both report to directors of the Office of Field in regions.

（一）行政管理。各个CEE直接隶属于美国海关总部现场业务办公室管理，该办公室下辖的20个地区现场业务办公室，负责对所辖地区的口岸海关和CEE进行业务指导。CEE与所在地口岸海关不存在行政隶属关系，10个CEE的主任分别向所在地的地区现场业务办公室主任汇报工作，其级别与口岸海关负责人平级。

In September 2014, the headquarters of U.S. Customs and Border Protection signed a declaration order which delegated all authorities provided by law, regulation or otherwise that are vested in port directors to directors of the CEEs. For instance, directors of the CEEs have the authority of issuing decisions on the legitimacy of rules of origin, tariff code and rate of commodities as well as trademarks; share authority with directors of the port in goods return and sampling analysis, etc.; exercise the concurrent power in duty collection. With certain exceptions, port directors still retain singular authority over those matters pertaining to movement,

2014年9月，美国海关总部颁布授权令，明确了CEE的主任与口岸海关负责人依法享有的管理权限一致。比如，有权对进口货物的原产地、税号、税率和商标等是否合法做出决定；其与口岸海关负责人均可决定货物是否需要被退运、是否需要取样分析等，在货物征税事宜上也享有同等权力。除个别情况外，货物的移动、查验及放行仍由口岸海关负责人决定。

examination and release of goods.

(2) Personnel. The CEEs bring all trade expertise to bear on a single industry in a location. They are staffed with trade positions classification, risk analysis and customs control skills. At present, there are 2000 people with each CEE staffed from a dozen to hundreds. A CEE may propose increasing the number of personnel to the Office of Field in that region based on trade volume and revenue collection requirements. The Office of Field is responsible for selection nationwide. Application for positions in the CEEs is voluntary provided that any customs officers have specific knowledge of commodities. After being selected, the staff will be trained by the CEEs.

（二）人员管理。CEE工作人员由具有相关行业和商品分析技能的专家以及海关商品归类、风险分析和通关监管等领域的专业人员组成，目前共有2000人左右，各CEE从数十人到数百人不等。各CEE根据贸易业务量和税收形势配置人员，如需增加人员，应向地区现场业务办公室提出，由其在全国选拔。有特定商品知识背景的海关关员也可自愿申请加入CEE。经选拔通过的，CEE对其培训后上岗。

The CEEs operate in a virtual environment. There is only 2 or 3 staff including Director and assistant Director working at the office of the Center. The other personnel of the Center are located in different ports of entry. For example, as for the Center in Houston, the number of staff is 54 who are located in 19 ports of entry; while there are 67 staff in the Center in Chicago who are located in 28 ports of entry. The personnel management, for example, the promotion of their career is within the jurisdiction of the CEEs.

CEE不实行集中办公，其办公室日常只有主任及助理主任等2-3名人员，其余人员分散在相关口岸海关工作。例如，休斯顿中心54名专家分散在19个口岸海关工作，芝加哥中心67名专家分散在28个口岸海关。但专家人员的职位晋升等人事管理由各CEE负责。

(3) Pilot enterprises. Application for the CEE program is voluntary. At the beginning

（三）试点企业。参与CEE试点的企业实行自愿加

of 2011, only members of the Customs-Trade Partnership Against Terrorism (C-TPAT) program and the Importer Self-Assessment (ISA) program were qualified to participate in the CEE program. As of August 2012, U.S. Customs and Border Protection expanded the scope of the participation of the businesses, which meant that all enterprises as long as their business and import commodities were the same as the scope of the Center applying for could apply for the pilot program.

入。在2011年试点之初，仅“海关和商界反恐伙伴计划”（C-TPAT）和“进口商自主评估项目”（ISA）成员企业有资格申请加入。2012年8月后扩大试点范围，所有企业都可以申请加入试点，但其所从事的行业、进口的商品须与申请加入CEE的分工行业或商品范围相一致。

Although all enterprises who meet the qualification standards could apply for the program, U.S. Customs and Border Protection will prioritize tier 2 and tier 3 members of C-TPAT and members of ISA. Participating companies will enjoy facilitation during clearance, but if they break laws or regulations, the Center Director has the authority to cancel their membership in writing. At the same time, the participating accounts may quit at any stage after joining in the CEE program. As for those non-participating accounts, entry procedures remain the same as before and are processed by the applicable ports.

尽管目前符合标准的企业都可向海关提出申请，但海关优先考虑C-TPAT的2级及3级企业和ISA成员企业。试点企业可以享受通关便利优惠，但如果试点企业在进口环节发生违法违规行为，CEE主任有权书面通知取消其参与资格。同时，参与企业可以在加入试点后的任何时段退出。凡是未加入CEE的企业，其通关流程与之前相同，由相关口岸海关负责。

III. Responsibilities

三、工作职责

(1) The CEEs focus on reviewing revenue issues after the release of goods, including: a) compliance with law, regulation or otherwise for proposing risk levels and follow-up activities; b) customs declaration,

（一）CEE重点负责货物放行后的税收问题。主要包括：（1）审查企业贸易合规性，提出风险等级及后续措施建议。（2）审核企业纳税申

such as classification of commodities, valuation, applicable duty rates, duty assessment, etc.; c) qualification for the treatment of preferential duty rates of Free Trade Zone Agreement; d) dutiable taxes confirmation and liquidations; e) questions answering, modifications or cancelations of declaration, dispute settlement and voluntary disclosure for breaching laws.

报，重点是商品归类、估价、适用税率、估算税额等是否准确、真实。（3）对进口货物是否具备享受自贸协定优惠税率资格进行审查。（4）确认企业应缴税款，进行税收清算。（5）受理企业咨询、纳税申报单修撤、异议，受理并审查企业主动披露的有关违规事项。

(2) The CEEs will gradually expand the scope of their responsibilities. It is said that transactions bonds are processed at ports, while duty drawback remains processed at the four centers of duty drawback, e.g. New York and Houston. In the next stage, all duty related issues will be gradually transferred to the CEEs. All authorities will be pursuant to Chapter 19 Code of Federal Regulations (CFR). The scope of the CEEs will be expanded to engage in all trade processes. For example, upon the arrival of goods and at the release stage, the CEEs analyze risks and propose control advice; the CEEs take charge of all post clearance matters, including declaration review, duty liquidation, disputes, consultation, duty drawback, and penalty; the CEEs target risks and threats; the CEEs provide the headquarters with any industry-related policy advice.

（二）CEE职责将逐步扩大。据介绍，目前税款担保等仍主要在口岸海关办理，退税仍在纽约、休斯敦等四个退税中心办理，今后所有涉税职能将逐步转移到CEE。联邦法规第19章修正案将为其提供更全面的管理授权，其业务范围将逐步扩大，直至融入贸易过程的各方面。例如，在货物到达和放行环节，分析贸易风险并提出监管建议；负责所有货物放行后的业务，包括纳税申报审核、税收清算、异议、磋商、退税、罚款；分析确定风险和威胁目标；向海关总部提交与行业相关的政策建议等。

(3) Operational procedures. The greatest feature of U.S. import entry is making full play of electronic declaration and guarantee system, and adopting the "two-step declaration" system, i.e. entry summary for the purpose of the release of goods and customs declaration for the purpose of duty collection and statistics. The CEEs serve for the latter purpose. That is to say, the CEEs deal with revenue issues after the release of the goods within their scope.

（三）业务流程。美国进口通关制度的最大特色就是发挥电子申报系统和担保制度的作用，实行"两步申报"制度，即：以满足海关放行货物为目的的提货申报和以满足海关征税、统计为目的的纳税申报。CEE在"两步申报"流程的第二步，处理分工范围内企业进口货物放行后的税收问题。

1) Customs declaration. Within 10 working days after the release of goods upon guarantee deposit, enterprises should make declarations to ports of entry through the Automated Commercial Environment (ACE). The documents should include receipt of goods claim, customs declaration form and other supporting documents used as evidence for meeting requirements such as duty collection and trade statistics.

1）企业申报。在货物担保放行后十个工作日内，企业应通过海关"自动商务环境"申报系统（ACE），向入境口岸海关进行申报。相关单证包括：提货申报单回执、申报单以及用于海关征税、贸易统计和证明货物已满足进口规定所需的其他单证。

In general, when making customs declarations, enterprises should deposit guarantee to ports of entry roughly the same amount of dutiable payment in advance electronically.

一般情形下，企业在申报同时应向口岸海关预缴金额相当于估算税款的保证金，可通过电子方式预付。

2) Electronic verification. The system automatically screens all declaration data and deals with shipments based on the levels of risks. As for the low risk shipments, the system

2）电子审核。系统对企业申报数据自动进行风险甄别，并按货物风险值高低区别处置。对低风险货物，系统直

issues release orders directly. And with regard to medium- high risk shipments, the system automatically transmits the declarations to the relevant CEEs for review.

3) Manual verification. The staff in the CEEs review the documents of declarations dispatched by the system. If it's necessary for additional documents, the staff can make such requests through the system and the enterprises can send the information through either the system or designated email accounts to the CEEs. If a customs declaration is rejected, the CEEs will issue a notification accordingly.

Once there are any concerns during the verification, the CEEs may ask enterprises to come and explain and even investigate on spots when necessary. Ports of entry will provide assistance when it comes to goods inspection. (Customs officers at ports of entry are only responsible for examining goods rather than verifying classification and valuation.) In addition, there are customs laboratories under the U.S. Customs and Border Protection. The CEEs have the authority to sample for analysis. The results of laboratories have legally binding force.

Once the CEEs discover any risk issues related to IPR during verification, all cases are transferred to ports. All ports will further investigate risk issues of shipments.

接发出放行指令。对中高风险货物，系统自动将涉及特定货物的纳税申报单派送至相关的CEE进行审核。

3）人工审核。CEE专家对系统派送的纳税申报相关单证进行分析与处置。如需企业补充提供相关文件，通过系统发出补充申报信息，企业须将有关文件通过该系统或CEE电子邮件系统传送至CEE。如企业申报被退回，CEE将制发退回通知。

在审核中如有疑问，CEE专家可请企业人员当面解释，确有必要时可到企业实地调查；需要实地验核货物的，口岸海关查验关员予以协助（只负责验核实货，不负责验核归类、价格等征税要素）。另，美国海关设有化验室，CEE有权要求其对货物进行取样化验，该化验结果具有法律效力。

CEE对审核中发现的侵犯知识产权等安全准入风险问题，移交口岸海关。口岸海关将进一步验核货物的安全准入属性，进行相应处置。

4) **Duty liquidations.** The CEEs will check and verify the declaration data. As long as the extension application is not approved, in principle, the amount of duty is settled within one year after the release of goods. The result of liquidation is published on Customs Bulletin Board. According to the result of liquidation, overcharged duty will be returned and interests will be paid. The U.S. Customs and Border Protection will issue notification for claiming back duties once errors are discovered in classification, duty exemption and appraisement.

4）**税收清算**。CEE将企业纳税申报数据与根据审核结果所做出的商品归类、估价等进行核对，只要未经特许延长手续，原则上在货物放行后1年内决定最终税款，清算的结果在海关公告栏公告。根据清算结果，多缴的税款将予以返还并支付利息；因企业归类、减免、估价等错误而少缴的税款，海关将发出追税通知。

5) **Post audit– after clearance.** the U.S. Customs and Border Protection retains the power of auditing within a certain period of time. It is known that the CEEs focus on such issues as classification and valuation and correcting mistakes. The staff shall not shoulder responsibilities for errors incurred during verification because the post-audit may help minimize such human errors.

5）**后续稽核**。在清关后，海关保留在一定期限内进行稽核的权力。据介绍，CEE专家在审核中重点关注归类、价格等问题，对审核结果可能不正确或漏审要素的，审核人员不必负责，通过后续抽核复查来减少问题的发生。

Certainly, the U.S. Customs and Border Protection has some other remedy measures, such as declaration withdraw/cancelation, reconsideration, appeal and consultation in the name of rule of law. The Automated Commercial Environment provides technical assistance.

当然，美国海关还有一些救济措施，如申报单退撤、申请复议、诉讼、协商等，并以法制为保障，自动商务环境平台提供技术支撑。

From the above information, we can clearly see that during import and export supervision,

通过以上介绍，我们可以清楚地看到，美国海关

U.S. customs combines the comprehensive control at the border and industry-specific control. Using information technology and intelligence, its control has a focus on risk analysis and risk management, which enable U.S. customs to allocate its resources more effectively to preventing security risks, and high-risk cargos that pose a threat to border security, consumer health and safety. It also prioritizes duty collection, cracking down on violation of trade regulations and IPR infringement, and the consistency of customs enforcement. All these practices will provide references for advancing China Customs' national clearance integration and establishing the two centers (Risk Management Center and Duty Collection Center).

对进出口货物的监管，将口岸综合管理和商品专业分类监管相结合，依托计算机信息技术和情报，突出风险分析和风险管理，将监管资源更有效地集中于防控准入风险、防范高风险货物对国家边境安全、消费者健康与安全的威胁，强化税收征管，打击违反贸易相关法律和侵犯知识产权的行为，提升海关执法统一性。另外，CEE也是对海关内部执法活动的相互制约和监督。这些，为我们扎实推进全国通关一体化改革，有效建立“两个中心”（风险防控中心和税收征管中心）提供参考。

海关专员俱乐部研讨会

2014年2月25日

The Customs Attachés' Club Seminar

February 25, 2014

The Customs Attachés' Club (CAC) Seminar opened successfully this morning. With great pleasure, I attended the Seminar with a keynote speech and gave my heartfelt appreciation to the Israeli Embassy for its support. The theme of my speech at the Seminar was Customs MLA (Mutual Legal Assistance)-MAA (Mutual Administrative Assistance) and AEO.

今天上午，海关专员俱乐部研讨会成功举行。我很高兴参加了研讨会，做了专题发言，并对以色列大使馆给予的支持表示感谢。研讨会上，我讲的主题是“海关执法和行政互助以及经认证的经营者互认”。

As proposed by the current rotating chair, Minister Counselor Gabriel Shemouny from Israel Customs, the Seminar this morning discussed a number of pragmatic issues including Customs mutual legal assistance, mutual administrative assistance,

根据会议轮值主席、以色列公使衔海关参赞加布里埃尔·谢默尼的提议，这次研讨会主要讨论海关实务方面的一些议题，包括海关法律互助、行政互助、AEO项目及其互

the AEO program and the practice of mutual recognition. Over the years, China Customs has been advocating "mutual exchange of information, mutual recognition of control and mutual assistance in enforcement" (3Ms) in its cooperation with international partners. We hope to work with Customs, businesses and other government authorities for enhanced connectivity and enforcement capability, more effective control and a transparent, fair and dynamic trade environment, so as to advance global trade security and facilitation. Thus, topics discussed at today's Seminar were of particular significance. At the invitation of the rotating chair, at the Seminar, China Customs introduced the policies and measures in the China (Shanghai) Pilot Free Trade Zone and shared our experience in customs control enforcement and technical operation with other members.

认。多年来，中国海关在与其他海关开展国际合作的过程中，一直倡导"信息互换、监管互认、执法互助"（3Ms）的理念。我们希望通过海关之间、海关与企业和与其他政府部门的合作，加强沟通，提升执法能力，促进有效监管，营造一个透明、公平、充满活力的贸易环境，以推进全球贸易安全与便利。因此，今天的研讨会讨论的议题具有特别重要的意义。应轮值主席的邀请，中国海关还在会上介绍了中国（上海）自由贸易试验区的政策和措施，与参会同行分享我们在海关执法监管和技术应用方面的经验。

2014年2月，北京，在海关专员俱乐部研讨会上与各国海关驻华专员交流。

February 2014, sharing with foreign Customs Attachés at the CAC Seminar.

This year marks the 6th anniversary of the CAC. We are greatly heartened by the fact that the Club is thriving with new members, better mechanisms and bigger influence. It is now a big customs family with more than 40 members from 29 countries and regions, including the attachés not only based in embassies in Beijing, but also in consulates general in Shanghai, Guangzhou and Hong Kong.

By having members rotating for chairmanship, hosting exchange activities of all kinds to share latest developments and new ideas in the international customs community, the Club is playing an increasingly important role in facilitating exchanges among customs attachés as well as between attachés and China Customs. Up till now, the Club has held more than 50 seminars, field visits and other activities, covering almost all major areas of customs operation, with participants totaling at 1500.

Members of the Club are very active in playing a positive role in deepening bilateral cooperative relations between their own customs authorities and China Customs. Beyond that, members of the Club have also provided a lot of support and assistance for China Customs development. In addition, all the Counselors and Attachés have offered

今年是海关专员俱乐部成立六周年。俱乐部新成员正在蓬勃发展，并不断完善机制，提升影响力，对此我们备受鼓舞。现在俱乐部成了一个海关大家庭，共有来自29个国家和地区的40多名成员，不仅有各国驻北京大使馆的海关专员，还包括常驻上海、广州和香港等地总领事馆工作的海关专员。

通过成员轮值主席制度，举办各种交流活动、分享在国际海关领域的最新进展和最新思想，俱乐部在促进海关专员之间的工作交流以及与中国海关的沟通方面正发挥着愈发重要的作用。截至目前，俱乐部总共举行了50多场研讨会、实地考察及其他类别活动，涵盖了海关实务操作的几乎所有议题，参与者总计达1500人。

在深化各国海关与中国海关的双边合作方面，俱乐部成员也发挥了积极作用。与此同时，俱乐部成员还为中国海关事业发展提供了许多支持和帮助。此外，在中国海关代表团赴其派出国访问期间，所有的海关参赞和海关专员都提供了

great assistance to China Customs delegations during visiting in their countries. Actually, we have built deep friendship, caring for each other and helping each other.

极大的支持和便利。实际上，我们已经建立起了深厚的友谊，彼此关怀，相互帮助。

For instance, Israeli Minister Counselor of Customs Mr. Gabriel Shemouny has done outstanding work in mutual assistance regarding anti-smuggling cases. Meanwhile, German Customs Attaché Mr. Manfred Hofmann, in fighting against smuggling; Russian Customs Counselor Mr. Konstantin Toporkov, Kazakhstan Customs Counselor Ms. Saule Nurgaliyeva, and Representative of EU Customs Mr. Christophe Besse, in negotiating bilateral cooperation documents; Canadian Customs Attaché Mr. William R. Hetherington, in anti-money laundering; U.S. CBP Attaché Mr. Kent Krul and ICE Attaché Mr. James P Nagle, in supply chain security and facilitation; Japan Customs Attaché Mr. Masataka Dei, Korean Customs Attaché Mr. Kim Jeong and Italian Customs Attaché Mr. Marco Mamone in twinning cooperation, have made great contributions to deepening the bilateral cooperation between China and their mother countries.

比如，以色列公使衔海关参赞加布里埃尔·谢默尼先生在反走私执法互助方面做了出色的工作。同时，德国海关专员曼弗雷德·霍夫曼先生在打击走私方面、俄罗斯海关顾问康斯坦丁·托波可夫先生和哈萨克斯坦海关顾问索勒女士及欧盟海关代表克利斯多夫·贝斯先生等在双边合作文件磋商方面、加拿大海关专员威廉·海瑟林顿先生在反洗钱方面、美国海关与边境保护局专员肯特·克鲁尔先生及美国移民和海关执法局专员詹姆斯·纳格尔先生在供应链安全与便利合作方面、日本海关专员出井昌孝先生和韩国海关专员金郑其先生及意大利海关专员马可先生在关际合作方面等等，都为深化中国与有关国家的双边海关合作做出了巨大贡献。

Beyond that, members of the Club have also provided a lot of support and assistance for China Customs development, including on

此外，俱乐部成员还对中国海关开展技术设备应用、国外海关查验率和查获率以及海

the researches carried out by China Customs on the application of technical equipment, inspection rate and seizure rate of overseas customs, and customs operation in free trade zones. During the investigation and study, China Customs has received a lot of useful information and valuable experience from Customs Counselor and Customs Attachés from different countries. All the information provided is of great significance and is very instructive to the reform and development of China Customs.

CAC is indeed a good platform for all member customs to exchange information and experiences, enhance mutual assistance and cooperation, and strengthen the friendship. China Customs will be ready to do more to support the work of CAC and continue to help with its development in the future.

关对自由贸易区的监管等研究给予了热情帮助。在执法调研期间，中国海关收到了很多来自各国海关专员的十分有用的信息和宝贵的经验。所有提供的信息对中国海关的改革和发展都具有积极的借鉴意义。

海关专员俱乐部确实是一个很好的合作平台。所有成员海关都可以在这个平台上交流信息和经验，加强互助与合作并深化友谊。中国海关将更加努力地支持海关专员俱乐部的工作，愿继续为海关专员俱乐部的蓬勃发展提供帮助。

首期中非海关“现代化管理”高级培训班

2016年2月29日

The 1st Seminar on China-Africa Customs Modernization

February 29, 2016

It was a great pleasure to be in Shanghai Customs College with so many friends for the 1st China-Africa Customs Seminar on Modernization in the wonderful season of spring on 29th February. The seminar is aimed to follow up on the achievements made by President Xi Jinping's visit to Africa and further boost customs cooperation between China and Africa by means of capacity building in customs law enforcement.

2月的上海，春意渐浓。我很高兴与来自非洲国家海关的新老朋友们在上海海关学院相聚一堂，共同出席第一期中非海关“现代化管理”高级培训班。我们举办这次培训班，目的是为了落实习近平主席访问非洲成果安排，通过海关能力建设促进中非海关执法合作。

President Xi Jinping visited Zimbabwe and South Africa in December, 2015 and co-held the Johannesburg Summit of the China-Africa cooperation forum with the President of South Africa. During the summit, the Chinese

2015年12月，中国国家主席习近平访问津巴布韦、南非，并与南非总统共同主持中非合作论坛约翰内斯堡峰会。峰会期间，中国政府发表了

government released China's second *Africa Policy Paper* and proposed 10 cooperation programs in 2016-2018 between China and Africa. The paper and programs highlight the content of customs cooperation, which goes "to promote trade and investment facilitation and continue to grant zero-tariff treatment to 97% of taxable items from the least developed countries that have established diplomatic relations with China; enhance customs cooperation between China and Africa, strengthen mutual exchange of information, mutual recognition of control and mutual assistance in enforcement; jointly combat commercial fraud and create a law-biding and convenient trade environment; to help African countries improve capacity building and promote trade facilitation. "

第二份《中国对非洲政策文件》，并提出了2016-2018中非十大合作计划。政策文件和合作计划强调海关合作内容，要求"促进中非贸易与投资便利化，继续对原产于与中国建交的最不发达国家97%税目产品实施零关；推动中非海关合作，加强信息互换、监管互认和执法互助；共同打击商业瞒骗行为，营造守法便利的贸易环境；帮助非洲国家加强海关等执法能力建设，提高贸易便利化水平"。

Therefore, many customs authorities from African countries attached great importance and paid actively response to this seminar. We had a total of 54 participants from 12 African countries (Ethiopia, Kenya, Malawi, Mauritius, Namibia, Nigeria, Rwanda, South Africa, Tanzania, Uganda, Zimbabwe) and regional organization (EAC, the East African Community). Most of the delegations were headed by director generals or commissioners and even commissioner-generals. By holding this seminar, we hope to build a platform for

因此，我们举办这次培训班得到了非洲国家海关的高度重视和积极响应。共有12个非洲国家（埃塞俄比亚、肯尼亚、马拉维、毛里求斯、纳米比亚、尼日利亚、卢旺达、南非、坦桑尼亚、乌干达、津巴布韦）和地区海关（东非共同体）54位代表前来参加，大多数还是由署、局领导亲自带队前来。通过培训班搭建起一个互相交流的平台，大家相互尊

exchanges. The cooperation between China and African customs can only go further if we have a better understanding of each other and learn from each other based on mutual respect and trust.

At the opening ceremony of the seminar, I firstly delivered a warm welcome speech on behalf of the General Administration of Chinese Customs and then gave the first lecture on "China Customs Today". That I chose this subject was mainly because in the new context of a complex and changing world, customs administrations were in need of reform and innovation in response to new challenges. I mainly touched upon three aspects: First, a brief introduction of China Customs. Second, our modern management philosophy and reforms and innovations. And last but not least, China Customs international cooperation. Through my introduction, we shared the experience and achievements gained in the recent development, reform and innovation of China Custom with all participants to realize joint progress, mutually-beneficial cooperation and common development of China-Africa Customs. We all hoped to continuously improve trade facilitation and safety between China and Africa and make more contributions to our socioeconomic development and people's welfare.

重、相互学习、相互借鉴，通过加强海关执法能力建设，进一步推进中非海关的务实合作。

在开班仪式上，我首先代表中国海关作了热情洋溢的欢迎致辞，随后就以“当今中国海关”为题，给学员们讲了第一课。我确定这个主题的演讲，主要是考虑在当今世界复杂多变的新形势下，海关如何面对新问题和新挑战，向管理现代化迈进。主要谈三个方面内容：一是中国海关概况；二是中国海关现代管理理念和改革创新；三是中国海关国际合作。希望通过我的介绍与各位海关同仁分享中国海关近年发展和改革创新的经验与成果，实现中非海关携手并进、合作共赢、共同发展，不断促进中非贸易便利与安全，为双方经济社会发展和人民的幸福作出海关积极贡献。

There is a saying in Africa, "Only a river with a living source can run deep." China and Africa enjoy longstanding friendship. Over the years, we have been friends, partners and brothers, respecting each other and working together for mutual benefit and common development. China has been Africa's largest trading partner for 7 consecutive years, with bilateral trade volume standing at USD 179.1 billion last year. China has granted zero-tariff treatment to 97% of the goods exported from 31 least developed countries in Africa that have diplomatic ties with China. China has built more than 20 economic and trade cooperation zones on the continent. Its investment in Africa has been growing at an annual average of 37%, with more than 3000 Chinese companies making an investment there. The rapid growth of China-Africa business and trade ties has opened up broad prospects for Customs cooperation.

非洲有句谚语，“河有泉水才深”。中非友好源远流长。中非有着传统而深厚的友谊，多年来坚持平等相待、合作共赢、共同发展，是好朋友、好伙伴、好兄弟。中国已经连续7年成为非洲第一大贸易伙伴，去年中非贸易额达到1791亿美元，中国向31个与我建交的非洲最不发达国家实施了97%输华产品零关税待遇，支持在非洲兴建了20多个经贸合作区，中国对非投资年均增长37%，超过3000家中国企业在非洲投资落户。中非经贸合作的跨越式发展为海关合作提供了广阔的空间。

Customs plays an irreplaceable role in safeguarding trade security and facilitation as well as promoting regional economic growth. Over the years, under the stewardship of international organizations such as the WCO, Customs cooperation has been prospering, ensuring border and trade security while facilitating cross-border flow of goods, people, currency and information, and making

作为全球供应链上的重要节点，海关在维护贸易安全与便利、促进区域经济合作方面发挥着不可替代的重要作用。近年来，在世界海关组织（WCO）等国际组织的推动和倡导下，各国海关间合作蓬勃发展，在促进商品、人员、货币、信息等跨国界高效快捷

significant contribution to global trade and regional economic integration, which is demonstrated in:

流动的同时，有效维护了边境安全和贸易安全，为促进全球贸易发展和区域经济一体化作出了重要贡献。突出表现在：

——**The sustained growth of global trade.** By reform and innovation, Customs administrations have achieved fairness and efficiency in tariff collection, as well as simplification and harmonization of clearance procedures, and thus boosted global trade. From 2011 to 2014, global trade in goods grew from USD 12 trillion to USD 37 trillion.

——**全球贸易额持续增长**。各国海关通过改革创新，实现关税征管公平、高效，通关手续简化、协调，助推国际贸易增长。2001年至2014年，全球货物贸易额从12万亿美元增长到37万亿美元。

——**Significantly improved trade facilitation.** By risk management, capacity building and the application of technologies, the Customs community has raised the effectiveness of supervision and control and cut trade costs. By the end of 2014, 175 Customs administrations around the world have put in place automation systems and 60% of all Customs administrations now exercise paperless clearance.

——**贸易便利化显著提高**。各国海关通过实施风险管理，加强能力建设和科技应用，提升监管效能，降低贸易成本。截至2014年，全球有175个海关建立了自动化系统，60％的海关应用电子化通关。

——**Enhanced supply chain security.** The Customs community has together effectively curbed cross-border crimes and enhanced supply chain security by strengthening enforcement cooperation. From June 2013 to June 2014 alone, 7 international Customs enforcement operations were launched by the WCO, including SkyNet and

——**供应链安全得到提升**。各国海关通过加强执法合作，有效遏制了跨国违法活动，提升了供应链安全水平。仅2013年6月至2014年6月，世界海关组织就先后协调发起国际海关执法行动7起，包括中国海关倡议发起的“天网行

Demeter III initiated by China Customs, which curbed the smuggling of drugs, hazardous waste, weapons and endangered wild species, as well as IPR infringement.

动”和第三期“大地女神”行动，有力打击了毒品、有害废物、武器、濒危野生动植物走私以及假冒侵权等跨国违法犯罪行为。

The seminar ended successfully on 11th, March. That day, I attended the closing ceremony for farewell speech and handed the certificates to each of the participants in the hall of Shanghai Customs College. From the playback of photos and video clips which played in the closing ceremony, we all felt precious and beautiful memories as well as deep friendship.

为期两周的中非海关“现代化管理”高级培训班于3月11日圆满结束。那天，我再次来到上海海关学院参加结业式致辞并为每一位学员颁发证书。从结业式上回放的照片、录像剪辑和我们交流，大家共同感受到了珍贵美好的回忆和深厚的友谊。

Over the past two weeks, we had in-depth discussions on a wide range of topics of modernization including tariff collection, Customs supervision and control, technological innovation, trade facilitation, crackdown on smuggling and statistics compilation. We were particularly impressed by the presentations on African customs reforms and modernization drives, as well as their insightful comments in class. Experience gained from modernization reforms was shared and field visits to Shanghai and Suzhou Customs operation sites were arranged. What's more, there were a large variety of cultural activities in the spare time including Chinese classes, table tennis matches, Tai Chi practices and calligraphy

在过去的两周里，大家围绕“海关现代化管理”这一主题，在税收征管、通关监管、风险管理、科技创新、贸易便利化、打击走私和贸易统计等业务领域进行了深入的研讨，与会非洲海关代表对各自海关改革发展情况的介绍和在课堂上的精彩发言，也给我们留下了深刻印象。我们对海关现代化改革与发展的经验做了全面的交流，还实地参观访问了上海海关和苏州海关监管现场。除业务研讨以外，课余期间大家还开展了学习中文、乒乓球友谊赛、太极拳、书法等丰富

lessons. I know they also visited the Bund, Lujiazui, the Huangpu River, the Humble Administrator's Garden and the Museum of Suzhou Embroidery Art. The seminar is short, but our friendship will go a long way into the future. Just as the President Xi Jinping said at the Johannesburg Summit, "When brother's work in one mind, nothing is too difficult for them."

多彩的文化交流活动，并游览了上海外滩、陆家嘴、黄浦江以及苏州拙政园、刺绣博物馆等著名的景点。培训班是短期的，但友谊是长存的。就如习近平主席在中非合作论坛约翰内斯堡峰会上所说的，“兄弟同心，其利断金。”

As a major event to follow through on the consensus of the Johannesburg Summit, the seminar is a new starting point for Customs cooperation. China customs will come up with plans which will help both sides realize mutual recognition of controls, mutual exchange of information and mutual assistance in China-African customs enforcement. Next, we will focus on the following areas:

本次培训班作为中非合作论坛约翰内斯堡峰会的后续工作，拉开了中非海关务实合作的序幕。中国海关将与非洲海关认真研究制定合作方案，全面推进“监管互认、信息互换、执法互助”合作。下一步我们将着重加强以下合作：

Firstly, we wish to enhance connectivity and promote trade facilitation through win-win cooperation. China is working on the "Belt and Road" initiative to achieve exchanges on policies,the connection of infrastructure, fast flow of trade, enhanced cooperation in finance and deepened the friendship between the peoples. Meanwhile, Africa's *Agenda 2063* aims to build a prosperous Africa with inclusive growth and sustainable development. The aligned targets of ours present an opportunity for closer

第一，坚持互联互通、互利共赢，促进中非海关贸易便利化合作。中国正在大力推进“一带一路”建设，推动与各国之间实现政策沟通、设施连通、贸易畅通、资金融通和民心相通；非洲制定了《2063年议程》，努力建设以包容性增长和可持续发展为基础的繁荣非洲。双方发展目标相互呼应，为合作向更高水平发展提供了契机。中非海关在促进人

cooperation. China and African Customs share responsibilities and needs in speeding up cross-border movement of people, goods, capital and services. We are willing to work together on building "Single Window", improving the facilities of Customs clearance, implementing the WTO *Trade Facilitation Agreement*. Establishing and improving AEO programs and even mutual recognition of them will help us build a partnership with the private sector. Also, we need to facilitate the development of cross-border e-commerce, economic cooperation parks and other emerging forms of business, in an effort to better facilitate trade.

员、商品、资金和服务跨境流通、降低贸易成本方面有着共同的责任和需求。我们愿与非洲海关推进国际贸易"单一窗口"建设，改善边境口岸通关设施条件，支持WTO贸易便利化协定的实施，建立和完善"经认证的经营者"（AEO）制度并推动互认，与企业构建伙伴合作关系，并积极促进跨境电子商务、经贸合作园区建设等新型业态发展，提高贸易便利化水平。

Secondly, we wish to deepen China–Africa Customs enforcement cooperation through concerted efforts. Offenses and crimes including commercial fraud, IPR infringement, drug and wildlife trafficking pose serious challenges to both China and African Customs. China Customs is willing to sign and implement bilateral CMAAs with African Customs, which provide a legal framework for intelligence exchange, case investigation assistance, joint supervision and targeted joint operations. We will also explore new models of anti-smuggling cooperation with our African partners. Additionally, we hope that an effective platform and mechanism for information exchange will be established

第二，坚持协同防范，深化中非海关执法合作。商业瞒骗、侵犯知识产权、毒品和濒危野生动植物走私等违法犯罪活动，是中非海关面临的共同挑战。中国海关愿与更多非洲国家海关签署和实施双边海关行政互助协定，共同探索新的缉私合作模式，在协议框架下积极开展情报交换、案件协查、联合监管和专项执法行动等执法合作。同时，我们愿依据国际通行标准和各自职责，与非洲海关研究建立行之有效的信息数据交换平台和工作机制，逐步实现对贸易统计数

by China and African Customs based on international standards and their respective mandates, through which we can exchange statistics, Customs clearance data and case seizure data in a systematic and regular manner, making our cooperation more effective and better targeted.

据、海关通关数据、查获案件信息等数据的系统化、机制化交换，提高合作的针对性和有效性。

Thirdly, China Customs will commit itself to closer capacity building cooperation with African Customs. More seminars will be held to discuss issues of mutual interest, such as valuation, risk management, bonded operation, supervision of customs special control areas, the use of scanners and combating the trafficking of drugs and endangered wild species. The seminars will target officers of different levels. We also plan to send experts abroad for lectures and invite officers to China for attachment programs to share knowledge and experience with African Customs that face similar challenges as we do. We will continue to explore good ways to offer aid and do what we can in seeking to have some of the government's foreign aid budget directed toward helping African Customs. Meanwhile, we will seek to support the capacity building efforts of African Customs with the WCO China Fund.

第三，全面开展中非海关能力建设合作。我们将围绕非洲海关普遍关注的估价、风险管理、保税与海关特殊监管区域监管、集装箱扫描技术、打击毒品和濒危野生动植物走私等主题举办一系列面向非洲海关不同层次官员的培训班、研讨班、专家讲学和跟班作业等项目，愿与更多和中国海关面临同样挑战的非洲国家海关深入交流分享边境口岸监管通关经验。在中国政府对非援助框架下，积极协助非洲海关提出的援助申请，提供力所能及的支持与协助。此外，将加大WCO中国能力建设基金项目下的合作，支持非洲海关的能力建设。

Fourthly, we wish to enhance cooperation in Customs reform and modernization by

第四，坚持交流互鉴，推动中非海关改革与现代化管理

learning from each other. Reform and innovation are core philosophies of China Customs. Over the past few years, China Customs has been working on integrated Customs clearance scheme by introducing paperless clearance, regional integrated clearance, Customs-Quarantine cooperation featuring "one declaration, joint inspection and single release" aiming to facilitate trade. We have accumulated experience in customs international cooperation in joint Customs control, mutual recognition of AEOs, Smart and Secure Trade Lane (SSTL) project, risk management, data exchange, joint enforcement, intelligence exchange and capacity building. We are willing to share our experience and learn from the experience of African Customs in management, reforms and innovation, and the practice in line with international standards, so as to jointly improve customs enforcement and administration.

合作。改革创新是中国海关的核心理念之一。近年来，中国海关全面推进大通关建设，开展了通关作业无纸化、区域通关一体化、关检“三个一”，即“一次申报、一次查验、一次放行”等改革，不断提高贸易便利化水平。面向国际，我们通过多双边国际合作平台，与相关海关开展了联合监管、AEO互认、安全智能贸易航线、风险管理、数据交换、联合执法、情报信息交换、能力建设等宽领域、多层次的海关国际合作， 积累了合作共赢的成功经验。我们愿通过组织实施能力建设合作项目，与非洲海关共同分享这些经验，并希望学习借鉴非洲海关在管理方式、改革创新以及与国际接轨等方面的经验和做法，共同提高海关的执法和管理水平。

辑二

政治、经济、外贸

Politics, Economy and Foreign Trade

实现"中国梦" 人人须行动

2013 年 5 月 20 日

Pitch in for the "Chinese Dream"

May 20, 2013

After the 18th CPC National Congress, the Chinese National Museum held a grand exhibition themed "The Road of Rejuvenation". The exhibition covered China's modern history starting from the Opium War in 1840. Through 1200 plus cultural relics and over 870 photos, it depicts the hard-fought battles against Imperialism oppression. It hails a glorious and arduous journey of the Chinese people, who following the leadership of the Chinese Communist Party, explored with unremitting efforts to build the People's Republic of China, a strong modernized socialist country that is independent, democratic and prosperous. It shows the

党的十八大胜利闭幕后，中国国家博物馆举行了一场主题为"复兴之路"的专题展览。该展览回顾了自1840年鸦片战争以来的中国近代史，通过展出1200余件文物和870余张照片，描绘了中国人民反对帝国主义压迫的浴血奋斗，叙述了中国人民在中国共产党的领导下为建立新中国和建设发展一个独立、民主、繁荣的社会主义现代化强国而艰辛探索、不懈努力的光辉历程，体现了中国人民自强不息、勇往直前的民族精神。也正是在参

perseverant and courageous spirit of the Chinese nation. It was during the visit to the exhibition that General Secretary Xi Jinping put forward the "Chinese Dream" of the great rejuvenation of the Chinese nation – the dream that reflects the interests of the Chinese people as a whole.

观此次展览期间，习近平总书记首次提出了中华民族伟大复兴的梦想，这是反映全体中国人民利益的"中国梦"。

History proves that any individual's future and destiny is closely connected with the future of his country. People can only live well when the country and nation enjoy sound development. This glorious dream requests tireless efforts of generations of the Chinese people. We firmly believe that a moderately prosperous society in all respects will be realized by the time when the Communist Party of China celebrates its 100th anniversary. And by the centenary of the People's Republic, we can definitely build it into a prosperous, democratic, culturally advanced and harmonious modern socialist country. We admit that there will be twists and turns on the future journey of the Chinese nation, but in the end, we will be successful.

历史告诉我们，每一个人的个人前途命运都与国家的未来紧密相连。只有国家和民族不断发展，人们才能过上好日子。这个光荣的梦想需要一代又一代的中国人不懈努力。我们坚信，在中国共产党成立100周年之时，我们将会实现全面建成小康社会的宏愿；待到新中国成立100周年，中国将成为富强、民主、文明、和谐的社会主义现代化国家。虽然中华民族的未来之路免不了曲折与困难，但最终我们一定会走向成功。

The realization of the Chinese Dream not only involves political, economic and social development, but a lot more areas such as technology, culture, education, environmental protection, people's wellbeing, military, as well as national unity, and peace

实现中国梦，不仅体现在政治、经济和社会发展进步上，还体现在科技、文化、教育、环保、民生、军事以及祖国统一、世界和平发展等方方面面。以构建社会主义市场经

and development of the world. Take building the socialist market economy system for an example. The market cannot always grow at a constant speed, and a curve with rise and fall is a normal one in keeping with the market law. Therefore, regarding the relations between the market and the government, we have to first abandon the old policy-dependent mindset to cut back on the abuse of administrative measures to bail out or stimulate the market. Instead, we should build an open, fair, well-regulated, competitive, orderly, stable and healthy business environment, so that market resources can be allocated in the most effective way and all market elements can be stimulated. Meanwhile, we need to better play out the role of the government, not by interference or substitution, but by macro guidance and supervision. Too much or improper government intervention will hinder the development of a fair and just market. Meanwhile, regulators should strictly punish illegal business activities including inside trading. Only when the regulator completely separates itself from specific market activities and resume its original role as a supervising and administrative body, can a fair and transparent market order find the space to grow. We should give full play to the market's own functions and allocate more resources

济体系为例，市场不可能总是呈直线增长，有起有落才是符合市场规律的正常曲线。因此，在处理市场与政府的关系上，我们应该抛弃原先高度依赖政策的思维方式，减少一味地采取行政手段或救市来刺激市场，而应通过营造公开公平、法制规范、竞争有序、稳定健康的营商环境，使市场资源得到最有效的合理配置，充分激发市场各要素活力。与此同时，又要更好地发挥政府的作用，不是干预或替代，而是宏观指导和监督。政府干预过多或不当，市场便永远无法实现公平公正。同时，监管部门应当严厉惩罚内幕交易等非法商业活动。只有当监管机构从特定的市场活动中完全剥离出来，回归监督管理的角色，公平透明的市场秩序才有可能逐步成长起来。充分发挥市场自身的功能，将更多资源向遵纪守法、促进经济社会发展的企业和部门倾斜，逐步优胜劣汰，经济才能持续健康发展，为中国梦的实现打下坚实的基础。

to compliant companies that help promote socioeconomic development while eliminating backward ones, so as to secure sustained and sound economic growth, laying a solid foundation for the realization of the Chinese Dream.

"The Chinese Dream" is the dream of the people. We all have to pitch in for the dream to come true. I would like to say a few words from the perspective of our country's youths. Youths should contribute to the Chinese Dream. Most people understand the Chinese Dream in a general sense. Yet in fact, it is more than a dream of the country and the nation, but also a demonstration of the various dreams of the Chinese people. Only by fully integrating our individual dreams with the national one, integrating "the Chinese Dream" with people's needs for a better life and advancing them simultaneously, can we constantly find the positive driving force in our work, study and life.

“中国梦”是人民的梦。实现“中国梦”，人人须行动。关于这一点，我特别想站在年轻人的角度说上几句。年轻人应当为中国梦贡献自己的力量。人人都在谈中国梦，大多数人对这一概念的认识仅仅停留在宏观层面的理解上，但实际上中国梦不仅是国家和民族的梦，也是每个中国人实现个人梦想的集中体现。只有把个人的“小梦”与民族的“大梦”充分融合，也就是把实现“中国梦”与人民对美好生活向往的追求结合起来，共同推进，我们才能在自己的工作、学习、生活中不断找到昂扬向上的动力。

The young generation, with their firm will, strong sense of responsibility and outstanding professional competence, is the main force in realizing the Chinese Dream and where our hope lies. The young Chinese people from all walks of life, no matter an

从现实看，年青一代拥有坚强的意志、强烈的责任感和出色的专业能力，是实现中国梦的主力军和希望所在。中国各行各业的年轻人，无论是企业家还是公务员，空间技术

entrepreneur or a public servant, a space technology engineer or a farmer, a soldier or a migrant worker, a doctor or a teacher, should dare to dream and work assiduously to fulfill their dreams in order to contribute to the revitalization of the nation. When facing adversities, young people should stay steadfast to their faith, embrace the challenges optimistically and tenaciously, continuously refine their professional skills through hard work and build up their noble characters, until the dawn of success falls upon them.

工程师还是农民，是军人、农民工、医生还是人民教师，都应当敢于梦想，不懈努力去实现梦想，从而为民族复兴作出贡献。在困境中，年轻人应当坚定信念，保持定力，秉持乐观和顽强的奋斗精神，迎接挑战，同时用勤奋与坚持不断完善自己的专业技能，培养高尚的道德情操，直至迎来成功的曙光。

A nation will prosper if its young generation is ambitious and reliable. Actually, in the course of China's road towards modernization in the last century, youths had made an important contribution in social transformation and national rejuvenation. In the current information era, China's development still calls for the commitment and sacrifice of its young people. The Chinese Dream can be attainable only through down-to-earth work.

如果一个国家的年青一代踏实而上进，这个国家将走向繁荣。事实上，在中国20世纪走过的现代化历程中，便离不开年轻人对社会转型和民族复兴所做的巨大贡献。在当今信息时代，中国的发展仍然呼唤年轻人的投身与奉献。只有脚踏实地地肯干苦干，中国梦才有可能成为现实。

China is expecting to realize its own intelligent digital dream. I still remember the first time when I saw the wallpaper of a Shanghai subway station turned into a "digital shelf". I simply scanned the barcode of an item on the "shelf" and paid, and by the time I got home, the product I ordered was already on my doorway. Moreover, while traveling

中国期待实现属于自己的智能与数字梦想。我还记得，第一次看到上海地铁车站内的墙上出现了一批“数字货架”，我只需简单地扫描“架上”的条形码下单，下了地铁回到家时，就能在家门口发现刚才购买的商品。乘坐地铁

on the light rail, we will always notice that most people are focusing on the screen of their mobile phones. They are either browsing microblogs and news, playing games or messaging with their friends. Today, more than half of all access to the Internet occurs on mobile devices. Technology is revolutionizing the way we interact with the world.

We live in a time of great possibilities. The advent of new information technology provides China with more solutions to its problems and more opportunities for future development. In the past, benefits from information technology were mostly related to productivity and efficiency gains. Today, China is on its way to building the world's largest e-commerce market and further improving people's well-being. Driven by technical progress, more and more innovators are creating new businesses in completely new ways. In this process, they really combine the Chinese Dream with their own conscious actions

China is willing to share its dream with the world, provide positive energy for global peace and prosperity. The Chinese Dream will bring peace, development, cooperation and opportunities, but by no means any threats to the world.

Each country has its own problems.

时，也很难不注意到许多人都紧盯着手机的数字屏幕：他们或是全神贯注于微博、新闻，或是玩手机游戏，或与朋友发微信。今天，超过一半的互联网访问是通过手机等移动设备实现的。技术彻底改变了中国与世界的互动方式。

我们生活的时代充满了各种可能性。新的信息技术的诞生，为中国各类问题带来了更多解决方案，也创造了更多发展机会。过去，信息技术通常与生产力和效率效益相关。而今，得益于技术进步，中国正在发展世界上最大的电子商务市场，人们的生活质量不断改善。在技术进步的驱动下，越来越多的创新者们正在通过全新的方式实现成功创业。在这个过程中，他们切切实实地将中国梦融入了自身的自觉行动。

中国愿与世界分享梦想，为全球的和平与繁荣提供“正能量”。中国梦将为世界带来和平、发展、合作和机会，但绝不给世界造成任何威胁。

每个国家都面临各自的问

China has become the world's second-largest economy, but its per capita GDP remains low because of a huge population. Besides, China still has a long way to go in many fields. There are many more factors other than GDP growth that will equally influence the realization of the Chinese Dream, such as technological innovation, improvement of people's wellbeing, environmental protection, and coverage of college education and medical insurance. Some other "soft measurements" are even more important, including China's innovating capability and global influence. Furthermore, the realization of a beautiful dream also requires a country with improved social morality and legal environment.

The Chinese Dream is a vision, the realization of which needs the efforts of every Chinese. We should all share General Secretary Xi Jinping's vision for the great rejuvenation of the Chinese nation, more diligently fulfill the responsibilities in work and contribute towards the final realization of the Chinese Dream.

题。中国已成为世界第二大经济体，但由于人口基数庞大，其人均国内生产总值仍然不高。除此之外，中国在许多领域还有较大的进步空间。除了国内生产总值，还有很多其他因素对中国梦的实现起着同等重要的作用，包括科技创新、民生改善，也包括环境保护、高等教育和医保覆盖范围等。一些“软指标”更为重要，比如国家的创新能力和全球影响力。同时，美好梦想的实现，还需要国家总体道德水平和法治环境的不断提升。

中国梦是一个愿景，需要通过每一个中国人的努力才能变为现实。我们应当积极响应习总书记提出的中华民族伟大复兴的号召，在各自的岗位上恪尽职守、加倍努力，为实现中国梦作出应有的贡献。

关于“四个全面”战略布局

2015年3月10日

The Four-pronged Comprehensive Strategy

March 10, 2015

The 12th National People's Congress (NPC), China's national legislature, opened its Third Plenary Session on the morning of March 5 at the Great Hall of the People in Beijing. Nearly 3,000 NPC deputies from across the country attended the Session along with top Party and state leaders.

Premier Li Keqiang delivered his annual government work report at the opening meeting, made an objective review of the work of the government in 2014, analyzed the situation we are facing and put forward tasks, objectives and the new plan for the work in 2015. I listened to the report carefully that day and specially focused on the four-pronged

3月5日上午，中国的立法机构——第十二届全国人民代表大会在北京人民大会堂举行了第三次全体会议。党和国家领导人、来自各地的近3000名全国人大代表参加了会议。

会议期间，李克强总理做了关于政府工作的年度报告，客观回顾了2014年工作，分析了当前面临的形势，又为我们呈现了2015年新的政府工作任务、目标和路线图。当日，我认真听取了报告全文，并重点关注了“四个全面”战略布局

comprehensive strategy.

The four-pronged comprehensive strategy refers to a political concept, which comprises "comprehensively building a moderately prosperous society in all respects, comprehensively deepening reform, comprehensively advancing the rule of law, and comprehensively supervising the Communist Party of China". This strategy represents the basic direction of building a strong modern socialist society of China.

Here I'd like to share some thoughts about the main idea and key words of the four-pronged comprehensive strategy.

The strategic goal. Comprehensively building an overall moderately well-off society is the strategic goal of China's modernization drive, which is aimed at solving people's livelihood problems. At the launch of reform and opening-up in 1978, Deng Xiaoping emphasized the importance of raising people's living standards. Thanks to the reform and opening-up, China has succeeded in the primary stage of building a moderately well-off society by the beginning of this century. Now its goal is to comprehensively build an overall moderately prosperous society by 2020. To achieve this goal, the Party and the government will propel social and economic development in order to improve people's

的有关内容。

“四个全面”战略布局包括“全面建成小康社会、全面深化改革、全面依法治国和全面从严治党”四个方面。这一战略布局体现了中国建设社会主义现代化强国的基本方向。

在此，我想重点谈谈对“四个全面”战略布局主旨和内容中几个关键词的理解：

一是战略目标。全面建成小康社会是中国现代化建设的战略目标，旨在解决人民群众生活中遇到的各种问题。1978年起，中国开始实施改革开放政策，其时邓小平同志便高度重视人民生活水平的提升。改革开放带来了巨大进步。21世纪初，中国已经进入小康社会，现在的目标是到2020年全面建成小康社会。为实现这一目标，党和政府将不断推动社会和经济发展，进一步改善人民生活。这一发展目标也同时表明，中国的现代化建设并非一味追求GDP的高增长率，而

livelihoods. Also, China's goal makes it clear that its modernization drive is not to pursue high GDP. Instead, it is to improve the lives of the Chinese people, which is exactly what General Secretary Xi Jinping's governing philosophy is all about.

是改善中国人民的生活质量，这也是习近平治国理政理念的核心思想所在。

An all-round in-depth reform. China has reached a crucial stage in its effort to comprehensively build a moderately prosperous society through its reform and opening-up. The main problem at this stage is to overcome the deep systematic obstacles hindering its development. And only comprehensively deepening reform can remove these obstacles. The Third Plenum of the 18th CPC Central Committee in 2013 released a roadmap and timetable for comprehensively deepening reform. More importantly, the general objective of comprehensively deepening reform has been established, which is the modernization of state governance. This objective is also part of General Secretary Xi Jinping's governance philosophy. What China's modernization pursues is not only social and economic in nature, but also the building of a sound and mature modern state. Reform shall be pushed forward, with a focus on cutting government red tape, reforming the tax and financial sector, as well as reforming state-owned enterprises and assets.

二是全面深化改革。中国加大改革开放、全面建成小康社会的事业已经来到了一个关键阶段。现阶段面临的主要问题在于解决阻碍发展的深层次系统性难题。只有全面深化改革，才能妥善解决这些问题。2013年召开的中共十八届三中全会公布了全面深化改革的时间表和路线图，并提出了全面深化改革的总目标，即推进国家治理体系和治理能力现代化，这也是习近平治国理政理念的重要组成部分。中国的现代化建设，本质上说不仅仅是为了追求经济和社会领域的进步，也涉及建设一个健康成熟的现代化国家。改革需要不断推向前进，重点在于简政放权、实施税收和金融领域改革及国有企业和国资改革。

For example, China plans to lower the annual GDP growth target to around 7 percent from 7.5 percent, the slowest in 22 years, and to keep increase of consumer price index (CPI) at around 3 percent. We will continue to implement proactive fiscal policy and prudent monetary policy in 2015, while noting policy flexibility to sustain economic growth. The government will further liberalize interest rate and make steady progress to make the yuan freely convertible under the capital account including setting up a pilot program to allow individual investors to directly invest in overseas markets. China will encourage qualified private investors to establish, in accordance with the law, small and medium-sized banks and other financial institutions. On the other hand, the government will pay much more attention to environmental protection, pledge to accelerate the promotion of cleaner and renewable sources of energy and tackle pollution by restricting the use of coal and cutting carbon emission. The consumption of coal will have zero growth in key areas, while the intensity of carbon dioxide will be cut by at least 3.1 percent. Premier Li Keqiang also emphasized green, safe, and efficient development of the agricultural sector.

例如，中国的GDP年增长率目标已经从7.5%调整至7%，是22年内的最低值，并力图将居民消费价格指数保持在3%左右。2015年，中国将继续实施积极的财政政策和稳健的货币政策，并注意政策灵活性，确保经济持续增长。政府将进一步解放利率，稳步实现人民币资本项目可兑换，包括开展个人投资者境外投资试点等。此外，中国还将推动具备条件的民间资本依法发起设立中小型银行等金融机构。另一方面，政府还将加大环境保护力度，加快清洁能源和可再生能源的使用，限制煤炭使用，减少碳排放，从而更好解决污染问题。政府将促进重点区域煤炭消费零增长，二氧化碳排放强度要降低3.1%以上。李克强总理还强调，中国要努力实现绿色、安全、高效的农业发展。

A comprehensive framework for promoting the rule of law. The rule of law is the basic characteristic of a modern state and

三是全面依法治国。依法治国是现代化国家的基本特征，也是确保民主和公平的前

a prerequisite for guaranteeing democracy and fairness. Governing the country in accordance with the law will be determined by the overall goal of comprehensively deepening reform, which is the basic foundation of reform in every aspect. President Xi has been reiterating the importance of governing the country in accordance with the law, saying that governance should be according to the Constitution and we should jointly promote integrated construction of the country, government and society with the rule of law. The Fourth Plenum of the 18th CPC Central Committee has systematically laid out the tasks of comprehensively strengthening the rule of the law in 2014.

提。依法治国是全面深化改革总目标的题中之义，也是各方面各领域改革的根本基础。习近平总书记对依法治国的重要性加以反复强调。他指出，治理国家必须遵照宪法规定，要坚持法治国家、法治政府、法治社会一体建设。2014年举行的中共十八届四中全会系统部署了全面依法治国的各项任务。

China is now working on the *Legislation Law*. The draft of a revised version of the law was handed over to the NPC for discussion and is scheduled for a vote on Mar 15. The *Legislation Law* is a basic set of rules, with its judicial significance only after the *Constitution*. Although it is so high-profile a law, it is related to the life of everyone: it can make the lawmaking process more scientific and democratic, standardize and restrain governments' administration, and make people feel happier.

中国正在推进《立法法》的相关工作。经修改的草案已经提交全国人大3月15日投票表决。《立法法》包括一系列基本规定，其法律意义仅次于《宪法》。虽然《立法法》规格很高，但它与我们每个人的生活息息相关，这部法律可以确保立法过程更加科学民主，规范约束政府行政活动，为人民群众创造更加幸福的生活。

An all-out effort to enforce strict Party discipline – Zero tolerance for corruption is important for the future destiny of the Party

四是全面从严治党。坚持以零容忍态度惩治腐败，关乎党和国家的前途命运。自党的

and our country. Since the 18th CPC National Congress, the leadership has stressed the need for supervising the Party. The Party has issued "eight rules" to improve its working style and has started an intensive anti-corruption campaign to re-establish a healthy political environment. In this sense, comprehensively supervising the Party will help purify and build a stronger Party, improve workstyle and work efficiency, and strengthen social morality.

In short, the four-pronged comprehensive strategy is a dialectical unity, and each aspect of that unity is indispensable. It forms a complete and competent strategy to build a modern socialist society with Chinese Characteristics. As the national supervisor on the border, customs has the responsibilities to safeguard the country and serve the people. Therefore, we must uphold the ideal and faith, follow the four-pronged comprehensive strategy in our own line of work, and make unremitting efforts to achieve the "Two Centenary Goals" and realize the Chinese Dream of the great rejuvenation of the Chinese nation.

十八大以来，党和国家领导人始终高度重视全面从严治党，出台了“八项规定”，转变工作作风，并大力开展反腐败行动，重塑健康的政治生态。在这个意义上，全面从严治党有利于纯洁党的队伍、加强党的建设，有利于改进作风、提高工作效率，有利于提升全社会的道德水平。

简言之，“四个全面”是一个辩证统一的整体，缺一不可，它是建设中国特色社会主义现代化的总体战略。海关作为国家进出境监督管理机关，肩负着为国把关、为人民服务的神圣职责，因此我们必须坚定理想信念，按照党中央提出的“四个全面”战略布局扎实做好本职工作，为实现“两个一百年”奋斗目标、实现中华民族伟大复兴的中国梦而不懈努力。

"十三五"规划的新目标新发展

2015年11月9日

New Target and Development in the 13th Five Year Plan

November 9, 2015

The just-concluded Fifth Plenary Session of the 18th Communist Party of China Central Committee, with its decision on major reforms, has set new goals and mapped out the blueprint for China's future development.

According to a communiqué released by on October 29, 2015, the four-day Session adopted the proposal for formulating China's 13th Five-year Plan (2016-2020), which outlined the new targets and requirements for completing the building of a moderately prosperous society in all respects: China will target "medium-high economic growth" in the five years from 2016, and aim to double its 2010 GDP and per capita income of both

刚刚结束的中国共产党第十八届中央委员会第五次全体会议所做出的重大改革决定，为中国的未来发展确定了新的目标，勾画出了新的蓝图。

根据2015年10月29日发布的会议公告，为期四天的全会通过了《中共中央关于制定国民经济和社会发展第十三个五年规划的建议》，提出了全面建成小康社会新的目标要求：经济保持中高速增长，在提高发展平衡性、包容性、可持续性的基础上，到2020年国内生产总值和城乡居民人均收入比

urban and rural residents by 2020 by ensuring more balanced, inclusive and sustainable development, with a view to ensuring that the country can realize a moderately prosperous society in an all-round way by 2020. The country will promote greater sophistication in its industrial sector and significantly raise the contribution of consumption to economic growth.

2010年翻一番，旨在确保2020年能实现全面建成小康社会的目标。国家将加大力度促进工业结构优化，提高消费对经济增长的拉动作用。

The urbanization ratio calculated based on the number of registered residents will also rise at a faster pace. The ratio of registered urban residents to total population stood at 35.9 percent at the end of 2014. A national plan to promote urbanization has set a target of raising the ratio to 45 percent.

常住人口城镇化比例也将呈现快速发展态势。2014年底，城镇化人口占全国总人口的35.9%。国家计划推动城镇化发展，将目标设定在45%。

At the Session, the CPC Central Committee also discussed modernizing agriculture and raising the people's quality of life. It plans to bring all rural people out of poverty by 2020 and shorten the list of counties officially categorized as poor by more than 600.

会议还讨论了农业现代化和提高人民生活质量的问题，计划到2020年消灭农村贫困人口，超过600个贫困县全部摘帽。

The communiqué also says that China aims to maintain a mid- to high-level economic growth rate in the next five years and significantly increase consumption's contribution to the economy. The goals will be crucial to ensure that the country fulfills its target of becoming a "well-off society in an

公报还称，中国将在未来五年经济保持中高速增长，拉动消费对经济的贡献。该目标对确保全面建成小康社会至关重要，这也意味着到2020年国内生产总值和城乡居民收入比2010年翻番。根据国家统计局

all-round way", which refers to doubling the gross domestic product and per capita income of urban and rural residents by 2020, from the 2010 level. In 2010, the per capita disposable income of urban residents was 19,109 yuan ($3,000) and that of rural residents was 5,919 yuan, according to the National Bureau of Statistics.

数据，2010年城市居民可支配收入是19109元（折合3000美元），乡镇居民可支配收入是5919元。

At present, economic transformation and restructuring cannot be ensured without sufficient growth, while a very ambitious target is unlikely, taking into account the downward pressure and rising costs. So, we should stress on significantly increasing the share of consumption to GDP as the country is stepping up the transition from an export-and-investment-driven economy to a consumption-driven one. In 2014, consumption accounted for 51.2% of China's GDP. Next, the service sector and green industries will become the major drivers propping up China's growth. The growth of such industries as e-commerce, medicine and health, environmental protection, new energy, tourism and entertainment all outpaced China's overall growth, becoming the new indicators that should be closely watched.

目前，面对经济下滑压力加之成本上涨，没有足够的增长率，经济转型和调结构将无法实现，要实现所设定的宏大目标几无可能。所以，我们应强调大幅度提高消费占国内生产总值比例，加速从出口和投资驱动型经济向以消费为驱动模式的转型发展。2014年，消费占国民生产总值51.2%。下一步，服务业和绿色工业将成为中国经济增长的新驱动力。包括电子商务、医疗、环保、新能源、旅游和娱乐业在内的产业发展将全面超过中国整体增长速度，成为新增长指标，这应受到密切关注。

At the same time, traditional economic indicators such as coal prices, electricity consumption and cargo volume have gradually lost their significance, as they are closely-

同时，传统的经济指标，如煤炭价格、用电消耗、货物量已逐渐退出舞台，因为这些指标和不断减少的高污染、高

related to the declining high-polluting and energy-guzzling industries. Recently, economists widely agreed that China's GDP has to maintain a 6.5% growth rate during the 13th Five-Year period, so as to realize the GDP and income goals. The target will be announced next March.

能耗产业密切挂钩。经济学家近来广泛认同，在“十三五”期间，中国的国内生产总值需要保持6.5%的增速，才能实现其国内生产总值和收入目标。具体目标将在明年3月公布。

The proposal of the 13th Five-Year Plan also mentioned making new contributions to global ecological security by sticking to green development. It vows to stick to the basic policies of resource conservation and environmental protection, building a highly efficient modern energy system and promoting demonstration projects for zero emissions. It is encouraging to see that the factor of the environment has really been incorporated into China's economic plan.

“十三五”规划还提到将坚持走绿色发展的道路，为全球生态安全做出新的贡献。我们将坚持节能环保的基本政策，努力建设高效现代化的能源体系，推动开展零排放试点项目。令人振奋的是，环境因素已被切实纳入中国经济规划中。

In addition, the proposal refers to other important issues, such as average annual income, employment, education, housing, medical care, the two-child policy as well as judicial reform.

此外，对于其他重要问题的建议，例如平均年收入、就业、教育、住房、医疗、二胎政策以及司法改革等。

From my point of view, the new development targets set in the 13th Five-Year Plan are in keeping with our national conditions, in line with our people's interests and designed to tackle the key problems and challenges. Customs is a government agency that supervises and administrates all imports

我认为，“十三五”规划提出的新发展目标符合国情，贴近群众利益，直面问题和挑战。海关是国家进出境监督管理机构，我们必须对国家的新发展目标作出更多贡献。特别要在经济结构转型、创新驱动

into and exports from the customs territory. We have to do more for the new development targets of our country. Especially, we have to play a bigger role in areas of the economic structure transformation, innovation-driven development, deepened opening-up, balanced import and export, as well as social harmony and progress, so as to serve as the "Iron Great Wall" in protecting national economic interests and wellbeing of the people.

发展、进一步扩大开放、平衡进出口贸易及促进社会和谐进步等领域发挥更大的作用，成为维护国家经济利益和人民福祉的钢铁长城。

For instance, adapting to the new round of science and technology reform, China Customs has to transform and enrich our administration philosophy, regime and implementation of law enforcement. We should further implement the "3Ms" (mutual exchange of information, mutual recognition of control, mutual assistance in enforcement), the FTA strategy, "single window" of international trade, in order to continuously score trade facilitation to a new height.

例如，为适应新一轮的科技改革，中国海关必须改革和充实监管理念、体系和执法。我们应该进一步落实“信息互换、监管互认、执法互助”的“三互”制度、自贸区战略、国际贸易“单一窗口”，不断提升贸易便利化水平。

For another example, we should make new grounds for opening-up in all areas and promote the building of the "Belt and Road". We should promote a new customs cooperative mechanism among coastal, inland and border areas, and improve the innovation of cross-border multimodal transport regulations (sea-air-land-rail-mail-web) to improve the international logistics system. It can be called a

另一方面，我们应推动形成全面开放新格局，推进“一带一路”建设。我们应在沿海、内陆和边境之间促进新的海关协同机制，完善跨境多式运输（海—空—陆—铁—邮—网络）制度创新，便利国际物流发展。这可被称为双向开放的内外联通。同时，随着经

"two-way open internal and external linkage". At the same time, in the context of economic globalization, we should make good use of the two markets and two kinds of resources both home and abroad, and constantly promote the innovation and development of processing trade to extend the industrial chain and improve the added value.

济全球化发展，我们应充分利用内外两个市场和两种资源，不断促进加工贸易的创新和发展，延伸产业链，提升增值空间。

It's also important to build a sound business environment featured by legalization, internationalization and facilitation. For this purpose, we should not only continue to simplify customs procedures, but also optimize customs services of imports and exports administration. On the one hand, we have to further standardize customs law enforcement activities through establishing the power list, positive list and negative list, so as to ensure that law is enforced in a procedure-based, impartial, and civil manner. On the other hand, we have to participate in the international customs cooperation in a more proactive way. We should make our successful management models and experience known by the international customs community and provide our support for Chinese enterprises to go global for new development. At the same time, we should also uphold the overall national security theories, and continue to crack down on the smuggling of drugs, weapons and ammunition,

必须强调，营造完善法制化、国际化和便利化的商业环境也是很重要的。为此，我们不仅要继续推动简化海关手续，而且还要优化海关进出境监管。一方面，我们要通过建立权力清单、正面清单和负面清单进一步规范海关执法行为，确保依法行政、公正执法、文明服务。另一方面，我们要更积极地参与国际海关合作，向国际海关界介绍我们成熟的管理模式和海关执法经验，大力支持中国企业走出国门，寻求发展。同时，我们也要贯彻落实国家安全理念，继续打击毒品、武器弹药、固体废物、濒危动植物以及高税额的工业、农业产品走私违法活动，确保国家的政治安全、经济安全、生

solid waste, endangered species of wild fauna and flora, as well as some high-tax industrial and agricultural products in accordance with the law, so as to ensure national political security, economic security, environmental and ecological security, food security and global supply chain security, and build China into a beautiful, healthy and peaceful country.

态环境安全、食品安全和全球供应链安全，打造美丽、健康、安全的中国。

再创历史的伟大远征

2016 年 10 月 21 日

Recreate the Great Expedition in History

October 21, 2016

I still remember the stories about the Long March that I heard from grown-ups in my childhood some 50 years ago. And later in Chinese classes in primary school, teachers also told us the heroic stories of the Long March of the Red Army. Back then, I was impressed by how the Red Army had stuck to their faith, and braved danger and hardship. They had climbed over snow-covered mountains, trekked through grasslands, eaten belts and grass for food, and gone through all sorts of adversity before finally breaking through enemy's siege and successfully arriving at the destination after a 25-thousand-li long march.

50多年前，记得我们还是孩童时，就常听长者们讲长征的故事。上小学后，老师也在课堂上给我们讲起了语文课本中红军长征的英雄史诗。当时，我印象最深的是红军战士们坚持信仰、不畏艰险，爬雪山、过草地，煮皮带、吃野草，受尽了苦，最后打破了敌军的重重“围剿”，胜利地完成了两万五千里长征。

I was too young to understand the reason

尽管那时我们还小，还不

and the great significance of the Long March, yet since then, we have been with full of respect for the brave and fearless Red Army soldiers, and a golden seed started to grow in me, giving me the confidence and determination to conquer any obstacle.

懂得为什么要长征和长征的深刻意义，但也就是从那时起，在我们的脑海中已经充满了对红军战士那种英勇无畏精神的无限崇敬，同时也在我幼小的心灵里播下了金色的种子——面对任何艰难险阻，都要有克服和战胜它的信心与决心。

Today, at the gathering to commemorate the 80th anniversary of the victory of the Long March, Xi Jinping, General Secretary of the Communist Party of China (CPC) Central Committee, affectionately talked about the bitter yet glorious journey, spoke highly of the arduous yet great expedition, and hailed the Long March as a “stately monument” in the history of the great rejuvenation of the Chinese nation. He pointed out that the Long March was a “great expedition to seek ideal and faith”, “to test truth”, “to awake the people”, and “to break new ground”. Its victory signifies the strength of the Chinese Communists’ ideals and faith. “Rain and wind chills to the bone yet our bone grows harder, weed and grass fills the stomach yet our mind gets stronger; we march through thick and thin, with our revolutionary ideal higher than the sky.” On the stormy path of the Long March, noble cause and solid faith had always been inspiring and leading the Red Army’s way forward. During the expedition,

今天，在纪念红军长征胜利80周年的大会上，习近平总书记深情回望了80年前那段苦难辉煌的壮阔进程，高度评价了那场艰苦卓绝的伟大远征，赞扬长征是中华民族伟大复兴历史进程中的“巍峨丰碑”。他指出，长征“是一次理想信念的伟大远征”“是一次检验真理的伟大远征”“是一次唤醒民众的伟大远征”，也“是一次开创新局面的伟大远征”。实践证明，长征的胜利是中国共产党人理想的胜利，是中国共产党人信念的胜利。“风雨浸衣骨更硬，野菜充饥志越坚；官兵一致同甘苦，革命理想高于天。”就在那风雨如磐的长征路上，崇高的理想，坚定的信念，时时激励和指引着红军一路向前。长征途中，英雄的红军血战湘江，四

heroes of the Red Army fought a bloody battle at Xiangjiang River, made four attempts across Chishui River, crossed Jinsha River through ingenious planning, faced the foe head-on at Dadu River, miraculously took the Luding Bridge, engaged in a fierce skirmish at Dushu Town, bravely took over Baozuo Village, and successfully transferred to Wumeng Mountain, defeating millions of vicious enemies that attempted to hunt down or stop the Red Army. On average, a soldier died every 300 meters in the leading Red Army troop. It is safe to say that the crimson ribbon of the Long March is dyed by the blood of countless Red Army soldiers.

渡赤水，巧渡金沙江，强渡大渡河，飞夺泸定桥，鏖战独树镇，勇克包座，转战乌蒙山，击退了上百万穷凶极恶的追兵阻敌。在红一方面军二万五千里的征途上，平均每300米就有一名红军牺牲。可见长征这条红飘带，是无数红军将士的鲜血染成的。

"Difficulty is the nurse of greatness." The time, scale, distance, difficulty and harshness of the Long March is unprecedented in Chinese history and is rarely seen globally in the history of war and human civilization. Hardship can destroy human flesh, death can take away life, yet no sort of power can shake the ideal and faith of the Chinese Communists.

"艰难困苦，玉汝于成。"长征历时之长、规模之大、行程之远、环境之险恶、战斗之惨烈，在中国历史上是绝无仅有的，在世界战争史乃至人类文明史上也是极为罕见的。艰难可以摧残人的肉体，死亡可以夺走人的生命，但没有任何力量能够动摇中国共产党人的理想信念。

Studying and understanding the important speech of General Secretary Xi Jinping has reinforced our belief in the strength of ideal and spirit. Spirit is the soul that keeps a nation alive. A man won't be independent

学习领会习近平总书记的重要讲话，让我们更坚定了信念的力量和精神的力量。精神，是一个民族赖以长久生存的灵魂。人无精神则不立，国

without spirit, and a state won't be powerful without it either. Only after reaching a certain spiritual level, can a nation be steadfast and courageously make it forward in the currents of history. "The Long March is a great achievement in human history. Its spirit, one that was forged by life and blood of Chinese Communists and the Red Army, is a precious legacy."

无精神则不强。唯有精神上达到一定的高度，这个民族才能在历史的洪流中屹立不倒、奋勇向前。"长征这一人类历史上的伟大壮举，留给我们最可宝贵的精神财富，就是中国共产党人和红军将士用生命和热血铸就的伟大长征精神。"

General Secretary Xi Jinping made an in-depth explanation about the connotative meaning of the Long March spirit, which can be summarized in 5 aspects: (1) It means putting the interests of the Chinese people and the nation above anything else, staying firmly to the revolutionary ideal and faith, and unswervingly believing that the just cause will prevail. (2) It means unflinchingly facing all hardship and obstacles, and the willingness to sacrifice everything to save the nation and its people. (3) It means staying independent, seeking the truth from facts, and doing everything in line with reality. (4) It means bearing in mind the overall interests, abiding by the disciplines, and closely working together. (5) It means relying firmly on the people, going through thick and thin with them, and working diligently. The great Long March spirit is the reflection of the revolutionary spirit of members of the CPC

习近平总书记对长征精神的内涵进行了深刻的阐述，概括起来主要体现在五个方面：（1）把全国人民和中华民族的根本利益看得高于一切，坚定革命的理想和信念，坚信正义事业必然胜利的精神；（2）为了救国救民，不怕任何艰难险阻，不惜付出一切牺牲的精神；（3）坚持独立自主、实事求是，一切从实际出发的精神；（4）顾全大局、严守纪律、紧密团结的精神；（5）紧紧依靠人民群众，同人民群众生死相依、患难与共、艰苦奋斗的精神。伟大长征精神，是中国共产党人及其领导的人民军队革命风范的生动反映，是中华民族自强不息的民族品格的集中展示，是以爱国主义为核心的民族精神的

and the people's army under its leadership, a demonstration of the characteristic of the Chinese nation to unremittingly improve itself, and the embodiment of the national spirit that is centered on patriotism.

The progression and development of China, whether during the founding of the country, the opening up and reform, or now, can be traced back to the Long March. As history keeps going forward, we still have to follow this predetermined road, pass the baton from generation to generation, and continue the long march to get to our goals. Surely, the road to the dream is never easy. We still have to climb many "mountains", cross many "grasslands", and win many battles such as the ones at Loushan Guan and La Zikou. Therefore, we should never rest on our laurels and stop working hard, and we should never indulge in self-complacency and stop marching forward.

Today, our work on development and reform is pressing and arduous. The two Centenary Goals and the Chinese dream of national rejuvenation are the tasks that are just as pioneering, difficult and complex as the Long March, if not more so. We must study and understand the essence of General Secretary Xi's important speech to remember, study, and practice the great Long March

最高体现。

今天中国的进步和发展，无论建国、改革开放，还是现在，都是从长征中走出来的。历史不断向前，要达到理想的彼岸，就要沿着我们确定的道路不断前进，继续接好棒、走好长征路。当然，通往梦想的道路从来不会平坦，在新的长征路上我们还有许多“雪山”和“草地”需要跨越，还有许多“娄山关”和“腊子口”需要征服，因此一切贪图安逸、不愿继续艰苦奋斗的想法都是要不得的，一切骄傲自满、不愿继续开拓前进的想法都是要不得的。

当前，我们发展的任务紧迫繁重，改革的攻坚艰苦卓绝，实现“两个一百年”奋斗目标、实现中华民族伟大复兴的中国梦，其开创性、艰巨性、复杂性，丝毫不亚于当年的万里长征。深入学习领会习近平总书记的重要讲话精神，为的就是要牢记伟大长征精

spirit. Only by doing so can we mitigate the "four risks", face the "four challenges", conquer the mountains and grasslands before us, and advance in the new long march of this generation.

神、学习伟大长征精神、弘扬伟大长征精神。只有这样，我们才能克服“四种危险”、经受住“四大考验”，才能跨越今天的雪山草地，才能走好我们这一代人的长征路。

Customs shoulders the great responsibility of safeguarding the country and its people. In the future, in order to put the Long March spirit into practice, we must remain true to the original aspiration, consolidate our faith, and work diligently towards our ideal and goals. We must have full confidence in the path, theory, system and culture of Chinese socialism. Faith in our heart gives us strength. We must strive for the national rejuvenation through controlling and serving the import and export. We must place the people above all else in our hearts, do everything for the people and with the help of the people, enforce the law for the people, and strive for the wellbeing of the people. We must follow the decision of CPC Central Committee and the State Council, work towards the right direction, make plans taking into account the overall situation, aim at the main tasks and strive for the main goals. We must reinforce the leadership of the CPC, run the Party with full and strict discipline, and strive for the great new project of Party building. During the Long March, the Red

海关肩负着为国家把关、对人民负责的重任。下一步，弘扬伟大长征精神，我们必须不忘初心、牢记使命，坚定理想信念，坚定中国特色社会主义的道路自信、理论自信、制度自信、文化自信。必须增强“四个意识”，自觉维护以习近平同志为核心的党中央的集中统一领导，认真贯彻落实党中央国务院的决策部署，牢固树立“执法为民”思想，通过海关对进出口的把关服务，为国家经济繁荣发展、人民过上更美好的生活、实现中华民族的伟大复兴而不懈奋斗。必须加强党的领导，坚持全面从严治党，惩治腐败，推进党的建设新的伟大工程。当年在长征途中，红军不拿群众一针一线，严格遵守“三大纪律八项注意”，我们要继承红军严明的纪律和优良的作风，把全面从严治党和从严治关紧密结

Army had strictly followed the "Three Rules of Discipline and Eight Points for Attention" and taken nothing from the people. It had succeeded in the revolution by combining the revolutionary ideal and the strict discipline. At present, rigid discipline and good practices are still at the core of running the Party with strict discipline. Therefore, Customs should take into account the disciplines while running the Party as well as Customs itself, and ensure impartial law enforcement and clean governance in order to provide political and organizational support for the recreation of the historical and great Long March,so as to live up to the expectations of Party and the People.

合，确保海关公正执法、廉洁从政，为再创历史的伟大远征提供政治、组织和纪律保障，以不辜负党和人民对海关的殷切期望。

重建丝绸之路经济带

2013年9月28日

Rebuild the Silk Road Economic Belt

September 28, 2013

The Eurasia region has ushered in a historic moment with the most intertwined interests and greatest opportunities for cooperation. The opening ceremony of the 2013 Euro-Asia Economic Forum （EAEF） was held on Sept. 26 in Xi'an, the capital of Shaanxi province. I had the privilege to participate in the Chinese Delegation led by Vice Premier Wang Yang to attend the ceremony. Wang Yang delivered a keynote speech at the Fifth Forum and called for countries in Eurasia to boost cooperation and re-make the Silk Road economic belt a benefit to the people from countries and regions along the route.

欧亚大陆迎来了一个利益相互交融、合作机会最佳的历史性时刻。2013年9月26日，欧亚经济论坛（EAEF）开幕式在陕西省会西安市举行。我有幸参加了由汪洋副总理率领的中国代表团出席了开幕仪式。汪洋在这次第五届论坛上发表了主旨演讲，呼吁欧亚所有国家加强合作、重建丝绸之路经济带、造福沿线国家和地区的人民。

The 2013 EAEF was held from September 26 to 29 in the historic city of Xi'an, China, under the theme "From Concrete Collaborations to Mutual Booming". Organized with help from the Shanghai Cooperation Organization (SCO) and the Xi'an municipal government, the forum aims to enhance the sharing of infrastructure construction and trade promotion, as well as a joint-venture demonstration zone to explore collaborations in the fields of energy, finance, science and technology, trade and business, education, and customs affairs as well. The three-day conference in Xi'an attracted about 2,000 delegates from 75 countries, regions and international organizations. Representatives from 19 Chinese ministries and 20 NGOs and relevant organizations from home and abroad attended this year's EAEF, which aims to stimulate real collaboration and sustainable development between European and Asian Countries to provide new economic solutions and opportunities for these two great continents and beyond.

这次欧亚经济论坛主题是“加强合作，共创繁荣”。在上海合作组织（SCO）的帮助和西安市政府的精心组织下，论坛旨在共享加强基础设施建设和促进贸易发展，建设合资企业示范区，探索能源、金融、科技、商贸、教育、海关事务领域的合作。在西安为期三天的会议，吸引了来自75个国家、地区和国际组织的2000多名代表。来自中国政府的19个部委、20个非政府组织和国内外的相关组织代表参加了今年的论坛。欧亚经济论坛是为了使欧洲和亚洲国家之间建立起务实的合作，为这两大洲及其他地区可持续发展提供新的经济解决方案和发展机会。

The Silk Road Economic Belt is the focus of this Forum. The Silk Road refers to the land trade route opened when Zhang Qian was sent west on a diplomatic mission more than 2,000 years ago. Starting from the city known today as Xi'an, the ancient Silk Road

丝绸之路经济带成为了此次欧亚经济论坛的热点。丝绸之路是指2000多年前张骞被派西行执行外交使命而开辟的一条商贸之路。古代的丝绸之路是以今天众所周知的西安作为

ran through northwest China's Gansu Province and Xinjiang Uygur Autonomous Region, and Central and Western Asia, before reaching the Mediterranean. The Silk Road was not only a trade route, but also a route of culture and peace.

起点，越过中国西北部的甘肃省、新疆维吾尔自治区和亚洲中部和西部，到达地中海。丝绸之路不仅是一条贸易之路，也是文化与和平之路。

In early September, Chinese President Xi Jinping put forward the proposal of the Silk Road Economic Belt to deepen cooperation and make economic ties closer among European and Asian nations. His proposal for the Silk Road Economic Belt has brought unprecedented opportunities for regional development. Actually, themed "deepening pragmatic cooperation and promote common prosperity", this Forum featured eight main seminars on cultural heritage, ecological safety, economic growth, education, energy development, financial cooperation, new technology and tourism development.

9月初，中国国家主席习近平提出了建设丝绸之路经济带的倡议，深化相互合作，使欧洲和亚洲国家之间的经济更加紧密相连。建设丝绸之路经济带的倡议为该区域发展带来了前所未有的机遇。实际上，这次论坛围绕“深化务实合作，促进共同繁荣”主题，还分设了文化遗产、生态安全、经济增长、教育、能源开发、金融合作、新技术和旅游开发等八个专题的研讨会。

Vice Premier Wang Yang urged that Eurasian countries should push forward broader regional cooperation on a higher level with a firmer resolve and more practical measures, to actualize the ideal picture as soon as possible for the benefit of the people. He stressed mutual political trust and common development in the region, calling for opening up and fighting protectionism in all forms, promoting mutual understanding and

汪洋副总理呼吁欧亚国家应该在更高层次上推进更广泛的区域合作，以更坚定的决心和更务实的举措，尽快将美好的愿景变为现实，造福人民。他强调，加强区域的政治互信和共同发展，呼吁开放和反对各种形式的保护主义，促进相互理解，加深友谊，扩大在教育、文化和旅游方面的交流。

deepening friendship by expanding exchanges in education, culture and tourism. Currently, infrastructure along the Silk Road such as roads and pipelines been initially completed, but more efforts in mechanisms for trade and investment are needed. China remains a developing country to the whole world and China's development brings opportunities to other countries.

目前，沿线的道路、管道等基础设施已经初步完成，但还需要在贸易和投资机制上作出更多的努力。对整个世界来说，中国仍然是一个发展中国家，中国的发展会给其他国家带来发展机会。

With regard to customs cooperation, we have built closer ties and cooperation mechanisms with other customs among European and Asian nations. The focus of our mechanisms is to ensure each customs administration will provide more secure and facilitated customs clearance and services for import and export, travelling, and technological and cultural exchanges in accordance with their respective customs laws and regulations.

关于海关合作，我们已经建立了一个与欧亚国家其他海关间更加紧密的联系合作机制。各海关机构按照各自海关的法律、法规，将为进出口贸易、人员进出、技术和文化交流提供更为安全便利的海关通关和服务。

Personally speaking, the most prominent precondition for development is to have an open, inclusive and win-win mindset. And the most important way to enhance cooperation among the countries is to have pragmatic, pioneering, and mutually-beneficial measures. The Silk Road Economic Belt will be rebuilt and its future will be bright.

我认为，开放、包容、共赢的理念，是一个国家发展的首要前提。务实、开拓、互惠的措施是创造机会、促进各国合作发展的重要途径。丝绸之路经济带必将重建，它的未来是光明的。

一次有意义的国防大学研讨会

2014年7月3日

An Interesting Symposium in NDU

July 3, 2014

There is a regular symposium with foreign military officials and experts during my training at the National Defense University (NDU) for the exchange of views, discussion on issues and enhancement of understanding. It's also an important activity with foreign military.

参加国防大学进修班学习，通常会有一次外事研讨交流活动，旨在与外国军官和军事专家开展学习交流、探讨问题、增进了解。这也是十分重要的军事外交活动。

On the afternoon of July 1, the symposium was held between Chinese ministerial-leader students and the foreign military officials in the hall of the National Defense University. The theme of the exchange meeting was "How to promote China's relations with other countries around the world". From the Chinese side, there were 56 ministerial-leader students attended. And from the foreign side, there were 2 classes:

7月1日下午，国防大学会议厅里举办了这样一次由中国省部级领导干部学员与外国军官共同参加的研讨会。会议的主题是"如何促进中国与世界其他国家的关系"。中方有56名省部级领导干部学员参加。外方参加的军官分为两个班级：一是第32班（英语），共

one was No. 32 (English), in which there were 84 military officers from 54 countries in Asia, Africa and Europe; and the other was No.33 (French) with 24 students from 19 countries mainly in Africa. Totally, there were 108 foreign military officials (generally in the colonel ranks or brigadier general above) from 73 countries studying in the NDU for one year.

有来自亚洲、非洲和欧洲54个国家的84位军官；二是第33班（法语），包括主要来自非洲19个国家的24名学员。这次外方总共有来自73个国家的108名军官（基本为校官、准将军衔以上），他们在国防大学参加为期一年的学习。

The first speaker was a brigadier general from Pakistan. He touched upon China's foreign policy, which focused on China's independent diplomacy of peace, explored China's strategic pursuit and refuted the theory of "the threat from China's rise". The third speaker was a senior colonel officer from Mali. He mainly talked about "how to promote China's relations with African countries" through analysis of the achievements of China-Africa relations and the ways to promote mutually-beneficial cooperation and establish a comprehensive strategic partnership for common development.

第一位演讲者是一名巴基斯坦准将。他演讲的主题是中国的外交政策，重点关注中国独立自主的和平外交政策，探索中国的战略追求以及批驳“中国崛起威胁论”。第三位演讲者是来自马里的大校军官，他通过分析中非关系的发展成果，讲述了“如何促进中国与非洲国家的关系”，以及如何加强互利合作，建立全面战略伙伴关系并推进共同发展。

I was arranged as the second speaker. In my speech, from the Customs perspective, I mainly highlighted two aspects: one was about the high interdependency between China's economy and the world economy, and the other was peaceful development was China's own choice. Countries around the world should share the responsibility and answer the call of the times.

我被安排在第二个演讲。我的演讲从海关的角度出发，主要聚焦两个重点：一是关于中国与世界经济的高度相互依存；另一个是和平发展是中国的自主选择，世界各国都应承担的共同责任，回应时代要求。

With regard to the high interdependency between China's economy and the world economy, I mentioned the following four characteristics:

关于中国与世界经济间的高度相互依存，我阐述了以下四个方面特征：

1. Exchange of goods. The exchange of goods usually refers to barter trade in ancient times. From caravans on the Silk Road to modern logistics networks, trade is now taking a different form, and it brings prominent benefits. According to China Customs statistics, China's foreign trade in 2013 topped US$4.16 trillion, up by 7.6% year on year. Exports stood at US$2.21 trillion, up by 7.9%; imports US$1.95 trillion, up by 7.3% (world trade grew by an average 2.5%), making China the No.1 country in trade in goods The U.S. foreign trade in 2013 was more than US$3.91 trillion, falling short by US$249.93 billion compared with China. But the U.S. registered more than US$1.13 trillion of trade in services, up by 3.7%, while that of China was only about US$539.6 billion, but up by 14.7%.

第一，商品的交换。商品交换古时代一般是易货贸易。从丝绸之路上的商队发展到现代物流网络，贸易的形式正在发生变化，它带来的好处也显而易见。据中国海关统计，2013年，中国对外贸易达到4.16万亿美元，同比增长7.6%。其中，出口2.21万亿美元，增长7.9%；进口1.95万亿美元，增长7.3%（世界贸易平均增长2.5%）。中国也因此成为第一大货物贸易国。美国对外贸易在2013年超过3.91万亿美元，比中国少2499.3亿美元。但美国的服务贸易达到了1.13万亿美元，增加了3.7%，而中国服务贸易额仅为5396亿美元，增长14.7%。

2. Complementarity of markets. China's largest trading partners in 2013 were the E.U. (US$559.1 billion, up by 2.1%), the U.S. (US$521 billion, up by 7.5%), ASEAN (US$443.6 billion, up by 10.9%), Chinese Hong Kong (US$401 billion, up by 17.5%), Japan (US$312.6 billion, down by 5.1%), and

第二，市场的互补性。2013年，中国最大的贸易伙伴分别是欧盟（5591亿美元，增长2.1%）、美国（5210亿美元，增长7.5%）、东盟（4436亿美元，增长10.9%）、中国香港（4010亿美元，增长

South Korea (US$274.2 billion, up by 7.0%). China's trade with these six partners (US$2.708 trillion) accounted for 65% of its total. Chinese exports took bigger market share in both major developed countries and emerging economies. In 2013, Chinese exports accounted for 16.5% of the E.U.'s total imports, up by 0.4% year-on-year. It showed that the world's trade market was open, diverse, and dynamic, and that players, although competitors to each other, were highly complementary to one another.

17.5%）、日本（3126亿美元，下降5.1%）、韩国（2742亿美元，增长7.0%）。中国与上述六个贸易伙伴（2.708万亿美元）的贸易额占其贸易总额的65%。中国的出口商品在主要发达国家和新兴经济体都占有了较大的市场份额。2013年，我国出口商品占欧盟进口总额的16.5%，同比上升0.4%。这体现出了世界贸易市场开放、多元和动态化的特征，而参与者们彼此具有较强的竞争性，但更多的是互补性。

3. Investment for mutual benefit. As the world's second largest importer, China is emerging as a "world market", buying products from across the globe. Statistics showed that in 2011 China's FDI (Foreign Direct Investment) grew for the 10th consecutive year, reaching US$74.65 billion, with its share of the world's total rising from less than 0.5% in 2002 to 4.4%. China's foreign exchange reserve, which stood at US$3.82trillion by 2013, as a share of the world's total, rose from 8.6% in 2000 to 31.2% in 2011. China, shifting from a net capital importer to a major capital exporter, has become a new source of global investment. In 2013, newly approved businesses directly

第三，互利的投资。作为世界第二大进口国，中国正在成为一个“世界市场”，购买来自世界各地的产品。统计数据显示，2011年中国的对外直接投资已连续增长十年，达到746.5亿美元，其占世界总量的份额从2002年的不到0.5%上升到4.4%。中国外汇储备截至2013年为3.82万亿美元，占全世界份额从2000年的8.6%上升到2011年的31.2%。中国从资本净进口国转变为主要资本输出国，并已成为全球投资的新来源。2013年，非金融

funded by foreign investors in the non-financial sector stood at 22773, down by 8.6%; paid-in FDI reached US$117.6 billion, up by 5.3%; China's outbound FDI in the non-commercial sector was US$90.2 billion, up by 16.8%. China pursued mutual benefit both in attracting investment and in investing abroad.

领域新批准的由外商直接投资的企业数量达到22773，下降了8.6%；实际利用外商直接投资1176亿美元，增长了5.3%；中国在非商业领域的对外直接投资达902亿美元，上升了16.8%。中国追求的是在吸引外资和对外投资两方面的共赢。

4. Complete industrial chains. Though there is the global division of labor, all links on the industrial chains are connected, with countries serving as different links. China, for example, does processing. In 2013, China's processing trade amounted to US$1.36 trillion, up by 1%, taking up 32.6% of China total trade volume. Of course, three facts deserve our attention. First, China has remained a major country in processing trade. Exports of traditional products are seeing steady growth while exports of hi-tech products are gaining competitiveness. Second, China is still at the mid-to-lower end of industrial chains with few core technologies, making it difficult to export high added-value goods while creating an extra burden on the resources and the environment. Third, restructuring processing trade is needed for deepening reform. We need to further extent our reach in the processing chain, step up

第四，完整的产业链。虽然有全球劳动分工，产业链上的所有环节是相连的，不同国家在不同的链接上发挥着作用。例如，中国的加工贸易。2013年，中国加工贸易达1.36万亿美元，增长1%，占中国贸易总额的32.6%。当然，有三个因素值得我们关注。首先，中国仍然是加工贸易的主要国家，我们可以看到传统出口产品稳步增长，而高新技术产品出口竞争力也在提升；其次，中国仍处于产业链的中低端，核心技术较少，因此难以出口高附加值产品，同时也在不断增加资源和环境的负担；再次，调整加工贸易是深化改革的需要，我们要不断延伸加工贸易产业链，通过创新提升核心竞争力，增加产品的附加值。

innovation to enhance competitiveness so as to increase the value added to the products.

These four characteristics point to the same conclusion: China's economic growth is intertwined with the economic growth of countries around the world. They are the inevitable results of economic globalization. And they are also the embodiment that China and the world are interdependent, interconnected, and interacting to one another.

以上四个特征归结起来说明一点，就是中国经济发展与世界各国经济发展是融为一体的，这是经济全球化发展的必然趋势，也是中国与世界相互依存、相互关联、相互影响的具体体现。

During the course of economic development, China pursues peaceful development. So I moved on to the second topic, peaceful development. I pointed out that it is China's own choice and the call of the times, and all countries should see this as a shared responsibility. After 30 years of development since the reform and opening up policy was introduced, China is now the world's second largest economy and its imports and exports ranking the first in the world. However, some are worried whether China's growth would pose a threat to the rest of the world. China has long declared that we unswervingly pursue the path of peaceful development and safeguard world peace in order to maintain a peaceful environment for the world and its own development.

在经济发展的过程中，我们追求的是和平发展。紧接着，我开始讲第二个问题，即和平发展。我指出，和平发展是中国自主的选择，也是时代的要求，这是世界各国共同的责任。改革开放以来，经过30多年的发展，中国已经成为世界第二大经济体，其进口和出口在世界上都名列首位。然而，一些人担心中国的发展是否会对其他国家构成威胁。一直以来，中国都向世界宣示，我们坚定不移地追求和平发展道路，通过维护世界和平，谋求世界及中国的自身发展。

1. China has always pursued peaceful development. Peaceful development is deeply

第一，中国始终坚持和平发展。和平发展深深植根于中

rooted in the Chinese culture. It fits into China's development plans and reflects our understanding of the international landscape. Our ancestors already realized that a country, however strong, would collapse if it constantly sought wars. China, for a long time in history, used to be one of the most prosperous countries in the world, but had no record of invasion or colonialism.

国文化。它符合中国的发展路线，也体现了中国对国际形势的理解。我们的祖先早已认识到，一个国家无论多么强大，若不断寻求战争最终必将走向瓦解。中国历史上有很长一段时间是世界上最繁荣的国家之一，但没有任何入侵别国和殖民主义的记载。

2. Peaceful development is the calling of our times. Today's world is defined by peace, development and cooperation for mutual benefit. On the one hand, old colonialist systems have collapsed and the cold war has long passed; on the other, countries are more interdependent than ever before. Therefore, hegemony and colonialism no longer work, while at the same time conventional security threats, including hegemony and power politics, are increasingly entwined with non-conventional threats such as terrorism and cyber espionage. We, therefore, face a long way ahead in maintaining world peace and promoting common development.

第二，和平发展是当今时代的要求。当今世界被定义为和平、发展、合作，实现互利共赢。一方面，旧殖民体系崩溃和冷战早已逝去；另一方面，各国之间的相互依存度空前。因此，霸权和殖民主义失去了存在的条件。但也应看到，霸权主义和强权政治等传统安全威胁越来越多地与恐怖主义和网络间谍活动等非传统威胁纠结在一起。因此，我们在维护世界和平、促进共同发展方面仍任重而道远。

3. China's role in peaceful development. China's economic growth is pivotal to the world economy. According to the IMF, from 2008 to 2012, China's economy grew by 9.3%. The Chinese economy's net growth accounted for 29.8% of that of the world. In 2012, China

第三，中国在和平发展中的作用。中国经济的增长对于世界经济至关重要。根据国际货币基金组织的数据，从2008年到2012年，中国经济增长了9.3%。中国经济的净增长

saw a growth of 7.8%, taking up 60.9% of the world's net growth. The Chinese Dream is benefiting the Chinese people as well as the world. In the coming 5 years, China is expected to import more than US$10 trillion of goods and invest more than US$500 billion abroad. Five-hundred million outbound visits will be made by the Chinese. This is the sound development opportunity China offers to the world. For another example, since 2001 China has given preferential tariff treatment to 41 Least Developed Country (LDCs) with diplomatic ties with China, covering most of their exported goods to China. Starting from July 1, 2013, China started to collect zero tariffs on 95% of exported products from the LDCs (7831 items) which have completed the necessary procedures.

占世界的29.8%。2012年，中国增长7.8%，占世界净增长的60.9%。“中国梦”正在惠及中国人民以及全世界。未来5年，中国将进口超过10万亿美元的商品并吸纳5000亿美元国外投资。中国出境游将达到5亿人次。这是中国向世界提供发展的好机会。另一个例子，自2001年以来，中国给予了与中国建交的41个最不发达国家优惠关税待遇，覆盖了这些国家出口到中国的大部分货物。从2013年7月1日开始，中国对来自最不发达国家且已完成相关手续的95%的出口商品（7831个税号）实施零关税优惠待遇。

4. Joint efforts for peaceful development. Peaceful development is our shared responsibility. In the face of changing international situations, all countries should work together for a new type of international relations focusing on mutual benefit. Joint efforts are needed in addressing new challenges. Security issues are threats to peaceful development. No country can effectively address them on its own. Military forces only complicate the situation instead of providing the solution. Working together for common security is the

第四，和平发展的共同努力。和平发展是我们共同的责任。面对国际形势的深刻变化，各国应该共同推动建立以合作共赢为核心的新型国际关系。新的挑战需要大家共同努力来应对。安全威胁是破坏和平发展的因素，任何国家都不能独善其身，军事力量并不能解决问题，反而只能使局势变得更为复杂，只有共同开展安全合作才是唯一的出路。人类

only way out. Human beings today are in a better position than ever before to forge ahead towards peaceful development. The goal can only be achieved by mutually beneficial cooperation. We should all play our due part. As a saying goes, “Strength doesn’t come from force, but from unity.”

比以往任何时候都更适合和平发展的道路。只有通过互利合作才能达成目标。我们都应尽自己的一份力量。正如一句谚语所说，“力量不来自于武力，而来自于团结”。

In this regard, China Customs is also earnestly carrying out its duty of safeguarding national security, maintaining world peace, elevating global trade facilitation and enhancing the common prosperity of the global economy.

在这方面，中国海关也正在认真履行自身职责，保护国家安全，维护世界和平，推动世界贸易便利化水平不断提升，促进全球经济共同繁荣发展。

The last agenda item of the symposium was free exchanges. Anyone could raise any questions for any speaker. I was asked to answer five questions. In more than two hours of communication, our both sides exchanged views in an in-depth way, increased mutual understanding and trust and achieved expected outcomes. It was really an interesting symposium and an unforgettable experience with foreign military officials in the National Defense University.

研讨会的最后一个环节是自由交流，即大家可以对任何人提任何问题。我回答了五个问题。在两个多小时的交流过程中，中外双方交换了意见，增进了相互了解与信任，达到了预期目标。此次在国防大学与外国军官的研讨活动的确很有意义，给我留下了难忘的印象。

贸易保护主义损人害己

2018年4月20日

Trade Protectionism Will Benefit None

April 20, 2018

Disputes or frictions in international trade are a kind of market conducts among trading bodies during trade activities. They should be resolved through rules-based consultations or negotiations under the multilateral framework of the World Trade Organization （WTO）. While in the past few months，the provocative acts and aggressive attitude of the U.S. government are extremely disappointing and worth thinking.

国际贸易争端或摩擦，是国际贸易主体之间在贸易活动中所产生的一种市场行为，它理应在WTO多边贸易框架下，按照规则通过磋商或谈判来得以解决。但这一段时期以来，美国政府一系列的贸易挑衅行为和咄咄逼人的架势，不得不让人失望和深思。

On August 14, 2017, U.S. President Donald Trump signed an executive memorandum, directing U.S. Trade Representative (USTR) Robert Lighthizer to launch an investigation into China's alleged theft of U.S. intellectual

去年8月14日，美国总统特朗普就签署行政令，指示美国贸易代表罗伯特·莱特希泽按照美国《1974年贸易法案》第301条款对中国发起调查，

property and forced technology transfer policies under Section 301 of the *Trade Act of* 1974.

On November 28, 2017, the U.S. Department of Commerce self-initiated antidumping duty and countervailing duty cases against common alloy aluminum sheet from China.

On November 30, the USTR's office announced that it had formally told the WTO that it opposed granting China market economy status, due to the state's pervasive role in the Chinese economy, including rampant granting of subsidies.

On March 22, 2018, Trump announced plans to impose 25% tariffs on US$50 billion of Chinese imports and new restrictions on Chinese investment in U.S. science and technology. Trump also ordered Lighthizer to publish a list of targeted products within 15 days, involving 1300-odd items. Trump even claimed that the U.S. would further impose extra tariffs on US$100 billion of Chinese goods.

To this end, the Chinese government clarified its position, that is, we firmly opposed the U.S.'s act of unilateralism and trade protectionism. China would never sit idly and let its lawful rights and interests

内容包括中国是否侵犯美国知识产权以及强制美国进行技术转让。

去年11月28日，美国商务部宣布对中国产普通合金铝板发起反倾销和反补贴调查。

去年11月30日，美国贸易代表办公室宣布，已正式通知世界贸易组织（WTO），反对给予中国市场经济地位，因为中国政府在经济中发挥了重大的作用，包括大量发放补贴等。

今年3月22日，美国总统特朗普宣布将对500亿美元中国商品加征25%关税，并将限制中国对美国科技产业投资。特朗普指派贸易代表莱特希泽在15天之内宣布进口关税实施的产品种类，涉及产品种类达1300多项。特朗普甚至还称，将视情将征税商品扩大至1000亿美元。

对此，中国政府表明严正立场，坚决反对美方这种单边主义和贸易保护主义行径，表示绝不会坐视合法权益受到损害，必将采取所有必要措施，

be undermined and would surely take all necessary measures to firmly safeguard its legitimate rights and interests.

坚决捍卫自身合法权益。

On March 23, the Ministry of Commerce （MOFCOM） issued a product list of termination and concessions against the U.S. Section 232 measures for imported steel and aluminum products and solicited public comments, planning to impose tariff on part of U.S.'s imports so as to balance China's loss caused by the U.S. 232 measures. This list tentatively contained 128 tax products across 7 categories. According to the 2017 statistics, it involved U.S. exports to China of some US$3 billion. The first part covered a total of 120 taxes involving US$977 million in U.S. exports to China, including fresh fruits, dried fruits and nut products, wines, modified ethanol, American ginseng, and seamless steel pipes, which was expected to impose a 15% tariff. And the second part covered a total of 8 taxes involving US$1.992 billion of US exports to China, including pork and its products, recycled aluminum and other products, with a proposed 25% tariff.

3月23日，中国商务部发布了针对美国进口钢铁和铝产品232措施的中止减让产品清单并征求公众意见，拟对自美进口部分产品加征关税，以平衡因美国对进口钢铁和铝产品加征关税给中方利益造成的损失。该清单暂定包含7类、128个税项产品。按2017年统计，涉及美对华约30亿美元出口。第一部分共计120个税项，涉及美对华9.77亿美元出口，包括鲜水果、干果及坚果制品、葡萄酒、改性乙醇、花旗参、无缝钢管等产品，拟加征15%的关税。第二部分共计8个税项，涉及美对华19.92亿美元出口，包括猪肉及制品、回收铝等产品，拟加征25%的关税。

A MOFCOM spokesperson said, the fact that the U.S. imposed tariffs of 25% and 10% on imported steel and aluminum products on the grounds of "national security" actually constituted a safeguard measure that was

商务部新闻发言人表示，美方以"国家安全"为由对进口钢铁和铝产品分别征收25%和10%关税的行为实际上构成了有损贸易合作方保障措施。

harmful to trade partners. According to the relevant provisions of the WTO's *Agreement on Safeguard Measures*, China has formulated a list of suspension of concessions. If China and the U.S. fail to reach a trade compensation agreement within the stipulated time, China will exercise the right to suspend concessions for products mentioned in the first part; China will implement the second part list after further evaluating the impact of the U.S. measures on China. China reserves the right to adjust measures based on actual conditions and will implement necessary procedures in accordance with relevant WTO rules."

中方根据世贸组织《保障措施协定》有关规定，制定了中止减让清单。如果中美未能在规定时间内达成贸易补偿协议，中方将对第一部分产品行使中止减让权利；中方将在进一步评估美方措施对中国的影响后实施第二部分清单。中方保留根据实际情况对措施进行调整的权利，并将按照世贸组织相关规则履行必要程序。

On April 3, the U.S. government announced to impose a 25% tariff on imported products originating in China based on its unilateral findings of 301 investigation.

4月3日，美国政府依据301调查单方认定结果，宣布将对原产于中国的进口商品加征25%的关税，涉及约500亿美元中国对美出口。

On April 4, MOFCOM issued a statement on imposing tariffs on certain goods originating in the U.S. In response to the U.S.'s findings of 301 investigation, China decided to impose tariffs on 106 products across 14 categories such as soybeans and other agricultural products, automobiles, chemicals and airplanes originating in the U.S. at the rate of 25%, involving about US$50 billion China's imports from the U.S. The General Administration of China Customs participated in the special study

4月4日，中国商务部发布了关于对原产于美国的部分进口商品加征关税的公告。针对美国公布的301调查结果，中方决定对原产于美国的大豆等农产品、汽车、化工品、飞机等14类106项进口商品加征25%的关税，涉及中国自美进口金额约500亿美元。海关总署参加了相关问题的专题研究，并做好了随

of relevant issues and made due preparations for immediate implementation.

时执行的准备。

An official with China's Ministry of Finance stated that China's imposition of tariffs on certain U.S. imports is a righteous move in defense of its own lawful rights and interests and the multilateral trade regime, and a legal measure in accordance with the basic principles of international law. The decision was made based upon relevant provisions of the *Foreign Trade Law of the People's Republic of China* and the *Regulations of the People's Republic of China on Import and Export Duties*, while the current policy of taxation, tax relief, and tax exemption remained unchanged. The specific data of implementation of the tariffs will be separately released by the Customs tariff Commission of the State Council depending on the implementation of U.S.-imposed tariffs on Chinese imports.

中国财政部有关负责人表示，中国对美方部分商品加征关税是捍卫自身合法权益、维护多边贸易体制的正义行为，是符合国际法基本原则的正当举措。此决定系根据《中华人民共和国对外贸易法》和《中华人民共和国进出口关税条例》相关规定做出，现行保税、减免税政策不变。对这些商品加征关税的实施日期将视美国政府对我商品加征关税实施情况，由国务院关税税则委员会另行公布。

On April 16, the U.S. Department of Commerce banned American companies from selling components, products, software and technology to leading Chinese telecom equipment maker ZTE for seven years.

4月16日，美国商务部宣布，今后七年内，美国公司将被禁止向中兴通讯销售零部件、商品、软件和技术。

The trade war fomented by the U.S. has caused panic and alert worldwide. The world's economy has just stabilized and shown positive prospects in 2017, and global GDP, trade, investment and manufacturing have just

美国挑起的贸易战，已引起了全世界的恐慌和警觉。2017年全球经济刚开始企稳向好，全球GDP、贸易、投资以及制造业等开始摆脱十年低迷

walked out of a ten-year-long downturn. Such large-scale trade frictions between the largest two economies of the world, if not effectively controlled, are expected to exert severe impacts to the hard-won global economic recovery.

From the global perspective, since the Trump administration announced its increase of tariffs on imported steel, the international community has been criticizing its trade protectionism and made preparations for countermeasures. The German Chancellor Angela Merkel stated on March 21 that the E.U. would take unambiguous countermeasures against the U.S.'s tariff surges if necessary. She also accused U.S.'s moves as "unlawful", and said isolationism would finally harm everyone. At the G20 Finance Ministers and Central Bank Governors Meeting, Bruno Le Maire, the French Minister of the Economy and Finance, made it clear that "France is opposed to all types of protectionism". Haruhiko Kuroda, Governor of the Bank of Japan (Japan's central bank) pointed out, "There is a solid understanding within the global community that free trade is important." The former Japanese Prime Minister also stressed that China should learn a lesson from the Plaza Accord and raise its vigilance on the U.S. The E.U. is now ready to respond to the U.S.'s tariff plan, and with no progress in its

局面。这次世界前两大经济体发生如此大规模的贸易摩擦，如不有效管控，必将对来之不易的全球经济复苏带来不利影响和强大冲击。

从全球反映看，自特朗普政府宣布提高钢铁关税等行为开始，国际社会就发声批评贸易保护主义，纷纷准备采取措施予以回应。德国总理默克尔3月21日说，若有必要，将对美国加征钢铝关税的政策采取“明确的反制措施”。她还指责美国的做法是“非法”的，孤立主义最终将伤害所有人。法国经济和财政部长布鲁诺·勒梅尔在二十国集团（G20）财长和央行行长会议上表示，“法国反对任何贸易保护主义。”日本银行（央行）总裁黑田东彦称：“自由贸易非常重要，这个清楚的认识对各国来说是共通的。”日本前首相也强调，中国应吸取日本的“广场协议”教训，对美提高警惕。目前，欧盟已准备回应美国的关税计划。在寻求美国赦免钢铝关税进程并不顺利的情况下，已发布对美贸易制裁的10页清单，涉及产品

quest for tariff exemption on European steel and aluminum products, it has released 10-page sanctions against U.S. trade involving 2.8 billion euro of annual U.S. imports, which could jump to 6.4 billion should U.S. tariffs influenced the European economy too badly. Inside the U.S., the unwise decision of Trump also meets widespread and strong opposition from the political arena, business sector and general public.

From the look of it, Trump is most concerned about the huge trade deficit in China-U.S. economic and trade relations, but in fact, he is merely using intellectual property protection as an excuse to constrain the transformation and upgrading of China's manufacturing, strangle the take-off of China's emerging high-tech industries and create obstacles in the implementation of China's "Made in China 2025" strategy on its journey towards high-quality economic development. Here lies the fundamental goal of Trump's imposition of tariffs on Chinese goods. He once toughly demanded China slash U.S. trade surplus by US$100 billion on Twitter. Last year, U.S.'s official data showed that the difference in U.S.-China trade by commodities hit a record high of US$376 billion. But according to China's official statistics, U.S.'s trade surplus with China was a smaller US$275

价值每年在28亿欧元左右。如果美国关税对欧洲经济的影响突出，这一数字可能会增至64亿欧元。从美国国内看，特朗普不明智的决策，也受到了美国政界、企业和广大人民的强烈反对。

在中美经贸关系中，表面上看，特朗普较在意的是巨额的贸易赤字，但实质上就是打着保护知识产权幌子，企图限制中国制造业的转型升级，扼杀中国新兴高科技产业新的起步，给“中国制造2025计划”实现经济高质量增长制造障碍。这是他要对中国加征关税的根本原因。特朗普曾强硬地在推特上要求中国将对美贸易顺差减少1000亿美元。去年，根据美国官方统计，美中商品贸易差额达到创纪录的3760亿美元。不过，如果按照中方的统计，美国对中国的商品贸易逆差为2750亿美元。中国商务部部长钟山3月11日在两会记者会上指出，“美国官方统计的对华贸易逆差每年都被高估

billion. Zhong Shan, Minister of Commerce of China pointed out at a press conference during the National People's Congress on March 11 that the annual U.S. trade deficit with China was overestimated by about 20%, and it could be reduced by 35% if the U.S. eased export controls on certain products to China.

了20%左右”，“如果美国对华出口管制放宽，对华贸易逆差可减少35%左右”。

It's widely known that a big part of China's exports to the U.S. are from joint ventures, including U.S.-funded companies. Who after all will be the victims of the U.S.-provoked trade war? For instance, the U.S. imposed restrictions on steel and aluminum imports, while China isn't the largest resource of these commodities. China's steel export only takes up around 3% of the U.S.'s overall steel import; and Chinese-made aluminum products imported to the U.S. ranked after Canada, Russia and the UAE. Overcapacity is a common problem faced by many countries, and it needs concerted efforts from all parties to alleviate the situation. In fact, China has already managed to sharply slash its excess production capacity in the past few years. Another example is U.S. restrictions on Chinese investment in America. This kind of unilateralism and trade protectionism is completely meaningless in economic and political terms, and will only harm the interests of states, cities and counties of the U.S. itself,

众所皆知，我对美出口很大一部分比重是中外合资企业，其中包括美方投资的企业出口。美国突然挑起贸易战，受害者究竟是谁？比如，美对进口钢铁和铝产品采取限制措施，中国并不是美最大的钢铁和铝产品进口来源，中国对美国出口的钢铁产品仅占美进口钢铁总量的约3%；而来自中国的铝产品进口位列加拿大、俄罗斯、阿联酋之后。许多国家都存在产能过剩问题，去产能需要各方共同努力。事实上，中国在过去几年中大幅削减了过剩产能。又如，美限制中国企业在美投资，这种单边主义和贸易保护主义做法在经济上和政治上都毫无意义，到头来只会损害美国各州、市、县的利益，减少老百姓就业机会，最终伤害美国整体经济，这对任何人都没有好处。

reduce job opportunities and ultimately harm the U.S. national economy. This will definitely benefit no one.

As for intellectual property protection, China always respect laws and intellectual property protection, since this also relates to the building of a law-based environment needed by its own socioeconomic development. But China will only show respect to international law and internationally recognized business rules. We will not accept the unreasonable demands of the U.S. beyond laws and rules.

至于知识产权保护，中国十分尊重法律和知识产权保护，因为这是中国自身经济社会发展所必需的法律环境建设，但是中国只会尊重国际法和国际商业规则，我们不会接受美国政府超越那些法律和规则的无理要求。

The concept of so-called "non-market economy country" does not exist in the multilateral rules of the WTO, but only a phrase coined by some member countries during the Cold War. Countries and regions such as the U.S. and the E.U. keep referring to the idea of "market economy country", because they hope to avoid the obligation and responsibility enshrined in Article 15 of the *Protocol on the Accession of China to the WTO*. The said article stipulates that from December 11, 2016, member countries have to stop using surrogate country to decide the extent of dumping in anti-dumping cases against China. This is utterly clear and indisputable, and every WTO Member should honor their commitment.

所谓的“非市场经济国家”这个概念，并不存在于世贸组织的多边规则当中，只是个别成员冷战时期的国内产物。美国、欧盟等有关国家不停地引入“市场经济国家”这个概念，是想逃避履行中国加入世贸组织议定书第15条的义务和责任。中国加入世贸组织议定书第15条规定，自2016年12月11日起，在对华反倾销中，采用替代国价格计算倾销幅度做法必须终止。这一点是非常明确和不容置疑的，所有世贸组织的成员都应该重信守诺。

The harm of trade protectionism and

贸易保护主义的危害和

significance of free trade are self-evident. We only have one earth, and all countries share the same world. No country can stand aloof and there should be no unipolar hegemony. President Xi Jinping proposed the building of a community of shared future for mankind with a view to benefiting all people around the world. The "Belt and Road" initiative is a specific move for its realization, aimed at win-win and mutually beneficial development through cooperation among various countries. The meaning of economic globalization lies in the production of quality goods at low prices to benefit people of all countries. In effect, China-U.S. cooperation enjoys great potential and bright prospects. The key is that the two sides should adopt a collaborative and constructive manner to resolve problems, and address the potential disputes and differences between the two countries through dialogue and consultation. Confrontation will result in no good. Higher duty means higher costs, which will eventually trickle down to consumers. It will impact all sectors down the line including investment, production, and consumption. China does not look forward to a trade war with any country, but will not yield to any threat, force or intimidation. We will consider all possible options and adopt firm and necessary countermeasures to safeguard

自由贸易的重要性是不言而喻的。人类只有一个地球，各国共处一个世界，任何国家都不可能独善其身，也不应该出现单极霸权。习近平主席提出的人类命运共同体理念旨在让全世界所有人都幸福。“一带一路”建设便是一项具体行动，通过促进各国合作，实现共赢共享发展。经济全球化的意义，就是在于以低廉的价格生产质量好的产品，让世界各国人民都享用物美价廉的产品。其实，中美合作拥有良好的潜力和前景，关键是双方应采取合作和建设性的方式处理问题，通过对话协商解决两国间可能存在的争论和分歧，对抗性的方式对各方都不利。因为高关税势必抬高商品成本，最后会转嫁到消费者身上，从而导致投资、生产、消费等各环节受到不良影响。中方不想同任何一方打贸易战，但也绝不会屈从于任何威胁、强迫和恐吓。我们必须考虑所有选项，将采取坚决和必要的应对措施，维护好自身的正当权益。

our own lawful rights and interests.

The trade conflict between China and the U.S. must be settled through consultation and negotiation. We hope the U.S. side would restore its rationality, abandon its extreme practice of unilateralism and trade protectionism, and resolve trade disputes in accordance with rules and regulations under the WTO framework. We also have to fully realize that the trade conflict between China and the U.S. is not a temporary one and it will be complex and fierce in the long run. Therefore, we need to have a strong commitment and flexible strategies, meet the challenges head on, and take just and righteous countermeasures. The fact remains that trade protectionism will benefit no one, and there will be no winner in this trade war. Only by riding the wave of economic globalization and adopting the path of multilateral cooperation, trade and investment liberalization and mutual and win-win benefits, can we secure sound development for the country and welfare for the people.

中美双方的贸易争端，最终是要通过磋商和谈判协调解决问题。我们希望美方回归理性，放弃单边主义、贸易保护主义的极端做法，在世贸组织框架下遵循规则解决贸易争端问题。但同时，我们也要清醒地认识到，中美贸易分歧和摩擦不是一朝一夕的事，要充分认识到它的复杂性、艰巨性和长期性。因此，我们要以坚定的信念和对应的策略，有理有据有节地处理好问题。说实在的，贸易保护主义损人害己，贸易战没有赢家。我们唯有在经济全球化的大潮中，走多边合作、贸易和投资自由化、互惠共赢的路子，才能使国家发展得更好、人民更幸福。

跨境电子商务新政出台

2016年4月9日

New Tax Policy for the Cross-border E-commerce

April 9, 2016

In order to better support and improve the development of the cross-border e-commerce in China, a new import tax policy for its retail, formulated by the Ministry of Finance together with other government departments and approved by the state council, has been carried out since April 8. According to the new rules, retail goods purchased online through cross-border e-commerce platform will no longer be treated as personal postal articles but as imported goods for tariffs, VAT and consumption tax collection.

为更好地支持和促进我国跨境电子商务健康持续发展，由财政部牵头会同相关部门制定的跨境电子商务零售进口税收政策，经国务院批准于4月8日起施行。根据新规，零售商品在网上购买将不再被视为个人邮递物品，而是按进口商品征收关税、进口增值税和消费税。

According to the new policy the customs tariffs for all goods are zero, but the new policy only allows a maximum of 2,000

按新规，目前所有上述货物的关税为零，但新政策只允许最多每单跨境交易限值人

yuan per single cross-border transaction and a maximum of 20,000 yuan per person per year. The goods within the limits will be levied temporarily by 70% of the import VAT and consumption tax rates, while those exceeding the limits will be levied full tax rates as general trade does. The new policy will apply to a list of 1,142 commodities which are most often traded online. The list was published by the Ministry of Finance last Thursday.

民币2000元和每人每年人民币20000元。货物只要在限值以内的，进口环节增值税和消费税暂按70%征收；如超过限值的将按一般贸易全额征税。新政策适用于网上交易最频繁的1142种商品，清单已由财政部于上周四公布。

According to previous regulations on personal postal articles, parcels mailed from Hong Kong, Macau and Taiwan are limited to 800 RMB yuan; parcels from other countries or regions are limited to 1000 yuan. Parcels exceeding the above value are subject to clearance procedures as goods, or to be returned. Customs tariffs are exempted if payable duty is under 50 yuan. The change of China's tax policy to the retails sales on cross-border e-commerce platforms has triggered a heated discussion among buyers and sellers. Someone speculated that the policy was expected to raise retail prices, because it has bid farewell to the 'tax-free' era of cross-border e-commerce.

按原个人邮递物品监管规定，寄自港澳台的邮包每次限值800元，寄自其他国家地区的邮包每次限值1000元，超出限值的按货物办理通关手续或退运，税额在50元以下的可以免征税收。中国此项税收政策的变化在跨境电子商务平台上零售销售的买家和卖家之间引发了热烈讨论。部分人士预测新政将推高零售价格，因其为跨境电子商务“免税”时代画上了句号。

In my view, the new tax policy will bring some new changes to cross-border e-commerce importers and domestic traditional

我个人认为，这次新的税收政策将对跨境电子商务进口商和国内传统零售商在经营模

retailers in their business models and also bring new hopes for the consumers.

式上带来新的变化，给广大消费者带来新的希望。

During the past few years, China has witnessed a booming cross-border e-commerce sector, which registered more than 30 percent annual growth last year despite a sluggish foreign trade. China currently has over 5, 000 cross-border e-commerce platforms. The Ministry of Commerce predicted that the total amount of the cross-border e-commerce in 2016 will reach 6.5 trillion yuan and will soon account for 20 percent of China's foreign trade.

在过去的几年中，中国见证了跨境电子商务蓬勃的发展，尽管外贸面临下行压力，但企业注册数去年增长超过了30%。中国目前有超过5000个跨境电子商务平台。商务部预测，2016年跨境电子商务的总额将达到6.5万亿元人民币，将占中国对外贸易的20%。

The new policy will benefit traditional imports and physical economy. It will also prevent tax evasion and improve market order. In the past, some online purchasing agents have taken advantage of postal article tax and used new methods such as repackaging and mailing products separately to avoid tax. The consumers' rights will be better protected under the new policy, as products imported through online platforms will have to transfer their transaction, payment and logistics information to Customs. At the same time, the new policy will speed up customs clearance so consumers will receive orders from overseas within two weeks instead of two months.

新政策将有利于传统进口和实体经济，还将防止逃税和有利改善市场秩序。过去，一些网上采购代理人利用邮递物品税和重新包装及拆分邮寄等方法逃避税收。新政策下，消费者的权益将会得到更好的保护。作为进口产品的网络平台，必须向中国海关提交他们的交易、支付和物流信息。同时，新政策将加快海关通关，消费者在两周内将会收到大部分来自海外的货品，而不是之前的两个月。

Moreover, the cross-border e-commerce sector lacked entering threshold and oversight mechanism in the past. The new tax policy

此外，过去跨境电子商务行业缺乏准入门槛和监督机制。新的税收政策和在线零售

and the list of online retail imports encourage healthy development of e-commerce companies. Companies with more product variety and higher ability to readjust supply chains and products structure will get more chances for development, while those that solely relied on price competition and imported products through illegal means will be regulated effectively.

进口清单鼓励电子商务公司的健康发展。公司更多的产品种类和更高的能力调整供应链和产品结构将得到更多的发展机会，而那些仅仅依靠价格竞争或通过非法手段进口产品将得到有效的监管。

Next, Customs will implement the new policy conscientiously, formulate the rules of imports and exports for cross-border e-commerce retail, promote the application of information system, simplify the customs clearances, give a more convenient service for all imports and exports and strengthen collaboration with the relevant agencies so as to promote the healthy development of cross-border e-commerce.

下一步，海关将认真执行新政策规定，研究出台全国统一的跨境电子商务零售进出口监管制度，推进信息化系统应运，简化流程手续，便利合法进出，并加强与有关部门的协作配合，有力促进跨境电子商务健康有序发展。

亚投行与中国在全球经济中的角色

2015 年 8 月 25 日

AIIB and China's Role in the Global Economy

August 25, 2015

In an endeavor to promote the global economy, China has come up with the idea of establishing the Asian Infrastructure Investment Bank (AIIB). The response from the international community has been overwhelming.

为了进一步提振全球经济，中国发起了建立亚洲基础设施投资银行（简称亚投行）的倡议。国际社会对此反响热烈。

The AIIB was first proposed by Chinese President Xi Jinping in October 2013. A year later, 21 Asian nations, including China, India, Malaysia, Pakistan and Singapore, signed an agreement to establish the Bank. After a series of talks and negotiations, the signing ceremony of *Memorandum of Understanding on Establishing the Asian Infrastructure Investment Bank* was held in

2013年10月，中国国家主席习近平首次提出了建立亚投行的设想。一年后，包括中国、印度、马来西亚、巴基斯坦、新加坡在内的21个亚洲国家就建立亚投行签订了协议。经过一系列的磋商与谈判，2014年10月24日，《筹建亚洲基础设施投资银行备忘录》签

Beijing, October 24, 2014.

The chief negotiators, on behalf of founding members, met in Singapore meeting again to vie for the top five positions at the AIIB on May 20, 2015. Mr. Shi Yaobin, Vice Minister of China's Ministry of Finance, co-chaired the three-day meeting with Yee Ping Yi, deputy secretary of Singapore's Ministry of Finance.

Up till now, a total of 57 countries have joined AIIB as its founding members and have authorized capital of US$100 billion. Asian countries have contributed up to 75 percent of the total capital and been allocated a share of the quota based on their economic size. China, India and Russia are the three largest shareholders, with a voting share of 26.06 percent, 7.5 percent and 5.92 percent, respectively. But the United States, Japan and Canada remain absentees among the Group of Seven (G7) industrialized countries.

The purpose of the AIIB is to provide financial assistance to infrastructure projects in the Southeast, Central and Southern Asian regions. Investment priority will be given to the projects related to the power plants, ports, oil and gas, telecommunication sector, construction of schools, hospitals, airports, roads and railway networks. Details on the structure, functions, shares and fees of the

字仪式在北京举行。

2015年5月20日，亚投行创始成员国首席谈判代表再次汇聚新加坡，对亚投行的五个最高职位展开竞选。中国财政部副部长史耀斌与新加坡财政部副部长余秉义共同主持了为期三天的会议。

到目前为止，共有57个国家作为意向创始成员加入了亚投行，并达成一致按1000亿美元资本金认缴。其中，亚洲成员国股权占比约为75%，并按照其经济规模进行分配。中国、印度和俄罗斯是最大的三个股东，分别拥有26.06%、7.5%和5.92%的投票权。但在七国集团中，美国、日本和加拿大仍未加入亚投行。

亚投行的建立，旨在为东南亚、中亚和南亚地区的基础设施项目提供资金支持。投资将优先考虑发电厂、港口、石油和天然气、电信部门以及学校、医院、机场、道路和铁路网建设等项目。成员的架构、职能、股权和费用等细节尚未披露。但可以确定的是，亚投

membership are yet to be clarified. But it has been confirmed that the AIIB will have a registered capital amount of US$100 billion. Of this, half of the amount would come from China. Asian and Non-Asian member countries will provide the rest.

行资本金将达到1000亿美元，其中中国将出资一半，亚洲和非亚洲成员国将提供余下的部分。

The establishment of the AIIB has triggered a new debate among experts. A majority of the analysts think that the creation of the Bank will bring many advantages to the region. According to the Asian Development Bank （ADB）, Asia needs about US$8 trillion in infrastructure investment from 2010 to 2020. Correspondingly, the World Bank report on BRICS countries indicated that the bloc requires about US$1 trillion each year in infrastructure projects. Currently, the funding capacity of existing institutions, including the International Monetary Fund （IMF）, World Bank （WB） and the Asian Development Bank （ADB） is inadequate. Hence, the creation of the AIIB makes much economic sense.

建立亚投行在专家中引发了一场新的争论。多数分析人士认为，创建亚投行将给该地区带来许多好处。根据亚洲开发银行（亚行）的说法，2010年至2020年，亚洲仍然需要约8万亿美元的基础设施领域投资。同时，世界银行关于金砖国家的报告显示，金砖五国在基础设施项目上每年的资金需求约为1万亿美元。目前，包括国际货币基金组织、世界银行和亚洲开发银行在内的现有金融机构的融资能力远远不够。因此，从经济角度上看，设立亚投行意义重大。

Another argument in favor of the AIIB is that the existing financial institutions have failed to provide required assistance when the global economy was in trouble. The 2007 financial crisis is one of the most cited examples. When the United States and other large economies experienced the crisis, the

赞成设立亚投行的另一个论点是，当全球经济陷入困境时，现有的金融机构并未提供所需的援助。2007年的金融危机是最常被提及的例子。随着美国和其他大型经济体遭遇金融危机，全球金融机构资源根

global financial institution resources were far from adequate for addressing the issue.

本无法解决这一问题。

Many leaders of the world have expressed their opinions that the establishment of the AIIB will complement the existing financial institutions and it will bridge the gap between demand and supply. The IMF remarks, "The AIIB is good news since it can help sustain Asian and global economic growth."

世界许多国家的领导人表达了他们的看法——建立亚投行将对现有的金融机构形成有效的补充，并弥补供需之间的差距。国际货币基金组织认为："亚投行是个好消息，因为它可以帮助促进亚洲和全球经济的增长。"

What does the AIIB mean to China? Why does China want to establish a new institution and why is it willing to pay the mammoth amount of US$50 billion in lieu of registered capital? The answers are mainly as follows:

那么，亚投行对于中国来说意味着什么？中国为什么要建立一个新的机构，又为什么愿意支付500亿美元的庞大资金作为银行的资本金呢？原因有以下几点：

Firstly, China wants to promote its global image of a more opened country and create a like-minded community that addresses their own economic grievances and offers assistance when required. To this end, the roles of the IMF, the World Bank, the WTO and the ADB have often been questioned. It is alleged that the existing institutions are controlled by the developed economies and their policies serve these masters only. The IMF is the case in point. In the IMF, America, as the world's biggest economy, enjoys supreme power and it alone controls nearly 17 percent of total votes. Likewise, the seven

第一，中国希望树立进一步扩大开放的国际形象，建立起基于共识的合作共同体，以更好解决各自的经济难题，并在需要的时候提供帮助。在此问题上，国际货币基金组织、世界银行、世界贸易组织和亚洲开发银行常常受到质疑。人们认为，现有的金融机构都被操控在发达经济体手中，其政策仅仅服务于它们的主人。国际货币基金组织就是一个最好的例子：在该组织内，全球第一大经济体美国拥有至高无上

largest high-income countries (Canada, Italy, France, Germany, Japan, the U.K. and the U.S.) control almost 45 percent of the votes. Important decisions within the IMF are made by votes with the weight of each nation's vote proportional to its influence. Since the larger economies have a bigger share in the IMF, they exercise power on particular issues.

的权力，仅其一家就控制了17%的投票权。同样地，国民收入最高的七个大国（加拿大、意大利、法国、德国、日本、英国和美国）控制了45%的投票权。各国根据其影响力大小被分以不同的投票权力，在国际货币基金组织内部共同做出重要决定。因为较大的经济体拥有较大的投票权，它们便能够在特定事务上发挥影响力。

Secondly, the Chinese economy is going through a critical phase, where it needs to rebalance the economy. The key challenges are to shift from external demand to domestic demand, from government investment to private investment, from traditional elements of production to advance means of production. Traditionally, the Chinese economy has been driven by the gross fixed capital formation. Annually, China spends over 40 percent of its GDP on infrastructure development. And this had been the key drive of Chinese economic growth.

第二，中国经济进入了关键时期，需要重新达到经济平衡。最大的挑战是从外需到内需、从政府投资到民间投资、从传统生产元素到先进生产方式的转变。传统意义上，中国经济受到固定资本形成总值的驱动。中国每年都将国内生产总值的40%用于基础设施建设。长期以来，这一直是中国经济增长的关键动力。

Since the last couple of years, efforts have been made to shift the drivers of growth from an industry-led economy to a service-oriented economy. The new normal model has paid dividends but the growth rate has slowed

过去几年里，中国大力推动经济增长动力从产业引领到服务导向的转变。经济“新常态”模式带来了红利，但增长率却逐渐放缓。去年，中国的

down. Last year, China posted a GDP growth rate of 7.4 percent, marking the lowest pace of expansion since 1990. A slow growth rate could result in pressure on employment, low saving-low investment and widen the fiscal imbalance. Nevertheless, the Chinese economy enjoys sound macroeconomic fundamentals, and for that reason, a slow growth rate is not a serious concern among policy makers.

国内生产总值增长率为7.4%，是自1990年以来的最低值。低增长率可能导致就业压力增大，低储蓄低投资局面显现，进一步加剧财政不平衡。然而，中国的宏观经济基本面仍然向好。因此，即便增长率放缓，对于政策制定者来说并非太大的问题。

Thirdly, China is very eager to promote its economy and maintain the pace of economic growth to eliminate the fear of a mid-income trap. Some experts believe that China's demographic dividend is rapidly waning and the economy is gradually approaching the Lewis turning point. If Chinese authorities fail to re-structure its economy, it might fall into the middle-income trap. It is worth mentioning that some of the Latin America countries, Japan, and Malaysia have gone through this transformation, but they fell into the "middle-income trap" or the "high-income trap".

第三，中国致力于加快经济增长，保持稳定增长率，以消除"中等收入陷阱"的担忧。一些专家认为，中国的人口红利正在迅速减少，中国经济正逐步接近"刘易斯拐点"。如果政府没能完成经济结构调整，中国可能陷入"中等收入陷阱"。值得一提的是，一些拉美国家、日本和马来西亚都曾经历过这一过程，但它们都陷入了"中等收入陷阱"或"高收入陷阱"。

Many experts disagree with the above connotation. It is argued that the size of the Chinese economy is much bigger than the above cited economies. Furthermore, China enjoys huge domestic consumption, thus it is unlikely that the economy will go through the same transition or trap in any mid-

也有许多专家不同意上述说法。他们认为，中国的经济规模远远大于刚才提及的几个经济体。此外，中国还拥有巨大的国内消费市场，因此其经济不太可能会经历相同的演变，或陷入任何中

income gap.

Fourthly, external balance is another issue that China seeks to improve through the establishment of the AIIB. Economics dictionaries define "external balance" as a situation in which the money a country brings in from exports is roughly equal to the money it spends on imports. External balance also covers capital movement. In the light of the above definition, when we assess China's external balance, it is uneven. Conventionally, China carries huge trade surpluses over the years. In 2014, the Chinese trade surplus was more than USD 382.4 billion. Many countries stress China to improve its trade balance through the capital investment from its side. With the creation of AIIB, on one hand, the demand of many countries will be honored and on the other hand, China will be able to improve its external balance via its outbound investment.

The AIIB is not only significant to China. It means much more for Asia and the world in general. To some estimates, the creation of AIIB will generate approximately 180 million jobs across Asia. New job creation has empirical links to poverty alleviation. As is well known, Asia remains one of the poorer regions of the world. China is fighting an arduous battle against poverty. The situation

等收入陷阱。

第四，对外平衡是中国试图通过建立亚投行改善的另一个方面。在经济学词典中，"对外平衡"是指一个国家的出口收汇与进口成本大致相等的情况。对外平衡还涵盖了资本流动。根据上述定义，我们在评估中国现状时，便可得知其失衡的严重程度。多年以来，中国始终拥有巨大的贸易顺差。2014年，中国的贸易顺差规模达到了3824亿美元。许多国家向中国施压，要求其通过加大资本投资，促进贸易平衡。设立亚投行，一方面可以满足这些国家的需求；另一方面中国也得以通过对外投资，改善其对外平衡状况。

亚投行的重要意义，不仅限于中国。它对亚洲和整个世界都具有不同寻常的意义。据估计，亚投行的设立将在亚洲产生约1.8亿个工作岗位。新的就业机会又将极大推动减贫事业的进步。众所周知，亚洲仍是世界上较为贫穷的地区之一。中国脱贫解困的任务也很

in India is even worse, according to the Oxford Committee for Famine Relief (Oxfam) reports, half of the Indian population earn less than $1.25 dollar a day. Likewise, Pakistan, Bangladesh, the Philippines and other less developed Asian countries suffer from severe poverty. The proposed AIIB will provide new financial support for the developing Asia and help promote a global economy.

艰巨。印度的情况更为严重：慈善团体乐施会发布的报告指出，印度有一半人口每天的收入低于1.25美元。此外，巴基斯坦、孟加拉国、菲律宾和其他较不发达的亚洲国家也久为贫困所扰。筹建亚投行将为促进亚洲发展、提升全球经济水平提供资金支持。

Recently, the chief negotiators from 54 of the 57 founding members of the AIIB (with Sri Lanka, Switzerland and Amman absent) unanimously agreed to choose Jin Liqun, a former Chinese official as the official candidate for the bank's first president in Tbilisi, capital of Georgia. Mr. Jin was China's vice finance minister, vice president of the ADB, chairman of the Supervisory Board of China Investment Corp., and board chairman of China International Capital Corp Ltd.

近日，57个创始成员国中，来自54国（斯里兰卡、瑞士和安曼缺席）的首席谈判代表在格鲁吉亚首都第比利斯举行会议。大家一致同意，推举前中国政府官员金立群为亚投行首任行长候选人。金立群曾任中国财政部副部长、亚行副行长、中投公司监事长、中金公司董事长等职。

I am convinced that with the creation of the AIIB, more financial demands in infrastructure development across Asia will be effectively met. And it has a great potential to lure bulks of infrastructure funding worldwide to benefit the whole Asian region and people around the world.

我坚信，亚投行的设立将会有效满足全亚洲基础设施建设的资金需求。同时，亚投行拥有巨大潜力，在全球范围内吸引更多的基础设施投融资，惠及整个亚洲地区和世界人民。

促进贸易：将评估转化为行动

2014 年 2 月 16 日

Promote Trade from Valuation to Action

February 6, 2014

I spent this Spring Festival with my family in Shanghai and rushed back to Beijing before the vacation ended, because there was an important document from work waiting for me. The document was sent by Mr. Zhu Gaozhang, Director of the Directorate of Compliance and Facilitation of the World Customs Organization (WCO) in Belgium. Mr. Zhu was the Director General of the Department of International Customs Cooperation at the General Administration of China Customs. This time, he not only brought the greetings of the Spring Festival, but also attached a document about how to promote trade facilitation in the world. The

今年，我陪家人在上海度过了这个春节，但假期结束前我就赶回了北京，有一份重要的文件等着我去处理。这份文件是世界海关组织守法与便利司司长朱高章先生发来的，他也曾在中国海关总署任国际合作司司长。此次，他的邮件不仅带来了节日的问候，还附带了一份有关推动全球贸易便利化的文件——“促进贸易：将评估转化为行动”。文件指出，促进贸易发展已成为当前各国关注的重要议题。付诸实际行动远比仅仅做出评估重要

title of the document was "Enabling Trade from Valuation to Action". It means promoting trade development is a vital task now. It will be more significant to have practical actions than to have only the evaluation. So the document highlights that interest in better and smarter border management is at an all-time high.

得多。因此，文章强调应高度关注提升边境管理的质量和智能化水平。

There is the common need to facilitate trade to boost economic growth and development, while maintaining high levels of compliance to guarantee the security of people's interests as well as the collection of revenue. Governments in general, and customs more specifically, can contribute significantly to economic growth through modernization and automation, and through collaboration with other government agencies and trade, which will in turn lead to the highest levels of compliance.

目前，世界各国都在努力推动贸易便利化，以促进经济发展，维护守法环境，并保障人民利益和税收收入的安全。各国政府，特别是海关部门通常能够通过开展现代化、自动化改革，加强部门间以及与商界合作为经济增长做出巨大贡献，而关企合作又能反过来推动形成高度守法的贸易环境。

At the WCO, all members are committed to playing a vital role in stimulating the growth of international trade through fostering connectivity, innovation and communication, and developing global standards, instruments and tools for the modernization and automation of customs procedures. With all our efforts, we champion a partnership approach as one of the keys to building bridges between customs administrations and their partners, both in government and the private sector. An honest, transparent, facilitative and predictable

就世界海关组织而言，各成员海关都在致力于深化互联互通，加强创新与沟通，制定推动海关手续现代化和自动化的国际标准、文件及政策工具，以刺激国际贸易的发展。各方也在共同努力建立海关与各政府部门和商界的伙伴关系。诚信、透明、便利和可预测的口岸环境将对提升经济竞争力和各国社会的福祉起到直接的推动作用。

border environment directly contributes to the economic competitiveness and social well-being of states.

The recent deal at the WTO Ministerial Conference in Bali, Indonesia, with its emphasis on border management, reconfirmed that this is the first step to facilitating trade. Passing the border is one of the instances of direct interaction between business and government officials. Naturally, this interaction results in tensions. In particular, business sees an opportunity for border agencies to streamline activities and adopt more sophisticated information technology (IT).

近期在印尼巴厘岛召开的世贸组织部长级会议期间通过的贸易便利化协定，着重强调了边境管理的重要性，重申了协定的达成是通往贸易便利化之路上的第一步。货物进出境的过程也是企业与政府产生直接联系的过程。在此过程中，难免会引发摩擦，特别是企业一方希望边境管理部门能够简化手续，并采用更先进的信息技术手段。

The recent agreement by WTO emphasized again that accelerating customs reforms has clear benefits for both the public and private sectors. Reduced border delays means increased trade, leading to greater flows of investment, job creation and GDP growth. Working within the best practice guidelines provided by the Organization for Economic Co-operation and Development, World Bank, World Customs Organization and others for developing coordinated border management, governments should accelerate efforts to deploy e-customs capabilities. Exchange of ideas between public and private stakeholders on future e-logistics systems, and

世贸组织贸易便利化协定，再次强调海关改革有利于公共和私营部门发展。更快的边境通关速度意味着更多的贸易、投资、就业和 GDP 增长。在经合组织、世界银行、世界海关组织和其他致力于增进协调边境管理的国际组织的指导下，各国政府应加快提升海关的数字化能力。政府部门与企业界共同就未来数字化物流体系进行紧密合作和联合开发显得尤为重要。此外需要强调的是，政治层面的坚强领导和广泛汲取各方意见的管理流

co-development through close cooperation are valuable. Above all, strong political leadership and a management process that engages all relevant stakeholders are critical to achieving the shared vision of streamlined, and digitalized border management.

In China, we've already launched programs of promoting trade with other countries through border customs management. For example, the SSTL project has seen great progress. In 2005, WCO enacted the *SAFE Framework of Standards to Secure and Facilitate Global Trade* (SAFE Framework). China and the EU launched the Secure and Smart Trade Lane Pilot Project (SSTL) in 2006, which was the first pilot program to implement the SAFE Framework. Promoted by China and the EU, and has been promoting trade across Asia and Europe ever since. Another successful example is "Yu Xin Ou", the freight train on Chongqing-Xinjiang-Europe International Railway, and a new channel to Europe for notebook computers, machinery products, and car spare parts manufactured in Chongqing. The route starts from Chongqing, then through Xi'an, Lanzhou and Urumqi, goes outward of China Customs territory at Alataw Shankou, through Kazakhstan, Russia, Belarus and Poland, and finally ends in Duisburg in Germany, with the total length of 11,178

程将帮助我们实现简化和数字化边境管理这一共同目标。

中国海关现已开展了多个深化海关边境合作、推动贸易发展的项目。比如，中欧安智贸项目就取得了显著成效。2006年，中欧海关共同启动了安全智能贸易航线试点项目（简称安智贸），作为全面落实世界海关组织制定了《全球贸易安全与便利标准框架》（简称《标准框架》）的首个试点项目，安智贸对畅通欧亚大陆的贸易往来起到了积极的推动作用。另一个成功的合作案例是“渝新欧”。这是一条途经重庆、新疆并最终抵达欧洲的跨国铁路，也是中欧间运输产自重庆的笔记本电脑、机械设备和汽车零部件的战略要道。该铁路从重庆始发，途经西安、兰州、乌鲁木齐，经阿拉山口出境后途经哈萨克斯坦、俄罗斯、白俄罗斯和波兰，最终抵达德国杜伊斯堡，全长11178公里。全程约

kilometers. It takes some 16 days and about 10 thousand US dollars to cover the whole route, which is cheaper than air transportation and faster than sea transportation. Therefore, it is known as a secure, highly efficient, and low-cost route. This is also one of the best example of enabling the trade from valuation to action.

需16天，运输成本在1万美元左右，比空运便宜，且比海运快，是一条安全、高效、低成本的运输路线。这也是以实际行动促进贸易的典型范例。

The Trade Facilitation Agreement contains 3 Sections, 24 Articles, which cover import and export regulations, fees and charges, risk management, release and clearance of goods, formalities connected with importation, exportation and transit, boarder agency cooperation and Customs cooperation, single window, capacity building, and so on. A lot of these articles are directly related to the work of customs. Therefore, if the Agreement were to be ratified by the Chinese Government, China Customs would surely dedicate itself to the implementation of the Agreement: revise the improve regulations and schemes that are not in line with the Agreement, enhance international customs cooperation and boarder agency cooperation, strengthen enterprises' understanding towards the Agreement, and increase customs policy transparency and facilitation of customs procedures so as to promote the growth of international trade.

贸易便利化协定共分为3个部分、24项条款，提出的标准涉及进出口规费，风险管理，货物放行与结关措施，进出口和过境相关的法规或程序，海关及边境机构之间的合作，单一窗口，能力建设等内容。其中，许多内容都与海关工作直接相关。因此，如中国政府决定接受贸易便利化协定，中国海关将努力做好一系列落实工作，修订完善与《协定》不符的规章制度，加强国际海关和边境部门合作，增强企业对《协定》的理解与认识，提升海关各项政策措施透明度和海关业务便捷度，全力推动国际贸易发展。

中国对外资企业的吸引力

2014 年 1 月 26 日

China's Attraction to Foreign Invested Companies

January 26, 2014

A special report in an English magazine titled "China Loses Its Allure" has attracted my attention. The author, from the perspective of reality, reported the current plight for the development of foreign invested enterprises in China.

Generally speaking, comments from the western magazines on China are usually biased. This is not only because of political and economic factors, but also the cultural barriers and misunderstanding in some specific fields. But this time, the author analyzed the situation objectively though I didn't agree with all of the author's views. In the article, we can really find some useful ideas through critical reading.

最近，我在一本英文杂志上看到一篇题为《难道中国吸引力不再？》的文章，引起了我的极大关注。作者从现实的视角反映了当前外资企业在中国发展所面临的处境。

一般来说，西方杂志对中国的报道总是带有偏见的。这种偏见不仅带有政治目的、经济因素，也在某些领域有文化上的隔阂与理解上的问题等。但这一次,作者还是较为客观地分析了问题，尽管我不太同意他的所有观点。以批判性的眼光阅读文章，我们可以从中

They revealed some phenomenon which is worth considering.

得到一些有用的启示。文章所揭示的一些现象，值得我们去思考。

The author pointed out, “Life is getting tougher for foreign companies. Those that want to stay will have to adjust. More pain, less gain. The claim was over the top, but not absurd.”

作者指出，“对于外国公司，生存越来越艰难了。那些想要坚持下去的，必须做出调整。越来越痛苦，收获越来越少。这说得有些夸大，但并非荒谬”。

For the above opinion, how should we look at it? Admittedly, the phenomenon and problems the author reflected are mostly objective. But the key is how to put forward the countermeasures to solve the problems through analyzing the cause of them. Maybe the following analysis can give us the answers:

针对以上的观点，我们如何来看待？诚然，作者反映的现象和问题大多都是客观的，但关键是如何通过分析原因提出解决问题的对策。也许下面的分析可以给我们提供答案：

First, production costs. With the development of the economy, we will see, as a rule, the rising cost of labor, materials and production. Rising cost means that bosses must shift their growth models to enhancing productivity. So, we have to invest in labor-substituting technology, not only in manufacturing but also in service. At present, multinationals are falling behind local firms like Alibaba and Tencent in exploiting a surge of big data coming from e-commerce and smart-phones. Therefore, the problem is how to adapt to the new situation for foreign enterprises.

第一，关于生产成本。随着经济的发展，劳动力、原材料和生产成本的上升是一种规律。成本上升意味着必须转变增长方式来提高生产效率。所以我们必须投资于替代劳动力的技术，不仅在制造业也应在服务业。目前，跨国公司在利用电子商务和智能手机大数据上，正在落后于国内一些诸如阿里巴巴和腾讯等民营企业。因此， 对外国企业来说，问题是如何适应新形势。

Second, economic transformation. The economic structure has to be transformed in line with the law of development, namely the transition from manufacturing to service. This is the national strategy for sustainable development. It will bring a tough test inevitably for all companies, not just for foreign companies.

第二，关于经济转型。经济结构必须符合从制造业到服务业转型的发展规律。这是可持续发展的国家战略。这不可避免地会给所有企业带来考验，不仅仅是对外国公司。

Third, credibility and compliance. Perfecting the rule of law provides better security for companies, and a comprehensive constraint on compliance. As a good firm, it must be confident in its own management. If you have illegal operations in your business, of course, you would be punished. This is the rule in the market economy. It reflects social fairness and justice and is also responsible for both consumers and enterprises.

第三，关于诚信守法。完善法治是对企业全面发展的安全保障，但也是一种全面的守法约束。作为一个好公司必须有管理上的自信。如果你不守法开展业务，你当然要受到惩罚。这是市场经济的规则。它反映了社会公平和正义，也是对消费者和企业负责。

Fourth, supply and demand. Along with the social progress and people's living standard rising, people's concept of consumption and their needs for the high quality of products are changing and upgrading. They pay more attention to the brand, style, quality, and practicality of the products as well as their prices. So, innovation or reformation would be more welcome. To all enterprises, competition is inevitable and survival is just for the fittest.

第四，关于供需关系。随着社会进步和人民生活水准提高，人们的消费观念和他们对高质量产品的需求在变化和升级。人们更加注重品牌、样式、产品质量、实用性以及商品的价格。所以创新或改革将会更受欢迎。所有企业，竞争是不可避免的，只有适者才能生存。

Finally, the government management must be improved. It is the rule to give

最后，政府必须改善管理。这是充分发挥市场在资源

full play to the market in the allocation of resources, at the same time, give better play to the management, so as to provide a better condition and service for the firms.

Personally, I don't think China has lost its allure. The Chinese market is very large and full of potential, vitality and attraction for foreign companies. Just as the author finally pointed out, "China is still a rich prize. Firms that can boost productivity, improve governance and respond to local tastes can still prosper." Therefore, in a new round of economic development, foreign invested companies can even make greater progress in their business in China as long as they seize a good opportunity, adapt to the changeable market, invest in a good project, and improve their competitiveness as well.

配置中作用的规则。与此同时，也应更好地发挥政府管理作用，为公司提供更好的营商环境和服务。

从我个人角度看，我不认为中国已经失去了吸引力。中国市场非常大，很有潜力，对外国企业具有活力和吸引力。正如作者最后指出的，“中国仍然是一个大有可为的地方。企业仍可以通过提高生产力、改进管理及满足当地市场需求等途径获得成功”。因此，在新一轮的经济发展中，只要外资企业抓住好的机会、适应多变的市场、选择优质项目进行投资、提高竞争力，在中国发展业务仍可以取得更大的成功。

辑三

环保、科技、文体

Environment, Technology, Culture and Sports

绿水青山就是金山银山

——植树节来临时的联想

2015 年 3 月 11 日

Clean Water and Green Mountains are Golden and Silver Ones

—— Thoughts at the Tree Planting Day

March 11，2013

Grasses are tall with nightingales in the air. Everything around is blossoming. A lovely spring has come.

草长莺飞，万物复苏，春天来了。

Sowing the seeds of green and hope，we have a date of tree planting with thc spring.

洒下绿色，播种希望，植树是我们和春天不变的约定。

March 12 is China's Tree Planting Day. For the past few years, the Afforestation Committee of Central and State Organs has been organizing the "Voluntary Tree Planting Activity of Ministers of the People's Republic", which I found very meaningful and would attend as long as I was not on business trips.

每年的3月12日是我国的植树节。近年来，由中央国家机关绿化委员会组织的共和国部长义务植树活动很有意义。我只要在北京，就会报名参加这一植树活动。

I still remember the 2011 activity. It was on the morning of March 26，just after

记得2011年3月26日那天，清早起来，旭日初升，云

sunrise, when the clouds were pale and a light breeze was blowing. We arrived at the Binhe Park in Tongzhou District, Beijing by bus. As planned, several ministers and I picked the planting tools and went to the designated area. Under the guidance of forest zone staff, we began working in high spirits.

淡风轻。我们坐车来到了北京郊区通州区的滨河公园。按照工作人员的安排，我和几位部领导领取了植树的工具后，就赶紧到指定的区域，在林区职工的指导下，兴致勃勃地开始植树。

The trees we planted were mainly Chinese pines, gingkoes, Chinese ashes, lacebark pines, etc. The seedlings were in rows besides the shallow tree wells. And we just needed to dig the wells deeper and deeper, put the seedlings in the wells erect, fill the well with earth and compact it, and then water the seedlings.

我们种的树种主要有油松、银杏、白蜡和白皮松等。树种已一排排地放在了浅浅的树坑边，只要我们将树坑挖深、再挖深，把树种放入坑中竖直，压上土、再压实，然后浇上水就可以了。

There was a sea of people that day. The atmosphere was really festive and the scenes were spectacular. My companions and I cooperated with each other and worked hard without stopping. Sweat trickled down my forehead. Every time when we finished planting one tree, I felt happy and heartened beyond expression. Our action was indeed of value to the building of a beautiful China.

那天，人山人海、气氛热烈、场景壮观。我和我的同伴们相互配合、一刻不停、情绪高涨地忙乎得满头大汗。每当我们完成一棵树的种植，心里总有一种说不出来的高兴，感到劳动很有价值，建设美丽中国我们在行动。

It is true that building China into a beautiful country is a long-term strategy concerning the people's well-being and the nation's future. In recent years, as China's reform and opening-up goes to a deeper level, environmental protection has become a priority on the agenda. Leaders of the Party Central

的确，建设美丽中国是一个关系人民福祉、关乎民族未来的长远大计。近年来，随着国家的改革开放不断深化，环境保护问题已经提到了十分重要的议事日程。中央领导同志每年都会带头参加义务植树活

Committee set a good example by taking part in the voluntary tree planting activities every year. This reveals a profound truth that "Environment is livelihood, green mountains are beauty, and blue sky is happiness". This is in line with General Secretary Xi Jinping's instructions on upholding green development, advancing ecological progress in all respects, and bringing wealth to the people, prosperity to the country, and beauty to China.

动。这里其实揭示出了一个深刻道理，即"环境就是民生，青山就是美丽，蓝天也是幸福"。这是习近平总书记坚持绿色发展理念、全面推进生态文明建设、实现人民富裕、国家富强、美丽中国目标而提出的要求。

On August 15, 2005, when serving as secretary of Zhejiang Provincial Party Committee, Comrade Xi paid a field visit to Anji, Huzhou. There he put forward the scientific conclusion that "Clean waters and green mountains are golden and silver ones". After that, he further elaborated upon the three development phases of the relationship between "clean waters and green mountains" and "golden and silver mountains". The important thought of green development by Comrade Xi fully embodies the dialectical point of view of Marxism, systematically analyzes the interrelations between economy and ecology, human and the nature in their evolvement, and profoundly reveals the basic law of economic and social development.

2005年8月15日，时任浙江省委书记的习近平同志在浙江湖州安吉考察时，首次提出了"绿水青山就是金山银山"的科学论断。后来，他又进一步阐述了绿水青山与金山银山之间三个发展阶段的问题。习近平同志关于绿色发展的重要思想，充分体现了马克思主义的辩证观点，系统剖析了经济与生态、人与自然在演进过程中的相互关系，深刻揭示了经济社会发展的基本规律。

Mountains take up 70% of Zhejiang Province; rivers and lakes account for 10%;

浙江境内七山一水两分田，靠山吃山自古皆然。从

and the rest 20% is covered by farmland. It was the case since ancient times that local people depended on the local environment for a living. During 2005-2015, 10 years since the scientific conclusion of green development was drawn, officials and citizens of the province took "Beautiful Zhejiang" as the most precious capital for a sustainable development and made every effort to protect the clean waters and green mountains and consolidate the golden and silver mountains, continuously enriching the dialectical relationship between economic development and ecological protection. Translating the philosophy of the "Two Mountains" into a vivid reality through practical action has already become a conscious behavior of tens of millions of people. Rome is not built in one day. From selling ores to selling sceneries, from dependence on the environment to protection of the environment, people are turning the beautiful landscape into a thriving economy in their pursuit for development. Ecological progress has driven the overall growth across the board. Green mountains, clean waters and clear air have become a normal in people's lives.

2005年到2015年，坚持绿色发展的科学论断提出10年来，浙江干部群众把美丽浙江作为可持续发展的最大本钱，护美绿水青山、做大金山银山，不断丰富发展经济和保护生态之间的辩证关系。在实践中将“绿水青山就是金山银山”化为生动的现实，已成为千万群众的自觉行动。从卖矿石到卖风景，从靠山吃山到养山富山，久久为功谋求发展，使美丽风光变身美丽经济，生态引领了全域的提升，让青山常在、清水长流、空气常新成为现实生活的一种常态。

However, we should not ignore the ecological problems facing our country. For instance, **air pollution.** Smog caused mainly

但是，我们也切不可忽视我国当前存在的生态环境问题。比如，**大气污染**。PM2.5

by PM2.5 is the chief culprit of today's dirty air. Because of its small size, PM2.5 can easily stick to some bacteria, viruses and hazardous chemicals, and enter man's respiratory organs and lungs, thus resulting in sickness. Another example is **water loss and soil erosion,** China now suffers from the worst water loss and soil erosion in the world. The current situation is "sporadic improvement yet overall deterioration". Environmental protection can never catch up with pollution and damage, and the situation is only getting more severe. The third example is a **shortage of water resources and water pollution.** Competent agencies through monitoring warn that to some extent, underground water resources in most Chinese cities have been polluted in a spot-and surface-like way, and the pollution is worsening. This not only affects the using functions of water bodies, but also further aggravates the problem of water resource shortage of the country. And there are even more examples.

导致的雾霾天气是现今空气污染的直接因素，因其粒径小，可以很容易地附着在一些细菌病毒和有毒的化学物质上，通过人们的日常呼吸进入人体呼吸道及肺部，从而引发疾病。又如，**水土流失严重**。中国是世界上水土流失最为严重的国家之一。总的情况是：点上有治理，面上有扩大，治理赶不上破坏，水土流失的情况严峻。再如，**水资源短缺和污染**。据相关部门监测，目前全国多数城市的地下水资源受到一定程度的点状和面状污染，且有逐年加重的趋势，这不仅降低了水体的使用功能，而且进一步加剧了我国水资源短缺的矛盾，等等。

All these environmental problems reflect the impacts on the ecological system either of the traditional extensive form of economic growth, or from the exponential increase of population. The insufficient or weak countermeasures by various government departments as well as a lack of environmental

上述生态环境问题的产生，既有传统的粗放型经济增长方式对生态环境的影响；又有人口的指数型增长对生态环境的影响；同时，政府各部门对生态问题的治理力度不够和公民及全社会

protection awareness across the whole society only intensify the situation.

I would like to cite the Saihanba spirit here. The name Saihanba, a combination of the Mongolian language and Mandarin, means "beautiful highlands". It is located in Weichang County in the northernmost part of Hebei Province. In the past, Saihanba used to enjoy the vast land and towering trees, and was dubbed "thousand-li pine forest" in the Liao and Jin dynasties. In late-Qing Dynasty, the decreasing national strength, predatory logging by Japanese aggressors, mountain fires over many years and increasing agricultural and husbandry activities altogether gave rise to the tragic disappearance of the vast forests here. By the founding of the People's Republic, Saihaiban had degraded from a royal hunting ground into a sandy wasteland. Its legendary wilderness and natural harmony gave way to a sight of bleak desolation.

对加强生态环境保护的意识薄弱也有很大关系。

这里我特别想提一下弘扬塞罕坝精神。塞罕坝是蒙汉合璧语，意为“美丽的高岭”，她位于河北省最北部的围场县境内。历史上，这里就地域广袤，树木参天，辽金时期被称为“千里松林”。清朝后期由于国力衰退，日本侵略者掠夺性的采伐、连年不断的山火和日益增多的农牧活动，使这里的树木被采伐殆尽，大片的森林荡然无存。到新中国成立前夕，塞罕坝由“林苍苍，树茫茫，风吹草低见牛羊”的皇家猎苑蜕变成了“天苍苍，野茫茫，风吹沙起好荒凉”的沙地荒原。

After the founding of the People's Republic of China, the Ministry of Forestry carried out a series of researches and surveys and formulated a scientific design plan. In February 1962, a decision was made to establish the Saihanba Tree Farm. With the strenuous efforts of two generations of Saihanba people, a remarkable 1.12-million-mu man-made forest was created out of the

新中国成立后，林业部经过充分调研论证和科学规划设计，于1962年2月决定建立林业部直属的塞罕坝机械林场。通过塞罕坝两代人近50年的艰苦奋斗，在极端困难的自然条件下，在140万亩的总经营面积上，成功营造了112万亩人工林，使“黄沙遮天日，

1.4-million-mu operation area in extremely difficult natural conditions, turning the lifeless and sand storm-plagued desert land into a "source of rivers, home of clouds, world of flowers, sea of trees and paradise of birds". What a green miracle! Forest coverage rose from the initial 11.4% to 80%, and the total stand volume of forests tops 10.12 cubic meters. In the boundless northern wasteland, Saihanba people successfully built the largest concentrated man-made forest of the country.

飞鸟无栖树”的荒漠沙地，变为“河的源头、云的故乡、花的世界、林的海洋、鸟的乐园”，创造了一个变荒原为林海、让沙漠成绿洲的绿色奇迹。森林覆盖率由建场初期的11.4%提高到现在的80%，林木总蓄积量达到1012万立方米，塞罕坝人在茫茫的塞北荒原上成功营造起了全国面积最大的集中连片的人工林海。

The Saihanba Spirit is a complete spiritual system that is centered on hard work, supported by a scientific, practical, pioneering and innovative philosophy, and based upon selfless contribution and dedication. It incarnates the lofty sentiments and aspirations for the "green cause" of Saihanba people, as well as their unique ideal and pursuit. To this end, *People's Daily* did a special report in 2014. Building a beautiful China will benefit both current and future generations. The spirit of Saihanba bestows upon us a profound inspiration: every one of us should start from trivial issues and from today and take action to fulfill our responsibility and make contributions.

塞罕坝精神是以艰苦创业为核心，以科学求实和开拓创新为支撑，以无私奉献和爱岗敬业为价值取向的一个完整的精神体系。它既充满了塞罕坝人献身“绿色事业”的豪情壮志，又体现了塞罕坝人特有的理想追求。为此，《人民日报》于2014年进行了专题报道。塞罕坝精神给了我们一个深刻的启示：建设美丽中国，功在当代，利在千秋。我们每一个人都应从点滴做起、从现在做起，为此而努力践行、忠诚尽责、无私奉献。

Another Tree Planting Day is around the corner, and a new sense of urgency and mission wells up in my heart. Whenever we

植树节又来临了，一种新的紧迫感和使命感油然而生。每次当我们义务植树活动结束

were nearing the end of the voluntary tree planting activity, everyone would turn around and take a few more looks at the seedlings planted with our own hands. Tender leaves and twigs indicate new lives in the making. In time, it will grow into a forest, adding a dash of green to the city. This is the harmony between man and nature, a realization of our original aspiration for sustainable development. Clean waters and green mountains are golden and silver ones.

快要离开时，大家都会不停地回过头去，多看几眼自己亲手栽下的那片新树。嫩叶葱葱，枝枝成行，新的生命开始成长了。过些年，这里将变成森林，城市就多了一片绿色。这是人与自然的和谐共生，也是可持续发展的初衷使然。绿水青山就是金山银山。

人工智能给我们带来新的启示

2018 年 3 月 10 日

New Inspirations from Artificial Intelligence

March 10, 2018

Artificial Intelligence, or AI, is a new technical science on research and development of the theory, method, technology and application used for simulating, extending and expanding human intelligence.

人工智能（Artificial Intelligence），英文缩写为AI，它是研究开发用于模拟、延伸和扩展人的智能的理论、方法、技术及应用系统的一门新的技术科学。

AI is a subfield of computer science. It aims to understand the nature of intelligence, and produce a new intelligence machine that can respond in a similar way to human intelligence. AI research includes robotics, speech recognition, image recognition, natural language processing, expert system, etc. Since its advent, AI is seeing its theory and technology increasingly mature, and its

人工智能是计算机科学的一个分支，它企图了解智能的实质，并生产出一种新的能以人类智能相似的方式做出反应的智能机器。该领域的研究包括机器人、语言识别、图像识别、自然语言处理和专家系统等。人工智能从诞生以来，理论和技术日益成熟，应用领域

application fields enlarged. We can imagine that in future, the scientific and technological products brought by AI will provide a "reservoir" for human wisdom.

也不断扩大，可以设想，未来人工智能带来的科技产品，将会是人类智慧的“容器”。

This reminds me of a "man-versus-machine match" of Go on March 15, 2016, during which AlphaGo from Google took on the world's top Go player Lee Sedol in Seoul, Korea, for the fifth time. Final Score: AlphaGo 4 – Lee Sedol 1. I am a Go lover, and I enjoy playing a game or two on the computer in my spare time though I'm still an amateur. I take Go as a way to train and improve my mind. Then, will AI eventually surpass human wisdom? Is man still able to rein AI? I'd like to share some of my opinions on this.

联想到 2016 年 3 月 15 日一场“人机弈战”，谷歌 AlphaGo 在韩国首尔与世界围棋名将李世石进行第 5 场挑战赛。最终 AlphaGo 以总比分 4:1 战胜李世石。我也是围棋爱好者，尽管我是业余水平，但有空闲时也喜欢在计算机上对弈，主要是想通过下棋训练和提高自己的思维能力。那么，人工智能最终是否将超越人类智慧？人类还有没有能力驾驭 AI？对此，我想谈谈个人的看法。

First of all, we have to admit that AI represents human's own development. In essence, AI is a simulation of human's consciousness and the information process of thinking. Generally speaking, the simulation of human's thinking can be realized by two means: One is a structural simulation, which is to copy the structure and mechanism of the human brain and produce a "brain-like" machine, called "Brain-like AI". The other is a functional simulation, which is to simulate the functions and process of human

第一，应该承认人工智能的出现是人类进步的表现。人工智能就其本质而言，就是对人的意识、思维的信息过程的模拟。一般来说，这种对于人的思维模拟可有两个路径：一是结构模拟，即仿照人脑的结构机制，制造出“类人脑”的机器，被称为“脑型人工智能”。二是功能模拟，即暂时撇开人脑的内部结构，而从其功能过程进行模拟，通过分析

brain regardless of its internal structure, and get smarter through analyzing tremendous amounts of data, called “Big Data-based AI”. The “Big Data-based AI” is so far away from human mind, which is not good at quickly processing massive amount of data and making analysis or judgment due to physical limits. “Big Data-based AI”, however, excels in calculation and analysis, giving it an absolute advantage over human. The invention of modern computers was based upon the simulation of human brain’s thinking function and information process. This is indeed a profound “intellectual revolution”.

Second, the development of AI will change global competition. Previously, the competition was mainly among human, but it would be changed with the advent of AI. As the technology of “Deep Learning” comes into being, computers will become more capable of identifying images and playing a bigger role. AlphaGo’s win against Lee Sedol is attributed to “Deep Learning”, and its potential fully played out. Lately, I read a special coverage on the Internet about “automated vehicles”, which elaborates the operating principle, development progress, competitive situation and regulatory requirements. This offers us a totally new perspective on changing the future world. For instance, AI technology meeting head on with

庞大的数据而变得聪明，这是“基于大数据的人工智能”，因为它与人类相当不同，人类受生理局限，一般并不擅长在短时间内一下子识别大量数据，并作出某种分析判断，而“大数据人工智能”则擅长这种运算和分析，它与人类相比是占据绝对优势的。现代电子计算机的产生便是对人脑思维功能的模拟，是对人脑思维的信息过程的模拟。这确实是一场深刻的“知识革命”。

第二，人工智能的发展将改变未来世界竞争的方式。原先，世界竞争方式主要基于人与人之间的竞争。但人工智能出现后，竞争方式将要改变。随着“深度学习”技术的出现，计算机识别图像的能力和扮演的角色将获得飞跃性进步。AlphaGo能战胜李世石或其他著名围棋选手，就是因为人工智能有“深度学习”的功能，并将其发挥到了极致。最近，我在网上看到一篇有关“自动驾驶汽车”的特别报道，详细叙述了自动驾驶汽车的运行原理、发展历程、竞争

automobile manufacturing will thoroughly alter these two sectors, and will call for a new business operation mode. Another example is that the creation of automated vehicles will reshape the city's landscape. It will overthrow many of the vehicle-centered assumptions made in the 20th century, transforming the way of traveling, working, entertaining and social networking, changing the texture of our daily life, and perhaps also markedly alleviating road casualties, traffic delay and a waste of parking space. Surely, whether automated vehicles will prove a success is subject to well-conceived regulation. Smart regulation has to develop hand-in-hand with intellectual technology, while at the same time we have to guard against all kinds of risks stemming from the malicious use of AI.

态势及监管要求。这就给了我们一个对改变未来世界的崭新视角。比如，人工智能技术和汽车制造板块相互碰撞，将彻底地改造这两个行业，并将需要新的商业运作模式。又如，自动驾驶汽车的出现，将重塑城市蓝图，从而推翻人们在20世纪作出的许多以汽车为中心的假设，并改变人们的出行、工作、娱乐和社交等方式，改变人们日常生活的质感，也可能会使交通死亡人数、堵车时间和停车空间的浪费都显著下降。当然，自动驾驶汽车是否最终能成功，还取决于科学的监管，聪明的监管和智能技术必须携手并进，同时要预防人工智能被恶意使用所带来的各种风险。

Third, we should take a dialectical approach to the relations between AI and human wisdom. AlphaGo bested the world's top Go player Lee Sedol and proved its super intelligence; the invention and use of automated vehicles will change how competition takes place in future, which again reveals the advantage of AI. But I think we should see this in an objective and dialectical way. Human wisdom is the supreme

第三，辩证地看待人工智能与人类智慧关系。AlphaGo能战胜世界超一流围棋手李世石，这确实说明人工智能有超强的能力；“自动驾驶汽车”的出现和运行，将改变未来世界的竞争方式，这也说明人工智能的优势所在。但我认为要客观辩证地看待两者的关系。人类智慧是最高的智慧，它是

form of wisdom. It consists of the thoughts, theories, outlook on values, knowledge and skills that man has created and formed when transforming the objective world. And the powerful functions of AI are the very evidence of the superiority of man's scientific ideas, design philosophy, and abilities of procedures setting and calculating. Apparently, we can't jump to the conclusion that AI has surpassed human. Instead, it merely works under human guidance with new technology and methods to achieve goals of development set up by human. In other words, AI thinks like human and may overtake human intelligence in some areas, but it just extends the ideological and core values of human wisdom in the cost decreasing and benefit increasing process.

人们在改造客观世界中所创造和形成的思想、理论、价值观及知识技能等。人工智能之所以有如此强大的功能，恰恰证明了人类的科学理念、设计思想、程序设置能力和计算能力的优越性。我们不能简单地说人工智能超越人类，而应该把它定位于这是在人类智慧的指导下，运用新科技手段，创造新的工作方法，实现人类新的发展目标。换言之，人工智能能像人那样思考，也可能在某些方面超过人的智能，但它在实现“提效降本”的过程中，延续着人类智慧的思想和核心价值。

Fourth, the future development of AI should center on "cooperation with human". Since AI is unstoppable, the best attitude is to make the best use of it and adapt to the changes. In Customs' actual supervision and administration of inbound and outbound goods, articles, transport vehicles, etc., AI is also adopted to guard the border and provide customs services according to law. For example, China Customs has innovated its control methods, and implemented the "double random inspections" system. After the declaration of goods, a computer system

第四，未来发展方向应以“与人类合作”为重点。既然人工智能已成为一种不可阻挡的发展趋势，那么积极的态度就应该是因势利导、顺应发展。在海关对进出境货物、物品、运输工具等实际监管中，也有借用人工智能来实现依法把关服务的目的。比如，我们在监管制度创新中，实施“双随机”查验，就涉及这个问题。进出口货物申报后，查哪票货，由计算机随机布控，

will randomly target which goods to check. Namely, based on risk analysis and following clear operational standards and procedures, the system automatically and randomly selects the goods corresponding to the declaration form. Detail requirements such as quantity and sampling methods are also predetermined in the computer system. Meanwhile, the system will randomly pick customs officers to carry out the inspection for selected goods. This smart customs control system lets the computer to answer "what should be checked" and "checked by whom". This random but well-designed system makes customs control well targeted and effective, and it ensures unified and fair law enforcement. Another example is for the credit evaluation of import and export enterprises, we can totally conduct risk analysis by combining the abundant, actual, real-time and on-site import and export data and the Enterprise Resource Planning (ERP) resources. This AI-based method is also of great value in customs control for general trade goods, processing trade goods, as well as in Pilot Free Trade Zones, checkpoints in customs special control areas, and duty collection.

即基于风险分析，按照明确的业务参数标准和规范操作程序，由计算机自动随机选定需查验的报关单所对应的货物。查验要求、开拆数量、抽样方式等也都是由电脑设定好的。与此同时，海关针对需要查验的报关单证，由计算机系统随机选派查验人员实施查验。这种“查谁”和“谁查”都有计算机决定的智能化海关监管模式，体现了“随机不随意”，既实现了海关监管的针对性和有效性，也确保了执法的统一性和公正性。又如，对进出口企业诚信的考绩，我们完全可以利用充足、实际、即时的海关一线海量的进出口数据，结合企业ERP资源进行风险分析。这种借用人工智能的监管方法，在海关对一般贸易货物、加工贸易货物以及在自由贸易试验区、海关特殊监管区域卡口管理和征税等业务领域也有着很好的应用价值。

We hope that someday computers could solve pressing issues from our work to our study, from life to social contact, from medical diagnosis to environment models. We hope

我们还希望有一天它能延伸功能，给人类提供更多的从工作到学习、从生活到社交、从医诊用药到环境模型等

that as technology advances, AI will do many jobs for human including management and translation. Of course, some have expressed their concern over AI through science fictions. For example, AI may have independent consciousness or make a decision to threaten or kill, which may indeed be harmful to human. It means that effective control is needed to ensure AI develops in a controllable and orderly way, instead of chaotically and blindly.

方案。随着科技的发展，未来将有大量人类工作将被人工智能所取代，包括机器人管理、翻译等。当然，很多科幻作品对人工智能发展到一定程度时也表达了一些担忧，如AI拥有“自主意识”“自定权”的问题，倘若做出威胁或杀戮的决定，的确会伤害到人类，这就需要有效控制，使得AI的发展是一个循序渐进的、可控的发展，而非盲目的、无序的发展。

Finally, I think it is more like a battle for the future than just a game of Go between man and AI. It is mankind's answer to challenges from the future, as well as anticipation for the future itself. I believe future AI development should focus on "cooperation with human", and we should conduct research and development in a way accommodating human's life style, so as to better share the wonderful outcomes provided by AI, respond to the trend of the times, advance social development and benefit the mankind.

最后，我想说，“人机弈战”是一场围棋比赛，但它更让人感觉像是一场争夺未来的比赛。这既是人类对未来挑战的回应，也是对未来世界的期待。我认为，“人工智能”未来发展方向应以“与人类合作”为重点，研究开发能与人类生活方式相适应，以此来更好地共享人工智能给我们带来的美好成果，以顺应时代，推动社会发展，造福人类。

关于中国的春节

2013年2月18日

Chinese Spring Festival

February 18, 2013

The Spring Festival is around the corner. It is also called the Chinese New Year and is the most important traditional festival for the Chinese people.

春节又到了。春节又称中国新年，这可是中国人最重要的传统节日。

2013 is the year of the snake, beginning on February 10 on the Chinese lunar calendar.

今年是蛇年，春节是在阳历2月10日那一天。

Part One: Origin and Legends

一、由来与传说

Speaking of the Spring Festival, I would like to touch upon some tales and legends about its origin and development first.

说到春节，我想先说说它的由来与一些传说。

The Spring Festival has the longest history among all and is the grandest and most exciting occasion for the Chinese people. The concept of the Spring Festival and "Nian" originally derived from the cycle of agricultural

春节是我国历史最悠久、最隆重、最热闹欢庆的传统节日。春节和年的概念最初来自农业，古人把谷物的生长周期称为"年"。俗话说："年，

production. In ancient times, people called the growth cycle of grain "Nian" (literally meaning "year"), which meant, when grains got ripe, it was one year. In the Xia Dynasty (2070-1600 B.C.) and the Shang Dynasty (1600-1046 B.C.), the Chinese people regarded the cycle of the moon being full or not as a month, the day of each month without the moon as "Shuo", and the two hours between 11PM and 1AM on the day of Lunar January as the first hours of one year, namely, the start of the year or "Nian". The usage of the concept "Nian" started from the Zhou Dynasty (1046-256 B.C.), was officially adopted in the Western Han Dynasty (207B.C. to 25A.D.) and is still in use today.

谷熟也。"意思是说，谷物到了成熟时，方称年。在古代中国的夏（公元前2070–前1600年）和商（公元前1600–前1046年）时代，曾以月亮圆缺周期为月，每月不见月亮那天为"朔"，正月朔日子时称为岁首，即一年开始，也叫"年"。年的名称是从中国古代周朝（公元前1046年–前256年）开始的，西汉（公元前207年–公元25年）正式固定下来，延续至今。

According to traditional tales and legends, there was once an odd looking and ferocious monster called "Nian". Every 365 days, "Nian" would come to the residential areas to eat livestock and crops and wouldn't return to the forest until daybreak. But it turned out that the colour red, flames and explosions were what "Nian" feared the most. Hence from then on, on each New Year's Eve, each family would stick on the doors couplets written on red paper, blow up firecrackers, keep their houses brilliantly illuminated and stay up late into the night to scare "Nian" away.

关于"年"的传说，古代有一种叫"年"的兽，形貌奇特，凶猛异常，每隔365天即到人群聚居地偷吃尝鲜，直到鸡鸣破晓时才返回山林，但它最害怕红色、火光和炸响。因此，每年除夕家家贴红对联，燃放爆竹；户户烛火通明，守更待岁。

Have you heard of the twelve Chinese Zodiac Signs? The Chinese Zodiac, known

你听说过中国的十二生肖吗？生肖，作为一种中国的

as "Sheng Xiao" in Chinese, is an ancient component of the Chinese folk culture. There are many versions of where it came from. What people mostly say is that the Jade Emperor, the Emperor of Heaven, decided to select twelve guards as auspicious symbols of each year. The Jade Emperor gave notice to the animals that they must come to the Taihang Mountain for the signup. Since the Cat has got the habit of sleeping late, just one day before the signup he asked the Rat to wake him up the next day so that they could go together to the gathering place. The Rat promised to awake the cat. But in the morning when the Rat woke up, he was too excited to recall his promise and went directly to the Taihang Mountain alone. He completely forgot what the Cat had asked for him. It's said that the Cat and the Rat have become the worst enemies since then. When the Rat arrived at the Taihang Mountain, he found that the Tiger, the Ram, the Horse, the Pig, the Rooster, the Monkey, the Dog, the Rabbit, the Dragon, the Ox, the Snake and the Lion all came before him. At that moment, when the Elephant was trying to jump the queue, the Lion ran up to stop him and said: "Mr. Elephant, we are so sorry. Since we already have twelve animals here, you may have to wait for the next time." But the Elephant ignored the Lion and instantly stomped and trampled the Lion to death. Almost at the same

古老民俗文化事象，有关它的起源，众说纷纭。较多的说法是，传说中玉皇大帝要选出十二种动物护卫，做每年吉祥如意的象征。于是贴出告示，让动物们到太行山报名。报名的前一天，爱睡懒觉的猫请老鼠第二天一早叫醒它同去报名，老鼠答应了。可老鼠第二天起早后兴奋不已，直奔太行山，把猫拜托的事忘得一干二净。据说，从此猫和老鼠就成了大冤家。可等老鼠到了太行山，它发现虎、羊、马、猪、鸡、猴、狗、兔、龙、牛、蛇、狮十二种动物都已来齐了。这时一只大象吼着要挤进来，狮子忙跑上前去阻拦说，"大象，真对不起，十二种动物来齐了，你下次再来吧。"可大象不理会，没等狮子说完，就一脚把狮子踩成了肉饼。就在此刻，老鼠钻进了大象的鼻子，大象吓得落荒而逃。最后，老鼠搭上了末班车。这时，玉皇大帝乘着五彩祥云到来，十二种生肖便选定了。

time, the Rat sneaked into the long trunk of the Elephant. The Elephant was so shocked that he ran away. In the end, the Rat rode his luck into one of the twelve animals. As the Jade Emperor came travelling on the colourful clouds, the twelve Zodiac Signs were thus settled.

The twelve animal signs are repeated every twelve years, which can be classified into three types: First, six domestic animals including ox, ram, horse, pig, dog and rooster, which are of economic interest to man for agriculture and have been domesticated. The traditional Chinese concept of "six domestic animals thrive" represents auspiciousness and flourishing family population; second, wild animals that are familiar to people and closely linked to our daily life. They are tiger, rabbit, monkey, rat and snake; and third, a legendary creature in Chinese folklore, which is dragon. This year is the year of the Snake. In fact, the Snake is sometimes called the "little dragon" in Chinese Zodiac Signs. Both snake and dragon are symbols of divine authority, powerful deity, splendour and luck in China. Nevertheless, the Dragon has different interpretations in the western culture. Anyway, that is what we call the cultural differences between the East and the West.

十二种生肖动物，每12年轮回一次。大致可分为三类：一类是已被驯化的“六畜”，即牛、羊、马、猪、狗、鸡，它们是人类为了发展经济而驯养的，在中国的农业文化中是一个重要的概念。又称“六畜兴旺”，代表着家族人丁兴旺、吉祥美好。第二类是野生动物中为人们所熟知的、与日常社会、人的生活有着密切关系的动物，它们是虎、兔、猴、鼠、蛇。第三类是中国传统的象征性吉祥物——龙，今年是蛇年，蛇也被称为“小龙”。龙和蛇是人们想象中的“灵物”，是权威、巨能、荣华之象征，也是吉祥、喜气之物。不过在西方，龙又有了其他别的概念，这就是中西文化的差异。

Part Two: Customs of the Festival

People are used to making special

二、节日中习俗

在中国过年，人们习惯于

purchases for the Spring Festival in China. Naturally, food and drinks are the main components of the special purchases. All dishes are prepared before the Spring Festival, including main dishes, side dishes, and dry, fresh, raw and cooked foods. For example, upon entering the 12th lunar month, the Chinese people prepare the Laba rice congee; on the 23rd day of the 12th lunar month, people offer sacrifice to the kitchen god. After that day, people start to prepare pork, lamb, chicken, duck, fish and egg dishes. In addition, rice cake, dumplings, candies, melon seeds, preserved fruits and gifts to friends and relatives are all put in place before the festival.

年前备年货。很自然，吃喝饮食类是年货中的重头戏，即要把主食、副食、干的、鲜的、生的、熟的在年前都准备好。比如，一进腊月门就先准备熬“腊八粥”；腊月廿三要“祭灶神”；接着开始备猪肉、牛羊肉、鸡鸭、鱼蛋等。此外，年糕、饺子、糖果、瓜子、蜜饯以及走亲戚要送的礼盒也要在节日前准备好。

As for clothing, people typically wear new clothes from head to toe, especially children.

在穿戴方面，过年都讲究穿新衣、戴新帽，尤其是小孩过年盼着高兴地穿上新衣服。

Certainly, some necessities like firecrackers, lanterns and New Year paintings are essential for the Spring Festival as well. For one custom, people would put up spring couplets on the doors. Spring couplets, known as antithetical couplets, pairs or peach wood charms against evil, are pairs of antithetical phrases written on sheets of paper, cloth or engraved on bamboo and woods. In Spring Festival, each household selects spring couplets to post on their doors. On the couplets, good wishes and joyfulness are expressed.

当然，春节的一些特殊用品也是不可少的。如鞭炮、灯笼等。又如贴春联。春联，也叫门对、对联或桃符，是写在纸、布上或刻在竹子、木头上的对偶语句。每逢春节，家家户户都要精选春联贴于门上，为节日增加喜庆气氛和对新的一年的祝愿。

These traditions are quite common in China's rural areas, particularly in the middle and western parts of the country. Some even stick paper cuts to windows and paste New Year paintings on doors. But such customs as staying up late on the New Year's Eve, eating dumplings, setting off firecrackers, paying ceremonial calls and giving gift money remain popular in both rural and urban areas.

这些在中国的农村比较盛行，尤其在中国的中西部地区这种风俗更浓，有的还要贴窗花、挂年画等。但全家吃年夜饭、除夕守岁、吃饺子、放鞭炮、相互拜年和给压岁钱，这倒是全国无论是农村还是城市都比较普遍的。

Part Three: Heritage and Changes

三、传承与变化

I spent this year's Spring Festival with my family in Shanghai. On the New Year's Eve, we had a reunion dinner and then watched the live broadcast of CCTV's New Year Gala. We stayed up till midnight and started to eat dumplings, and then set off firecrackers at the front gate. We ignited the "Da Di Hong" or "Red Earth" firecracker and ushered in the New Year with the accompanying cracking and popping sounds of firecrackers.

今年春节我还是和我家人在上海过的。大年三十，我们一家吃了个热腾腾团圆饭。然后，收看中央电视台的春节文艺晚会直播。至晚上过了12点，吃饺子，接着就到院子大门前放鞭炮。我们点燃了一个叫“大地红”的鞭炮，在爆竹声声中，除旧迎新。

On the morning of the first day of the first lunar month, as usual, I paid a field tour to the Customs work sites, extending regards and best wishes to Customs officers and Customs police on duty. I also took the opportunity to learn the work at grass-root levels and their plans for the New Year.

正月初一上午，我如同往年一样去海关业务工作现场视察，慰问在节日期间加班的关警员，给他们拜年，向他们问新年好。同时，也了解基层的一些工作情况和新年打算。

Compared to the previous years, I noticed some changes during this Spring Festival. For instance, people made less extravagant

与往年相比，我觉得今年的春节也发生了一些变化。如办年货不太铺张了，送礼少

purchases and gave away fewer gifts. Banquets at restaurants were reduced significantly. More than half of the banquets booked were said to have been cancelled due to the central government's order that no public funds should be used for entertaining guests. Although there were still some people setting off firecrackers at defined places within the required time in cities like Beijing, Shanghai and Guangzhou, the quantity was clearly decreased for air pollution and safety reasons. Money gifts were getting more rational than before. Regardless of the size of red envelops, as long as given with love and affection, they are blessings for seniors' longevity and juniors' fruitful new year. Apart from that, I also noticed that people began to be concerned about quality service, comfort, cleanliness and health when travelling and entertaining during the festival. They would read travel forecasts and consult each other so as to avoid peak time, though 200 million migrants' returning to their hometowns is undoubtedly a test for our transport system. It is a reflection of the changes brought by industrialization and urbanization as a result of socioeconomic development. The key is that we must handle these changes with care. We must not only have emergency response plans, but also a long-term development blueprint.

了；酒店宴请明显减少，听说原预定的宴席有一半多都取消，因为中央要求不得用公款请客；放鞭炮的还是有，如在北京、上海、广州等大城市在规定的时间段和地点容许燃放，但也明显减少，为的是减少空气污染，更注重安全；给压岁钱也趋于理性，红包不论大小，只要有心、有情、有孝即可，压岁钱对老年人来说是增福长寿，对晚辈来说是祝愿新年美好。另外，我也注意到外出旅游和休闲娱乐也讲究服务质量、舒适、卫生与健康了，大家都在看旅游预报和注意咨询，尽量避开人流高峰。当然，两亿多城里的农民工返乡，这一流动大潮还是在考验着我国的铁路和交通，这正是我国经济社会发展向工业化和城镇化转变的一个必然过程。关键是我们要应对好，处理好，既要有应急，更要有长远的规划和建设。

Part Four: Praying for Happiness Around the World

When the year of the Snake came, all Chinese or ethnic Chinese from home and abroad celebrated the Spring Festival. In the U.S., California has more than 1 million ethnic Chinese residents. They were beating drums in the business street on the early morning of Lunar New Year's Day. The lion dance is the highlight of the celebration. The "Lions", covered with colourful silk fabrics on their bodies, were dancing to the rhythm of drums, bidding New Year greetings to people by vigorously waving their heads, bodies and tails. During the Golden Dragon Parade in LA's Chinatown, there even appeared two American kids in red jackets with skullcaps in the marching band, which was composed of percussion instruments. It gave out an exotic flavour when foreign kids dressed up as Chinese "young boys and girls". And in U.K., red lanterns, reunion dinners, lion and dragon dance parades, Chinese hot dim sum, etc., all these immersed the London city in a joyful Chinese festive atmosphere. In Thailand, Singapore, Canada, Australia, Argentina, South Korea and South Africa, red lanterns, Chinese knots, New Year paintings, Chinese dumplings, red envelops and New Year's greetings became popular words at every street corner. People

四、海内外共祈福

在中国农历癸巳蛇年新春到来之际，国内外凡有中国人或华裔居住的地方也同样过上浓浓的春节。如美国，在华裔人口超过百万的加利福尼亚州，大年初一大清早华人在商街敲起了震耳欲聋的锣鼓声。典型的就是舞狮表演，身披彩缎的狮子踏着铿锵鼓点，精神抖擞，摇头摆尾地向大家贺春贺喜。在洛杉矶中国城“金龙大游行”中，洋鼓洋号组成的方阵里还出现了两个顶着瓜皮帽、身穿大红袄的美国儿童，洋孩子装扮“童男童女”别有一番风味。另外，在英国，红灯笼、团圆饭、舞龙舞狮长街巡游、热腾腾的中国小吃，也使伦敦始终处于浓浓的中国春节欢庆气氛中；在泰国、新加坡、加拿大、澳大利亚、阿根廷、韩国及南非等地，红灯笼、中国结、年画、饺子、红包、拜年等字眼，也流行在了街头巷尾，大家尽情享受，追求快乐，共祈幸福。

there were enjoying lives, pursuing their joy and praying for happiness, which is certainly the same as China pursuing the dream of the national rejuvenation.

In China, the art shows on CCTV and some local TV channels also live broadcast foreign friends' participation in learning Chinese songs, dances and even Chinese cross-talks, which bring jubilant spirits and the warmth of spring.

在中国，中央电视台和一些地方电视台在播放文艺演出中，也频频播放外国朋友参与我联谊活动的镜头，有的学唱中国歌，有的学跳中国舞，也有的学说相声，一派喜气，春意暖心。

As a matter of fact, holidays are the manifestation of a country or a nation's culture. The power of culture not only lies in its uniqueness and inheritance, but also in its dissemination and influence. Wish people around the world a happy, lucky and peaceful new year!

其实，节日就是一个国家或民族对于一种文化的展现。文化的力量不仅仅在于它的独特和传承，更在于它的传播与影响。祈求全世界人民新年和谐快乐，吉祥平安！

人是要有点精神的

——中国女排勇夺里约奥运金牌

2016 年 9 月

One Must Have Some Spirit

—— Chinese Women's Volleyball Winning Gold in Rio Olympics

September, 2016

At 9:15 AM Beijing time, August 21, women's volleyball final of the 2016 Olympic Games began in Rio de Janeiro. After losing the first set against Serbia, China improved its serving and blocking, and went on a winning streak, turning the tables on its strong opponent, and snatching the first Olympic gold medal in twelve years. The floor of the Maracanãzinho Stadium trembled as the team jumped and hugged with tears of joy in a red sea of Chinese national flags. People across the country cheered with them, and the national anthem echoed above Rio.

北京时间8月21日上午9点15分，2016年里约热内卢奥运会女子排球决赛打响了。面对塞尔维亚强劲的挑战，中国女排在先输一局的情况下，加强了发球和拦网和大力扣杀，结果连扳三局，终以3:1逆转获胜，四局比分为19:25、25:17、25:22和25:23，时隔12年中国女排再度获得奥运金牌。这一刻，里约马拉卡纳奇诺体育馆的地板震响了，中国女排姑娘们抱作一团在一片红色的国旗中伴随喜悦的泪水跳跃着，全国人民也为之欢腾了，全世界回荡着雄壮洪亮的中华人民共和国国歌声。

"It was so intense that I could hardly take it myself. I haven't experienced such intense games either," China's Chief Coach Lang Ping said with excitement in an interview after the game. "We knew beforehand that it wouldn't be easy, so I told the team to 'play one score at a time and hold on to it as a team'. It's dead or alive for us, and we have indeed crawled our way out."

赛后，主教练郎平在接受采访时激动地说，"比赛如此胶着，我的心脏也受不了，我也没见过这么激烈的场面。""我们知道这几场球特别难，我和队员们说'打一分赚一分，我们一起顶。'我们真是咬着牙，杀出一条血路。"

"One score at a time, we go as a team" – how nicely put! Her words represent a kind of spirit and sense of responsibility. This spirit is no other than a courage and uprightness of indomitability and unyieldingness. This is just what we call the "fighting spirit of Chinese women's volleyball".

说得多好啊！"打一分赚一分，我们一起顶。"郎平的话其实道出了一种精神，道出了一种责任和担当，是一种不甘平庸、不甘落后、不甘放弃的血性和品节。这就是强大的"女排精神"。

I still remember in a winter's day 35 years ago when Chinese women's volleyball team won its first World Cup in Osaka, Japan. The following three and five successive championships have proved that Chinese women's volleyball team is at the top of the world with its courage and tenacity, and showed to the world that "China can". Selfless dedication, unity, diligence and self-discipline characterize the "spirit of the Chinese women volleyball" that has combined national spirit

记得35年前的一个冬日，中国女排姑娘在日本大阪首次荣获世界杯冠军。之后"三连冠""五连冠"，中国女排以她们无畏的拼搏精神跨上巅峰，向世界证明了"中国人能行"。无私奉献、团结协作、艰苦创业、自强不息的女排精神，是民族精神与时代精神的完美结合，成为一个时代的集体记忆、价值标签。今天我们又站在了奥运女排最高领奖台

and Zeitgeist, and has become the collective memory and label of values of a generation. Today, we have again stepped onto the highest podium of the Olympics, and the fighting spirit of Chinese women's volleyball radiated once more.

上，“女排精神”再放光彩。

That is true. One who is without spirit cannot survive, and a country without spirit cannot prosper. A nation must have some spirit, or else it will lose the backbone to stand erect. One who is without an enterprising spirit and a sense of duty will never find the value and meaning of his life.

是啊，人无精神不立，国无精神不强。一个民族要有点精神，否则就不能自强自立。一个人如果没有一种昂扬向上的精神，没有使命般的激情，不思进取，生命就失去了存在的价值和意义。

When looking from the volleyball court to the highest podium, listening to the national anthem and saluting the rising five-star flag, we could, once again, understand the "spirit of Chinese women's volleyball". In my opinion, this spirit, with a rich connotation, is a flag of China's sportsmanship. The most impressive aspects should be team spirit and persistence. For instance, team spirit is, as Ms. Lang Ping told her players during the pre-match mobilization, "We are not so strong to easily beat each rival we meet, but even if we were defeated, we should still try our utmost. At the court, you ought to understand, tolerate, trust and complement each other. " It's like twelve players finishing one jigsaw, each piece being significant and inseparable. Only through

从女排赛场到最高领奖台，从国歌奏响到五星红旗升起，我们再次领悟到了什么是“女排精神”。我体会，“女排精神”内涵很丰富，它就是中国体育精神的一面旗帜。其中，最为独特和可贵的莫过于“团队精神”和遇到困难“永不放弃”的精神。比如，“团队精神”，用郎平在赛前对队员们动员的话说：“我们的实力没有说一定能战胜每一个对手，但哪怕我输给你，也要把我的水平打出来。场上要互相理解、包容、相信队友，大家互相弥补。”这就好比12名队员在共拼一幅图，每一块拼板

concerted efforts and joint excellence, can a perfect picture be completed. For another example, persistence. That is, when in adversity or even on the verge of failure, you should still have the confidence in overcoming difficulties and persist to the very end. This means a great resilience, as well as a sublimation of the spirit and will of the Chinese people. In Rio, when they lost the first several matches in the group, the Chinese women's volleyball team showed no fear and struggled hard, winning strong opponents one by one. They fully inherited and carried forward the "spirit of Chinese women's volleyball", and thoroughly interpreted China's sportsmanship with "winning honor for the country" at its core and the Olympic spirit of "faster, higher and stronger". Surely, other than spirit, skills and strength are also needed to win a game.

都是十分重要且不可分割的，只有整体合力、各展其色，才能拼出一幅完美的好图。又如，“永不放弃”精神，那就是当你处于低谷、不顺或逆境，甚至到了将被战败的边缘时，仍然要有克服困难的自信，仍然要咬牙在坚持中再坚持，不离不弃、永不言败。这是一种强大韧劲的体现，也是中华民族精神和意志品质的升华。这次中国女排在小组赛初战不利的情况下，不畏强手，咬牙坚持，奋力拼搏，连克强手，充分继承和发扬了这一“女排精神”，也完美地诠释了以“为国争光”为核心的中华体育精神和“更快、更高、更强”的奥林匹克精神。当然，精湛的球技和高超的竞技能力也是必不可少的。要赢球，既要靠精神力量，也必须技术过硬。

One must have some spirit, the most important of which is confidence, self-improvement and self-reliance. With such spirit, one can maintain full passion in weal and woe. At all times and across the world, all great talents possess such spirit. As long as we believe in ourselves and stand on our own feet,

人是要有点精神的，最重要的是要有自信、自强、自立的精神品格。有了这种精神，不管身处顺境还是逆境，都能保持奋斗的激情。古今中外，大凡成大器者，都是具有这种品格的人。只要我们自信自强

unleash our potential and work hard, can we secure remarkable achievements and embrace a bright future.

With love, one will hang on. With a dream, one will forge ahead. The "spirit of Chinese women's volleyball" showcased the world again China's unity, patriotism and the will of self-improvement. As Hemingway wrote in *The Old Man and the Sea*, "...A man is not made for defeat. A man can be destroyed but not defeated." At the present time, China is striving forward the "five-in-one" overall layout and "Four Comprehensives" strategic layout. In the great course of realizing the "Chinese Dream", we, from all walks of life, should learn upon and develop the "spirit of Chinese women's volleyball", hold on to the dream of honoring our country and the spirit of seeking change and innovation. We should identify our direction with unswerving belief, enhance our capability with expertise, and inspire ourselves with the "Never give up" spirit. We should shoulder our responsibility, "remain true to our original aspiration, keep our mission firmly in mind and work tirelessly along the course".

自立，用勤劳的双手把聪明才智都发挥出来，就能干出一番大事业，闯出一片新天地。

有热爱就会坚持，有梦想就会追求。中国女排精神让世人再次看到了中国的集体主义、爱国精神和自强拼搏的意志。正如海明威在《老人与海》里所言：“人不是为失败而生的。你可以摧毁我，但你打不败我。”当前，全国上下正在全力推进“五位一体”总体布局和实施“四个全面”战略布局，在实现“中国梦”的伟大进程中，我们从事每一个行业、做每一项工作的人，都要学习和发扬“女排精神”，坚守为国争光的梦想，永葆求新求变的精气神，用坚定信念明确前进方向，以专业素养提升履职能力，以永不放弃精神不断激励自己，把责任扛在肩上，“不忘初心，牢记使命、不懈奋斗”。

辑四

其　他

Miscellaneous

千秋古关　沧桑巨变

2015 年 10 月

Vicissitudes of the Millennia-old Customs

October, 2015

Several years ago, when I visited China's inland provinces, officials from local governments would always ask me the same question: "Customs (in Chinese "Hai Guan", literally meaning "sea pass") should be close to the sea. Yet we are neither by the sea or the national border. Then why are we also called 'Hai Guan'?" This question, seemingly merely about the name and institution of customs, actually touches upon the origin of customs and its history and development.

前些年，每当我去内陆省份出差，地方政府的领导同志往往会问我一个同样的问题："海关应该靠海呀，我们内地（内陆）不靠海也不连边，为什么也叫海关？"这个问题面上看，问的是海关的称谓及设置，其实它涉及海关的起源和它的历史与发展。

Customs is an authority or agency in a country responsible for the supervision and administration of border entry and exit and symbolizes state sovereignty. Ever since the

海关是国家进出境监督管理机关，是国家主权的象征。自从国家出现、国际贸易兴起，世界各国

advent of countries and rise of international trade, institutions that perform functions of modern customs have been established around the world.

就设有履行现代海关职能的机构。

In foreign countries, the earliest customs authority appeared in Athens of ancient Greece in the middle of the 5th century B.C. In the 11th century, the Republic of Venice in Western Europe set up the first customs-named institution, Venetian Customs. In the long history of feudal society, western countries not only set up customs agencies along the sea and the borders, but also installed customs passes along vital land and water communications lines in inland areas. At the early stage of capitalist development (17th-18th century), customs carried out protective tariff policies, attached importance to duty collection, and formulated a set of complicated systems of customs administration and collection. By the 19th century, in order to boost foreign trade, European countries successively removed inland passes, abolished international tariffs and by and large stopped collecting export duties. Customs have long been in place in several developed countries, mainly including France, Britain, the Netherlands, Italy, Germany, Japan, the United States, etc.

从外国海关看，最早的海关机构出现在公元前5世纪中叶古希腊城邦雅典。11世纪以后，西欧威尼斯共和国成立以“海关”命名的机构即威尼斯海关。在漫长的封建社会，各国除继续在沿海、沿边设置海关外，在内地水陆交通要道也设置了许多关卡。资本主义发展前期（17－18世纪），海关执行保护关税政策，重视关税的征收，并建立一套周密烦琐的管理、征税制度。19世纪，为发展对外贸易，欧洲各国先后撤除内地关卡，废止内地关税，并且基本停止出口税的征收。海关历史悠久的发达国家主要有法国、英国、荷兰、意大利、德国、日本和美国等。

Customs enjoys an even longer history in China of 3，000-odd years. As early as the

中国“关”的历史更为源远流长，迄今已有3000

Western Zhou Dynasty （1046-771 BC）, "guans" and "jins" were set up on thoroughfares along land borders and at main waterway transport channels, which were outposts at key land passes and water ferries assuming the responsibility of safeguarding the country, as well as checking trade caravans and receiving envoys. After conquering the other six states and unifying China, the Qin Dynasty （221-207 BC） set 33 guans and jins, and deployed border officers to take charge of assets and personnel at guans and jins. According to research, the

余年历史。西周时期就在陆路边界和水路交通要道上设立了"关"和"津"，这个"关津"就是设在关口或渡口的关卡，主要承担守卫疆土的职责，兼顾稽查商旅、接待使节等任务。秦灭六国统一天下后，设关津33处，派关都尉掌管关津事务。据考证，记录公元前960年左右周穆王西征的《穆天子传》，反映了中原与西域进

鄂君启节

E Jun Qi Jie - the oldest existing clearance certificate

Biography of King Mu of the Zhou Dynasty, a record of King Mu's westward expedition in circa. 960 BC, reflects the communications between the Central Plains and the Western Regions, over 800 years earlier than Envoy Zhang Qian of the Han Dynasty (206 BC-AD 220) was sent there.

行交流的情况，比张骞通西域早了800多年。

In the China Customs Museum, there is the earliest clearance and duty-free certificate found in China – the 2, 500-year-old "E Jun Qi Jie". It's also the oldest existing clearance certificate across the world. Also exhibited in the Museum is China's earliest decree for passes and ferries, the "Jin Guan Ling" of the early Western Han Dynasty (202 BC-8 AD), which dates back to about 2, 200 ago. It clearly stipulates the setup of passes, exit and entry of people, horses and prohibited goods, smuggling, and punishment on customs officers for dereliction of duty.

在中国海关博物馆里，有中国最早的通关免税凭证——距今约2500年的“鄂君启节”，它也是世界上现存最早的通关凭证。展出的还有中国现存最早的关津管理制度——西汉初期“津关令”，距今已有约2200年历史，明确规定了当时津关设置、人员出入、马匹出入、禁物出入以及私度偷渡关塞、关吏失职的处罚措施等。

关字瓦当

The Guan-character eaves tile in China Customs Museum.

The most precious treasure of the Museum is the Guan-character eaves tile previously hanging on the arch of the Han'gu Pass of the Han Dynasty 2，200 years ago. The Han'gu Pass，located in Xin'an County，Henan Province，was the eastern starting point of the glorious ancient Silk Road at that time. Yin Xi – the first recorded customs commissioner （equivalent to today's customs director-general） in China used to be commissioner of the Han'gu Pass. Another exhibit，the "Zhiyuan Rules" was China's first regulation on seaborne foreign trade，like today's foreign trade law. Promulgated in 1293，the regulation clearly outlined tax rates among other issues.

中国海关博物馆里还有一件镇馆之宝，就是汉代函谷关门楼上的篆体“关字瓦当”。它距今已有2200年了。函谷关是汉代西北陆上丝绸之路的东起点，位于今河南省新安县，它见证了陆上丝绸之路的辉煌。中国第一个在史籍上留下姓名的关令（相当于现在的关长）就是函谷关令尹喜。另外，馆内珍藏的《至元市舶法则》是我国现存最早的海上对外贸易管理法规，相当于现在的《外贸法》。它是1293年颁布的，详细规定了征税的税率等。

There is also the Spanish currency that came into Fujian Province from Southeast Asia during 14th-19th centuries. These Spanish Dollars are made of Mexico-produced silver by the Spanish after they colonized the Americas. Early customs agencies in ancient China only collected tax in kind. Namely, they took a certain share of exported or imported goods as taxation. It was not until the 16th and 17th centuries when they began collecting tax in money. Since then, Chinese and foreign merchants could pay tariffs in Ming notes or Spanish dollars, etc.

展品还包括14至19世纪从南洋流入广东福建一带的西班牙本洋，是西班牙殖民者占领美洲后利用墨西哥的白银铸造的货币。在中国，早期关津都征收实物税，就是从进出口货物中抽取一定比例的货物作为税收；到了16至17世纪才改征货币税。此后，中外商人可缴纳大明宝钞、西班牙本洋等作为关税。

The Museum's "Jiujiang Customs House"

当然，馆藏的九江关

blue-and-white porcelain bowl is also worth mentioning. Made in Jingdezhen, it depicts the scene of Jiujiang Customs House in the 18th century. Supervised by Jiujiang Customs House, porcelains made in Jingdezhen were exported to the world. So Jiujiang Customs House commissioner of the Qing Dynasty was also responsible for supervising porcelain production. Tang Ying, a distinguished artist whose calligraphy and painting works were collected by the Palace Museums in Beijing and Chinese Taipei, once served as Jiujiang customs commissioner. His deep insights brought the porcelain production at Jingdezhen's imperial kilns during his tenure onto an unprecedented level. The nicknamed "Tang Kiln porcelain" witnessed the evolution of the ancient Maritime Silk Road.

青花瓷碗也很值得一提。它绘有清代乾隆时期的九江关衙署场景。当时，景德镇的瓷器都是经九江关监管外销的，因此清代九江关监督曾长期兼任景德镇督陶官，同时管理关务和窑务。著名的唐英就曾担任这一职务，他琴棋书画俱佳，至今北京故宫、台北故宫都保存有他的书法、绘画作品，而且他对瓷器烧造造诣颇深，在任时使景德镇官窑达到了一个前所未有的高度，号称“唐窑”。它见证了海上丝绸之路的发展历程。

From the Western Zhou Dynasty to the "guan and jin", from the "Bureau of Foreign Shipping" to the four coastal customs offices in Fujian, Guangdong, Shanghai and Zhejiang, from the New Customs (Foreign Customs) to the people's customs of the People's Republic, the name, mission and structure of China's customs have changed with the times, but its basic role as the guardian of the national gate never alters. Moreover, different times also gave it a different portfolio. For instance, it is within customs' spectrum of duty to administer

随着历史的变迁，从西周起，历经关津、市舶司、沿海四海关（闽粤江浙）、新关（“洋关”），直至新中国人民海关成立，海关的名称、任务、设置有所不同，但它的基本职能和作用发挥相对聚焦，即国门的把守者。另外，根据不同时代，它还兼管其他事项。比如，对进出境运输工具、货物、行李物品、邮递物

inbound and outbound means of transportation, cargoes, passenger items, postal items and other items, collect duty and taxes, combat smuggling, compile customs statistics. While in modern times, customs agencies have seen their jurisdiction extended to the administration of maritime and port services, navigation channels, lighthouses, inspection and quarantine, postal services, trademark registration, and so on. The collection of "Large Dragon" stamps issued by customs in 1878 was the first of its kind in China. It marks the beginning of China's modern postal service, and was among the 73 earliest national stamps listed by the International Society of Postmasters.

品和其他物品进行监管、征收关税、打击走私、编制海关统计是海关重要的基本职责，但在近代海关还管理海务港务、航道、灯塔、检验检疫、邮政、商标注册等事务。1878年由海关印刷发行的中国历史上第一套邮票——“大龙邮票”，就标志着中国近代邮政的开端，它现被国际邮政局长协会列入73种世界各国最早邮票之一。

In the long development of ancient customs from inland to coastal areas, to the dishonor of customs being controlled by foreign countries in modern days, then to today's strong customs contributing to a prosperous China, the vicissitudes of China Customs has always been closely connected to the destiny of the country and the nation.

从古代海关由内陆关向沿海关的漫长演变过程中，到近代海关被洋人控制的屈辱经历，直至现代海关兴关强国的辉煌历程，中国海关的沧桑巨变，始终与国家和民族的命运紧紧相连。

With the founding of the People's Republic of China, the key to the national gate has been in the charge of our own hands. We can take a look at the customs emblem comprising a golden key and the caduceus of Mercury, god of commerce: as is universally recognized, the caduceus represents foreign trade, and a key crossing it

新中国成立后，国家大门的钥匙掌握在了自己的手里。我们从金钥匙与商神手杖交叉为基本图案的海关关徽就可以看出，商神手杖代表对外贸易（国际公认标志），用金钥匙与之交

means the people's customs has taken charge of the economic gate of the country; and the three cuts of the key represent the three major missions of supervision, collection and anti-smuggling. China's State Council approved the design plan submitted by the GACC in April, 1953.

义，意寓人民海关已经掌握了新中国的经济大门，钥匙的三个齿代表海关监管、征税、缉私三大任务。1953年4月，政务院正式批复海关总署提交的关徽设计使用方案。

中国海关关徽
China Customs emblem

According to Article 3 of the *Customs Law of the People's Republic of China*, "The State establishes the customs at the ports open to foreign countries and other localities where customs affairs are concentrated. Administratively customs offices are not subordinate to the government administration of various levels. The local customs shall perform its functions and exercise its powers independently and be accountable only to the Customs General Administration." It clarifies that customs offices can be set up at both ports

根据《中华人民共和国海关法》总则第三条规定，"国家在对外开放的口岸和海关监管业务集中的地点设立海关。海关的隶属关系，不受行政区划的限制。海关依法独立行使职权，向海关总署负责。"这表明海关的设立既可以在对外开放的口岸，也可以在海关监管业务集中的地点。因此，内地（内陆）只要符合以上条

open to foreign countries and other localities where customs affairs are concentrated, including inland localities that match the relevant condition. China Customs adopts a vertical management regime.

件，就可以设立海关。海关的管理体制实行垂直的领导体制。

中国海关关衔

China Customs Ranks

In 2003, China Customs launched the ranking system. Customs became the third institution after the army and the police to have ranks. The customs ranks are classified into thirteen grades under five categories:

Customs Commissioner-General

Deputy Customs Commissioner-General

Customs Commissioner First Class

Customs Commissioner Second Class

Customs Commissioner Third Class

Customs Supervisor First Class

Customs Supervisor Second Class

Customs Supervisor Third Class

2003年，海关实施关衔制度，这是中国继军衔、警衔后实行的第三种衔级制度。关衔分为五等十三级：

海关总监

海关副总监

一级关务监督

二级关务监督

三级关务监督

一级关务督察

二级关务督察

三级关务督察

Customs Superintendent First Class

Customs Superintendent Second Class

Customs Superintendent Third Class

Customs Inspector First Class

Customs Inspector Second Class

These symbols distinguish the grades and titles of customs officers. They are an honor awarded by the state, and signify the responsibility and accountability of customs in safeguarding the national gate.

The millennia-old customs have undergone vicissitudes in its long history. We can see the passing and progress of the times by looking into the customs' origin and development. China Customs, a force that is absolutely loyal to the Party and to the Chinese people, is now implementing the requirements of the Party central leadership and the State Council, "conducting law-based administration, guarding the national gate, serving economic growth and facilitating development". It is making relentless efforts for the country's reform and opening up cause, for the development of the open economy and the people's well-being, and for the realization of the "Chinese Dream" of the great rejuvenation of the Chinese nation.

一级关务督办

二级关务督办

三级关务督办

一级关务员

二级关务员

以上是区分海关关员等级、表明海关关员身份的称号和标志，是国家给予海关关员的荣誉，也是海关把守国门的责任担当。

千秋古关，沧桑巨变。从海关的起源和它的历史与发展，我们看到了时空的穿越和时代的进步。海关，这支对党和人民绝对忠诚的队伍，正按照党中央、国务院的要求，认真“依法行政、为国把关、服务经济、促进发展”，在为国家的改革开放、为我国开放型经济发展和人民幸福、为实现中华民族伟大复兴的“中国梦”不懈奋斗。

从一个圣诞小礼物想到的

2012 年 12 月 25 日

Thinking from a Christmas Gift

December 25，2012

Christmas is a traditional holiday in the West. It is celebrated every year like Chinese people celebrate their Spring Festival. This religious holiday is usually observed on December 25th, while Christmas Eve, the evening before Christmas Day, is observed on the 24th.

It was already past 10 o'clock in the evening when I came home from work. Just as I was about to open the door, a small and colorful gift bag on the doorknob met my eyes. Who could have sent it to me? May be a Christmas gift? What a lovely surprise. I took the bag, went inside and opened it. There seemed to be a red paper bag and a

圣诞节是西方的传统节日，就像中国每年要过春节一样。这一宗教节日一般在每年的12月25日，而西方人都会先在24日过平安夜。

12 月 25 日晚，我加班回家已是夜里 10 点多了。我正要开门，忽然发现在门柄上挂着一个彩色的礼袋。这是谁送来的呢？是圣诞礼物吧？真让人有点喜出望外。我取下了彩袋子，进屋后赶紧打开，发现袋子里有一个红纸包和一封信。拆开红纸包，呈

letter. Inside the red paper bag, there was a cute little angel, which was golden from head to toe with two wings. It was smiling innocently and wearing a lovely bow. Looking up and down the adorable figurine, I realized there was a wick on the top of its head. It was a cute little angel candle. The letter in the bag answered my question from earlier. It was from my new neighbor, a foreigner. "Dear friend, I am your new neighbor in Room 1226. Please accept this small Christmas gift, my greetings and best wishes. Hope we could be good neighbors and be able to help each other. Merry Christmas!" The warmth from my new neighbor struck me. A foreigner and a complete stranger came to my door with a Christmas gift on this special day. Isn't it a symbol of the genuine affection and friendship between people? I would have gone over immediately and rung my new neighbor's doorbell to say hello and thank you, if it weren't already too late into the night.

现在我眼前的是一个可爱的小天使。这个小天使全身金色，有两个翅膀，神态天真，满脸微笑，还系着漂亮的蝴蝶结。我仔细打量着这可爱的小天使，突然又发现他的头顶上有一根捻子，原来这是一支小天使形状的蜡烛。读完了随附的信后，我才知道这圣诞小礼物是我的新邻居一位外国住客送的。他在信中说："亲爱的朋友，我住 1226 房，是你的新邻居。送给你一个圣诞小礼物并传达我对你的问候和良好祝愿。我希望我们会是好邻居，让我们互相帮助。圣诞快乐！"顿时，我感到一阵暖意。我的新邻居，一位毫不相识的外国人，在这一特殊的日子里，主动送来了圣诞小礼物。这不就是人与人间真诚的感情和友善的传递？要不是晚上太晚了，我真的想马上去按响隔壁家的门铃，向新邻居表示谢意和问候。

Night had come, and it was minus 15 degrees outside, but inside, I felt warm. Looking at the angel candle, I thought of a short Christmas story written by the famous American novelist O. Henry called *The Gift of the Magi*, a love story of a young husband

夜深了，室外的气温寒至零下15摄氏度，但我的心头始终涌淌着一股暖流。目视着蜡烛天使，我不禁想起了由美国著名文学家欧·亨利写的《麦琪的礼物》这篇短篇小说。小说讲述了

Jim and his wife Della. They both wanted to give each other a gift for Christmas but they didn't have the money. Eventually, Della had to sell her beautiful hair to buy a fob chain for Jim's pocket watch passed down by his father, while Jim bought ornamental combs for his beloved wife. What a coincidence! They were left with such wonderful gifts that neither one could use. In the story, Della picked up the combs and said: "I had my hair cut off and sold it. I couldn't live through Christmas without giving you a gift. My hair will grow again. It's Christmas, Jim. Let's be happy." "Let's put our Christmas gifts away and keep them a while. They're too nice to use now, " Jim replied. The story is a depiction of selfless love of the young couple. Although ironically, they couldn't use their Christmas gifts, they got something much more valuable —— Love.

吉姆和黛拉这对小夫妻彼此相敬相爱的故事。当圣诞节来临，他们俩都想赠送给对方一件礼物，但他们没有足够的钱。最后，黛拉卖掉了她漂亮的棕色长发，为她丈夫祖传的金表买了一根金表链；而吉姆则卖掉了他祖传的金表，为他心爱的妻子买了一套梳子作为圣诞礼物。这是多么的巧合啊！上好的礼物，但就在那一刻却变得毫无用处。黛拉拿起梳子，双眼充满着爱对吉姆说："我剪掉了我的头发，把它卖了。因为你可不能没有圣诞礼物啊。头发会很快长起来的，祝愿'圣诞快乐'。"吉姆温情地回答道："让我们收藏好彼此的礼物，因为它们太珍贵了"。这个故事反映了两个年轻夫妻真实无私的爱情。尽管结果阴差阳错，两人互赠的圣诞礼物都变成了无用的东西，但他们却得到了比任何实物都宝贵的财富——爱。

Today's gift and O. Henry's story made me think about our daily life: we need to be respectful and grateful for the love of others, and we need to learn to love others with sincerity.

今天的小礼物和欧·亨利的故事引发了我对现实生活的一点思考：要尊重和感谢他人的爱，也要学会真诚地去爱他人。

写在清明前夕

2014年4月4日

On the Eve of the Tomb-sweeping Day

April 4, 2014

The annual Tomb-sweeping Day is coming. Qingming Festival is one of our traditional festivals in China and it's the most important holiday of sacrifice too. It usually falls on April 4-6 each year. In addition, Qingming Day is also called "Ta Qing Jie". As the spring comes and flowers blossom, people will often travel, relax, and pray for blessing. As the name of the festival indicates, the Tomb-sweeping Day is the most important day for ancestor worship and tomb sweeping when people pay tribute and express nostalgic feeling.

一年一度的清明节又要到来了。清明节是我国传统的节日之一，也是最重要的祭祀节日。清明节也叫"踏青节"，一般在每年4月4日至6日。清明也通常是人们外出旅游的日子，踏青回归大自然，以此休闲，放松心态，祷告吉祥。当然，从节日的本意上说，清明节最主要还是祭祖和扫墓的日子，人们借以追思亲人，表达思念。

There is an English poem circulated on the Internet recently. The name of the

近日，在网络上流传一首英文诗，诗名叫《但是你没有》。

poem is "But You Didn't." The author is a common American woman. Her husband served in the army in Vietnam when her daughter was only four years old, she lived in difficulties with her daughter together. Later, her husband died on the battlefield. As a widow, she had not remarried until she died of illness and old age. Her daughter found her mother's poem to her father when she was clearing up her belongings. The poem was titled "But You Didn't".

诗的作者是一位普通的美国妇女，她的丈夫在女儿四岁时应征去了越南战场，从此她便和女儿相依为命。后来，她的丈夫在战场上不幸身亡。她终身守寡，直至年老病逝。她的女儿在整理遗物时，发现了母亲当年写给父亲的这首诗，题目就是《但是你没有》。

The full text of the poem is as follows:

诗的全文如下：

But You Didn't.

《但是你没有》

Remember the day I borrowed your
brand new car and dented it?
I thought you'd kill me,
but you didn't.

还记得那天，
我借用你的新车，我撞凹了它？
我以为你一定会杀了我的，
但是你没有。

And remember the time
I dragged you to the beach,
And you said it would rain, and it did?
I thought you'd say, "I told you so."
But you didn't.

还记得那天，
我拖你去海滩，而真如你所说的
天下了雨？
我以为你会说"我告诉过你"，
但是你没有。

Do you remember the time
I flirted with all the guys to
Make you jealous, and you were?
I thought you'd leave,

还记得那天，
我和所有的男人调情好让你嫉妒，
而你真的嫉妒了？
我以为你一定会离开我，

But you didn't.

但是你没有。

Do you remember the time
I spilled strawberry pie all
Over your car rug?
I thought you'd hit me,
But you didn't.

还记得那天，
我在你的地毯上洒满了草莓饼？
我以为你一定会厌恶我的，
但是你没有。

And remember the time I forgot to
Tell you the dance was formal and
You showed up in jeans?
I thought you'd drop me,
But you didn't.

还记得那天，
我忘了告诉你那个舞会是要穿礼服的，
而你却穿了牛仔裤？
我以为你一定要抛弃我了，
但是你没有。

Yes，there were lots of things
You didn't do it.
But you put up with me,
And love me,
And protect me.

是的，
有许多的事你都没有做，
而你容忍我，
钟爱我，
保护我，

There were lots of things
I wanted to make up to you
When you returned from Vietnam.
But you didn't.

有许多许多的事情我要回报你，
等你从越南回来，
但是你没有。

After reading this poem, I was deeply moved. The poem is a plain one, but it has told us so many vivid stories again and again, and expressed a particular feeling

读完这首诗，我被深深地打动了。诗如平常，但讲述了一个又一个动人的故事，抒发出一次再一次的思念之情。一个男人

of missing someone. A man with his ambition and strength of tolerance, love and protection, gave a deep love to his dear wife. But he didn't come back while she wanted to return her endless love to her husband. What a pity and how sad it was. It was so real and moving.

以包容、钟爱、保护的胸怀和力量，给妻子以深深的爱；而妻子想要给予无尽的回报之时，却又等不来心爱之人。这是多么的遗憾和伤感，又是那样的真切与动人。

I think there must be so many similar stories in real life. They reflect not just common people's life, but reveal a kind of cultural connotation and the pursuit of social values. The poem is full of negative sentences, but with certain semantic conclusion. To be kind, honest, tolerant, loving, perseverant and grateful.... They are the virtues of a nation and the mental strength of a society.

我觉得，在现实的生活中，也一定有许许多多类似的故事。故事反映的不仅仅是普通人的生活，其实它是一种文化内涵的揭示，是一种社会价值观的追求。上述诗以疑问和否定句型出现，但却以肯定语意结论。善良、诚实、宽容、厚爱、坚韧、感恩……这些不就是一个民族、一个社会所需要的美德和精神力量吗?

On the eve of the Tomb-sweeping Day, I've written some words here to remember the past, express the feelings, and look forward to the bright future, to pursue the dream of realizing the value of life.

在清明节前夕，我写下这些。思念故人，抒发情怀，期望未来，以追求人生价值梦想的实现!

学亦有益　学而时习　学以致用

2012年6月14日

Learn It, Review It and Put It into Practice

June 14, 2012

By the arrangement of the Organization Department of the Central Committee of the CPC, I attended the 7th Intensive English Training Program (IETP-7) at Chinese Academy of Governance from March to June. The three-and-a-half-month course and teachers from Beijing Foreign Studies University have greatly helped me improve my English.

经中央组织部安排，我于3月至6月在国家行政学院参加了为期三个半月的第七期省部级干部英语强化班（IETP−7）学习。在培训课程和北京外国语大学老师的帮助下，自己在英语学习上又进了一步，颇有收获。

Twelve trainees with an average age of 53 and from different state-owned enterprises and government agencies have come to share a firm belief in the value of English study. We learnt from our teachers through the day, getting up at five or six o'clock to read

强化班的12位学员来自企业和政府，虽然平均年龄在53岁，英语的基础也各有不同，但我们始终坚定信念，与老师们朝夕相伴，清晨五六点钟就起床开始朗读，白天上课，

English, going to classes for the day, and studying in the evening and often late into the night. Although we all had different starting points in learning the language, we managed to overcome the challenges, and immersed ourselves in an "English only" environment. From my own perspective, the course had four distinct features:

晚上辅导、自习过了半夜才休息。大家克服了种种困难，全身心地投入到了"全英文、全浸泡、全封闭"的学习之中。我归纳学习的特点主要在以下几点：

Firstly, the course had a clear goal and focus. The main purpose of this class was to improve trainees' listening and speaking skills. According to the requirements of the Organization Department of the Central Committee of the CPC, the course focused on twenty-four situational dialogues, complemented by phonetics, listening comprehension, oral English, frequently used expressions regarding foreign affairs, and news English. Many experienced professors personally delivered enlightening lectures. The course was systematically designed and custom-made to address key challenges in studying English.

第一，目标明确，重点突出。本期学习的主要目标定位于提高英语的听、说能力。根据中组部领导在开班仪式上提出的要求，课程重点围绕24个情景对话，旨在矫正语音、语调，强化听力、口语、外事常用语和新闻英语。不少经验丰富的北外老教授还亲自为我们授课。教学既有系统性又有针对性，突出解决主要问题。

Secondly, there was effective communication between teachers and students so that concrete results could be achieved. We set up an effective communication mechanism for teaching and learning to meet the needs of trainees. The Class Committee solicited suggestions from trainees and gave monthly feedback to the

第二，教学沟通，注重效果。针对学员需求不一，基础不一，我们建立了教与学的沟通机制。由班委及时征求学员意见，每月一次向教学组反馈。国家行政学院和北外领导以及教师组团队高度重视、精

teachers. Teachers and officials from Chinese Academy of Governance and Beijing Foreign Studies University all put great importance to the program and course design, and made adjustments to the teaching plans based on trainees' feedback, thus creating an effective communication system between teaching and learning so as to achieve maximum results.

心安排，根据学员意见及时研究提出教学调整计划。教学沟通、注重效果，达到了更好的学习目的。

Thirdly, field trips were arranged to make us put English into use. The Class Committee offered nine field trips to companies, government agencies, universities, and news agencies to integrate learning with practice through English inductions, Q&A and discussions. We even had chances to talk with American and British editors and officials at *China Daily* and get together with the Yale Glee Club from the U.S. All have significantly improved our practical language skills.

第三，结合实践，强化应用。我们实施开门教学，班里组织课外教学实践活动共9次。先后到有关企业、政府部门、大学及报社等单位参观访问，用英语进行介绍、问答和讨论。在《中国日报》社还与社领导及美英外籍编辑用英语交流，并与来华访问的美国耶鲁大学学生合唱团交流联欢，大大提高了英语应用的实战能力。

Fourthly, students helped each other for common progress. Students all had the same vision for this course: seize the opportunity and every moment to improve ourselves. In class, we read English aloud and made presentations with passion; on campus, we listened attentively and practice after English audio; in dorms, we watched English TV programs and practice with our tutors; and in the cafeteria, we share what we had learned at the "English corner." We respected

第四，互帮互学，共同提高。本期学习，大家都有一个共同的心愿：抓住机会，珍惜分秒，强化自我。课堂教室里，有大家琅琅书声和激情演讲；校园路上，有大家头戴耳机练听跟读的背影；宿舍里，学员们收看收听英语电视广播，助教辅导陪练；食堂餐厅，更成了大家练习交流的"英语角"。大家尊师爱校，严守纪律，互

our teachers, exercised self-discipline, learned from each other and improved ourselves.

帮互学，团结向上。

In spite of the tight training schedule and mounting pressure, we all had a very productive time in the happy family of IETP-7. This will be a valuable memory for us to cherish in the future. We also learned that study is not only a necessity. Rather, it is should be our goals in life and a state of mind. Senior officials and executives need to learn English to understand and to be more exposure to the outside world. IETP's mission is not only to improve our English skills, but also to help us become ambassadors of cross-cultural exchange and international cooperation and to create an image of Chinese officials. Therefore, we wish to extend our sincere gratitude to all the officials, teachers and faculties that helped us during the course.

尽管三个半月英语学习的课程比较紧张，压力也很大，但我们都感到在IETP-7这个“幸福大家庭”里，十分充实，很有收获，这一段将成为我们记忆中的永远珍藏。我们深深体会到，学习不仅是一种需要，更是一种追求，一种境界。领导干部加强外语学习，是深入了解、研究并融入世界的需要。IETP的使命，不仅帮助我们提高英语水平，还有利于我们能成为跨文化交流和促进国际合作的使者，在世界上树立中国官员的良好形象。因此，我们对关心和帮助我们学习的各级领导、各位老师以及相关工作人员表示深深的谢意和敬意。

A poet once said, “The road will seem rather long if one rides over the Guan Mountain for the first time.” The end of IETP7 is not the end, but a new beginning of work and study. “Learning is important for you”. It enriches our soul and improves our mind. Yet we cannot forget that it is even more important to review and put what we've learnt into practice. We should keep in mind that “To study means

“关山初度路犹长”。IETP-7学习的结业并非学习的终止，而是新的工作学习里程的开始。“学亦有益”，学习丰富我们的精神，提升我们的境界。同时，我们不能忘记“学而时习”和“学以致用”更加重要。我们应时刻谨记，“学必日新，不日新者，

to progress every day. You will fall behind if you can't move forward", and that it is never too late to study; we should keep in mind the mission entrusted to us by a new era and our obligations in a time of globalization; and we should keep in mind using what we've learnt for the nation's prosperity and the people's well-being.

必日退”，学习应陪伴我们终身；我们应时刻牢记，新时代赋予我们的神圣使命和全球化进程中我们应尽的责任；我们应时刻铭记，用学到的知识和技能为国家繁荣和人民幸福多作奉献！

附录一

Appendix I

一、重要词汇释义（按字母顺序排列）

1. Important Terms and Definitions

序号	英文名称	中文名称	页码
1	ACE (Automated Commercial Environment)	自动化商业环境系统	465
2	AEO (Authorized Economic Operator)	经认证的经营者	465
3	Belt and Road	一带一路	468
4	CAC (Customs Attachés' Club)	海关专员俱乐部	470
5	CMAA (Customs Mutual Administrative Assistance)	海关行政互助	471
6	CRM (Customs risk management)	海关风险管理	471
7	CSI (Container Security Initiative)	集装箱安全倡议	473
8	C-TPAT (Customs Trade Partnership Against Terrorism)	海关—商界反恐伙伴计划	474
9	Customs Special Control Area	海关特殊监管区域	476
10	Dual Investigtions	一案双查	478
11	Global Supply Chain Security	全球供应链安全	478

序号	英文名称	中文名称	页码
12	Green Channel for Fast Clearance	快速通关绿色通道	479
13	Intellectual Property Rights (IPR) Border Protection	知识产权边境保护	480
14	Joint Customs Cooperation Committee (JCCC)	联合海关合作委员会	482
15	Megaports Initiative	特大型港口计划	483
16	3Ms	三互合作理念	484
17	National Targeting Center (NTC)	美国国家布控中心	486
18	Origin Declaration by Approved Exporter	原产地自主声明	487
19	Paperless Customs	海关通关无纸化	487
20	Paramilitary Disciplined Customs Force	准军事化海关纪律部队	488
21	Pilot Free Trade Zone (PFTZ)	自由贸易试验区	489
22	Radiation Detection Training Center (RDTC)	辐射探测培训中心	491
23	Reform of National Customs Clearance Integration	全国海关通关一体化改革	491
24	SAFE Framework of Standards to Secure and Facilitate Global Trade (SAFE Framework)	全球贸易安全和便利标准框架	492
25	Sub-Committee on Customs Procedures (SCCP) / APEC Customs-Business Dialogue (ACBD)	亚太经合组织海关手续分委会/海关与商界对话会	493
26	Smart and Secure Trade Lane Pilot Project (SSTL)	安全智能贸易航线试点项目（安智贸）	494
27	Trade Facilitation Agreement	贸易便利化协定	495
28	World Customs Organization (WCO)	世界海关组织	497
29	Double random inspections and prompt release of results	双随机、一公开	499
30	Exercising law-based administration, Safeguarding the border, Serving the economic interests and Promoting social development	依法行政，为国把关，服务经济，促进发展	499

1. Automated Commercial Environment (ACE)

The U.S. Automated Commercial Environment (ACE) is the primary system through which the trade community reports imports and exports and the government determines admissibility. Through ACE as the Single Window, manual processes are streamlined and automated, paper is being eliminated, and the trade community is able to more easily and efficiently comply with U.S. laws and regulations. ACE has modernized and streamlined trade processing across all business capabilities, including Manifest, Cargo Release, Post Release, Export and Partner Government Agencies (PGAs).

1. 自动化商业环境系统

美国的自动化商业环境系统（ACE）是企业进行进出口申报以及政府部门决定是否同意准入的主要业务系统。ACE发挥着单一窗口的作用，能够简化和自动化人工操作流程，实现无纸化，确保企业按照美国法律法规更方便快捷地开展业务。ACE对进出口业务各个层面的流程进行了现代化和简化，如舱单申报、货物放行、放行后监管、出口申报以及与相关政府部门的合作。

2. Authorized Economic Operator (AEO)

The concept of AEO is firstly brought up by the World Customs Organization (WCO) in its *Framework of Standards to Secure and Facilitate Global Trade* (SAFE) in 2005: AEO is a party involved in the international movement of goods in whatever function that has been approved by or on behalf of a national Customs administration as complying with WCO or equivalent supply chain security standards. Authorized Economic Operators include inter alia manufacturers, importers, exporters,

2. 经认证的经营者

AEO概念最早由世界海关组织（WCO）在2005年通过的《全球贸易安全与便利标准框架》中提出：经认证的经营者指国际物流中，经海关或其授权部门批准为符合世界海关组织制定的或同等效力的供应链安全标准的企业。这些企业包括：生产商、进口商、出口商、报关行、承运人、货代、贸易中间商、港口、机场、码

brokers, carriers, consolidators, intermediaries, ports, airports, terminal operators, integrated operators, warehouses and distributors.

头经营者，综合经营者，仓库、分销商等。

As China's foreign trade blooms, China Customs are facing growing pressure in its operations. Therefore, it is essential for China Customs to roll out a classified enterprise management system based on AEO to increase control efficiency and foster secure and facilitated trade environment. On one hand, customs can grant facilitation to trusted traders, and allocate limited administrative resources to tackling illicit trade; on the other, customs-verified trusted traders can enjoy facilitations such as lower examine rate, prioritized clearance and streamlined procedure of document examination, which will encourage self-discipline in business operations, and bring about compliance and facilitation trade environment.

近年来，随着中国对外贸易不断发展，中国海关面临的业务压力日益增加。因此，以AEO理念为基础实施企业分类管理制度对海关提高监管效率，营造安全便利的贸易环境具有重要意义。一方面，海关能够对高资信企业给予通关便利，并将有限的行政资源用于查处违法行为，保障健康的贸易秩序；另一方面，经海关认证的高资信企业可以享受较低的查验率、优先办理海关手续、简化进出口单证审核等便利措施，这也有助于鼓励企业自律，营造守法便利的贸易环境。

In 2008, China Customs enacted *Measures of the Customs of the People's Republic of China on the Classified Management of Enterprises*, which converted the AEO scheme in SAFE into China's own scheme, and divided companies into five categories, i.e. AA, A, B, C, D from top to bottom. AA companies are credited ones with customs' evaluation, and equivalent to AEO status. In 2014, China Customs adopted *Interim Measures of the General Administration*

中国海关于2008年颁布《中华人民共和国企业分类管理办法》，将《标准框架》的AEO制度具体转化为国内制度，按照自高向低的顺序设置了AA、A、B、C、D五个管理类别。其中，AA类为经海关验证的信用突出企业，与AEO相对接。2014年，中国海关实施《中华人民共和国海关企

of Customs of the People's Republic of China for Enterprise Credit Management, converting the original 5 classes to Advanced Certified Enterprises, General Certified Enterprises, General-Credit Enterprise, and Class C and D enterprises, whose credit status should be re-determined by customs. Advanced Certified Enterprises are of the same status as AEOs.

业信用管理暂行办法》，将原来的五个企业管理类别转为高级认证企业、一般认证企业、一般信用企业以及需重新认定信用级别的原C类和D类企业，其中高级认证企业与AEO对接。

Up till October 2016, the number of Advanced Certified Enterprises is well over 3500, which is only 1% of all the import and export companies, but contributes to 1/3 of the trade volume and revenue collected during import and export. China Customs exercise a differentiated management on different companies. For instance, examine rate for goods imported by Advanced Certified Enterprises is about 0.8%, 90% lower than that for General-Credit Enterprise, significantly cutting logistic and clearance costs, while the rate for discredited companies is much higher. Customs also offers many other services for Advanced Certified Enterprises, including streamlining document review, fast clearance, and customs-business coordinators, while exercise tight control on discredited companies.

截止2018年，高级认证企业数量约有3500家，数量虽不足有进出口业务企业的1%，但进出口量和纳税额都占到了全部进出口的三分之一。中国海关对不同信用的企业实施差别化管理。以货物查验为例，海关对高级认证企业进口货物查验率约为0.8%，比一般信用企业低90%，大幅减少了企业物流和通关成本，而对失信企业则实施高比例查验。此外，海关对高级认证企业还有简化单证审核、优先通关、配备企业协调员等多项便利措施，而对失信企业，则会时时处处严密监管。

Meanwhile, China Customs has been proactively carrying out AEO cooperation and grant facilitation to each other's AEOs.

同时，中国海关积极开展AEO国际互认合作，相互给予对方的高资信企业便利化待

Up till June 2018, China Customs has signed and implemented AEO mutual recognition arrangements (MRA) with customs administrations from 35 countries or regions including the EU, Singapore, Korea, and Hong Kong SAR. Export to these countries or regions accounts for about 40% of China's total export.

遇。截至2018年6月，中国海关已同欧盟、新加坡、韩国、中国香港等35个国家和地区海关实现了AEO国际互认，出口贸易额约占我国出口总额的40%。

3. Belt and Road（The Silk Road Economic Belt and the 21st-Century Maritime Silk Road）

In September and October 2013 in Kazakhstan and Indonesia, Chinese President Xi Jinping successively proposed the important initiative of building the Silk Road Economic Belt and the 21st Century Maritime Silk Road. In March 2015, *Vision and Actions on Jointly Building Silk Road Economic Belt and 21st-Century Maritime Silk Road* was issued by the National Development and Reform Commission, Ministry of Foreign Affairs, and Ministry of Commerce of the People's Republic of China, with State Council authorization, setting forth 5 major goals of the Belt and Road cooperation: policy coordination, facilities connectivity, unimpeded trade, financial integration and people-to-people bonds.

3．“丝绸之路经济带”和“21世纪海上丝绸之路”（“一带一路”）

2013年9月和10月，中国国家主席习近平在出访哈萨克斯坦和印度尼西亚期间，先后提出共建“丝绸之路经济带”和“21世纪海上丝绸之路”的重大倡议，得到国际社会高度关注。2015年3月，国务院授权国家发展改革委、外交部、商务部联合发布《推动共建丝绸之路经济带和21世纪海上丝绸之路的愿景与行动》，提出以政策沟通、设施联通、贸易畅通、资金融通、民心相通为主要合作内容。

China Customs has been thoroughly

中国海关深入贯彻落实习

following the instructions of President Xi Jinping and the Central Government by making plans, setting key objectives to materialize the Belt and Road Initiative, and promote customs cooperation along the routes. It aims at the 5 major goals, and focuses on "Mutual exchange of information, Mutual recognition of control, Mutual assistance in enforcement", in order to make customs service accessible in a far greater area. May 2015 in Xi'an, China Customs held the Forum for Heads of Customs Administrations along the Belt and Road, attended by over 400 delegates, including heads and representatives from 63 customs administrations, 8 international organizations and over 100 participants from the business community. The forum built a primitive network for the Belt and Road customs cooperation, and customs cooperation and gained much publicity. May 2017, China held the Belt and Road Forum for International Cooperation. China Customs attended the Forum's opening ceremony and the parallel meeting on "Promoting Unimpeded Trade". China Customs also invited heads of customs administrations from 12 countries and international organizations, held bilateral talks with them, signed 4 cooperative agreements, and reached extensive consensus on promoting customs cooperation concerning the docking

近平主席和中央的部署要求，先后出台了海关总署推动落实"一带一路"倡议的实施方案、重点工作以及推进"一带一路"海关国际合作的指导意见，以促进"五通"为目标，以"信息互换、监管互认、执法互助"为合作重点，推动实现"关通天下"。2015年5月，中国海关在西安举办"一带一路"海关高层论坛，汪洋副总理出席论坛并发表讲话，共有包括63个国家和地区的海关、8个国际组织的负责人和代表，以及100多名商界代表在内共400余人参加论坛，初步构建起了"一带一路"海关合作网络，在国内外反响热烈。2017年5月，中国举办"一带一路"国际合作高峰论坛。中国海关参加了论坛开幕式以及"推动贸易畅通"平行主题会议，并于论坛期间邀请了12个国家海关和国际组织负责人来华开展双边会谈，签署了4份合作文件，并就深化机制衔接、监管创新、信息共享、贸易安全、能力建设等5个领域的合作达成了共识。

of mechanisms, innovation of customs control, exchange of information, trade security, and capacity building.

4. Customs Attachés' Club (CAC)

Proposed by China Customs, the Customs Attachés' Club (CAC) was founded on January 28, 2008 by China Customs and all Customs Attachés (CA) and representatives of customs affairs working in the Embassy, Consulate General, or Mission within China. There are 50 CAs and representatives from 32 countries and regions in the CAC. Members will take the Chair on a rotational basis in alphabetical order according to the name of their country or region and hold office for 3 months.

Since its establishment, the CAC has held nearly one hundred activities, including seminars, workshops, policy publication, onsite visits, and seasonal meetings, covering areas such as trade security and facilitation, combating the smuggling of drugs, cigarettes and hazardous waste, IPR protection, customs procedures, anti-fraud, combating money laundering, AEO, Coordinated Border Management (CBM), free trade zones, customs technological innovation, enforcement of the CITES Convention on endangered wild

4. 海关专员俱乐部

为加强与各国驻华海关专员之间的交流，促进合作，在中国海关的倡议下，2008年1月28日，由中国海关和各国（地区）驻华使（领）馆（团）海关专员或海关事务代表组成的“海关专员俱乐部”在北京正式成立。目前，俱乐部成员包括32个国家（地区）的海关专员和代表50余人。成员按照其代表国家（地区）的首字母顺序担任俱乐部轮值主席，任期3个月。

海关专员俱乐部成立以来，先后组织了活动近百次，包括研讨会、座谈会、政策宣讲会、参观口岸、季度例会等，涉及贸易安全与便利、打击毒品、香烟、有害废物走私、知识产权保护、海关通关制度、反商业瞒骗和反洗钱、AEO制度、协调的边境管理、自由贸易园区、海关科技创新、濒危野生动植物种国际贸易公约（CITES）执法、跨

species, cross-border e-commerce, valuation, training and capacity building, and so on.

境电子商务海关监管、海关估价、海关教育培训与能力建设等专题。

5. Customs Mutual Administrative Assistance (CMAA)

Customs Mutual Administrative Assistance (CMAA) means that customs administrations of two countries or regions provide assistance to each other, according to the CMAA agreements or other agreements signed by their governments or organizations, to the provisions concerning CMAA affairs in international conventions that they are parties to, or based upon the needs of their cooperation. The World Customs Organization has formed a model bilateral agreement as a recommendation to its members. Assistances include providing cargo information upon a party's own initiative or on request, verifying the authenticity of import and export information, providing declaration forms and documents, controlled delivery, and so on.

5. 海关行政互助

海关行政互助是指两国（地区）海关根据双方政府或海关签订的行政互助协定、其他合作协议以及所加入的有关国际公约中涉及行政互助的相关条款的规定，或根据国际合作实际需要，相互提供协助。世界海关组织制定了海关行政互助双边协定示范文本，推荐给成员使用。协助的主要形式包括应对方请求提供或主动提供有关货物信息、核实有关进出口信息是否属实、提供货物有关报关单证、控制下交付等。

6. Customs risk management (CRM)

Customs risk management is to systematically utilize risk management philosophy, methodology and technology to effectively identify, measure, analyze, assess, address and monitor all kinds of risks

6. 海关风险管理

海关风险管理是对海关工作领域存在的各类风险，系统地运用风险管理理念、方法和技术，有效进行识别、度量、分析、评估、处置和监控，以

in Customs-related areas, so as to prevent, control, mitigate or avoid harm and loss caused by risks to the largest extent. The World Customs Organization (WCO) defines the basic procedures of Customs risk management as: establish the context, risk identification, risk assessment, risk analysis, risk evaluation/prioritization, risk treatment, as well as risk monitoring and review through risk management process.

最大限度地防范、控制、减少或者避免风险造成的危害和损失。世界海关组织将海关风险管理的基本程序概括为：建立风险环境，风险识别，风险分析，风险评估，风险处置，并对整个风险管理流程进行风险监控和复查评估。

The *Agreement on Trade Facilitation* of the WTO, the *Revised Kyoto Convention* of the WCO and the WCO SAFE Framework of Standards all incorporate Customs risk management as a specific measure to streamline and coordinate Customs procedures. Risk management has now become an important management tool to tackle such challenges as growing trade volume and worsening safety risks for Customs administrations around the world.

世贸组织《贸易便利化协定》、世界海关组织《经修订的京都公约》和《标准框架协议》中均纳入了海关风险管理内容，作为简化和协调海关手续的一项具体措施。目前，风险管理已成为各国海关为应对贸易量增长、安全风险加剧等挑战所采取的重要管理手段。

China Customs' exploration of risk management can be dated back to the 1980s, starting with the "Red and Green Channels" in passenger inspection. The *Decisions on Establishing a Modern Customs System* by the General Administration of China Customs released in 1998 specified that customs should take building and improving the risk management mechanism as a key link in the

中国海关对风险管理的探索始于20世纪80年代，首先在旅检工作中开始推行“红绿通道”验放制度。1998年下发的《海关总署关于建立现代海关制度的决定》，明确提出把建立健全风险管理机制作为海关现代化发展战略的中心环节。2003年海关总署党组提出全面

modernization development strategy of China Customs. In 2003, the Party Leading Group of the General Administration of China Customs made the decision of modernizing China Customs in an all-round way and realizing the Step-2 development goal in the modernized Customs system. One major policy of that decision was to widely use risk management method and build and improve the risk management mechanism.

建设现代化海关，实现现代海关制度第二步发展目标，其中重要决策之一就是广泛运用风险管理方法、建立健全风险管理机制。

In recent years, China Customs has been working on the clearance integration reform across the country and speeding up the establishment of risk management centers in order to conduct risk management in a centralized, unified and intelligent way, increase risk prevention and control efficiency, and provide more effective and facilitated Customs clearance for the business sector.

近年来，中国海关正着力进行全国海关通关一体化改革，加快推进风险防控中心建设，以实现风险防控业务的集中、统一、智能处置，提升风险防控效能，为企业提供更有效的通关便利。

7. Container Security Initiative（CSI）

In the aftermath of the terrorist attacks on September 11, 2001, U.S. Customs Service began developing antiterrorism programs to help secure the United States. Within months of these attacks, U.S. Customs Service had created the Container Security Initiative (CSI). CSI addresses the threat to border security and global trade posed by the potential for terrorist use of a maritime container to deliver

7. 集装箱安全倡议

2001年9·11恐怖袭击事件后，美国海关开始着手制定保障美国国土安全的一系列计划。2002年1月，美国海关公布了集装箱安全倡议（CSI）。该倡议旨在防范恐怖分子通过海运集装箱运送武器并对边境安全和国际贸易造成威胁。集装箱安全倡议的核

a weapon. CSI proposes a security regime to ensure all containers that pose a potential risk for terrorism are identified and inspected at foreign ports before they are placed on vessels destined for the United States. CBP has stationed teams of U.S. CBP Officers in foreign locations to work together with our host foreign government counterparts. Their mission is to target and prescreen containers. Those foreign administrations use non-intrusive inspection (NII) and radiation detection technology to screen high-risk containers before they are shipped to U.S. ports.

心理念是针对具有恐怖主义风险的集装箱在外国口岸装运并前往美国以前进行查验。为此，美国海关与边境保护局向已开展合作的国家派驻官员，提前布控和筛查集装箱，而国外相关部门据此实施非侵入式查验并使用辐射探测技术在高风险集装箱离港前往美国前进行检查。

China and U.S. Customs started the CSI program in ports in Shanghai and Shenzhen in 2005. Since then, no weapon of mass destruction (WMD) has been found in the 58 CSI ports around the world. According to the cooperation agreement between China and the U.S., China Customs is planning to deploy officers to U.S. ports reciprocally to guarantee the security of shipments from the U.S.

2005年起，中美CSI项目在上海和深圳的港口启动实施。项目启动后，美方在全球开展CSI项目的58个港口均未发现大规模杀伤性武器。根据中美CSI合作协议，中国海关正计划对等地向美国口岸派驻CSI官员，以加强对美国输华海运集装箱的安全监管。

8. Customs Trade Partnership Against Terrorism (C–TPAT)

8. 海关—商界反恐伙伴计划

Through Customs Trade Partnership Against Terrorism (C-TPAT) program, U.S. Customs and Border Protection's (CBP) works with the trade community to strengthen

海关—商界反恐伙伴计划由美国海关与边境保护局发起，旨在与商界加强在国际贸易供应链领域的合作，提升美

international supply chains and improve United States border security. C-TPAT is a voluntary public-private sector partnership program which include principle stakeholders of the international supply chain such as importers, carriers, consolidators, licensed customs brokers, and manufacturers. From its inception in November 2001, C-TPAT continued to grow. Today, more than 11,400 certified partners have been accepted into the program. Some of the benefits of the program for verified partners include: reduced number of CBP examinations, front of the line inspections, fast release and shorter wait times at the border

国边境安全水平。该伙伴计划由企业自愿选择参加，参与方包括进口商、承运商、集运商、报关行和生产商等在国际供应链上的重要环节。2001年11月启动以来，海关—商界反恐伙伴计划参与方数量不断增长，现已超过1.14万个。经该计划认证的企业能够享受到减少查验、优先查验、便捷放行、缩短口岸滞留时间等一系列便利化措施。

In March 2008, China Customs and CBP signed a cooperative agreement, which stipulated that a joint C-TPAT verification group would be set up to carry out onsite verifications of Chinese companies that were suppliers of American C-TPAT companies. The group was spearheaded by China Customs, and supported by CBP. Currently, there are 373 verified Chinese companies that are exporting the U.S. These suppliers would be able to enjoy the benefits of the program when entering the U.S. After the September 2015, joint verification was brought to a halt as China Customs and CBP have directed their focus to promote the AEO mutual recognition program.

2008年3月，中国海关与美国海关与边境保护局签署合作文件，组成C-TPAT联合验证组，采用中国海关主导验证，CBP提供支持的模式，对C-TPAT美方企业的中国供应商企业实施实地验证，目前，中方共有373家货物输美企业通过了C-TPAT验证，其货物可以享受在美便利通关待遇。2015年9月以后，双方未再开展C-TPAT联合验证，重点推动AEO互认磋商。

9. Customs Special Control Area

According to the *Customs Law of the People´s Republic of China*: customs special control areas such as bonded areas authorized by the State Council to be established in the territory of the People's Republic of China, shall be in the execution of control by the Customs in accordance with the relevant national provisions. The establishment of customs special control areas is the mandate of the State Council. A customs special control area is a physically enclosed area controlled by the customs with special tax and duty arrangements, set up by the State Council, and managed with a computerized system.

Since the first Bonded Zone at Wai Gaoqiao in Shanghai in 1990, there have been 6 kinds of customs special control areas in China: Bonded Zones, Export Processing Zones, Bonded Logistics Zones, Cross-border Industrial Zones, Bonded Ports, and Comprehensive Bonded Zones, which have played important roles of supporting economic and trade growth in different times. After almost three decades, customs special control areas have become the ideal platforms of opening-up with preferential duty policies, facilitated clearance, sophisticated supervision facility, and sound environment for businesses. Up till May 2018, there are a total of 136

9. 海关特殊监管区域

根据《中华人民共和国海关法》规定："经国务院批准在中华人民共和国境内设立的保税区等海关特殊监管区域，由海关按照国家有关规定实施监管"。其中，海关特殊监管区域是指由国务院批准设立，实行特殊税收政策、建有封闭围网和信息化管理系统的海关特定监管区域。

自1990年上海外高桥保税区设立以来，我国先后设立了6类海关特殊监管区域：保税区、出口加工区、保税物流园区、跨境工业区、保税港区、综合保税区，为国家在不同时期的外经贸发展做出了重要贡献。经过近30年发展，海关特殊监管区域已逐步成为税收政策优惠、通关手续便捷、监管设施完备、营商环境优良的对外开放平台。截至2018年7月，中国已批准设立了137个海关特殊监管区域，分布在29个省、自治区、直辖市。中

customs special control areas in 29 provinces, autonomous regions and municipalities across the country. And China Customs has already built a sophisticated system, and set forth a list of preferential policies, for instance: foreign goods entering the area are subject to bonded supervision; domestic goods entering the goods enjoy tax refund; foreign equipment entering the area is exempted from duty, with a view to encouraging R&D, design, manufacturing of key components, and logistics. In 2017, import and export of customs special control areas totaled 4.64 trillion RMB yuan with a year-on-year increase of 19.7%, accounting for16.7% of China's overall trade volume.

国海关也已建立了较为完善的海关特殊监管区域管理体系：政策上，实行境外入区货物保税、境内入区货物退税、进口设备免税等规定；功能上，鼓励开展研发、设计、核心元器件制造、物流等业务。2017年，海关特殊监管区域进出口总值达4.64万亿元人民币，同比增长19.7%，占同期我国外贸进出口总额的16.7%。

In order to further promote the scientific development of customs special control areas and improve the quality of their development, the GACC has been earnestly carrying out the decision and plans of the CPC Central Committee and the State Council to integrate and optimize customs special control areas by standardizing types and names of customs special control areas, promoting the upgrade of industrial structure and supervision services, applying more stringent criteria on new applicants, and setting up an exit mechanism for underdeveloped areas, has achieved satisfying outcomes .

为进一步推进海关特殊监管区域科学发展，提高其发展质量，2012年以来，海关总署认真贯彻党中央、国务院关于海关特殊监管区域整合优化的决策部署，整合规范海关特殊监管区域类型和名称，推动优化产业结构和监管服务，严格设立审核，实施退出管理，整合优化工作取得了良好成效。

10. Dual Investigations

Where there is smuggling, there is often corruption. Therefore, customs enforcement agencies should explore the source of unlawful acts through smuggling cases, and carry out investigations into smuggling activities and violations of Party discipline and the law by customs officers simultaneously. To this end, China Customs has established and improved a "Dual Investigations" mechanism on fighting against smuggling and corruption at the same time, which means that while an anti-smuggling case is under investigation, clues on customs internal violations and disciplinary misconducts should also be examined so as to ensure the customs force is impartial and clean.

10. 一案双查

走私行为往往与腐败行为相伴而生。在侦办走私案件的过程中，海关执法部门应通过走私案件挖掘违法根源，外查走私行为和内查执法队伍违法违纪同步进行。为此，中国海关建立完善了反走私与反腐败的“一案双查”机制，明确规定任何一起走私案件在查期间，应该同时调查海关内部相关违法违纪线索，以确保海关队伍的公正廉洁。

11. Global Supply Chain Security (GSCS)

Economic globalization generates social and economic development. Yet unstable and uncertain factors are significantly increasing. And unconventional risks of finance, environment, information security, epidemic, and terrorism, have become major threats to national security, and are profoundly affecting the ways of economic and social development, which requires us to put in more efforts to enhance the security of the supply chain, the transport and logistics system for the world's

11. 全球供应链安全

经济全球化带来了社会的发展和经济的繁荣，但影响和平与发展的不稳定、不确定因素明显增多，金融、环境、信息安全以及流行疾病、恐怖主义等非传统安全因素，已经构成了对国家安全的重要威胁，也深刻影响到各国的经济社会发展。因此，从全球层面提升供应链、运输工具和物流安全水平，以保障国际货物贸易安

cargo on a global scale.

To this end, the World Customs Organization adopted the *SAFE Framework of Standards to Secure and Facilitate Global Trade* (SAFE Framework) in 2005. There are two pillars in the SAFE Framework to ensure supply chain security: Customs-to-Customs network arrangements and Customs-to-Business partnerships. The first pillar covers all areas of customs operations such as supply chain management, inspection technology, risk management and targeting, electronic data exchange, performance and security assessment, integrity, etc. The second pillar involves mutual recognition of Authorized Economic Operators, information sharing and security among others.As times change, it is more and more important for customs to collaborate with other government agencies and relevant stakeholders.

全则显得尤为重要。

为此，世界海关组织于2005年通过了《全球贸易安全与便利标准框架》，其中主要包括了保障供应链安全的两大支柱，即海关与海关之间的合作安排和海关与商界之间的伙伴关系。第一个支柱涉及供应链管理、查验技术、风险管理和布控、电子信息交换、绩效和安全评估以及工作人员的廉政等海关监管工作的各个方面。第二个支柱包括AEO互认、信息交换与安全等内容。随着形势的发展，海关与其他政府部门及相关方的协作配合也日显重要。

12. Green Channel for Fast Clearance

Green Channel for Fast Clearance in a broad sense means the channel set up by the customs for a specific group of cargo or passengers.

In customs international cooperation, it can also mean a specific cooperation program with some of China's neighboring countries to facilitate the clearance of certain commodities.

12. 绿色通道

绿色通道广义指海关为特定货物和旅客设立的快速通关通道。

在具体工作中，绿色通道还指与部分周边国家开展的重点商品快速通关合作项目。目前，中国海关在边境口岸分别

For instance, China Customs is working with Kazakhstan, Tajikistan, Kyrgyzstan on a "Green Channel" project to set up special windows for the declaration of agricultural products, prioritize the review of relevant documents, and clear vehicles with the "Green Channel" label without unnecessary delay, in order to reduce the time for clearance.

与哈萨克斯坦、塔吉克斯坦、吉尔吉斯斯坦开展了农产品快速通关"绿色通道"项目合作，在口岸设置专用农产品进出口报关报检窗口，第一时间对企业递交的报关单据进行审核，快速通过贴有绿色通道标识的车检通道，尽量缩短货物通关时间。

On May 14, 2017, President Xi Jinping gave a speech at the opening ceremony of The Belt and Road Forum for International Cooperation. His speech, titled *Work Together to Build the Silk Road Economic Belt and the 21st Century Maritime Silk Road*, specifically mentioned the achievements China Customs administrations made in areas of trade and investment facilitation and business environment with countries along the Belt and Road. He said that for Kazakhstan and other Central Asian countries alone, customs clearance time for agricultural produce exporting to China had been cut by 90%.

2017年5月14日，国家主席习近平在北京出席"一带一路"国际合作高峰论坛开幕式，并发表题为《携手推进"一带一路"建设》的主旨演讲，其中特别提到，近年来中国同沿线国家大力推动贸易和投资便利化，不断改善营商环境，仅哈萨克斯坦等中亚国家农产品到达中国市场的通关时间就缩短了90%。

13. Intellectual Property Rights (IPR) Border Protection

13. 知识产权边境保护

Convention Establishing the World Intellectual Property Organization (effective from April 26, 1970) indicates that intellectual property rights (IPR) include the rights

根据《建立世界知识产权组织公约》中规定，知识产权包括：文学、艺术和科学作品的权利；表演艺术家的演出、

relating to: literary, artistic and scientific works; performances of performing artists, phonograms, and broadcasts; inventions in all fields of human endeavor; scientific discoveries; industrial designs; trademarks, service marks, and commercial names and designations; protection against unfair competition; and all other rights resulting from intellectual activity in the industrial, scientific, literary or artistic fields. *General Principles of the Civil Law of the People's Republic of China stipulates that* IPR includes rights relating to authorship (copyrights), patents, trademarks, discoveries, and inventions or other achievements in scientific and technological research, which are all protected by law. China's *Criminal Law* and laws on patent, trademark also set forth ways to protect IPR.

As the national organ for import and export supervision, China Customs is responsible for IPR border protection. In recent years, following the plans of the CPC Central Committee and the State Council, China Customs has focused its enforcement resources onto special crackdown operations, targeted, efficient and stringent punishment to IPR infringement, carried out a wide array of international cooperation, targeted IPR infringement during import and export with stringent punishment, therefore effectively

录音和广播的权利；人们努力在一切领域的发明的权利；科学发现的权利；工业品式样的权利；商标、服务商标、厂商名称和标记的权利；制止不正当竞争的权利；以及在工业、科学、文学或艺术领域里一切其他来自知识活动的权利。《中华人民共和国民法通则》中规定了6种知识产权类型，即著作权（版权）、专利权、商标权、发现权、发明权和其他科技成果权，并规定了知识产权的民法保护制度。我国的刑法、专利法、商标法等法律法规也对知识产权的保护做出了规定。

中国海关作为进出境监管管理部门，承担着知识产权边境保护的重要职责。近年来，中国海关根据党中央、国务院部署，大力进行专项整治，广泛开展国际合作，严厉打击进出口环节侵权行为，有效维护了进出口经贸秩序，营造法治化营商环境。海关打击侵权假冒工作的成绩也得到了外界的高度评价。2011年6月，全球反假冒组织将中国海关评为

protecting international trade order and the business environment based on the rule of law. In June 2011, China Customs won the National Public Body Award of the Global Anti-Counterfeiting Network (GACN), the only government agency among the winners that year. In September 2015, China Customs received Interpol's global anti-counterfeiting award and the award for international cooperation on the investigation of IP crimes. In the U.S. Chamber's *2018 International IP Index Report*, China Customs got a perfect score for IP enforcement transparency.

2011年度"反假冒最佳政府机构奖"，中国海关是该年度全球唯一获此奖项的政府机构；2015年9月，国际刑警组织为中国海关颁发"国际知识产权犯罪调查合作奖"。美国商会发布的《2018年国际知识产权指数报告》中，对中国海关知识产权执法透明度给予了满分评价。

14. Joint Customs Cooperation Committee (JCCC)

In 2005, the General Administration of China Customs and the General Directorate of Taxation and Customs Union (DG TAXUD) of the European Commission established the China-EC Joint Customs Cooperation Committee (JCCC). JCCC is an important mechanism and means for China-EU Customs international cooperation. It emphasizes on sharing the information of recent reforms and development and experience, reaching agreements on key issues concerning customs cooperation, discussing and implementing substantial cooperative programs. The Committee holds an annual meeting in China

14. 联合海关合作委员会

2005年，中国海关总署与欧委会税收与海关同盟总司成立了中欧联合海关合作委员会。联合海关合作委员会是中欧海关开展国际合作的主要机制与途径，旨在相互通报最新改革发展情况和经验，就海关合作的重大问题进行协商，探讨并开展务实合作项目。委员会每年择期举行一次会议，由双方轮流在中国和比利时举办。机制下设有知识产权、安智贸、AEO、反瞒骗、贸易统计、风险管理、信息技术

and Belgium on a rotational basis. It houses several working groups in specific areas such as IPR, SSTL, AEO, anti-fraud, statistics, risk management, IT and solid waste control as well. It is the first mechanism for dialogue between ministerial-level officials of China and EU customs administrations, and it serves as a useful consultation platform for important cooperation matters.

和固体废物监管等多个专项工作组。该会议机制的建立标志着中欧海关部级对话机制的形成，为协调解决中欧海关合作的重要问题提供了有效平台。

China Customs has also set up similar dialogue platforms on different levels with our major trade partners, for instance the Customs Cooperation Sub-committee under the Committee on Regular Meetings between Chinese Premier and Russian Prime Ministers, China UK Customs Joint Work Group, etc.

此外，中国海关还与重要贸易伙伴国海关在各个工作层级建立了类似的对话机制，例如中俄总理定期会晤委员会下设的海关合作分委会，中英海关联合工作组等。

15. Megaports Initiative

The Megaports Initiative is a cooperation mechanism among the General Administration of China Customs, the then Administration of Quality Supervision, Inspection and Quarantine, and U.S. Department of Energy (DOE). It works with foreign customs, port authorities, and other relevant entities in partner countries to install radiation detection systems at the port in order to prevent illegal nuclear and other radioactive materials in containerized cargo transiting the global maritime shipping network, and ensure global

15. 特大型港口计划

"特大型港口计划"是中国海关总署、原国家质检总局与美国能源部开展的机制化合作，旨在加强各国海关、港务部门及其他相关方合作，通过在港口安装辐射检测系统，防止海运集装箱渠道中核和其他放射性物质的非法贩运，保障国际贸易供应链安全。2011年12月，该项目正式在上海洋山港启动实施，由美方出资，在洋山港出境海关卡口全部安装

supply chain security. The Initiative was commenced at Yangshan Port in Shanghai in December 2011. Portal radiation detection equipment financially sponsored by U.S. DOE was installed at every outbound customs checkpoint to detect and intercept nuclear and other radioactive materials. Since the Initiative started, no smuggling activities of such materials have been found. But China Customs has detected concealed explosives such as fireworks. It has served as a useful deterrence against illicit transportation of radioactive materials

门户式辐射探测设备，监测、拦截核材料及放射性物质。项目启动以来，虽未发现走私核及其他放射性物质的情况，但查获过夹藏烟花爆竹等危险爆炸物，并对放射性物质非法贩运起到了有效的威慑作用。

16. 3Ms

3Ms is the abbreviation of the three principles of China Customs' international cooperation with domestic and foreign port management authorities, i.e. "Mutual exchange of information, Mutual recognition of control, Mutual assistance in enforcement".

"Mutual exchange of information" means sharing the clearance data of inbound and outbound means of transportation and cargo, conducting pre-arrival risk analysis, in order to reduce the time at port and improve clearance efficiency.

"Mutual recognition of control" means setting and applying common risk rules and minimum standards for customs control,

16. “三互”合作理念

三互合作理念具体指国内和国际口岸管理部门开展的“信息互换、监管互认、执法互助”合作（简称“三互”）。

信息互换：对进出境运输工具、货物等通关数据共享，将进出口货物风险分析前置，减少货物滞港时间，提高通关效率。

监管互认：执行协商一致的共同风险规则和最低监管标准，相互认可对方海关和口岸

recognizing the results of other customs and border management authorities, in order to reduce redundancy of control and lower costs for the business.

管理部门的查验结果，减少重复查验，降低企业成本。

"Mutual assistance in enforcement" means combating illegal activities during import and export through the exchange of intelligence and verification of case information.

执法互助：通过情报交换、案件核查等方式打击进出境环节中的违法行为。

Domestically, China Customs carries out the 3M cooperation with management agencies to achieve Coordinated Border Management (CBM) at the port by advancing reforms such as the Single Window. On February 25, 2015, the State Council issued a Plan for the building and reform of the whole clearance system following the 3M principles. The plan requires enforcement agencies to build an integrated and coordinated clearance system, modernize border management systems and enhance management capacity.

国内层面，三互合作主要指口岸管理相关部门通过推进国际贸易单一窗口等改革项目实现“协同边境治理”。2015年2月25日，国务院印发《落实“三互”推进大通关建设改革方案》，旨在深入推进口岸大通关建设，推进口岸治理体系和治理能力现代化。

Internationally, the 3Ms cooperation includes bilateral and multilateral cooperation mechanisms in customs enforcement, quarantine, certification, standards, and statistics among others. It has become a core concept for China Customs' international cooperation to mitigate the impact of economic crisis, and create a fair, efficient, and facilitated clearance environment for businesses around

国际层面，合作包括各国各地区口岸执法机构通过建立国际协调机制，在海关执法、检验检疫、认证认可、标准计量、统计信息等方面的多双边合作。三互合作方案经多年完善和发展，现已成为中国海关开展国际交往合作的重要理念，旨在积极应对经济危机的

the world. China Customs is also taking advantage of many important occasions to actively promote the 3Ms principles, which have been welcomed by foreign customs administrations, and incorporated in many cooperative agreements.

负面影响，为各方企业营造公平、高效、便利的通关环境提供保障。中国海关在多种重要场合，广泛宣传三互理念，获得外国海关的积极回应，并已将此合作理念广泛体现在对外签署的海关合作文件中。

17. National Targeting Center (NTC)

Part of the U.S. Customs and Border Protection (CBP)'s layered strategy for securing U.S. borders, the NTC is responsible for identifying timely, actionable information before borders are crossed. Originally, the NTC grew out of federal efforts to develop risk targeting practices to protect ports from drug and currency smuggling. But after the 9/11 terrorist attacks, targeting techniques were re-focused on anti-terrorist concerns. NTC began 24/7 operations in November, 2001, tasked with supporting CBP's mission to prevent terrorists and their weapons from crossing US borders while also enabling public travel and international trade. In 2007, NTC was divided in two: NTC-Passenger and NTC-Cargo. NTC-P screens inbound and outbound commercial airline passengers to spot potential high-risk individuals, while NTC-C focuses on high-risk cargo that might conceal ingredients for weapons of mass destruction, chemical

17. 美国国家布控中心

美国国家布控中心属于美国海关与边境保护局实施的多层次安全策略体系，主要负责在货物通过美国边境前及时有效地进行识别。美国政府最初设立国家布控中心时主要负责对口岸毒品和现金走私进行风险布控。9・11恐怖袭击事件后，国家布控中心的重点转向反恐。2001年11月起，国家布控中心开始7×24小时不间断运行，主要协助美国海关与边境保护局在保障国际旅客和货物正常流动的同时防范恐怖分子及其武器进入美国境内。2007年，国家布控中心设立了两个分支——旅客布控中心和货物布控中心。旅客布控中心负责筛查乘飞机入境的高风险旅客；货物布控中心则侧重布控可能藏匿大规模杀伤性武器

precursors of illegal drugs or conventional weapons or explosives.

原材料、毒品化学前体、普通武器和爆炸物的高风险货物。

18. Origin Declaration by Approved Exporter

Origin Declaration by Approved Exporter (Self-declaration of Origin) means that during import and export, approved manufacturers, suppliers, or traders can print their own origin declaration on an invoice or another commercial document, instead of providing a certificate of origin issued by an approved third party in chrge of origin, which saves the time and cost for the business, rendering improved clearance efficiency, and solving the frequent delay of documents after goods arrive.

Origin Declaration by Approved Exporter applies to goods traded under the free trade agreements between China and Switzerland, and China and Iceland. The *China–Switzerland Free Trade Agreement* is also China's first free trade agreement using Origin Declaration by Approved Exporter, which covers more than 90% of the imported goods from Switzerland.

18. **原产地自主声明**

"经核准出口商原产地自主声明"（简称原产地自主声明），是指在货物进出口时，由资信较高的制造商、供货人或进出口商，在商业发票或者其他单证上对该货物原产地进行标注，而不必提交原本由原产地主管机构签发的证书，减少了企业往返签证机构及办理原产地证明所需的时间和费用，提高通关效率，也解决了受惠贸易文件赶不及物流速度的困扰。

目前，原产地自主声明适用在中国与瑞士和冰岛的自由贸易协定。其中，原产地自主声明作为《中国–瑞士自由贸易协定》的内容之一，也是我国首次在自贸协定中采用企业自主声明模式。目前，我国自瑞士进口的货物中，90%以上均采用原产地自主声明。

19. Paperless Customs

The reform of paperless customs aims

19. **海关通关无纸化**

海关通关无纸化改革是指

to reinvent the way that customs operates using classified management of enterprises and risk analysis. Customs now reviews the computerized data of declaration and its attached documents instead of hardcopies, exercises different control on goods with different risk levels, and clear the goods with the help of information technology. Since the pilot of the reform began on August 1, 2012, all systems and work have been advancing orderly and smoothly. The reform has been well received by the public and significantly improved the efficiency of customs clearance and control.

海关以企业分类管理和风险分析为基础，按照风险等级对进出口货物实施分类，运用信息化技术改变海关验核进出口企业递交纸质报关单及随附单证办理通关手续的做法，直接对企业报关单及随附单证的电子数据进行无纸审核、验放处理的通关作业方式。海关通关作业无纸化改革试点工作自2012年8月1日启动以来，各项工作有序推进，系统运行较为平稳，社会各界反响积极，对提高通关效率，提升监管效能起到了积极的促进作用。

20. Paramilitary Disciplined Customs Force

China Customs, a paramilitary disciplined force led by the Communist Party of China, fulfills its law-based duty of guarding the border and providing services at entry-exit ports. Its nature defines its most essential characteristic as a paramilitary disciplined force following the Party's command, loyal to the Party, servicing the people, impartial in law enforcement and strictly disciplined. It exercises a centralized management structure to enforce the law independently. The management of the paramilitary disciplined

20. 准军事化海关纪律部队

中国海关是中国共产党领导下的人民海关，是一支依法履行进出口把关服务职责的准军事化纪律部队。从队伍性质上看，听党指挥、对党忠诚、服务人民、执法公正、纪律严明是人民海关准军事化纪律部队最本质的特征。从领导体制上看，海关实行垂直统一领导，依法独立行使职权。从管理方式看，海关从政治建设，组织建设，能力建设，纪律建

customs force involves the building of political stand, organization, capacity, discipline, regulations, and it borrows a series of standardized and well-regulated management measures from the military. Members of the force are required to wear uniforms. And it is the only force that applies a ranking system other than the military and the police.

设，章制建设的实际需要出发，仿效军队正规化、规范化管理模式，统一着装，是我国除军队和警察以外唯一一支采用衔级制度的队伍。

21. Pilot Free Trade Zone

China's PFTZ is a unique innovation in the country's restructuring of the economic system, expansion of opening-up and transformation of the government functions. As an important platform of China's open economy, it focuses on expanding the scope of business, providing new functions, and creating new operation models. It is an area combining the functions of special customs control areas that facilitate the trade in goods, and areas that focus on expanding investment, finance and trade in services. September 29,2013, China (Shanghai) Pilot Free Trade Zone was founded by the State Council. With the approval of the State Council on December 31, 2014, 3 new PFTZs were officially founded in Tianjin, Fujian and Guangdong on April 21, 2015. Seven more were founded in Liaoning, Zhejiang, Henan, Hubei, Chongqing, Sichuan and Shaanxi Province in September 2016. Up

21. 自由贸易试验区

自由贸易试验区是我国近年来为在新形势下加快经济体制改革、扩大开放和转变政府职能过程中特有的创新产物。它作为我国开放型经济的重要平台，旨在拓展新领域，完善新功能，创新新模式，是一种以货物贸易便利化为主的海关特殊监管区域和以扩大投资、金融、服务贸易开放为主相结合的特定区域。2013年9月29日，经国务院批准中国（上海）自由贸易试验区正式成立。2014年12月31日，国务院又批复同意设立天津、福建、广东3个自贸试验区。2016年9月，我国在辽宁省、浙江省、河南省、湖北省、重庆市、四川省、陕西省再次新设立7个自贸试验区。截至目前，11个

till now, a total of 11 PFTZs cover an area of 1,314 square kilometers.

Since the establishment of the PFTZs in Shanghai, Tianjin, Fujian, Guangdong and the other 7 Provinces, General Administration of China Customs has been carrying out the decisions and plans of the CPC Central Committee and the State Council. Aiming at creating a sound business environment that guarantee internationalization, facilitation, and the rule of law, focusing on reforms of customs clearance facilitation, control over bonded operations, enterprises management, duty collection, as well as expanding the functions of special customs control areas, China Customs streamlined administration, delegated more powers to lower-level government and society, improved regulation and optimized services. China Customs vigorously promoted the innovation of customs control schemes, issued 187 innovative and supportive supervision measures, actively draw upon and spread experience, and won recognition in the business sector. May 23, 2018, the State Council issued a circular extend 30 schemes in the PFTZ across the country, which tasked Customs with 14 of them (13 are spearheaded and coordinated by Customs).

自贸试验区面积总计约1314平方公里。

上海和天津、福建、广东以及新的7个自由贸易试验区设立后，海关总署认真贯彻落实党中央、国务院决策部署，按照营造国际化、便利化和法治化营商环境的目标，围绕通关便利化、保税监管、企业管理、税收征管等改革和海关特殊监管区域功能拓展等方面，积极推进“放管服”改革，大力实施海关监管制度创新，共出台了187项制度创新，积极总结推广可复制的经验，受到广大企业的欢迎。2018年5月23日，国务院就做好自由贸易试验区第四批改革试点经验复制推广工作发布通知。通知中明确，下一步自贸试验区30项复制推广任务中海关就有14项，其中海关牵头13项。

22. Radiation Detection Training Center (RDTC)

On September 27, 2012, the Qinhuangdao Radiation Detection Training Center (RDTC) was open. The opening of the RDTC is part of the pragmatic longstanding cooperation between the General Administration of China Customs and the National Nuclear Security Administration (NNSA) of U.S. DOE in their joint efforts to counter nuclear terrorism. The training hosted there will promote and enhance the skills and knowledge base of customs officers charged with detecting and interdicting illicit shipments of nuclear and other radioactive materials at key ports of entry. The RDTC also hosts China-US Commodity Identification Training to improve the capabilities of customs officers in tackling illicit transportation of weapon of mass destruction (WMD), relevant materials, equipment, components and technologies.

22. 辐射探测培训中心

2012年9月27日，秦皇岛辐射探测培训中心正式开始运行，进一步丰富了中国海关总署和美国能源部国家核安全署在打击核恐怖主义领域的长期务实合作。培训中心旨在加强海关关员在重点口岸对核及其他放射性物质非法贩运进行探测和拦截的能力。此外，该中心还举办中美商品识别培训课程，以提升海关关员打击非法贩运大规模杀伤性武器相关的材料、设备、部件和技术的能力。

23. The Reform of National Customs Clearance Integration

The primary objective of the reform of national customs clearance integration is to carry out the reform of customs control systems required by the Third Plenary Session of the 18th Central Committee of the Communist Party of China. It aims

23. 全国海关通关一体化改革

全国海关通关一体化改革，主要目的是为贯彻落实党的十八届三中全会关于“改革海关监管管理体制”的要求，进一步优化营商环境、促进外经贸健康发展。海关总署制定

to improve the business environment and promote the healthy development of foreign trade. The GACC put forth the *Overall Plan to Deepen Customs Reforms in all Areas*, and the *Framework for the Reform of National Clearance Integration*.

了《海关全面深化改革总体方案》和《全国通关一体化改革框架方案》。

Main tasks of the reform are: set up the Risk Management Center and the Duty Collection Center, build a clearance system that requires declaration only once and allows the fast release of goods before step-by-step supervision measures, in order to separate the procedures of security control and duty collection; reinvent the way of revenue collection; created a new coordination model within different units in China Customs, and among border management agencies.

改革的主要内容包括：建设风险防控中心和税收征管中心；采取“一次申报、分步处置”的通关管理模式，相对分离安全准入和税收征管作业；改革税收征管方式；创新海关内和跨部门间的协同监管制度。

Starting from July 1, 2017, the reform of national customs clearance integration has covered all customs districts, modes of transport, and HS codes. The reform was in place and effetire towards the end of 2017.

自2017年7月1日起，中国海关通关一体化改革覆盖全关境、全运输方式及全商品章节。2017年底，该项改革已基本到位，效果显现。

24. SAFE Framework of Standards to Secure and Facilitate Global Trade (SAFE Framework)

24. 全球贸易安全和便利标准框架

The greatest challenge facing today's customs administrations is how to strike a find balance between effective control and facilitated trade. After 9/11, the World Customs

当前，对各国海关的最大挑战就是如何处理好海关有效监管和便利贸易之间的矛盾。美国9・11事件以后，世界海

Organization (WCO) issued guidelines on how to protect trade security, i.e. enhancing risk management, using more advanced technology, and stepping up international cooperation. In December 2004 the guidelines were developed into the *SAFE Framework of Standards to Secure and Facilitate Global Trade (SAFE Framework)*, which was later adopted by the WCO during its annual Council Session in June 2005. 168 member customs administrations, including China Customs, agreed on the implementation of the SAFE Framework.

关组织提出了应对贸易安全问题的指南，包括增强风险管理、应用高科技、国际合作等三个要素。2004年12月世界海关组织政策委员会基于上述指南初步形成了《全球贸易安全和便利标准框架》（简称《标准框架》）。该《标准框架》于2005年6月召开的世界海关组织理事会年会上获得通过，包括中国海关在内的168个成员海关正式表达了实施《标准框架》的意向。

The SAFE Framework is designed to promote global supply chain security through pre-arrival submission of cargo information, risk management, nonintrusive inspection equipment, mutual recognition of Authorized Economic Operators (AEO), Customs-to-Customs and Customs-to-Business partnership. Covering customs operations and reforms in all areas, it is a blueprint to plan for customs modernization, and it sets the direction of customs future development.

标准框架通过预先提交货物信息、应用风险管理、使用非侵入式货物扫描设备、推广“经认证的经营者”互认项目以及推广海关之间、海关及商界的伙伴关系来努力推动全球供应链安全，内容涉及海关的全面业务和全方位的改革方向，描述和规划了现代海关发展的蓝图，代表海关未来的发展方向。

25. Sub-Committee on Customs Procedures (SCCP)

The APEC Sub-Committee on Customs Procedures (SCCP) was established in 1994. Its main objectives are to simplify and harmonize

25. 亚太经合组织海关手续分委会

亚太经合组织（APEC）海关手续分委会成立于1994年，是APEC成员为简化、协

regional customs procedures to ensure that goods and services move efficiently, effectively and safely through the region. Over the past 20 years, the SCCP has carried out a series of initiatives and achieved fruitful outcomes in Single Window, intellectual property rights (IPR) enforcement, Authorized Economic Operator (AEO) programs, etc.

调地区海关手续，保障货物和服务高效、顺畅、安全流通进行专门讨论的机构。成立20多年来，海关手续分委会在单一窗口、知识产权保护、经认证的经营者等领域开展了一系列卓有成效的工作。

SCCP has also been holding the APEC Customs-Business Dialogue (ACBD) since 2001 to strengthen and deepen customs-business partnership, discuss measures and ways to maintain and enhance the competitiveness of the region, advocate for globalization and brave economic challenges emerged from a new age.

此外，海关手续分委会还自2001年起举办海关与商界对话会，加强和深化海关与商界的伙伴关系，共同商讨维护和增强亚太地区经济竞争力的对策和途径，迎接经济全球化和新经济的挑战。

26. Smart and Secure Trade Lane Pilot Project (SSTL)

In 2005, WCO enacted the SAFE Framework of Standards (SAFE). As the first pilot program to fully implement the SAFE, SSTL was launched by China and the EU customs in 2006 in order to better connect the Asia and Europe continents. This pilot project adopted the core elements of the SAFE Framework and introduced such new concepts and approaches as supply chain security, mutual recognition of customs control, AEO mutual recognition and Unique Consignment

26. 安全智能贸易航线试点项目（安智贸）

2005年，世界海关组织制定了《全球贸易安全与便利标准框架》（简称《标准框架》）。2006年，中欧海关共同启动了安智贸项目。作为全面落实《标准框架》的首个试点项目，安智贸对畅通欧亚大陆的贸易往来起到了积极的推动作用。该试点计划充分参照了《标准框架》的核心要素，引入了供应链安全、监管互

Reference (UCR) promoted by the WCO.

认、经认证的经营者互认和货运唯一识别代码等新理念、新措施。

When the SSTL started in 2006, the first phase of the program included 3 ports in China, the Netherlands and the UK. Entering the Third Phase, the Project included 27 ports of 10 countries (regions) by the end of 2017.

项目自2006年起，第一阶段合作包括中国、荷兰和英国的3个港口。目前项目已进入第三阶段。截至2017年底，共用10个国家（地区）的27个港口参与合作。

27. Trade Facilitation Agreement

27. 贸易便利化协定

In order to address the vast amount of barriers that still exist in moving goods across borders, members of the World Trade Organization (WTO) commenced the negotiation of the trade facilitation agenda in October 2004. In December 2013, The Ministerial Conference of the WTO in Bali agreed on the *Trade Facilitation Agreement* (hereinafter referred to as the Agreement). China ratified the Agreement on September 4, 2015, and the Agreement entered into force on February 22, 2017, as two thirds of the members (112) ratified the Agreement, which met the number of members required by the Agreement.

为消除货物跨境流通过程中遇到的障碍，世界贸易组织成员自2004年10月起正式展开贸易便利化议题的谈判。2013年12月，世贸组织巴厘部长级会议上通过了《贸易便利化协定》（简称《协定》）。我国于2015年9月4日同意接受《协定》。2017年2月22日，累计112个成员接受该协定，超过了《协定》规定的三分之二成员接受的生效条件，协定正式生效。

As the first multilateral agreement at the WTO since its establishment nearly 20 years ago, the Agreement bears great significance and will bring far reaching impact on the world and China's economy. International institutes

《协定》作为WTO成立近20年来达成的首个多边贸易协定，对世界和我国经济具有重要意义和深远影响。根据国际机构测算，有效实施

estimate that the effective implementation of the Agreement will bring down trade costs by 10% for developed countries, and by 13%-15.5% in developing countries. The Agreement can generate an annual increase as much as 9.9% (around $569 billion) for developing countries, and 4.5% (around 475 billion) for developed countries, drive global GDP to grow $960 billion, and create 21 million jobs.

《协定》将使发达国家贸易成本降低10%，发展中国家成本降低13%−15.5%。《协定》最高可使发展中国家出口每年增长9.9%（约5690亿美元），发达国家增长4.5%（4750亿美元），带动全球GDP增长9600亿美元，增加2100万个就业岗位。

The Agreement contains 3 Sections, 24 Articles. Section I (Article 1 through 12) is for import and export regulations, fees and charges, release and clearance of goods, formalities connected with importation, exportation and transit and so on. Article 8 and Article 12 are about boarder agency cooperation and Customs cooperation. Section II (Article 13 through 22) includes provisions for a transitional period of implementation and capacity building, in order to differentiate the implementation of Section I in developing and least developed countries. Section III (Article 23 and 24) contains some final provisions about setting up permanent bodies for the implementation of the Agreement.

《协定》共分为3个部分、24项条款。第一部分（第1至12条）涉及进出口规费、货物放行与结关措施、进出口和过境相关手续等内容。其中，第8条、12条主要涉及海关及边境机构之间的合作。第二部分（第13至22条）规定了发展中和最不发达国家在实施第一部分条款方面可享受的差别待遇，主要体现在过渡期和能力建设两个方面。第三部分（第23至24条）规定了《协定》实施机构设置等内容。

China Customs will dedicate itself to the implementation of the Agreement: revise the improve regulations and schemes that are not in line with the Agreement, enhance international customs cooperation and boarder

中国海关将进一步抓好《协定》的实施工作，修订完善与《协定》不符的规章制度，加强国际海关和边境部门合作，增强企业对《协定》的

agency cooperation, strengthen enterprises' understanding towards the Agreement, and advance the "Internet + Customs" service to increase customs policy transparency and facilitation of customs procedures.

理解与认识，推进“互联网+海关”服务，提升海关各项政策措施的透明度和海关业务便捷度。

28. World Customs Organization (WCO)

The World Customs Organization, formerly known as the Customs Co-operation Council (CCC), was founded in 1952. In 1994, the CCC decided to change the name of the working body of the organization to the "World Customs Organization". WCO is the only intergovernmental organization that studies on customs matters. It studies all customs related issues, including: examine the technical aspects, as well as the economic factors related thereto, of Customs systems with a view to proposing to its Members practical means of attaining the highest possible degree of harmony and uniformity; Prepare draft Conventions and ensure the uniform interpretation and application of the Conventions; Make recommendations, in a conciliatory capacity, for the settlement of disputes concerning the interpretation or application of those Conventions; Ensure the circulation of information regarding Customs regulations and procedures; Co-operate with

28.世界海关组织

世界海关组织前身是成立于1952年的海关合作理事会。1994年，海关合作理事会决定将“世界海关组织”作为该组织的工作名称。WCO是世界范围内唯一一个专门研究海关事务的国际政府间组织。它负责研究所有涉及海关合作的问题，包括从技术角度对海关制度和相关的经济因素进行审议，以便提出促进海关制度协调和统一的实际方法；起草公约并确保公约的统一解释和实施；从调解的角度出发提出建议，协调解决涉及公约解释和实施方面的争议；成员提供海关事务方面的资料或意见；就其主管范围所涉及的事务与其他国际组织进行合作。

other inter-governmental organizations as regards matters within its competence.

Up till June 2017, the WCO, which has 6 regional capacity building or intelligence liaison offices, represents 182 Customs administrations across the globe that collectively process approximately 98% of world trade. The WCO's official working languages are English and French. The WCO organization include: the Council, Policy Commission, Finance Committee, and other Committees for specific customs operations. The WCO Secretariat, which is based in Brussels, Belgium, runs the WCO's day- to-day operations. There are 3 Directorates in the Secretariat, i.e. Tariff and Trade Affairs Directorate, Compliance and Facilitation Directorate, Capacity Building Directorate. The WCO Secretariat is under the leadership of the Secretary General.

截至2017年6月，世界海关组织总共有182个成员，在全球6个地区设有区域性的能力建设办公室和情报联络中心，覆盖全球约98%的贸易往来。世界海关组织使用两种正式语言（英语和法语）。世界海关组织的组织机构包括:理事会、政策委员会、财政委员会以及各专业领域委员会。世界海关组织日常工作由秘书处承担，秘书处设在比利时布鲁塞尔，下设守法与便利司、关税及贸易事务司（简称税贸司）和能力建设司。秘书长是秘书处负责人。

China Custom officially became a member of the WCO on July 18th, 1983. It Customs has been actively engaged in dialogues with senior officials of the WCO, contributing to decision making, and holding important conferences and activities. In 2010, Mr. Zhu Gaozhang from the General Administration of China Customs was elected Director for the Compliance and Facilitation Directorate. And in 2015, Mr. Liu Ping from

中国海关自1983年7月18日正式成为世界海关组织成员以来，一直积极通过高层会晤、参与规则制定、承办重要会议与活动等方式积极参与世界海关组织事务。海关总署朱高章同志2010年成功当选守法与便利司司长，刘平同志2015年当选税贸司司长。

GACC was elected Director for Tariff and Trade Affairs Directorate.

29. Double random inspections and prompt release of results

In November 2013, Premier Li Keqiang announced that the Government would reform and reinvent ways of supervision, and promote inspections of randomly-selected entities. July 2015, the State Council issued a circular, requiring government agencies carry out the new oversight model across the board, which means inspections of randomly-selected entities by randomly-selected inspectors and the public release of inspection results. The new oversight model makes regulation more effective and impartial, and ensures that power will not be used as one pleases and the exercise of power will always be supervised. Towards the end of 2017, good results of the reform were secured. Nearly 98% of China Customs inspections were randomly targeted, and 100% of the inspectors were randomly dispatched.

29. 双随机、一公开

2013年11月，李克强总理提出要改革创新监管方式，推行随机抽查。2015年7月，国务院办公厅印发通知，要求全面推行“双随机、一公开”的监管模式。“双随机、一公开”，指在监管过程中随机抽取检查对象，随机选派执法检查人员，抽查情况及查处结果及时向社会公开，目的是保障监管公平高效，实现有权不可任性，用权必受监督。截至2017年底，中国海关随机布控查验已占查验总量的近98%，并已实现100%随机派员查验，取得良好监管效果。

30. Exercising law-based administration, Safeguarding the border, Serving the economic interests and Promoting social development

The principle guideline for the work of China Customs is “exercising law-based

30. 依法行政、为国把关、服务经济、促进发展

“依法行政、为国把关、服务经济、促进发展”是指导

administration, safeguarding the border, serving the economic interests and promoting social development". It is also dubbed the "16-character Guideline for Customs work". In order to effectively enhance supervision, tackle smuggling and corruption, China Customs laid down a working guideline to "exercise law-based administration and safeguard the border". At the turn of the century, as economic globalization and China's open economy developed, customs administrations around the world and their governments were faced with a common question: how to strike a balance between trade security and facilitation? To address this, China Customs added "serving the economic interests and promoting social development" to the existing guideline, which was a more complete and comprehensive summary of its line of work in supervision and services, suited the needs of China's social and economic development, and was in line with the modernization of international customs administration.

海关全面工作的总原则，也被称为“海关工作16字方针”。1999年，为切实加强实际监管、打击走私、惩治腐败、中国海关确立了“依法行政、为国把关”的工作方针。进入新世纪，随着经济全球化的推进和中国外向型经济的不断发展，在贸易安全与便利之间寻求平衡点成为摆在国际海关乃至各国政府面前的一道共同命题。为此，中国海关于2001年在原有工作方针基础上进行了丰富和完善，加入“服务经济、促进发展”的内容。这样既更全面地体现海关把关服务的职责，符合我国经济社会发展的需要，也顺应了国际海关管理现代化发展的趋势。

二、组织机构、公约协议、合作机制对照表（按字母顺序排列）

2. Organizations, Agreements and Mechanisms

序号	英文缩写	英文全称	中文名称
1	ACE	Automated Commercial Environment	（美国海关）自动化商业环境系统
2	ADB	Asian Development Bank	亚洲开发银行
3	AIIB	Asian Infrastructure Investment Bank	亚洲基础设施投资银行
4	AmCham China	American Chamber of Commerce in China	中国美国商会
5	APEC	Asia-Pacific Economic Cooperation	亚太经济合作组织
6	ASEAN	Association of South and East Asian Nations	东南亚国家联盟（东盟）
7	ASEM	Asia-Europe Meeting	亚欧会议
8	Belt and Road	Silk Road Economic Belt and 21st Century Maritime Silk Road	丝绸之路经济带和21世纪海上丝绸之路（一带一路）
9	BIP	Basic Implementation Procedures for CSI Cooperation	中美海关集装箱安全倡议合作基本实施程序
10	BRICS	Acronym for Brazil, Russia, India, China and South Africa	金砖国家
11	CAC	The Customs Attachés' Club	海关专员俱乐部
12	CBP	U.S. Customs and Border Protection	美国海关与边境保护局
13	CBSA	Canada Border Services Agency	加拿大边境服务署
14	CCF-China	Customs Cooperation Fund-China	中国能力建设合作基金
15	CEE	Centers of Excellence and Expertise	美国海关商品分类监管中心

序号	英文缩写	英文全称	中文名称
16	CEPA	Closer Economic Partnership Arrangement	（内地与香港、澳门）关于建立更紧密经贸关系的安排
17	CITES	Convention on International Trade in Endangered Species of Wild Fauna and Flora	濒危野生动植物种国际贸易公约
18	CMAA	Customs Mutual Administrative Assistance	海关行政互助
19	CPPCC	Chinese People's Political Consultative Conference	中国人民政治协商会议
20	CSI	Container Security Initiative	集装箱安全倡议
21	C-TPAT	Customs Trade Partnership Against Terrorism	海关—商界反恐伙伴计划
22	DEA	U.S. Drug Enforcement Administration	美国缉毒署
23	DHS	U.S. Department of Homeland Security	美国国土安全部
24	DOE	U.S. Department of Energy	美国能源部
25	DOP	Declaration of Principles	原则声明
26	EAC	East African Community	东非共同体
27	EAEF	Euro-Asia Economic Forum	欧亚经济论坛
28	EAEU	Eurasian Economic Union	欧亚经济联盟
29	EC	European Commission	欧盟委员会（欧委会）
30	EC DG TAXUD	Directorate-General for Taxation and Customs Union of the European Commission	欧盟委员会税务与海关同盟总司
31	ECFA	Economic Cooperation Framework Agreement	海峡两岸经济合作框架协议
32	EU	European Union	欧洲联盟（欧盟）
33	FTA	Free Trade Agreement/Free Trade Area	自由贸易协定/自由贸易区
34	G20	Group of 20 Summit Meeting	二十国首脑峰会

序号	英文缩写	英文全称	中文名称
35	GACC	General Administration of Customs of the People's Republic of China	中华人民共和国海关总署
36	GACN	Global Anti-Counterfeiting Network	全球反假冒组织
37	HED	China-EU High Level Economic and Trade Dialogue	中欧经贸高层对话
38	ICE	U.S. Immigration and Customs Enforcement	美国移民与海关执法局
39	IMF	International Monetary Fund	国际货币基金组织
40	INTA	International Trademark Association	国际商标协会
41	INTERPOL	International Criminal Police Organization	国际刑警组织
42	ISA	Importer Self-Assessment Program	（美国海关）进口商自主评估项目
43	JCCC	Joint Customs Cooperation Committee	（中欧）联合海关合作委员会
44	Kyoto Convention	International Convention on the Simplification and Harmonization of Customs Procedures	关于简化和协调海关业务制度的国际公约（京都公约）
45	LDC	Least Developed Country	最不发达国家
46	Megaports	Megaports Initiative	特大型港口计划
47	NPC	National People's Congress of the P.R.C.	中华人民共和国全国人民代表大会
48	NSS	Nuclear Security Summit	核安全峰会
49	NTC	National Targeting Center	美国国家布控中心
50	OLAF	French: Office européen de lutte antifraude （English: European Anti-fraud Office）	欧盟反瞒骗办公室
51	PIP	Partners in Protection	加拿大海关与商界供应链安全合作项目

序号	英文缩写	英文全称	中文名称
52	RCEP	Regional Comprehensive Economic Partnership	区域全面经济伙伴关系协定
53	RDTC	Radiation Detection Training Center	辐射探测培训中心
54	SAFE Framework	WCO SAFE Framework of Standards to Secure and Facilitate Global Trade	全球贸易安全和便利标准框架
55	SCC	Scottish Crime Campus	英国（苏格兰）打击犯罪执法中心
56	SCO	Shanghai Cooperation Organization	上海合作组织（上合组织）
57	SED	Strategic and Economic Dialogue	中美战略与经济对话
58	SOI	Statement of Intent	意向声明
59	SSTL	Smart and Secure Trade Lane Pilot Project	中欧安全智能贸易航线试点项目（安智贸）
60	TIR	Convention on International Transport of Goods Under Cover of TIR(Transports Internationaux Routiers) Carnets	国际公路运输公约
61	UCR	Unique Consignment Reference Number	货运唯一识别代码
62	UNCTAD	United Nations Conference on Trade and Development	联合国贸易和发展会议（贸发会议）
63	USTR	U.S. Trade Representative	美国贸易代表
64	WB	World Bank	世界银行
65	WCO	World Customs Organization	世界海关组织
66	WCO TCRO	WCO Technical Committee of Rules of Origin	世界海关组织原产地技术委员会
67	WIPO	World Intellectual Property Organization	世界知识产权组织
68	WTO	World Trade Organization	世界贸易组织

三、海关专用术语对照表

3. Customs Terminology

序号	英文	中文
1	Take a clear political stand in customs work, Improve customs with reforms, Exercise law-based supervision, Vitalize customs with technology and Govern the customs force with strict discipline	政治建关、改革强关、依法把关、科技兴关、从严治关
2	Exercising Law-Based Administration, Safeguarding the Border, Serving the Economic Interests and Promoting Social Development (Guideline for China Customs Work)	依法行政、为国把关、服务经济、促进发展（中国海关工作方针）
3	Safeguarding the Border, Providing Quality Service, Preventing Potential Risks and Building A Qualified Workforce (China Customs Missions)	把好国门、做好服务、防好风险、带好队伍（中国海关工作总体要求）
4	Patriotism, Virtue, Integrity, Innovation and Dedication (Core Value of China Customs)	爱国、厚德、增信、创新、奉献（中国海关核心价值观）
5	Politically Committed, Professionally Qualified and Fully Accountable (Principle of Team Building)	政治坚强、业务过硬、值得信赖（中国海关队伍建设要求）
6	Paramilitary Disciplined Force	准军事化纪律部队
7	Customs Supervision and Control	海关监管
8	Entry-Exit Health Quarantine	进出境卫生检疫
9	Entry-Exit Animal and Plant Quarantine	进出境动植物检疫
10	Entry-Exit Food Safety	进出口食品安全
11	Entry-Exit Commodity Inspection	进出口商品检验
12	Inspection of Cargo	货物查验
13	Non-intrusive Inspection (NII)	非侵入式查验
14	Collect (Levy) Customs Duty	征收关税
15	Prevent and Counter Smuggling	打击走私

序号	英文	中文
16	Compiling Customs Statistics	编制海关统计
17	Customs Risk Management	海关风险管理
18	Post Clearance Audit (PCA)	稽查
19	Inward and Outward Goods and Articles	进出境货物、物品
20	Paperless Customs	海关通关无纸化
21	The Reform of National Customs Clearance Integration	全国海关通关一体化改革
22	Single Window	单一窗口
23	Customs Special Control Area	海关特殊监管区域
24	Pilot Free Trade Zone (PFTZ)	自由贸易试验区
25	Free Trade Zone (FTZ)	自由贸易园区
26	Intellectual Property Right (IPR) Border Protection	知识产权边境保护
27	Detain the Means of Transport in Violation of the Law	扣留违法船只
28	Interrogate Those Suspected of Violating the Law	调查违法行为
29	Examine Contracts, Invoice Accounts and Bill	查阅合同、发票、账册和单据
30	Withhold Articles in Violation of The Rules	扣留违规物品
31	Search the Place Suspected of Concealing Smuggling Goods	检查涉嫌藏匿走私货物的场所
32	Hand Over to the Judicial Organ	移送司法机关
33	Enter or Leave the Customs Territory	进出关境
34	Unless Otherwise Provided for	除另有规定外
35	Goods Declared and Duties Paid	货物申报和纳税
36	The Agent Shall Abide by all the Provisions of The Law	代理人应当遵守法律各项规定
37	Make an Accurate Declaration to The Customs	向海关如实申报
38	Present Papers and Documents and Be Subject to Customs Control.	交验单证接受检查

序号	英文	中文
39	Without Prior Permission by the Customs	未经海关许可
40	Loading and Unloading of Inward and Outward Goods	装卸进出境货物
41	Be Subject to Customs Control	接受海关监管
42	Pending the Completion of Customs Formalities and Payment	在完成办理海关手续并缴纳关税之前
43	Not to Be Transferred or Devoted to Other Uses	不得转让和移作他用
44	By Reason of Force Majeure	由于不可抗力的原因
45	Transit, Transshipment and Through Goods	过境、转运和通运货物
46	Consignee and Consignor	收货人和发货人
47	Import and Export License	进出口货物许可证
48	Cargo Restricted or prohibited by the State	国家限制、禁止货物
49	Commodity Identification Training (CIT)	出口管制商品识别培训
50	Not to be Released by the Customs	海关不予放行
51	Re-Examine the Goods and Take Samples	复验货物并取样
52	Misdischarged and Overdischarged Cargo	误卸和溢卸货物
53	Abandoned Cargo	放弃货物
54	Storage, Processing and Assembling of Bonded Goods	保税货物储存、加工、装配
55	Foreign Direct Investment (FDI)	对外直接投资
56	Small and medium enterprises (SME)	中小企业
57	Enterprise Resource Planning (ERP)	企业资源计划
58	Consignment Sales	寄售业务
59	Repacked, Mortgaged and Transferred Goods	改装、抵押和转让货物
60	Seals Affixed by the Customs	海关施加的封志
61	Storage of Goods Under Customs Control	海关监管货物储存
62	Goods Involved in Small Volumes of Border Transactions	边境小额贸易

序号	英文	中文
63	Inward and Outward Luggage Carried by Travelers	个人携带进出境行李物品
64	Inward and Outward Postal Items	进出境邮寄物品
65	Inward Postal Items Which Can Neither be Delivered nor be Returned	无法投递又无法退回的进境邮递物品
66	Diplomatic Privileges and Immunities	外交特权和豁免
67	Import and Export Tariff	进出口税则
68	Goods Permitted to be Imported or Exported	准许进出口货物
69	Articles Permitted to Enter or Leave the Territory	准许进出境物品
70	Origin Declaration by Approved Exporter	原产地自主声明
71	Most Favored Nation (MFN)	最惠国
72	Dutiable Value	完税价格
73	Cost Insurance and Freight (CIF) Price	到岸价格
74	Free on Board (FOB) Price	离岸价格
75	Duty Reduction or Exemption	关税减征或免征
76	Temporarily Imported or Exported Goods	暂时进出口货物
77	Fee for Delayed Payment	滞纳金
78	Deduct the Amount of Duties	扣缴税款
79	Sell off the Goods for Compensation	变卖货物抵缴（税款）
80	Donation for Public Welfare Undertakings	用于公益事业的捐赠物资
81	Evasion of Customs Control	逃避海关监管
82	Narcotic Drugs, Weapons and Counterfeit Currencies	毒品、武器和伪造货币
83	Weapon of Mass Destruction (WMD)	大规模杀伤性武器
84	New Psychoactive Substance (NPS)	新精神活性物质
85	Canine (K-9)	工作犬、缉私犬
86	Endangered Wildlife/Endangered Species of Wild Fauna and Flora	濒危野生物种/濒危野生动植物
87	Precious Cultural Relics	珍贵文物

序号	英文	中文
88	Obscene Items	淫秽物品
89	Smuggling for the Purpose of Profit-Making or Dissemination	以牟利、传播为目的走私
90	Armed Smuggling of Goods	以武装掩护走私货物
91	Resistance by Violence to Customs Examination	以暴力抗拒海关检查
92	A Crime of Smuggling	走私罪
93	Confiscated Goods	没收货物
94	Illegal Incomes	非法收入
95	Fines, Penalties	罚金，罚款
96	Turn Over to the State Treasury	上缴国库
97	Customs Decision of Punishment	海关处罚决定
98	Notification of Punishment	处罚决定书
99	Application for Reconsideration of the Case	案件复议申请
100	File a Lawsuit to the People's Court	向人民法院起诉
101	Compulsory Execution	强制执行
102	Make Up for the Actual Loss from Damage	赔偿实际损失
103	Abuse One's Power	滥用职权
104	Neglect One's Duties	玩忽职守
105	Connive at Smuggling	放纵走私
106	Administrative Sanction	行政处分
107	Criminal Liability	刑事责任
108	Operation Demeter	大地女神行动（打击固体废物走私）
109	Operation SKY-NET	天网行动（打击毒品走私）
110	Impartial and Clean	公正廉洁
111	Enforce the Law in a Civil Manner	文明执法

附录二

Appendix II

主要学习文献和参考资料

Main References

1. 《习近平谈治国理政》，2014年9月，外文出版社

Xi Jinping the Governance of China, September 2014, Foreign Languages Press

2. 《习近平谈治国理政》第二卷

Xi Jinping the Governance of China Volume Two, November 2017, Foreign Languages Press

3. 《习近平总书记重要讲话文件选编》，2016年4月，中央文献出版社

Selection of Important Speeches by General Secretary Xi Jinping, April 2016, Central Party Literature Press

4. 决胜全面建成小康社会　夺取新时代中国特色社会主义伟大胜利——在中国共产党第十九次全国代表大会上的报告

Secure a Decisive Victory in Building a Moderately Prosperous Society in All Respects and Strive for the Great Success of Socialism with Chinese Characteristics for a New Era- Report to the19th National Congress of the Communist Party of China

5. 坚定不移沿着中国特色社会主义道路前进 为全面建成小康社会而奋斗——在中国共产党第十八次全国代表大会上的报告

Firmly March on the Path of Socialism with Chinese Characteristics and Strive to Complete the Building of a Moderately Prosperous Society in All Respects- Report to the 18th National Congress of the Communist Party of China

6. 《十九大报告辅导读本》，2017年10月，人民出版社

Guidebook on Learning the Report to the 19th CPC National Congress, October 2017, People's Publishing House

7. 《十八大报告辅导读本》，2012年11月，人民出版社

Guidebook on Learning the Report to the 18th CPC National Congress, November 2012, People's Publishing House

8. 《总体国家安全观干部读本》，2016年4月，人民出版社

Reader for Officials on a Holistic Approach to National Security, April 2016, People's Publishing House

9. 《中国共产党章程》

Constitution of the Communist Party of China

10. 《中华人民共和国宪法》

Constitution of the People´s Republic of China

11. 中华人民共和国国民经济和社会发展第十二个五年规划纲要

The 13th Five-Year Plan for Economic and Social Development of the People’s Republic of China

12. 中华人民共和国国民经济和社会发展第十二个五年规划纲要

The 12th Five-Year Plan for Economic and Social Development of the People’s Republic of China

13. 《推动共建丝绸之路经济带和21世纪海上丝绸之路的愿景与行动》

Vision and Proposed Actions Outlined on Jointly Building Silk Road Economic Belt and 21st–Century Maritime Silk Road

14. 2013–2018年政府工作报告

Reports on the Work of the Government (2013-2018)

15. 《中华人民共和国海关法》

Customs law of the People´s Republic of China

16. 《中华人民共和国进出口关税条例》

Regulations on Import and Export Tariff of the People´s Republic of China

17. 《中华人民共和国进出口税则》

Import and export Tariff of the People´s Republic of China

18. 世界贸易组织《贸易便利化协定》

WTO *Trade Facilitation Agreement*

19. 世界海关组织《全球贸易安全和便利标准框架》

WCO *SAFE Framework of Standards to Secure and Facilitate Global Trade*

20. 《关于简化和协调海关业务制度的国际公约》（《京都公约》）

International Convention on the Simplification and Harmonization of Customs Procedures（Kyoto Convention）

21. 2013–2018年全国海关关长会议工作报告

Reports on the National Customs Director Generals' Meeting (2013-2018)

22. 2013–2018年全国海关党风廉政建设和反腐败工作会议报告

Reports on the National Customs Meeting for Party Building, Integrity and Anti-corruption (2013-2018)

23. 《中国海关统计年鉴》（2015年、2016年、2017年）

China Customs Statistics Yearbook (2015, 2016, 2017)

24. 《马列主义经典著作选编》，2011年6月，党建读物出版社

Selected Works of Marxism–Leninism, June 2011, Party Building Book Publishing House

25. 《辩证唯物主义和历史唯物主义原理》，中国人民大学出版社，

Principles of Dialectical Materialism and Historical Materialism, China Renmin University Press

26. 陈诗启，《中国近代海关史》，2002年8月，人民出版社

Chen Shiqi, *Contemporary History of China Customs*, August 2002, People's Publishing House

27. 《中国海关通志》， 2012年12月，方志出版社

Chorography of China Customs, December 2012, Chorography Press

28. 孙毅彪，《海关风险管理理论与应用研究》，2007年7月，复旦大学出版社

Sun Yibiao, *Studies of Theory and Application of Customs Risk Management*, July 2007, Fudan University Press

29. 报刊：人民日报、中国日报

Newspaper: People’s Daily, China Daily.

30. 网站：新华网、人民网、海关总署网站

Websites: xinhuanet.com, people.cn, customs.gov.cn

后　记

Epilogue

English is a very important and widely used tool in the work of customs. Because of my work, I've kept learning English by myself and reading English documents, letters and materials relevant to the work of WCO and its members. I have accumulated more experience in terms of English study and come up with more effective ways to write.

英语在海关工作中十分重要且应用广泛。基于工作需要，我一直坚持自学英语，并阅处日常来自世界海关组织及其成员海关的英文文件、信函和相关材料。日积月累，我在英语学习有了更新的体会，在写作上也掌握了更多的方法：

First of all, I will decide on the theme of writing, which covers a lot of areas including reform of customs operations and customs international cooperation, and other topics such as politics, economy, trade, technology, culture and sports. But there are two things that help me decide what to write. First, we could

首先，选择写作的主题。选择主题内容较为广泛，如海关业务改革、海关国际合作，以及涉及政治、经贸、科技、文体等。但我选择主题一般从两个角度考虑：一是以兴趣为目的选题，即选题并不需要某

choose based on our interest. It's not necessary to come down to a very specific topic. A general area will do, but it must be something that we are interested in. Second, we could choose for the purpose of learning. Some topics may be too sensitive or not familiar to us. But since these are brand new areas, and conducive to building our vocabulary and learning special expressions, we may as well select them. It would also be a good cause for us to learn new things.

个非常具体的领域，有个大类即可，但必须是你感兴趣的话题。二是以学习为目的选题，即某些话题可能并不那么熟悉，但却是全新的领域，有利于扩大词汇量，训练写作的特殊用法等，不妨也可以选择，这也有利于自己增强学习新事物的动力。

Secondly, gathering materials. Once we've settled on the subject, we have to find relevant materials and data from newspapers, magazines or columns on line. I have been subscribing to the English edition of "China Daily" and "The Economist" among others and gained a lot of information reading them. Although I am always too busy with my work to have enough time to peruse every article, I can still get some keywords or main ideas by browsing. I usually take notes on the computer, not all of the content all at once, but only the part that's important and useful. Honestly, it's tough work. But all these materials and data I've collected over the years will give me a head start and a good basis for the next step of writing and help develop the habit of learning.

其次，搜集材料。一旦确定了主题，就开始从报纸、杂志或网上专栏搜集相关材料和数据。我订阅了《中国日报》《经济学人》，通过每天的阅读获得了大量的信息。当然，由于工作繁忙没有足够的时间细读每一篇文章，但我可以通过快速浏览获取关键字和主要内容，在电脑上做笔记，不求一时的完整，只求突出重点和实际实用。说实话，这也是一件苦差事，但长期积累，收集的材料或数据将为你下一步的写作打下良好的基础，同时也养成了一种好的学习习惯。

Thirdly, selecting materials or data. Faced with a sea of information, we have to

再次，材料和数据选用。在大量的材料数据面前，我得区分需要什么，不需要什么，

divide and classify what we need and what we don't. After that, we can start writing. It's a key step to spot ideas from the materials. Usually, the materials serve for the ideas that we choose and the data will be used to prove those ideas. And it's essential to highlight the theme of the article, as well as keep the whole article in a logical order and structure. Surely, there should be some comments on the subject reflecting our own opinions, i.e. things we'd like to say or discuss, so that the article can be more profound, targeted, and closer related to reality.

Finally, practice writing. Vocabulary, patterns and structure of sentences, expressions as well as grammar, are all key points of practice. In other words, we have to write things in different areas even though they are not always familiar to us, in order to expand our reservoir ot terms and special expressions. It will enlarge our vocabulary and help us construct sentences skillfully. Meanwhile, I try as hard as I can to learn the way of thinking of native speakers, learn expressions from English speakers and reduce grammatical errors. It's without a doubt the hardest part for Chinese students. But fortunately, my teachers helped me proofread the writings every time, and every time I took it very seriously to correct the errors. When I wrote, I would carefully

然后才能开始写作。其中一个关键的步骤就是在材料中找出观点。一般情况下，材料应服务于你所选择的观点，而数据则用来证明这些观点。此外，还应该在突出文章主题的同时，兼顾整篇文章的构架及其逻辑性。当然，文章中更应反映出你自己的观点，即你想要述说或评论的东西。这样，文章就会写得更有深度，更有针对性、也更切合实际。

最后，写作练习。词汇、句式与结构、表达方式和语法都是练习的重点。换句话说，即使对有些选题并不熟悉，也得写不同领域的文章，为的是增加专业术语和训练表达方式，拓宽词汇量，提高写作技巧。同时，尽可能模仿母语国家的思维模式，学习地道的英语表达方式，并减少语法错误。这些对中国学生无疑是最难的了，但幸运的是我的老师每次都会帮助校核我的文章，我十分珍惜每一次的改正。只要校对检查出文章中的错误，我就会认真地改正并把它记录下来，争取下次不犯同样的错误，以不断完善和提高自己。

correct the mistakes found during proofreading and reviewing. I would then note them down and try to keep it in mind not to make the same mistake again in order to improve and enhance my skills.

For me, writing in English is not only about learning the language, but also getting more new knowledge through writing. It is also a test for a person's will and determination. It is critical to cultivate the mind and stick to that routine. People will lose the passion and interest, or even grow tired of doing the same thing over and over again for a long time. Truly, we all have so much responsibility and pressure at work that we can only spare so much time for English. However, once we’ve set a goal, we ought to stick to it till the end. There is a golden rule: “practice makes perfect.” We will be rewarded if we make unremitting efforts.

I sincerely hope this book can get readers to learn more about China Customs and support its work in the future. And I hope my experience in English learning can be an inspiration to the readers. To conclude, “It’s never too old to learn." It all depends on our determination and perseverance.

对我来说，坚持英语写作不仅仅是为了英语学习，重要的是想通过这种方式学习更多更新的知识，同时也是对自己决心和毅力的考验。对一个人来说，心境磨练和坚持如一很重要。通常，人们会因为长期做同一件事而渐渐地对它失去热情、兴趣甚至产生厌倦。的确，在繁忙的工作压力下学习英语的时间不是很多，但你一旦有了明确目标，就应该长期坚持。有这么一条黄金法则，叫做“熟能生巧”。久久为功，必有成效。

衷心希望本书能够帮助各位读者更好地了解和支持中国海关，更希望我的学习体会能够给大家带来启示。总而言之，“活到老、学到老”，一切取决于自己的决心和毅力。

图书在版编目（CIP）数据

学亦有益：海关英语学习随笔拾集 / 孙毅彪著 . --北京：中国文史出版社，2018.6

（政协委员文库）

ISBN 978-7-5205-0433-1

Ⅰ . ①学… Ⅱ . ①孙… Ⅲ . ①海关—英语 Ⅳ . ① F745

中国版本图书馆 CIP 数据核字（2018）第 171381 号

责任编辑： 程　凤

出版发行：**中国文史出版社**

社　　址：北京市西城区太平桥大街 23 号　邮编：100811

电　　话：010—66173572　66168268　66192736（发行部）

传　　真：010—66192703

印　　装：北京地大彩印有限公司

经　　销：全国新华书店

开　　本：710 毫米 ×1000 毫米　1/16

印　　张：34

字　　数：516 千字

版　　次：2018 年 12 月北京第 1 版

印　　次：2018 年 12 月第 1 次印刷

定　　价：106.00 元